Therapy

SECOND EDITION
REVISED AND EXPANDED

Advance Praise for *Principles of Trauma Therapy*, 2nd edition

Briere and Scott have taken a solid, powerful first edition and made it even more indispensable. Their deep understanding of the nature of this work, including the ways in which the therapist's own experiences and history are activated by engagement with trauma survivors, comes through in a volume that is both clinically wise and scientifically informed. I particularly appreciate the new chapter on mindfulness-based approaches to working with trauma, as well as the authors' careful attention to issues of ethics in practice. This will be required reading for trainees at my clinic.

—Laura S Brown, Ph.D. ABPP, Director
Fremont Community Therapy Project, Past President
American Psychological Association Division of Trauma Psychology

This book provides a deeply human, highly informative resource in the psychology of trauma. The principles set forth are guided by an excellent synthesis of the research literature along with a deep appreciation of clinical realities. This is one of the few books that are essential reading for clinicians working with trauma patients.

—Marylene Cloitre, Ph.D., National Center for PTSD
and Professor of Psychiatry and Child & Adolescent Psychiatry
New York University Langone Medical Center

Briere and Scott have made another remarkable contribution to the treatment of trauma with their extensively revised and updated book. The first edition of this book is already a classic, and the second edition offers an up-to-date compendium on trauma, its various manifestations, and its treatment. It includes attention to the most contemporary treatment applications, from which it draws broadly on the emerging neuroscience and clinical literature. It is noteworthy in terms of the empathy and compassion directed towards the traumatized client and applies principles of mindfulness to both client and therapist. A stellar accomplishment!

—Christine A. Courtois, PhD, ABPP, Psychologist, Private Practice, Courtois & Associates
PC, Washington, DC, Author: *Healing the incest wound: Adult survivors in therapy (Revised edition)*
Recollections of sexual abuse: Treatment principles and guidelines
Treating complex traumatic stress disorders: An evidence-based guide (with Julian Ford

This text is quite simply the best overview of trauma treatment that I have ever read. It combines clinical sophistication with compassion and evenhanded speculation about research trends to create a final product that is unrivaled in the literature. I will make it a goal to encourage every student and colleague that I have to read this book.

—Constance Dalenberg, Ph.D.
Director, Trauma Research Institute, Alliant International University
San Diego; Author, *Countertransference and the Treatment of Trauma*

Briere and Scott have a new comprehensive text that provides state-of-the-art information on the assessment and treatment of trauma. This is essential reading for both experienced trauma therapists and those who are new to the field. Trauma treatment continues to evolve, as exemplified by the authors' attention to innovative affect regulation and mindfulness interventions.

—Victoria Follette, PhD.
Foundation Professor, University of Nevada, Reno

Briere and Scott have admirably updated what already was a remarkably thorough and clinically savvy clinician's guide. By addressing a wide range of trauma-related symptoms, problems, and disorders, and offering evidence-based principles and tactics for assessment, psychotherapy, and pharmacological treatment, this volume provides an invaluable resource for every clinician who treats adults with posttraumatic disorders. Bravo!

—Julian D. Ford, Ph.D.
Professor of Psychiatry, Graduate School Faculty
University of Connecticut Health Center

The writers of this book have made a major contribution, providing great value for those looking to evaluate, treat, and teach others about trauma. It includes a careful, thoughtful approach to understanding both the diagnosis of trauma and, more importantly, the psychology of trauma patients. The section on Clinical Interventions is invaluable, including a careful description of what is known and unknown about the brain, and the potential benefits of psychiatric medication. I heartily recommend this book.

—Marcia Kraft Goin, M.D., Ph.D.
Professor of Clinical Psychiatry, Keck School of Medicine
University of Southern California, Past President, American Psychiatric Association

PRINCIPLES OF
Trauma Therapy

A GUIDE TO SYMPTOMS, EVALUATION, AND TREATMENT

SECOND EDITION
REVISED AND EXPANDED

John N. Briere • Catherine Scott

University of Southern California,
Keck School of Medicine

Los Angeles | London | New Delhi
Singapore | Washington DC

Los Angeles | London | New Delhi
Singapore | Washington DC

FOR INFORMATION:

SAGE Publications, Inc.
2455 Teller Road
Thousand Oaks, California 91320
E-mail: order@sagepub.com

SAGE Publications Ltd.
1 Oliver's Yard
55 City Road
London EC1Y 1SP
United Kingdom

SAGE Publications India Pvt. Ltd.
B 1/I 1 Mohan Cooperative Industrial Area
Mathura Road, New Delhi 110 044
India

SAGE Publications Asia-Pacific Pte. Ltd.
3 Church Street
#10-04 Samsung Hub
Singapore 049483

Acquisitions Editor: Kassie Graves
Editorial Assistant: Courtney Munz
Production Editor: Laura Stewart
Copy Editor: Terri Lee Paulsen
Typesetter: C&M Digitals, Ltd.
Proofreader: Sarah J. Duffy
Indexer: Ellen Slavitz
Cover Designer: Gail Buschman
Marketing Manager: Lisa Sheldon-Brown
Permissions Editor: Adele Hutchinson

Printed in the United States of America

Library of Congress Cataloging-in-Publication Data

Briere, John.

Principles of trauma therapy : a guide to symptoms,
evaluation, and treatment / John Briere, Catherine
Scott. — 2nd ed.

p. cm.

Includes bibliographical references and index.
ISBN 978-1-4129-8143-9 (pbk.)

1. Post-traumatic stress disorder—Treatment.
2. Psychic trauma—Treatment. I. Scott, Catherine,
1968- II. Title.

RC552.P67B7495 2013
616.85′21—dc23   2012017337

This book is printed on acid-free paper.

MIX
Paper from
responsible sources
FSC® C014174

12 13 14 15 16 10 9 8 7 6 5 4 3 2 1

Contents _____

Acknowledgments_____

We thank Janelle Jones and Heidi Ardern for their written contributions to this book and for their colleagueship throughout its writing; Katherine Avila, Courtney Bancroft, Laura Brown, Marylene Cloitre, Christine Courtois, Constance Dalenberg, Victoria Follette, Julian Ford, Warren Garner, Natacha Godbout, Marcia Goin, Monica Hodges, Cheryl Lanktree, Marsha Runtz, Randye Semple, and Weiguo Zhu for their detailed reviews and suggestions (errors remain our own); and Erin Eadie and Manny Zetino for much appreciated technical assistance. We are also very grateful to SAGE acquisitions editor Kassie Graves, for her continuing advice and patience in this and prior projects, as well as to SAGE production editor Laura Stewart and editorial assistant Courtney Munz.

JB thanks Cheryl Lanktree for her love, sustenance, and collaboration; the Briere, Lanktree, and Manson extended families for refuge and good times; and Colin Dias, Anne Galbraith, Natacha Godbout, David Kim, Sebastien Malette, and Marsha Runtz for their friendship and support during the writing process.

CS would like to thank John Jimenez for love and support in all things, and her mother, Martha Ford Brady Petrou, who was, and remains, her inspiration. During the writing of this second edition, CS had a newborn baby on her lap. He made many contributions, often creating chaos on her computer screen. This book would not have been completed without the help and love of the people who cared for her son while she worked: Dr. Jorge and Mrs. Alicia Jimenez, Gail Gordon and Richard Drapkin, Shana Blake Hill, Margarita Nicolas, Laura Cortez, and Heidi Trinidad.

Introduction _____

The history of humankind is not only a story of art, science, and culture, but it is also about war, interpersonal violence, oppression, and a plethora of disasters, both natural and human-caused. In fact, most people in Western society will experience one or more potentially traumatic events during their lives. Of these, a significant number will suffer lasting psychological distress, ranging from mild lingering anxiety to symptoms that interfere with almost all aspects of functioning.

As compared to other areas of psychology and behavioral science, the systematic study of the human response to trauma is relatively new. The modern field of studying traumatic stress was born in the aftermath of the Vietnam War, and the term *posttraumatic stress disorder* (PTSD) was introduced into the mental health lexicon only in the mid-1980s. Since that time, we have learned that trauma is pervasive, that it can occur at almost any point in the human life span, and that the human response to trauma can be extremely complex. As our knowledge has grown, researchers and clinicians have developed a variety of approaches to the treatment of posttraumatic stress and other trauma-related conditions. This information can be found in journal articles, books, and treatment manuals. Yet these sources are widely dispersed and are not always easily available to the practicing clinician. In addition, they tend to refer to a single theoretical orientation, generally focus on a single group of traumatized individuals (e.g., sexual abuse survivors, motor vehicle accident victims), and often do not provide sufficient information on how to actually implement a given treatment approach.

In response, we wrote this book to be a hands-on guide for clinicians—as well as trainees in psychology, psychiatry, and social work—who need information on the actual practice of effective trauma-focused therapy. At the same time, it provides an overall theoretical basis for trauma assessment and intervention, one that calls upon the various scientific and humanistic domains that impact the treatment of trauma. It is designed to be useful both for those clinicians working with clients who suffer from straightforward symptoms due to a one-time adult trauma and for those treating clients with more complex presentations, including the effects of extensive childhood maltreatment. Whenever possible, we take into account the psychosocial

1

and cultural environment in which the trauma survivor finds himself or herself, since such sociocultural forces (e.g., poverty, social marginalization, racism) can encourage or exacerbate trauma and its effects as well as serve as forms of trauma themselves.

The approach we outline in this book combines aspects of trauma-relevant cognitive-behavioral therapy, relational psychotherapy, mindfulness practices, and a general, nonpathologizing perspective on human suffering. Also included is a chapter on trauma psychopharmacology, intended for medical practitioners and psychiatric trainees, as well as for nonmedical clinicians, who are often critical to their clients' pharmacological treatment.

This second edition significantly expands on the first, reflecting recent advances in trauma research, theory, and practice, and enlivened discussions with clinicians and researchers since the first edition. In addition to updated material on existing topics, we provide new information in a number of areas, including:

- a new chapter on empirically based mindfulness interventions for trauma;
- traumatic brain injury (TBI) as it complicates posttraumatic presentations;
- treatment of trauma in inpatient burn units and emergency rooms;
- acute stress responses and early interventions;
- ethics of trauma practice;
- potential trauma contributions to psychosis, including the possible triggering and exacerbation of schizophrenia;
- additional information on trauma-relevant medications, including for TBI and acute stress;
- additional material on the use of psychoactive medications with pregnant women;
- interventions for those assaulted while under the effects of "date rape" drugs or heavy alcohol intoxication; and
- an introduction to the *pain paradox,* another perspective on pain, suffering, and avoidance.

Many of the interventions presented in this book are based on clinical research and reflect current science relevant to work with traumatized individuals. However, clients seen in public mental health centers and general clinical practices are often more complex and potentially more challenging to work with than those who are screened and selected to participate in randomized clinical trials (RCTs; Briere & Lanktree, 2011; Lanktree et al., in press; Spinazzola, Blaustein, & van der Kolk, 2005; Westen, Novotny, & Thompson-Brenner, 2004) and may be less responsive to RCT-developed treatment methodologies (Zayfert et al., 2005). An oft-cited meta-analysis concludes, in fact, that, due to sample screening, participant dropout, and other issues, the results of randomized clinical trials provide less guidance to clinicians in "real-world" settings than might be expected (Bradley, Greene, Russ, Dutra, & Westen, 2005). Another meta-analysis concludes that the various empirical ("bona fide") psychotherapies all appear to have more or less equivalent efficacy in the treatment of PTSD (Benish, Imel, & Wampold, 2008), although see Ehlers et al. (2010) for a critique.

Although we believe that some therapeutic approaches are more effective in treating trauma effects than others—hence this book—we agree that the current treatment outcome literature may be incomplete. As a result, we do not limit ourselves to describing interventions that have been fully validated in outcome studies. For example, we include some ideas from modern psychodynamic or relational therapy, even though the complexity and, often, longer duration of such approaches do not lend themselves well to controlled scientific studies. We also integrate the growing empirical literature on the benefits of mindfulness training for individuals who suffer from adverse experience and/or psychological disorders, even though this area of study and practice is relatively recent in Western cultures. In each of these cases, we provide research-based support for their inclusion in modern trauma therapy. There are, however, other, relatively experimental trauma treatment approaches that are not covered in this book, primarily because they appear to lack meaningful (that is, empirically supportable) theoretical underpinnings. This does not mean that they, too, may not be the empirically validated therapies of the future, only that we cannot recommend them at present.

Although specific treatment components receive detailed attention here, we believe that, as emphasized by the treatment outcome literature (e.g., M. J. Lambert & Barley, 2001; Martin, Garske, & Davis, 2000), the therapist's nonjudgmental, empathic attunement to the client, compassionate stance, and attention to the therapeutic relationship are also critically important. For this reason, we devote considerable discussion to an overbridging philosophy of treatment that, we believe, not only facilitates recovery from psychological trauma for the client, but also makes this work meaningful, even growthful, for the clinician.

Because effective intervention requires accurate understanding and assessment of trauma and its effects, we begin this book with chapters on the nature of psychological trauma; the problems, symptoms, and disorders that can follow traumatic events; and an overview of the primary trauma-focused assessment strategies and instruments used in the field. We have tried to make this information as relevant to the hands-on treatment of traumatized individuals as possible.

Working with trauma survivors can be challenging, and sometimes even vicariously traumatic. It often exposes us to the pain and suffering that comes from observing the worst that human beings can do to one another. At the same time, this work also can be deeply satisfying and rewarding. Trauma survivors show us that human beings have a capacity to heal, to overcome enormous challenges, and to grow. As we engage this process as clinicians, we almost inevitably learn important existential lessons about life and the workable bases of human suffering. We hope that this book will not only provide tools for those who work with traumatized clients, but that it also—along the way—affirms the tremendous optimism and value inherent in this endeavor.

PART I

Trauma, Effects, and Assessment

The first part of this book outlines the major types of traumatic events, their potential effects, and the ways in which trauma and its outcomes can be assessed. Each of these areas is important to effective trauma therapy. Awareness of the major types of traumatic events and their known psychological effects can help the clinician to understand what the client has undergone and what his or her current psychological experience is likely to be. In addition, knowledge of the relevant diagnostic interviews and psychological tests allows the clinician to pinpoint, in an objective way, specific targets for clinical intervention.

1

What Is Trauma?

The *Diagnostic and Statistical Manual of Mental Disorders,* 4th edition, Text Revision (*DSM-IV-TR;* American Psychiatric Association [APA], 2000) defines a trauma as

> direct personal experience of an event that involves actual or threatened death or serious injury, or other threat to one's physical integrity; or witnessing an event that involves death, injury, or a threat to the physical integrity of another person; or learning about unexpected or violent death, serious harm, or threat of death or injury experienced by a family member or other close associate (Criterion A1). The person's response to the event must involve intense fear, helplessness, or horror (or in children, the response must involve disorganized or agitated behavior) (Criterion A2). (p. 463)

DSM-IV-TR provides a list of potentially traumatic events, including combat, sexual and physical assault, robbery, being kidnapped, being taken hostage, terrorist attacks, torture, disasters, severe automobile accidents, and life-threatening illnesses, as well as witnessing death or serious injury by violent assault, accidents, war, or disaster. Childhood sexual abuse is included even if it does not involve threatened or actual violence or injury.

Although this definition is useful, some have criticized the requirement that trauma be limited to "threatened death or serious injury, or other threat to one's physical integrity," since many events may be traumatic even if life threat or injury is not an issue (Anders, Frazier, & Frankfurt, 2011; Briere, 2004). The earlier *DSM-III-R* (APA, 1987) definition also included threats to *psychological* integrity as valid forms of trauma. Because *DSM-IV-TR* and the proposed *DSM-V* (American Psychiatric Association, 2012a) do not consider events to be traumatic if they are merely highly upsetting but not life threatening—for example, extreme emotional abuse, major losses or separations, degradation or humiliation, and coerced (but not physically threatened or forced) sexual experiences—they undoubtedly underestimate the extent of actual trauma in the general population. They also reduce the availability of a stress disorder diagnosis in some individuals who experience significant posttraumatic distress, since Criterion A is a prerequisite for the diagnosis of posttraumatic stress disorder (PTSD) and acute stress disorder (ASD).

The issue of whether an event should have to satisfy current diagnostic definitions of trauma in order to be, in fact, "traumatic" is an ongoing source of discussion in the field (for example, Kubany, Ralston, & Hill, 2010; O'Donnell, Creamer, McFarlane, Silove, & Bryant, 2010). Our own conclusion is that an event is traumatic if it is extremely upsetting, at least temporarily overwhelms the individual's internal resources, and produces lasting psychological symptoms. This broader definition is used throughout this book, since people who experience major threats to psychological integrity can suffer as much as those traumatized by physical injury or life threat, and can respond equally well, we believe, to trauma-focused therapies. This is solely a treatment issue, however; the *DSM-IV-TR* version of trauma should be adhered to when making a formal stress disorder diagnosis.

Major Types of Trauma

Surveys of the general population indicate that more than half of adults in the United States have experienced at least one major trauma (Elliott, 1997; Kessler, Sonnega, Bromet, Hughes, & Nelson, 1995; Norris, 1992). Were threats to psychological integrity (for example, major losses and other very upsetting, but not physically harming, events) also included, this proportion would be even higher. Although traumatic stressors are common, their ability to produce significant psychological symptoms and disturbance varies as a function of a wide variety of other variables, as is discussed in Chapter 2. The following pages detail most of the major types of traumatic events potentially experienced by those seeking mental health services. There are myriad ways in which an individual can be psychologically hurt, of course, not all of which are easy for the client to disclose or express in an initial clinical interview. This is important to keep in mind—frequently, clients will not report events they have experienced unless they are specifically asked about those events in a nonjudgmental, supportive context (see Chapter 3). Each type of trauma is described only briefly here; the reader is referred to the Suggested Reading section at the end of the chapter for references to more detailed information.

Child Abuse

Childhood sexual and physical abuse, ranging from fondling to rape and from severe spankings to life-threatening beatings, is quite prevalent in North American society. Studies of retrospective child abuse reports in the United States suggest that approximately 25 to 35 percent of women and 10 to 20 percent of men, if asked, describe being sexually abused as children, and approximately 10 to 20 percent of men and women report experiences congruent with definitions of physical abuse (Briere & Elliott, 2003;

Finkelhor, Hotaling, Lewis, & Smith, 1990). Several studies suggest that 35 to 70 percent of female mental health patients self-report, if asked, a childhood history of sexual abuse (Briere, 1992). Many children are psychologically abused and/or neglected, as well, although these forms of maltreatment are harder to quantify in terms of incidence or prevalence (Hart et al., 2011).

As is described later in this and following chapters, child abuse and neglect not only produces significant, sometimes enduring, psychological dysfunction; it is also associated with a greater likelihood of being sexually or physically assaulted later in life, often referred to as *revictimization* (Classen, Palesh, & Aggarwal, 2005; Duckworth & Follette, 2011). Because it occurs early in life, when the child's neurobiology may be especially vulnerable (Pechtel & Pizzagalli, 2011; Pratchett & Yehuda, 2011) and enduring cognitive models about self, others, the world, and the future are being formed (Messman-Moore & Coates, 2007), child abuse and neglect is likely to constitute one of the greatest risk factors for later psychological difficulties of all traumatic events.

Mass Interpersonal Violence

Intentional violence that involves high numbers of injuries or casualties— but does not occur in the context of war—is a newer category in the trauma field. The Oklahoma City bombing on April 19, 1995 (North et al., 1999), the terrorist attacks on the World Trade Center and the Pentagon on September 11, 2001 (Galea et al., 2002), and the July 7, 2005, attacks on the London mass transit system (Salib & Cortina-Borja, 2009) are obvious cases of mass trauma in Western society. There is an unfortunately large number of other examples, however, including terrorist attacks throughout the world and mass human rights abuses (Hoffman et al., 2007; Johnson et al., 2010; Pfefferbaum et al., 2001). The September 11 attacks stimulated a dramatic increase in North American research on the effective short-term treatment of mass trauma, as described in Chapter 11. As noted later, this research suggests that it is as important to know what *not* to do as it is to know what to do when working acutely with victims of mass trauma. It is a goal of international groups like the International Society for Traumatic Stress Studies (http://www.istss.org) to disseminate this information worldwide, since there is little reason to believe that terrorist attacks or other mass casualty events will decrease in the foreseeable future.

Natural Disasters

Natural disasters can be defined as large-scale, not directly human-caused, injury- or death-producing environmental events that adversely affect a significant number of people. Disasters are relatively common in the United

States; surveys suggest that between 13 and 30 percent of individuals have been exposed to one or more natural disasters in their lifetimes (Briere & Elliott, 2000; Green & Solomon, 1995). Typical disasters include earthquakes, large fires, floods, tsunamis, avalanches, hurricanes, tornadoes, and volcanic eruptions. Although some disaster-exposed individuals either are initially unaffected or recover relatively rapidly, a significant proportion suffer significant long-term effects (for example, Briere & Elliott, 2000; Holgersen, Klöckner, Boe, Weisæth, & Holen, 2011). The extent of physical injury, fear of death, death of loved ones, and property loss during disasters appear to be the most traumatizing aspects of these events (Briere & Elliott, 2000; Maida, Gordon, Steinberg, & Gordon, 1989; Shear et al., 2011; Ursano, Fullerton, & McCaughey, 1994). When mental health workers are involved in assisting disaster victims, it is usually within the context of governmental (for example, the Federal Emergency Management Agency) or quasi-governmental agencies (for example, the Red Cross) that have been mobilized relatively soon after the event. At such times, as described in Chapter 11, the clinician's initial job usually involves triage and providing support, comfort, and psychological "first aid," as opposed to trauma therapy, per se.

Large-Scale Transportation Accidents

Transportation accidents include events such as airplane crashes, train derailments, and maritime (for example, ship) accidents. These events often involve multiple victims and high fatality rates (Maeda & Higa, 2006). Although the incidence of such events is not easily determined, large-scale transportation accidents can be especially traumatic to survivors (Lundin, 1995; Maeda & Higa, 2006), since such events frequently occur over a relatively extended period of time, during which the victims are exposed to ongoing terror and fear of death. Immediate response to airplane accidents in the United States is controlled primarily by the Federal Aviation Administration and the National Transportation Safety Board, who work in concert with local emergency services, the relevant airline company, and others in providing assistance to traumatized survivors and their families.

Fire and Burns

Although large-scale fires are often listed as disasters in the trauma literature, a significant number of survivors seen by trauma clinicians have been injured by smaller fires. These include house fires, often caused by smoking in bed, electrical short circuits, or leaking/malfunctioning propane tanks, stoves, or heaters. In other cases, serious burns may result from automobile accidents, industrial fires, fireworks, barbeque accidents, or even intentional burning by others. Physical injuries from fire can be particularly traumatic. The lasting physical effects of serious burns—extreme pain, a long recovery period, multiple surgeries, the presence and persistence of visible and/or painful scars, disfigurement, amputation, and reduced mobility—mean that the traumatic event, in some ways, continues and repeats over time (Gilboa, Friedman, Tsur, & Fauerbach, 1994), often leading to severe and chronic psychological outcomes (Browne, Andrews, Schug, & Wood, 2011; Davydow, Katon, & Zatzick, 2009; Fauerbach et al., 2009).

Motor Vehicle Accidents

Approximately 20 percent of individuals in the United States have experienced a serious motor vehicle accident (MVA; Blanchard & Hickling, 1997), and more than half of American adults will have a car accident by age 30 (Hickling, Blanchard, & Hickling, 2006). A substantial number of these people go on to develop significant psychological symptoms, especially if the accident involved major injury or resulted in the death of others. In the latter case, grief and self-blame may increase subsequent psychological effects. In addition, as noted in Chapter 2, survivors of major MVAs may sustain traumatic brain injury, which can further complicate assessment and treatment (Harvey & Bryant, 2002; Hickling, Gillen, Blanchard, Buckley, & Taylor, 1998; Kim et al., 2007). Despite the fact that serious MVAs are more likely than some other noninterpersonal traumas to produce PTSD and other forms of dysfunction, clinicians often inappropriately overlook such traumas when interviewing clients about negative life events.

Rape and Sexual Assault

Rape can be defined as nonconsensual oral, anal, or vaginal sexual penetration of an adolescent or adult (if the victim is a child, see "Child Abuse") with a body part or object, through the use of threat or physical force, or when the victim is incapable of giving consent (for example, when under the influence of drugs or alcohol, or when otherwise cognitively impaired). The term *sexual assault* sometimes denotes any forced sexual contact short of rape, although we will define it more broadly as any forced sexual contact, including rape. Using definitions similar to these, the prevalence of rape against women in the United States is reported to be 14 to 20 percent (Black et al., 2010; Kilpatrick & Resnick, 1993; Tjaden & Thoennes, 2000; White, Koss, & Kazdin, 2011).

Peer sexual assault against adolescent women is quite common; Singer, Anglin, Song, and Lunghofer (1995) found that, among students in six geographically and economically diverse high schools, 12 to 17 percent of women reported having been made to engage in at least one sexual act against their wishes. Similarly, the National Survey of Adolescents suggests that approximately 12 to 13 percent of female adolescents in America has experienced sexual assault or rape (Elwood et al., 2011). Sexual assault rates for males are less clear, due in part to only recent social awareness that men can be sexually victimized, but are estimated to range between 2 and 5 percent (Black et al., 2010; Elliott, Mok, & Briere, 2004; Tjaden & Thoennes, 2000).

Recently, clinicians and researchers have examined the phenomenon of *military sexual trauma* (MST), referring to sexual coercion, sexual harassment, and sexual assaults against active service-people by their peers or superiors in the military. Such events are much more common than had previously been assumed: One study of returning Operation Enduring Freedom and Operation Iraqi Freedom veterans, for example, indicated that 15 percent of women and 1 percent of men had experienced MST while on active duty (Kimerling et al., 2010).

Women who are refugees or live in war-torn countries often have experienced rape as well, partially because sexual violence may be used by invading forces as a way to humiliate civilians, devastate morale, foster "ethnic cleansing," or reward soldiers (Berman, Girón, & Marroguín, 2006; Human Rights Watch, 2009; Turner, Yuksel, & Silove, 2003; Stiglmayer, 1994). In addition, significant numbers of women and children are raped or sexually assaulted during illegal immigration, for example, by *coyotes* (human traffickers) who rape women and children as they smuggle them across the Mexican border (Amnesty International, 2010; Segura & Zavella, 2007).

Stranger Physical Assault

Stranger physical assault refers to muggings, beatings, stabbings, shootings, attempted strangulations, and other violent actions against a person not well known to the assailant. The motive for such aggression is often robbery or the expression of anger, although in gang and "drive-by" situations the intent may also be to define or protect turf or to otherwise assert dominance. Although many acts of violence in relationships are directed more toward women than men, the reverse appears true for stranger physical assaults (Amstadter et al., 2011). In one study of urban psychiatric emergency room patients, for example, 64 percent of men reported having experienced at least one nonintimate physical assault, as opposed to 14 percent of women (Currier & Briere, 2000). Similarly, Singer et al. (1995) found that, depending on the research site, 3 to 33 percent of male adolescents described being shot at or shot, and 6 to 16 percent reported being attacked or stabbed with a knife.

Intimate Partner Violence

Also known as *wife battering, spouse abuse,* or *domestic violence,* intimate partner violence is usually defined as physically or sexually assaultive behavior by one adult against another in an intimate and often (but not inevitably) cohabiting relationship. In the vast majority of cases, there is emotional abuse as well, including humiliation, degradation, extreme criticism, stalking, and/or threats toward or violence against children, pets, and/or property (Black et al., 2010; Kendall-Tackett, 2009; D. K. O'Leary, 1999; Straus & Gelles, 1990). In a large-sample survey of individuals in the United States who were married or living with a partner, 25 percent reported at least one incident of physical aggression in a domestic context, while 12 percent reported incidents of severe physical violence such as punching, kicking, or choking (Straus & Gelles, 1990). Similarly, the results of the National Violence Against Women Survey suggest that 20 percent of women in the general population have been physically assaulted by their current or former partner, as compared to 7 percent of men (Tjaden & Thoennes, 2000).

Rates of sexual assault of women by partners or spouses—irrespective of their history of physical battering—range from 9 to 17 percent (Black et al., 2010; Elliott & Briere, 2003; Finkelhor & Yllo, 1985). Among women who are physically assaulted by a partner, concomitant rates of sexual assault as high as 45 percent have been reported (Campbell & Soeken, 1999). According to the National Center for Injury Prevention and Control's National Intimate Partner and Sexual Violence Survey (Black et al., 2010), when all forms of intimate violence are considered simultaneously, 36 percent of women and 28 percent of men in the United States have experienced rape, physical violence, and/or stalking by an intimate partner. The prevalence of intimate partner violence among women who have psychiatric disorders or requesting psychological services is even higher, sometimes exceeding 50 percent (for example, Chang et al., 2011). As might be expected, the impacts of such violence are significant, both medically and psychologically (Black et al., 2010; Okuda et al., 2011; see Hien & Ruglass, 2009, for a review).

Sex Trafficking

Sex trafficking can be defined as the forced or coerced recruitment, transportation, transfer, harboring, or receipt of individuals for the purposes of commercial sexual exploitation (The Protection Project, 2011). Although exact numbers are impossible to determine, it is estimated that 600,000 to 800,000 people are trafficked for sex or forced labor across international borders each year, with 14,500 to 17,500 trafficked into the United States (U.S. Department of State, 2005). Once trafficked, women and girls (as well as, less frequently, boys) are forced into a variety of activities, including prostitution (in brothels, "out calls," and on the streets), pornography, strip shows, massage parlors, escort services, mail-order bride networks, and sex tourism. It can be argued that local prostitution, when coerced or forced by a pimp or brothel, is also a form of sex trafficking, albeit one not involving physical relocation (for example, Leidholdt, 2003).

The effects of sex trafficking are often severe. Involvement in prostitution, and the associated effects of the trafficking process (being kidnapped or coerced into slavery; raped and beaten as punishment for noncompliance; and transported illegally to another county without documents, where a different language may be spoken and isolation is severe) have been associated with high rates of depression, posttraumatic stress, substance abuse, and other symptoms and disorders (Farley, 2004; Freed, 2003; Reid & Jones, 2011).

Torture

The United Nations Convention Against Torture defines *torture* as "any act by which severe pain or suffering, whether physical or mental, is intentionally inflicted on a person for such purposes as obtaining from him [*sic*] or a third person information or confession, punishing him for an act he has committed or is suspected of having committed, or intimidating him or a third person" (United Nations Treaty Collection, 1984). The current U.S. Code (Title 18, Part I, Chapter 113C, Section 2340) defines it as "an act committed by a person acting under the color of law specifically intended to inflict severe physical or mental pain or suffering (other than pain or suffering incidental to lawful sanctions) upon another person within his (sic) custody or physical control."

Regardless of function or context, methods of torture involve both physical and psychological techniques, including beatings, near strangulation, electrical shock, various forms of sexual assault and rape, crushing or breaking of bones and joints, water-boarding, sensory deprivation, threats of death or mutilation, mock executions, being made to feel responsible for the death or injury of others, sleep deprivation, exposure to extreme cold or heat, stress positions, mutilation, and being forced to engage in grotesque or humiliating acts (Hooberman, Rosenfeld, Lhewa, Rasmussen, & Keller, 2007; Punamäki, Qouta, & El Sarraj, 2010; Wilson & Droždek, 2004). Most politically based torture involves police officers following arrest or violence at the hands of military forces. The incidence of torture is not known, although Amnesty International (2008) estimates that more than 81 nations currently sanction the use of—or at least tacitly allow—torture. Further:

> some of the measures that governments have taken in response to the attacks of 11 September 2001, as well as attacks or the threat of attacks in other countries since then, have amounted to a serious assault on the framework of human rights protection. States have used torture and other ill-treatment and have tried to justify this in the name of security, and to conferring impunity on the perpetrators. (Amnesty International, 2012, para. 4)

Torture victims are dramatically overrepresented among refugees (Baker, 1992). It is estimated that 500,000 torture survivors from Africa, Eastern Europe, the Middle East, South America, and Southeast Asia currently live in the United States (U.S. Department of Health and Human Services, 2012), although such individuals are rarely questioned about a potential torture history when they come in contact with North American mental health systems.

War

War is a common and relatively powerful source of trauma and enduring psychological disturbance. Posttraumatic difficulties have been described by veterans of a number of modern wars, including both world wars; those in African countries such as Angola, Somalia, and Rwanda; as well as wars in Afghanistan, Korea, Vietnam, Cambodia, the Persian Gulf (including Iraq), Israel, Armenia, Northern Ireland, the Falklands, and Bosnia. Combat involves a very wide range of violent and traumatic experiences, including immediate threat of death and/or disfigurement, physical injury, witnessing injury and/or death of others, and involvement in injuring or killing others (Kulka et al., 1988; Weathers, Litz, & Keane, 1995). For some, war includes witnessing or participating in atrocities, as well as undergoing rape, capture, or prisoner-of-war experiences such as confinement, torture, and extreme physical deprivation. These traumas, in turn, can produce a variety of symptoms and disorders (Institute of Medicine, 2010; Pizarro, Silver, & Prause, 2006). The majority of North American war veterans who seek psychological services today were combatants or support personnel in Afghanistan, Iraq, Vietnam, or Korea. Although the Veterans' Administration (VA) provides care for many U.S. war veterans with service-connected injuries or disabilities in the United States, others may not qualify for such treatment, and it is not uncommon for veterans to present to non-VA mental health centers and clinicians.

War can also profoundly affect the people indigenous to where it takes place. A number of studies indicate that living in a war-torn area (or armed-conflict zone) is associated with significant and lasting anxiety, depression, PTSD, and other—sometimes culture-specific—adverse outcomes, for both children and noncombatant adults (Bracken, Giller, & Summerfield, 1995; Eytan, Guthmiller, Durieux-Pailard, Loutan, & Gex-Fabry, 2011; Heidenreich, Ruiz-Casares, & Rousseau, 2009; Krippner & McIntyre, 2003). Excepting clinicians who travel on humanitarian missions to war-involved areas, the vast majority of survivors of war are seen clinically as refugees and/or torture survivors who have immigrated to safer environments (for example, Baker, 1992; Wilson & Drožðek, 2004).

Witnessing or Being Confronted With the Homicide or Suicide of Another Person

As described in the *DSM-IV* criteria for PTSD and ASD, trauma can involve witnessing or being confronted with (American Psychiatric Association, 2000) death or serious injury of another person. Witnessing such events can produce significant psychological distress and symptomatology, especially when, as noted later, the injured or deceased person is a friend, relation, or otherwise loved one, and the death or injury is intentional. Perhaps two of the most disturbing of such events are murder and suicide of significant others.

Murder

The Federal Bureau of Investigation (2010) estimates that there were 14,748 homicides in the United States in 2010 alone, a rate of 4.8 per 100,000 people. In such cases, multiple closely associated individuals (for example, friends, spouses, parents, offspring) are typically affected by the crime, either by directly witnessing it or learning of it soon after it occurs, resulting in a significant proportion of homicide survivors in the general population. For example, in a study of 1,753 American young adults reached in a telephone survey, 15 percent had experienced the loss by homicide of a family member or close friend (Zinzow, Rheingold, Hawkins, Saunders, & Kilpatrick, 2009). The psychological effects of murder on others are wide, including posttraumatic stress, extended grief, depression, anger, and substance abuse (Zinzow et al., 2009). Homicide survivors frequently experience not only the impacts that accrue from any relational loss, but also the results of sometimes intense media coverage, the level of violence implicit in the crime, the possibility that the survivor was the one to find the deceased victim, feelings of anger and desire for revenge, and, in some cases, prolonged involvement with law enforcement and judicial systems.

Suicide

Witnessing or being confronted with the suicidal death of a family member or close friend can be a highly traumatic event, particularly for children or youth exposed to suicide of a parent (Brent, Melhem, Donohoe, & Walker, 2009; Hung & Rabin, 2009; Wilcox et al., 2010), as well as for those whose partner or family member has committed suicide (Kaltman & Bonnano, 2003; K. Ogata, Ishikawa, Michiue, Nishi, & Maeda, 2011; Melhem, Walker, Moritz, & Brent, 2008). In addition to responses associated with loss and trauma (see *Complicated or Traumatic Grief* in Chapter 2), there also may be feelings of anger or betrayal directed at the deceased, and preoccupation with the possibility that the survivor somehow could have prevented the suicide. Such responses are often accompanied by corresponding guilt and shame.

Life-Threatening Medical Conditions

Although not always listed as such in the literature, illnesses and invasive medical procedures associated with overwhelming pain and/or potential life threat can be very traumatic events. Examples of traumatic illnesses or events include heart attacks, cancer, HIV/AIDS, stroke or brain hemorrhage, and miscarriage. Potentially traumatic medical procedures include heart surgery, treatment in intensive care units, surgery and nursing care for severe burns, major dental surgery, and other medical interventions that produce significant pain or fear (for example, O'Donnell, Creamer, Holmes, et al., 2010). Recently, the phenomenon of unexpected awareness or awakening under general anesthesia during surgery also has been discussed as a medical trauma (for example, Leslie, Chan, Myles, Forbes, & McCulloch, 2010).

Those individuals with life-threatening illnesses often undergo invasive medical procedures; this can make it difficult to ascertain which aspect of the person's illness or treatment is responsible for his or her posttraumatic difficulties. Regardless of its source, there is a growing recognition that trauma is not uncommon among those with major medical problems, and clinicians are increasingly advised to screen patients undergoing major medical procedures for possible posttraumatic stress, depression, or severe anxiety (for example, S. Lee, Brasel, & Lee, 2004).

Emergency Worker Exposure to Trauma

Because emergency workers often encounter potentially traumatic phenomena, including fatal injury, traumatic amputation, disembowelment, severe burns, and extreme victim distress, it is not surprising that those who help the traumatized can become traumatized themselves. Among those known to be at risk for such work-related stress are firefighters, rescue workers, paramedics and other emergency medical personnel, individuals involved in the identification and handling of deceased trauma victims, emergency mental health and crisis intervention workers, and law enforcement personnel (Benedek, Fullerton, & Ursano, 2007; Fullerton, Ursano, & Wang, 2004; LaFauci Schutt & Marotta, 2011; Rivard, Dietz, Martell, & Widawski, 2002). Psychotherapists who treat trauma survivors may also develop a form of vicarious traumatization (Dalenberg, 2000; Goin, 2002; Pearlman & Saakvitne, 1995).

_____ The Problem of Combined and Cumulative Traumas

This list of separately described traumas may give the erroneous impression that such events are independent of one another—in other words, that undergoing one trauma does not necessarily increase the likelihood of experiencing another. This is generally true of noninterpersonal traumas such as disasters or fires. However, a number of studies demonstrate that victims of interpersonal traumas are at statistically greater risk of additional interpersonal traumas (for example, Rees et al., 2011). This is especially true in what was described earlier as *revictimization:* Those who have experienced childhood abuse are considerably more likely to be victimized again as adolescents or adults (Amstadter et al., 2011; Classen et al., 2002; Tjaden & Thoennes, 2000; see a detailed review by Duckworth & Follette, 2011). In addition, many clinicians have noticed that some clients seem to have more than their normal share of adult traumas: Environmental, social, and behavioral issues appear to increase the likelihood of the individual being repeatedly victimized, as described below.

The relationships among different traumas—and the symptoms and difficulties they cause in a given individual's life history—can be complex. Childhood abuse and/or neglect may produce various symptoms and maladaptive behaviors in adolescence and adulthood (for example, substance abuse, running away from home, indiscriminate sexual behavior, attachment issues, and reduced danger awareness via dissociation or denial) that, in turn, increase the likelihood of later interpersonal victimization (Dietrich, 2007; Hetzel & McCanne, 2005; McCauley, Calhoun, & Gidycz, 2010; McIntyre & Widom, 2011; Messman-Moore, Walsh, & DiLillo, 2010; Reese-Weber & Smith, 2011). These later traumas may then lead to further behaviors and responses that are additional risk factors for further trauma and subsequent, potentially even more complex mental health outcomes. Because both childhood and adult traumas can produce psychological difficulties, current symptomatology in adult interpersonal trauma survivors may represent (1) the effects of childhood trauma that have lasted into adulthood, (2) the effects of more recent sexual or physical assaults, (3) the additive effects of childhood trauma *and* adult assaults (for example, flashbacks to both childhood and adult victimization experiences), and/or (4) the exacerbating interaction of childhood trauma and adult assault, such as especially severe, regressed, dissociated, or self-destructive responses to the adult trauma.

This mixture of multiple traumas and multiple symptomatic responses is well known to trauma-focused clinicians, who sometimes find it difficult to connect certain symptoms to certain traumas, and other symptoms to other traumas, or, in fact, to discriminate trauma-related symptoms from less trauma-specific symptoms. Although this task is often daunting, the remaining chapters of this book describe assessment and treatment approaches that clarify these various trauma-symptom connections and, in some cases, provide alternative ways of approaching multitrauma-multisymptom presentations.

Suggested Reading

Breslau, N., Davis, G. C., Andreski, P., & Peterson, E. L. (1991). Traumatic events and post traumatic stress disorder in an urban population of young adults. *Archives of General Psychiatry, 48,* 216–222.

Duckworth, M. P., & Follette, V. M. (Eds.). (2011). *Retraumatization: Assessment, treatment, and prevention.* London, UK: Routledge.

Koss, M. P., White, J., & Kazdin, A. (2011). *Violence against women and girls: Volume II: Navigating the solutions.* Washington, DC: American Psychological Association.

Norris, F. (1992). Epidemiology of trauma: Frequency and impact of different potentially traumatic events on different demographic groups. *Journal of Consulting and Clinical Psychology, 60,* 409–418.

Rees, S., Silove, D., Chey, T., Ivancic, L., Steel, Z., Creamer, M., . . . Forbes, D. (2011). Lifetime prevalence of gender-based violence in women and the relationship with mental disorders and psychosocial function. *Journal of the American Medical Association, 306,* 513–521.

2

The Effects of Trauma

John Briere, Catherine Scott, and Janelle Jones

This chapter is divided into two sections. The first discusses those individual, social, and trauma-specific variables most associated with the development of trauma-related symptoms in older adolescents and adults. These various contributors to, and moderators of, posttraumatic outcomes are relevant to clinical practice because, as it turns out, any two people exposed to a similar trauma may respond in remarkably different ways—for example, one may present with only mild, transient symptoms, whereas the other may develop a full-blown stress disorder that endures for months or years. Current research indicates that only a minority of those exposed to a Criterion A trauma, as defined by the *Diagnostic and Statistical Manual of Mental Disorders (DSM-IV-TR*; American Psychiatric Association [APA], 2000), go on to develop a posttraumatic stress disorder (Breslau, Davis, Andreski, & Peterson, 1991; Kubany, Ralston, & Hill, 2010)—the rest either are less affected or respond with other symptoms, such as depression or generalized anxiety. The specific extent and type of symptom expression is associated with a number of variables, often referred to as *risk factors for traumatic stress*. In some cases, intervention aimed at these risk factors may lead to decreased posttraumatic responses and less risk for future disorders.

The second section of this chapter describes the major forms that posttraumatic symptomatology can take. Clinical outcomes include not only the three major trauma-specific disorders (acute stress disorder [ASD], posttraumatic stress disorder [PTSD], and brief psychotic disorder with marked stressor [BPDMS]), but also a number of other, more generic responses or disorders that can arise from trauma.

What Makes Trauma Responses More Likely, More Intense, or More Complicated?

The amount and type of posttraumatic symptomatology an individual experiences are a function of at least three domains: (1) variables specific to the victim, (2) characteristics of the stressor, and (3) how those around the victim respond to him or her.

Victim Variables

Victim variables refer to those aspects of the victim that were in place before the relevant trauma but that nevertheless are associated with a likelihood of sustained posttraumatic difficulties. Some of these variables (for example, gender, race, and poverty) are risk factors largely because they are associated with social discrimination or marginalization of specific groups; others may arise from earlier trauma or maltreatment (for example, previous psychological disturbance and problematic coping).

Major victim-specific risk factors include the following:

- Female gender (Breslau, Chilcoat, Kessler, & Davis, 1999; Kimmerling, Ouimette, & Wolfe, 2002; Leskin & Sheikh, 2002)
- Age, with younger or older individuals being at greater risk than those in mid-adulthood (Atkeson, Calhoun, Resick, & Ellis, 1982; Koenen et al., 2002; McCutcheon et al., 2010)
- Race, with African Americans and Hispanics—as compared to whites—at higher risk (DiGrande, Neria, Brackbill, Pulliam, & Galea, 2010; Kulka et al., 1988; Ruch & Chandler, 1983)
- Poverty and low socioeconomic status (Carter, 2007; McLaughlin et al., 2009; Rosenman, 2002)
- Previous or coexisting psychological dysfunction or disorder (K. Brady, Killeen, Brewerton, & Lucerini, 2000; Kulka et al., 1988; Petrakis, Rosenheck, & Desai, 2011)
- Less functional coping styles (Fauerbach, Richter, & Lawrence, 2002; Hooberman, Rosenfeld, Rasmussen, & Keller, 2010; R. C. Silver, Holman, McIntosh, Poulin, & Gil-Rivas, 2002)
- Family dysfunction and/or a family history of psychopathology (Bassuk, Dawson, Perloff, & Weinreb, 2001; Breslau et al., 1991; Dierker & Merikangas, 2001)
- Previous history of trauma exposure (Breslau et al., 1999; Ozer, Best, Lipsey, & Weiss, 2003; Yuan et al., 2011)
- A hyperreactive or dysfunctional nervous system, especially involving the hypothalamic-pituitary-adrenal axis (McFarlane, Barton, Yehuda, & Wittert, 2011; Southwick, Morgan, Vythilingam, & Charney, 2003; Yehuda, Halligan, Golier, Grossman, & Bierer, 2004)

- Genetic predisposition (Bailey et al., 2010; Segman et al., 2002), including the interactive effects of environmental stress (including trauma) on the expression of genes, referred to as *epigenetic* effects (Mercer et al., 2011; Xie et al., 2010; Yehuda & Bierer, 2009)
- Peritraumatic dissociation, involving derealization, depersonalization, or cognitive disengagement at the time of the trauma (Lensvelt-Mulders et al., 2008; Ozer et al., 2003; Sugar & Ford, 2012), although it appears that persistent dissociation—beginning at the time of the trauma and continuing over time—may be a more powerful risk factor (Briere, Scott, & Weathers, 2005)
- Greater distress at the time of the trauma or immediately thereafter (Briere, Scott, et al., 2005; Roemer, Orsillo, Borkovec, & Litz, 1998)

This last characteristic, distress during or after the trauma (often referred to as *peritraumatic distress*), is a major predictor of risk for PTSD. In fact, as described by *DSM-IV-TR* Criterion A2, a stressful event is not considered to be a trauma unless the individual reports feelings of horror, fear, or helplessness at the time it happened or soon thereafter. Other peritraumatic responses, such as anger, shame, and guilt, are also likely to increase the risk of posttraumatic reactions (for example, Andrews, Brewin, Rose, & Kirk, 2000; Friedman, Resick, Bryant, & Brewin, 2011; Leskela, Dieperink, & Thuras, 2002). Although sometimes considered a trauma characteristic (as implied by *DSM-IV-TR*), peritraumatic distress (and peritraumatic dissociation) is probably as much a victim variable as it is an index of trauma severity. Those who experience especially high levels of distress at the time of a trauma would seemingly be more at risk for posttraumatic difficulties for a number of reasons, including preexisting problems in stress tolerance and affect regulation, prior trauma exposure, and a cognitive predisposition to view life events as outside of their control or as potential threats.

The Role of Gender and Race

It makes sense that many of the victim characteristics listed above would be associated with greater posttraumatic difficulties. For example, individuals with lower socioeconomic status, less functional coping styles, family histories of mental disorder, histories of previous trauma exposure, genetic predisposition to PTSD, and reduced stress tolerance, as well as those who are especially young or older, all might have greater vulnerability to traumatic events. On the other hand, the demographic variables of gender and race are less intuitively obvious risk factors. There is no reason to expect that women or people of color are inherently less hardy, or in some other way especially prone to trauma effects. Nevertheless, these groups are more likely than others to meet diagnostic criteria for PTSD in both clinical and nonclinical samples.

As it turns out, being a woman or a member of a racial/ethnic minority in American society is a risk factor for traumatic stress largely because women and racial/ethnic minorities are more frequently exposed to events that produce posttraumatic disturbance (Breslau et al., 1998; Briere, 2004; Read, Ouimette, White, Colder, & Farrow, 2011; Rees et al., 2011). In other words, the higher rate of PTSD in these demographic groups is unlikely to be due to an intrinsically lesser ability to handle stress, but rather to the fact that—as a result of broad social factors such as racial and sexual inequality—these individuals are more likely to experience trauma than other groups of people. For example, in the National Vietnam Veterans Readjustment Study (Kulka et al., 1988), the rate of PTSD in veterans was considerably lower for whites (14 percent) than for Hispanics (28 percent) or African Americans (19 percent). However, it was determined that Hispanics and African Americans were also more likely to be exposed to high combat stress than whites—and, although not highlighted in that study, undoubtedly more likely to be victimized prior to joining the military. When race differences in level of combat exposure were controlled for statistically, the difference in PTSD between whites and African Americans disappeared, and the white–Hispanic difference decreased significantly. Similarly, although Kessler and colleagues (1995) estimate the lifetime prevalence of PTSD to be 10.4 percent for women and 5.0 percent for men, they suggest that these sex differences are largely due to women's greater likelihood of exposure to PTSD-producing traumas—especially sexual abuse and rape.

When the likelihood of trauma exposure is equivalent for both sexes (for example, in the case of natural disasters), some studies suggest that PTSD rates are approximately equal between men and women (Yehuda, 2004). At the same time, other large-scale studies (for example, DiGrande et al., 2010) indicate that even among victims of terrorist attacks, women and minority groups are somewhat more likely to develop PTSD than men and whites. In these cases, pre-attack trauma histories, socialization for emotional expression (and thus greater symptom endorsement), and the effects of social marginalization may be mediating variables (DiGrande et al., 2010; Kimerling et al., 2002; Norris & Alegria, 2005).

Characteristics of the Stressor

In addition to victim variables, a number of trauma characteristics are associated with posttraumatic outcome. These include the following:

- Intentional acts of violence, as opposed to noninterpersonal events (Briere & Elliott, 2000; Green, Grace, Lindy, & Gleser, 1990; Poole et al., 1997)
- The presence of life threat (DiGrande, Neria, Brackbill, Pulliam, & Galea, 2010; Holbrook, Hoyt, Stein, & Sieber, 2001; Ullman & Filipas, 2001)

- Physical injury (Briere & Elliott, 2000; Foy, Resnick, Sipprelle, & Caroll, 1987; Haden, Scarpa, Jones, & Ollendick, 2007)
- In war, the extent of combat exposure (Goldberg, True, Eisen, & Henderson, 1990; Hoge et al., 2004; Kulka et al., 1988) and involvement in the killing others (Maguen et al., 2011)
- Witnessing death (Phillips, LeardMann, Gumbs, & Smith, 2010; Selley et al., 1997), especially when the scene is grotesque (Bills et al., 2009; R. S. Epstein, Fullerton, & Ursano, 1998)
- The loss of a friend or loved one due to a trauma (Green et al., 1990; O'Connor, 2010)
- Life-threatening illness and especially painful medical events and procedures (Bienvenu & Neufeld, 2011; Stramrood et al., 2011)
- Unpredictability and uncontrollability (E. B. Carlson & Dalenberg, 2000; Foa, Zinbarg, & Rothbaum, 1992)
- Sexual victimization (Breslau et al., 1991; Kang, Dalager, Mahan, & Ishii, 2005)
- Traumas of longer duration or greater frequency (Briere & Elliott, 2003; Naeem et al., 2011; Phillips et al., 2010)

The impact of these trauma characteristics on the development of posttraumatic stress is significant. Irrespective of victim variables, certain traumatic events (for example, rape) are known to produce a much greater likelihood of PTSD than others (for example, natural disasters). Thus, just as it is erroneous to consider only trauma variables when attempting to predict posttraumatic stress in an individual, it is also a mistake to assume that posttraumatic reactions are solely due to individual or demographic variables.

The Specific Role of Child Abuse and Neglect

Although many adult traumas are extreme in nature, and sometimes are associated with severe psychological outcomes, research suggests that, on average, childhood traumas are even more related to lasting psychosocial difficulties (Briere & Rickards, 2007; Gal, Levav, & Gross, 2011). This is likely due to the fact that childhood traumas occur at the most vulnerable point in human development, typically involve relational maltreatment (as opposed to noninterpersonal trauma), and may continue over a long period of time, involving multiple, separate victimization experiences (for example, sustained intrafamilial sexual abuse). As a result, child abuse and neglect can result not only in the disturbed mood, cognitive distortions, posttraumatic stress, and related symptoms sometimes found in survivors of adult traumas, but also in outcomes more specific to childhood victimization and disrupted parent-child attachment, including problems with affect regulation, identity disturbance, and difficulties in forming positive and lasting relationships with others (Briere & Rickards, 2007; Bureau, Martin, & Lyons-Ruth, 2010).

Because childhood trauma and neglect are also risk factors for additional victimization in adolescence and adulthood (for example, Amstadter et al., 2011), a significant proportion of child abuse survivors have experienced both earlier and later interpersonal violence, resulting in especially complex clinical outcomes (see *Complex Posttraumatic Presentations,* later in this chapter). This may involve not only the accumulation and summation of trauma effects over the life span (Briere, Kaltman, & Green, 2008; Follette, Polusney, Bechtle, & Naugle, 1996), but also the tendency for earlier trauma to exacerbate subsequent responses to later traumas (Breslau, Peterson, & Schultz, 2008; Salloum, Carter, Burch, Garfinkel, & Overstreet, 2011). Thus, although no one should discount the often major, lasting effects of rape, torture, or other atrocities committed against adults, it is important that these more recent traumas be evaluated and treated in the context of the client's earlier history of childhood victimization. As will be described in this and later chapters, these compound child-adult trauma effects may make treatment a more complicated endeavor, since a range of symptoms and problems may be present simultaneously, each potentially requiring different approaches and strategies.

Social Response, Support, and Resources

Psychological support from family members, friends, and others is known to reduce the intensity of posttraumatic outcomes. Such support includes accepting (that is, nonblaming) responses after the trauma disclosure, caring and nurturing from loved ones, and the availability of helpers and support or aid agencies after a traumatic event (for example, Berthold, 2000; Coker et al., 2002; A. Lee, Isaac, & Janca, 2002; Xu & Song, 2011). Social response to the victim is not independent of trauma characteristics or victim variables, however. Some traumatic events are more socially acceptable than others (for example, the victim of a hurricane or earthquake may be seen by some people as more innocent and worthy of compassion than a rape victim), and certain trauma survivors (for example, racial minorities, gays and lesbians, undocumented immigrants, prostitutes, and the homeless) are more likely to receive prejudicial treatment than others (L. S. Brown, 2008). Nevertheless, above and beyond these complexities, most studies suggest that social support is one of the most powerful determinants of the ultimate effects of trauma. This fact highlights the social/relational aspect of trauma recovery, including, as we will see, the importance of the therapeutic relationship in trauma treatment.

Types of Posttraumatic Responses _____

As noted previously, potentially traumatic events vary in type and frequency, and their psychological effects are moderated by a host of victim-specific and social/cultural variables. It is not surprising, therefore, that a number of different symptoms and disorders have been associated with exposure to traumatic events. The most significant of these are described in the following pages. It is important to note, however, that not all psychological impacts can be encompassed by a list of symptoms or disorders. Trauma can alter the very meaning we give to our lives and can produce feelings and experiences that are not easily categorized in diagnostic manuals. These more existential impacts can include a loss of meaning in life, a sense of being alone in the world, a realization of the fragility of life and the reality of death, loss of connection with one's spirituality or morality, and disruption in one's ability to hope, trust, or care about oneself or others (Drescher et al., 2011; Herman, 1992b; Rusiewicz et al., 2008; Shay, 1995). For this reason, rarely will a diagnosis or set of psychological test results encompass the full breadth of trauma impacts. On the other hand, diagnosis and symptom description allow clinicians to refer to a common language and knowledge base and can assist in the development of a useful treatment plan.

Depression-Related Disturbance

Exposure to traumatic events can produce a range of depressive symptoms (Kessler et al., 1995; Nanni, Uher, & Danese, 2012). When posttraumatic and depressive symptoms arise from the same trauma, victims often report themes of grief and loss, abandonment, and isolation. The significant overlap among posttraumatic stress, grief, and depression (Kersting et al., 2009; O'Connor, Lasgaard, Shevlin, & Guldin, 2010), as well as the connection between trauma-related depression and heightened suicide potential (Krysinska & Lester, 2010; Nrugham, Holen, & Sund, 2010), means that depression should always be considered in work with those who have been traumatized.

Complicated or Traumatic Grief

Grief is a normal response to loss and often resolves naturally over time. When the loss involves a sudden, traumatic, even violent death or disruption of an individual's life, however, this response may become more complicated and may be associated with lasting health and mental health problems. For example, traumatic loss may be accompanied by clinical depression, PTSD, substance abuse, or, in some cases, serious physical illness (for example, Shear & Smith-Caroff, 2002; Zisook, Chentsova-Dutton, & Shuchter, 1998). A "complicated" or "traumatic" grief disorder following traumatic loss was suggested in the late 1990s (Horowitz et al., 1997; Prigerson et al., 1999), a version of which has been proposed for *DSM-V* (Shear et al., 2011). The proposed *bereavement-related disorder* has a specifier, *traumatic bereavement,* wherein "following a death that occurred under traumatic circumstances (e.g., homicide, suicide, disaster, or accident), there are persistent, frequent distressing thoughts, images or feelings related to traumatic features of the death (e.g., the deceased's degree of suffering, gruesome injury, blame of self or others for the death), including in response to reminders of the loss" (American Psychiatric Association, 2012c).

Major Depression

A number of studies indicate that those who have been exposed to a major trauma are at risk of developing major depressive disorder, and depression is one of the most common comorbid disorders for PTSD (Breslau et al., 1991; Kessler et al., 1995). Some symptoms of major depression (particularly insomnia, psychomotor agitation, loss of interest in formerly enjoyable events, and decreased ability to concentrate) overlap with symptoms of PTSD (Gros, Simms, & Acierno, 2010), which may complicate assessment. In addition, many trauma survivors present with a chief complaint of depressed mood and may not initially report a history of trauma exposure. As a result, clinicians evaluating trauma victims should be alert to depressive symptoms, including the following:

- Extreme sadness or dysphoria related to irrevocable loss
- Hopelessness regarding the likelihood of future traumatic events
- Worthlessness, excessive guilt, or thoughts about having deserved a traumatic event
- Suicidality
- Loss of interest in former pleasurable activities
- Decreased ability to concentrate
- Psychomotor agitation or retardation
- Anorexia and/or weight loss
- Fatigue and loss of energy
- Sleep disturbance, either insomnia or hypersomnia

When depression is a significant component of an individual's posttraumatic picture, pharmacotherapy may be indicated in addition to psychotherapy (see Chapter 12).

Psychotic Depression

Trauma is known to be associated with psychosis as well as with depression (Read, van Os, Morrison, & Ross, 2005). It is not unexpected, therefore, that *major depression with psychotic features* (APA, 2000) has been linked to posttraumatic stress. What is more surprising is that PTSD is as much as four times more common among depressed individuals with psychotic symptoms than among depressed individuals without psychosis (for example, Zimmerman & Mattia, 1999).

This elevated risk of PTSD in those with psychotic depression may be explained in several ways. First, extreme trauma can produce both psychosis and depression, such that some individuals present with both sets of symptoms simultaneously. Second, those with a predisposition to psychotic depression may be at risk for PTSD by virtue of decreased affect regulation abilities or a tendency to become cognitively disorganized when stressed. Third, it is likely that some of the "psychotic" symptoms in those PTSD sufferers with comorbid depression actually represent severe intrusive symptomatology associated with posttraumatic stress. For example, victims of rape and domestic violence frequently report hearing the perpetrator calling their name or making derogatory comments, and victims of gun violence often report hearing gunshots. Regardless of the reasons for the associations among posttraumatic stress, depression, and psychosis, the assessing clinician should be alert to the possibility of significant trauma exposure in those who complain both of psychotic and depressive symptoms.

Anxiety

Because trauma involves the experience of danger and vulnerability, posttraumatic outcomes often involve symptoms of anxiety. Such responses can be divided into three clusters: generalized anxiety, panic attacks, and posttraumatic phobias.

Generalized Anxiety

Generalized anxiety disorder is known to be both a risk factor for developing posttraumatic stress in response to a trauma (for example, Koenen et al., 2002) and a syndrome that may follow trauma exposure (for example, Freedman et al., 2002). In addition, many individuals report an increase in nonspecific anxiety symptoms after a traumatic event (for example, Mayou, Bryant, & Ehlers, 2001). Because anxiety is probably a final common pathway for a variety of etiological factors, some of which are not trauma related, the presence of generalized anxiety in any given individual does not necessarily mean that he or she has a trauma history. In traumatized individuals, however, such nonspecific anxiety often reflects the impact of threatening events and should be addressed in any comprehensive trauma therapy.

Panic

Historically, panic attacks (usually lasting from 10 minutes to an hour and characterized by symptoms such as palpitations, shortness of breath, sweating, cold extremities, and feelings of impending doom) and panic disorder have not been considered trauma-related phenomena. Yet *DSM-IV* notes that panic attacks can arise from especially stressful events and major losses, and many trauma survivors report episodes of panic following victimization (for example, Cougle, Feldner, Keough, Hawkins, & Fitch, 2010; Falsetti & Resnick, 1997). According to *DSM-IV,* such episodes are not considered evidence of panic disorder, since diagnostic criteria require that panic attacks not be linked by the client to a specific event. Regardless of whether the diagnostic criteria for panic disorder are met, panic attacks can be overwhelming and terrifying experiences that require intervention from clinicians, including possible pharmacotherapy, as is discussed in later chapters.

Despite the decoupling of posttraumatic panic and formal panic disorder in *DSM-IV*, recent research suggests a significant comorbidity between panic disorder and posttraumatic stress in the general population (for example, Leskin & Sheikh, 2002). In other words, PTSD is often associated with panic attacks, even when such attacks are not obviously attributable to trauma-related triggers. As a result, the clinician should inquire about episodes of panic when evaluating those suffering from trauma exposure and should consider the possibility that panic attacks in a given trauma survivor may represent a form of posttraumatic stress.

Phobic Anxiety

Most models of the etiology of "irrational" fears (that is, phobias) tend to stress conditioned fear responses to stimuli associated with prior upsetting events, although some do emphasize more genetic aspects of phobia development (Kendler, Myers, & Prescott, 2002). In line with conditioning theory, many of the avoidant symptoms of PTSD and ASD are implicitly phobic: They involve efforts to avoid people, places, and situations that are reminiscent of a given trauma, primarily because of the fear that has become associated with those stimuli. In addition, both social phobias and specific phobias have been found to be comorbid with posttraumatic stress (Carleton, Peluso, Collimore, & Asmundson, 2010; Kessler et al., 1995; Zayfert, Becker, Unger, & Shearer, 2002) and to be more prevalent among those exposed to trauma (Cougle, Timpano, Sachs-Ericsson, Keough, & Riccardi, 2010; Mayou et al., 2001).

Stress Disorders

The hallmark of extreme traumatization is often considered to be PTSD or ASD, each of which is categorized as an anxiety disorder in *DSM-IV*. Although these responses represent only a subset of the symptoms that can arise from trauma, they are obviously quite prevalent among the trauma-exposed. A related disorder, BPDMS, is sometimes included among the stress disorders, but it is considered separately later in this chapter.

PTSD

Posttraumatic stress disorder is the best-known trauma-specific diagnosis in *DSM-IV*. As presented in Table 2.1, the symptoms of PTSD are divided into three clusters: reexperiencing of the traumatic event, avoidance of trauma-relevant stimuli and numbing of general responsiveness, and persistent hyperarousal. Typically, reexperiencing presents as flashbacks and intrusive thoughts and/or memories of the trauma, as well as distress and physiologic reactivity upon exposure to stimuli reminiscent of the event. Avoidance symptoms may be cognitive (for example, avoiding or suppressing upsetting thoughts, feelings, or memories), behavioral (for example, avoiding activities, people, places, or conversations that might trigger memories of the stressor), dissociative (for example, amnesia for all or parts of the stressor, depersonalization) and at least partially physiologic (for example, emotional numbing). The third PTSD symptom cluster, hyperarousal, may present as "jumpiness" (a lowered startle threshold), irritability, sleep disturbance, or attention/concentration difficulties. The reexperiencing symptoms of PTSD are often the first to fade over time, whereas avoidant and hyperarousal symptoms typically are more enduring (for example, Abbas et al., 2009; McFarlane, 1988).

Table 2.1   *DSM-IV* Diagnostic Criteria for Posttraumatic Stress Disorder

A. The person has been exposed to a traumatic event in which both of the following were present:

    (1) the person experienced, witnessed, or was confronted with an event or events that involved actual or threatened death or serious injury, or a threat to the physical integrity of self or others.

    (2) the person's response involved intense fear, helplessness, or horror. **Note:** In children, this may be expressed instead by disorganized or agitated behavior.

B. The traumatic event is persistently reexperienced in at least one of the following ways:

    (1) recurrent and intrusive distressing recollections of the event, including images, thoughts, or perceptions. **Note:** In young children, repetitive play may occur in which themes or aspects of the trauma are expressed.

    (2) recurrent distressing dreams of the event. **Note:** In children, there may be frightening dreams without recognizable content.

    (3) acting or feeling as if the traumatic event were recurring (includes a sense of reliving the experience, illusions, hallucinations, and dissociative flashback episodes, including those which occur on awakening or when intoxicated). **Note:** In young children, trauma-specific reenactment may occur.

(Continued)

(Continued)

C. Persistent avoidance of stimuli associated with the trauma and numbing of general responsiveness (not present before the trauma), as indicated by three (or more) of the following:

(4) intense psychological distress at exposure to internal or external cues that symbolize or resemble the traumatic event

(5) physiological reactivity on exposure to internal or external cues that symbolize or resemble the traumatic event

C. Persistent avoidance of stimuli associated with the trauma and numbing of general responsiveness (not present before the trauma), as indicated by three (or more) of the following:

(1) efforts to avoid thoughts, feelings, or conversations associated with the trauma

(2) efforts to avoid activities, places, or people that arouse recollections of the trauma

(3) inability to recall an important aspect of the trauma

(4) markedly diminished interest or participation in significant activities

(5) feelings of detachment or estrangement from others

(6) restricted range of affect (e.g., unable to have loving feelings)

(7) sense of foreshortened future (e.g., does not expect to have a career, marriage, children, or a normal life span)

D. Persistent symptoms of increased arousal (not present before the trauma), as indicated by two (or more) of the following:

(1) difficulty falling or staying asleep

(2) irritability or outbursts of anger

(3) difficulty concentrating

(4) hypervigilance

(5) exaggerated startle response

E. Duration of the disturbance (symptoms in Criteria B, C, or D) is more than 1 month.

F. The disturbance causes clinically significant distress or impairment in social, occupational, or other important areas of functioning.

Specify if: **Acute:** if duration is less than 3 months
Chronic: if duration is 3 months or more

Specify if: **With Delayed Onset:** if onset of symptoms is at least 6 months after the stressor

Source: Diagnostic and Statistical Manual of Mental Disorders, Fourth Edition, Text Revision (p. 467), 2000. Copyright 2000 by the American Psychiatric Association. Used with permission.

In contrast to ASD (described next), PTSD can only be diagnosed once 30 days have elapsed since the stressor. The symptoms do not have to appear within a certain time period after the trauma; in some instances "there may be a delay of months, or even years, before symptoms appear" (APA, 2000, p. 466). Such delayed PTSD appears to be relatively rare, however (for example, Bryant & Harvey, 2002).

As is noted more extensively later in this chapter, *DSM-IV* acknowledges several associated features of PTSD that are especially prevalent following interpersonal victimization. These include dissociation, cognitive distortions, and more personality disorder–like difficulties in areas such as identity and affect regulation. In addition, up to 80 percent of those with PTSD have at least one other psychological disorder (Kessler et al., 1995; Spinazzola et al., 2005). Common comorbidities include major depression, substance abuse, and the various anxiety disorders (Breslau et al., 1991; Kessler et al., 1995; Wisnivesky et al., 2011). For this reason, a detailed assessment for PTSD should consider these sequelae as well.

DSM-V PTSD

The suggested diagnostic criteria for PTSD in *DSM-V* are in many ways similar to those of *DSM-IV*. However, in the proposed *DSM-V*,

- Criterion A (trauma exposure) no longer includes the A2 peritraumatic distress (that is, terror, horror, or extreme helplessness) subcriterion required by *DSM-IV*,
- the *DSM-IV* avoidance cluster is divided into two separate criteria sets (numbing and effortful avoidance), and
- negative alterations in cognitions (for example, self-blame or low self-esteem) and mood (for example, anger or fear) are combined with the numbing cluster and will be required for a diagnosis of PTSD.

In most cases, these changes reflect recent research, especially the separation of effortful avoidance and numbing into different criterion sets (see Elhai & Palmieri, 2011). However, the proposed combination of numbing and dysphoric mood in the same symptom cluster (Cluster D) is not consistent with most factor analyses of PTSD symptoms (for example, Elhai & Palmieri, 2011; Elklit, Armour, & Shevlin, 2010) and is somewhat counterintuitive. In this regard, the proposed criteria consider sustained experiences of anger and fear, as well as low self-esteem, self-blame, dissociative amnesia, and feelings or detachment from others to all represent the same underlying symptom cluster (Cluster D).

ASD

The diagnosis of acute stress disorder first appeared in *DSM-IV*. The primary function of this category was to recognize and codify those intrusive, avoidant (especially dissociative), and hyperarousal-related psychological reactions to an acute stressor that occur relatively immediately after the traumatic event has transpired and that may help in identifying those who will progress to later PTSD. The relevant symptoms must last for at least 2 days but not exceed 4 weeks in duration. The specific symptoms of ASD are presented in Table 2.2.

Table 2.2 *DSM-IV-TR* Diagnostic Criteria for Acute Stress Disorder

A. The person has been exposed to a traumatic event in which both of the following were present:

  (1) the person experienced, witnessed, or was confronted with event(s) that involved actual or threatened death or serious injury, or a threat to the physical integrity of self or others

  (2) the person's response involved intense fear, helplessness, or horror

B. Either while experiencing or after experiencing the distressing event, the individual has three (or more) of the following dissociative symptoms:

  (1) a subjective sense of numbing, detachment, or absence of emotional responsiveness

  (2) a reduction in awareness of his or her surroundings (e.g., "being in a daze")

  (3) derealization

  (4) depersonalization

  (5) dissociative amnesia (i.e., inability to recall an important aspect of the trauma)

C. The traumatic event is persistently reexperienced in at least one of the following ways: recurring images, thoughts, dreams, illusions, flashback episodes, or a sense of reliving the experience; or distress upon exposure to reminders of the traumatic event.

D. Marked avoidance of stimuli that arouse recollections of the trauma (e.g., thoughts, feelings, conversations, activities, places, people).

E. Marked symptoms of anxiety or increased arousal (e.g., difficulty sleeping, irritability, poor concentration, hypervigilance, exaggerated startle response, motor restlessness).

F. The disturbance causes clinically significant distress or impairment in social, occupational, or other important areas of functioning or impairs the individual's ability to pursue some necessary task, such as obtaining necessary assistance or mobilizing personal resources by telling family members about the traumatic experience.

G. The disturbance lasts for a minimum of 2 days and a maximum of 4
     weeks and occurs within 4 weeks of the traumatic event.

H. The disturbance is not due to the direct physiological effects of a
     substance (e.g., a drug of abuse, a medication) or a general medical
     condition, is not better accounted for by Brief Psychotic Disorder, and is
     not merely an exacerbation of a preexisting Axis I or Axis II disorder.

Source: Diagnostic and Statistical Manual of Mental Disorders, Fourth Edition, Text Revision
(p. 471), 2000. Copyright 2000 by the American Psychiatric Association. Used with permission.

ASD is noteworthy for its similarity to PTSD, except that it is diagnosed
more acutely, has fewer effortful avoidance and hyperarousal requirements,
and includes more dissociative symptomatology. Especially prominent dissociative features listed in *DSM-IV* are psychic numbing and detachment, as well
as depersonalization and/or derealization. As these differences suggest, there is
not a one-to-one relationship between ASD and later PTSD. Some individuals
with severe acute responses, especially those with significant dissociation, will
initially meet criteria for ASD but will fail to meet criteria for PTSD once 30
days have elapsed. Conversely, some individuals who do not meet criteria for
ASD initially, because they do not have dissociative symptoms, will meet criteria for PTSD at 1 month posttrauma (Harvey & Bryant, 2002).

Individuals with acute stress reactions sometimes present with labile
affect and psychomotor agitation or retardation, although these symptoms
are not included in the *DSM-IV* criteria. Psychotic or near-psychotic symptoms also may be present, especially when the stressor is severe or the victim
is particularly vulnerable psychologically. These may include transient cognitive loosening, briefly overvalued ideas involving persecution or outside
control, and simple auditory hallucinations with trauma-related content.
When psychotic features are prominent, however, the appropriate diagnosis
is usually brief psychotic disorder, as noted later in this chapter, or major
depression with psychotic features.

Some have argued that there is insufficient evidence for the existence of
ASD as a disorder separate from early PTSD, and that the dissociative symptoms emphasized by the ASD diagnostic criterion set are not necessarily a
regular part of early onset posttraumatic stress (Bryant, Friedman, Spiegel,
Ursano, & Strain, 2011; Harvey & Bryant, 2002; Marshall, Spitzer, &
Liebowitz, 1999). Further, as noted in Chapter 11, a number of studies indicate that the dissociative components of ASD may be less powerful predictors of later PTSD than symptoms such as early hypervigilance, sleep
disturbance, and intrusive reexperiencing of the trauma (Dalgleish et al.,
2008; Halpern, Maunder, Schwartz, & Gurevich, 2011).

Regardless of whether ASD is discriminable from PTSD on any dimension
other than its time of onset, and whatever its specific ability to predict later

PTSD, it is a useful diagnosis for those suffering from severe symptoms immediately after accidents, major disasters, mass trauma, or interpersonal victimization. Interestingly, although the validity of ASD as separate from PTSD has been questioned, and several (including the first author) have suggested that it would not appear in *DSM-V,* it appears that this prediction is not true. At this time, the proposed *DSM-V* criteria for ASD are very similar to those of *DSM-IV*, except that, (a) as is also true for the new PTSD criteria, there is no longer any Criterion A2, and (b) rather than having several clusters of symptoms that have to be present, the criteria require simply that at least eight different symptoms, overall, be present (American Psychiatric Association, 2012a).

A Note Regarding Differential Diagnosis of Stress Disorders

Clinicians are sometimes unclear about how to describe someone who suffers from significant posttraumatic symptoms, but either (1) has not experienced a formal Criterion A event or (2) has experienced such an event, but his or her symptoms do not quite reach the threshold for PTSD. Generally, if an individual has not met Criterion A, but describes anxiety or depressive symptoms that meet criteria for another Axis I anxiety or depressive disorder, that disorder may best describe the person's clinical state. If symptoms do not meet anxiety or depressive disorder criteria, the diagnosis of *adjustment disorder* (a rather loosely defined diagnosis that captures anxiety, depressive, and behavioral disturbances in response to stressful life events) may be relevant. If the individual has experienced a Criterion A stressor, but does not fully meet all of the criteria for PTSD (perhaps reporting two avoidance symptoms instead of three, or describing significant avoidance and hyperarousal, but no reexperiencing)—in the absence of another codable Axis I diagnosis—the diagnosis of *anxiety disorder not otherwise specified* may be applied.

Dissociation

DSM-IV describes *dissociation* as "a disruption in the usually integrated functions of consciousness, memory, identity, or perception of the environment" (APA, 2000, p. 519). Central to most definitions is the notion of a variation in normal consciousness that arises from reduced or altered access to one's thoughts, feelings, perceptions, and/or memories, often in response to a traumatic event, that is not attributable to an underlying medical disorder (Briere & Armstrong, 2007).

DSM-IV lists five dissociative disorders:

1. *Depersonalization disorder,* involving perceptual alienation and separation from one's body

2. *Dissociative amnesia,* consisting of psychogenic, clinically significant inability to access memory

3. *Dissociative fugue,* characterized by extended travel with associated identity disturbance

4. *Dissociative identity disorder* (formerly multiple personality disorder), involving the experience of having two or more personalities within oneself

5. *Dissociative disorder not otherwise specified,* used when significant dissociative symptoms are present but cannot be classified into one of the preceding diagnostic categories

Despite the range of dissociative disorders, dissociative phenomena traditionally have been considered manifestations of a single underlying state, trait, or dimension, usually "dissociation" or "dissociative capacity." Some clinicians view dissociative symptoms on a continuum, such that dissociative identity disorder or fugue states are thought to represent more severe dissociation than, say, depersonalization (see, for example, I. H. Bernstein, Ellason, Ross, & Vanderlinden, 2001; Dell, 2006). Other researchers note, however, that dissociative symptoms tend to form a number of only moderately correlated clusters (for example, Briere, Weathers, & Runtz, 2005; C. A. Ross, Joshi, & Currie, 1991). These latter analyses suggest that "dissociation" is to some extent a misnomer—the construct appears to refer to a cluster of diverse, somewhat independent, phenomenologically distinct experiences that differ in form but ultimately may produce a similar outcome: mental avoidance of emotional distress. In this regard, it may not be sufficient merely to say that someone is dissociating, but rather *how* they are doing so.

Although the phenomenology of dissociative responses has yet to be resolved, it is clear that dissociation is often related to trauma. Each of the dissociative disorders (other than dissociative disorder not otherwise specified) is linked to traumatic events in *DSM-IV,* albeit not always exclusively. Among the stressors related to dissociative symptoms in the trauma literature are child abuse (for example, Carrión & Steiner, 2000; Şar, Akyüz, & Dogan, 2007), combat (for example, Bremner et al., 1992; Maguen et al., 2009), sexual and physical assaults (for example, Cooper, Kennedy, & Yuille, 2001; Elklit & Brink, 2004; Schalinski, Elbert, & Schauer, 2011), and, probably to a lesser extent, natural disasters (for example, Koopman, Classen, & Speigel, 1996; Simeon, Greenberg, Nelson, Schmeidler, & Hollander, 2005). This trauma-dissociation relationship probably explains the prominence of dissociative symptoms in the diagnostic criteria for ASD, as well as the significant comorbidity between persistent dissociation and PTSD (Briere, Scott, & Weathers, 2005; Murray, Ehlers, & Mayou, 2002). However, one study suggests that, although most dissociative responses occur in those with a trauma history, the majority of those exposed to a trauma—in the absence of other risk factors—will not describe major dissociative symptomatology (Briere, 2006). Instead, in order for dissociation to occur, there may need to be (a) trauma exposure, (b) associated peritraumatic distress, and (c) a relative inability to modulate or "handle" that distress psychologically or neurobiologically (Briere, 2006).

Interestingly, although most dissociative symptomatology can be linked to a *DSM-IV*-level trauma history, some dissociative responses appear to be associated with childhood neglect experiences and/or early, insecure parent-child attachment (Harari, Bakermans-Kranenburg, & Van Ijzendoorn, 2007; Main & Morgan, 1996; Ogawa, Sroufe, Weinfield, Carlson, & Egeland, 1997), sometimes irrespective of later traumatic experience. Especially relevant may be the individual's early "disorganized" attachment to caregivers, involving chaotic, shifting, and intrusive responses to grossly confusing, fear-inducing, and/or painful parental behaviors (Bureau, Martin, & Lyons-Ruth, 2010). Although such data might be construed to suggest that some dissociative symptomatology is not trauma-related, disorganized attachment is, itself, potentially a trauma syndrome—often arising from adverse events that occurred very early in the child's life (and that are therefore unavailable to later recall), or neglect, loss, or disattunement of such severity that it was terror-inducing, painful, and developmentally disruptive (Briere & Hodges, 2010). From this perspective, insecure attachment may be a marker for very early abuse, loss, or severe neglect.

Somatoform Responses

Somatoform responses are physical or bodily symptoms that are strongly influenced by psychological factors. Especially relevant to trauma survivors are somatization disorder and conversion reaction.

Somatization Disorder

Individuals with *somatization disorder* endorse a wide variety of symptoms (pain, gastrointestinal, sexual, and neurological) whose only commonality is their somatic focus and the fact that they cannot be explained based on medical phenomena alone. A related disorder, *undifferentiated somatoform disorder*, requires only one physical complaint for which no medical explanation can be found or for which the symptom(s) exceeds its expected intensity. Somatization has been linked repeatedly to a history of childhood maltreatment, especially sexual abuse (for example, Samelius, Wijma, Wingren, & Wijma, 2007; E. A. Walker, Katon, Roy-Byrne, Jemelka, & Russo 1993), as well as other traumatic events (Beckham et al., 1998; Ginzburg & Solomon, 2011; Luterek, Bittinger, & Simpson, 2011; Ursano, Fullerton, Kao, & Bhartiya, 1995). The reason for the connection between trauma and somatization is unclear. Possibilities include the effects of sustained autonomic arousal on organ systems especially responsive to sympathetic activation and preoccupation with somatic vulnerability when the trauma involved the survivor's body, such as chronic pelvic pain in sexual abuse survivors (Briere, 1992). In addition, somatization may serve as an idiom of distress, or a more direct representation of traumatic stress, for some cultures and subcultures relative to others (Kirmayer, 1996; Yeomans, Herbert, & Forman, 2008).

Although somatization is often related to trauma, many trauma survivors also present with physically verifiable medical problems (Del Gaizo, Elhai, & Weaver, 2011; Kendall-Tackett, 2009; Schnurr & Green, 2004). In such cases, somatic complaints may reflect underlying illness, immune disturbance, and, in some cases, physiologic sensitivity to bodily distress—perhaps especially in child abuse survivors with gastrointestinal and pelvic complaints (Paras et al., 2009; Videlock et al., 2009). For this reason, trauma survivors with significant medical concerns should be referred for a detailed medical work-up to rule out organic illness, as opposed to the clinician interpreting expressed somatic distress as solely psychological in nature.

Conversion

According to *DSM-IV, conversion* refers to "symptoms or deficits affecting voluntary motor or sensory function that suggest a neurological or other general medical condition" when "psychological factors are judged to be associated with the symptom or deficit because the initiation or exacerbation of symptoms or deficit is preceded by conflicts or stressors" and the symptom(s) cannot be fully explained medically (APA, 2000, p. 498). Typical conversion symptoms include paralysis, loss of ability to speak, abnormal movements, deafness, blindness, and seizures. Although conversion disorder was linked to guilt and conflict in the early psychoanalytic literature (Akagi & House, 2002), most empirically based analyses suggest stress and trauma factors. Traumas frequently implicated in the clinical literature are child abuse (for example, Roelofs, Keijsers, Hoogduin, Naring, & Moene, 2002; Şar, Akyüz, Dogan, & Öztü, 2009; Şar, Akyüz, Kundakci, Kiziltan, & Dogan, 2004), combat (for example, Mansour, 1987; Neill, 1993), and witnessing or experiencing torture (for example, Khan & Margoob, 2006; Van Ommeren et al., 2001). Both somatization and conversion appear to vary by culture and sometimes reflect ethnocultural models or explanations for psychological distress (Kirmayer, 1996). Whatever their cultural functions, conversion responses appear to be more frequent in some societies than they are in North America (Leff, 1988).

Psychosis

Although not especially common in the typical outpatient trauma population, psychotic symptoms (typically hallucinations, delusions, tangential or loosened mental associations, catatonic behavior) may follow exposure to overwhelmingly traumatic events. For example, it has been estimated that 30 to 40 percent of treatment-seeking Vietnam combat veterans with PTSD experience at least some hallucinations and/or delusions (David, Kutcher, Jackson, & Mellman, 1999), and psychotic symptoms have been documented among survivors of physical or sexual assaults (Burns, Jhazbhay, Esterhuizen, & Emsley, 2011; Kilcommons, Morrison, Knight, & Lobban, 2008) and child abuse (Alemany et al., 2011; Saha et al., 2011). Further, in analyses of psychotic individuals, the presence of childhood trauma is associated with more severe and varied psychotic symptoms as well as more disturbed behavior (Álvarez et al., 2011; Ramsay, Flanagan, Gantt, Broussard, & Compton, 2011; A. Thompson et al., 2010; Vogel et al., 2011).

In *DSM-IV* (as well as the proposed *DSM-V*), there is one trauma-related psychotic disorder (BPDMS), and one mood disorder (major depression with psychotic features) that has been associated with trauma and PTSD.

BPDMS

Brief psychotic disorder with marked stressor appeared in *DSM-III-R* (APA, 1987) as "Brief Reactive Psychosis." BPDMS is noteworthy for the fact that it often begins quite abruptly and may be quite florid in nature. The diagnosis requires at least one of four psychotic symptoms: delusions, hallucinations, disorganized speech, or grossly disorganized or catatonic behavior. Like other acute psychotic conditions, BPDMS is sometimes accompanied by extreme agitation, emotional distress, and confusion. *DSM-IV* lists suicide attempts as an associated feature and notes that those with this disorder may require close supervision. The duration of BPDMS ranges from 1 day to less than 1 month, although, as noted below, this time frame is somewhat questionable. See Table 2.3 for the *DSM-IV-TR* criteria for this disorder.

It is not always clear whether a psychotic episode that follows a traumatic stressor is, in fact, BPDMS. In some cases, for example, the psychosis may be trauma related but persists for several months or longer (APA, 2000, p. 331). Because these symptoms exceed the somewhat arbitrary 1-month limit required by *DSM-IV*, they cannot be diagnosed as BPDMS—regardless of how trauma-related they appear. In other instances, apparent psychotic responses to a marked stressor may represent the trauma-related activation of a latent predisposition toward psychosis, or the acute exacerbation of an already existing—but previously undetected—psychotic illness. It also is not uncommon for a severe trauma to produce or trigger depression with psychotic features, as noted earlier in this chapter—a diagnosis that takes precedence over BPDMS (APA, 2000, p. 332). As well, as noted above, some more chronic psychotic states are associated, at least in part, with childhood traumatic events (J. Read, Agar, Argyle, & Aderhold, 2003; Schäfer & Fisher, 2011), suggesting that not all trauma-related psychosis is necessarily "brief." Finally, some cases of severe posttraumatic stress may include psychotic symptoms (for example, paranoid ideation, looseness of thought, or hallucinations) in the context of a more prominent ASD or PTSD presentation (J. R. T. Davidson, 1994; Pinto & Gregory, 1995). In all of the latter cases, of course, BPDMS is not a diagnostic option, since the 1-month period has obviously passed.

Table 2.3   *DSM-IV-TR* Criteria for Brief Psychotic Disorder

A. Presence of one (or more) of the following symptoms:

  (1) delusions

  (2) hallucinations

  (3) disorganized speech (e.g., frequent derailment or incoherence)

  (4) grossly disorganized or catatonic behavior

Note: Do not include a symptom if it is a culturally sanctioned response pattern.

B. Duration of an episode of the disturbance is at least 1 day but less than 1 month, with eventual full return to premorbid level of functioning.

C. The disturbance is not better accounted for by a Mood Disorder With Psychotic Features, Schizoaffective Disorder, or Schizophrenia and is not due to the direct physiological effects of a substance (e.g., a drug of abuse, a medication) or a general medical condition.

Specify: **With Marked Stressor(s)** (brief reactive psychosis): if symptoms occur shortly after and apparently in response to events that, singly or together, would be markedly stressful to almost anyone in similar circumstances in the person's culture

  Without Marked Stressor(s): if psychotic symptoms do not occur shortly after, or are not apparently in response to events that, singly or together, would be markedly stressful to almost anyone in similar circumstances in the person's culture

  With Postpartum Onset: if onset within 4 weeks postpartum.

Source: *Diagnostic and Statistical Manual of Mental Disorders, Fourth Edition, Text Revision* (p. 332), 2000. Copyright 2000 by the American Psychiatric Association. Used with permission.

Trauma and Schizophrenia: The Controversy

Although psychotic symptoms have been associated with trauma exposure, generally it has been assumed that the most common psychotic disorder, *schizophrenia,* does not have a significant trauma etiology. Instead, schizophrenia, like bipolar affective disorder, is often viewed as arising from genetic factors, with elevated rates found among identical twins and children whose parents suffer from schizophrenia (see a review by Sullivan, 2005).

In contrast to most models of schizophrenia, however, some recent studies and analyses implicate trauma, especially severe childhood abuse (see reviews by C. Morgan & Fisher, 2007; J. Read, van Os, Morrison, & Ross, 2005; Schäfer & Fisher, 2011). For example, in a meta-analysis of 20 studies examining the relationship between a diagnosis of schizophrenia and a reported history of childhood abuse, C. Morgan and Fisher (2007) found that 42 percent of women and 28 percent of men diagnosed with schizophrenia reported a childhood history of sexual abuse, and that 50 percent, across gender, had histories of sexual or physical abuse. Similarly, an extensive review of studies examining childhood abuse rates among those diagnosed with schizophrenia or another psychotic disorder found that 435 of 1,536 studies (a weighted average of 28.3 percent) documented a childhood sexual abuse history, and 542 out of 1,081 (a weighted average of 50.1 percent) indicated a physical abuse history (J. Read et al., 2005).

These studies do not demonstrate that schizophrenia (or another psychotic disorder) arises directly from childhood trauma exposure, of course. Some "hallucinations" identified in trauma survivors may actually reflect posttraumatic flashbacks, some "delusions" may involve trauma-based cognitive distortions and hypervigilance, and some of the seemingly negative signs of schizophrenia actually may be due to posttraumatic dissociation (Briere, 2004). However, given the *neural diathesis-stress* model of schizophrenia (E. F. Walker & Diforio, 1997), it seems likely that at least some individuals who ultimately manifest schizophrenic symptoms do so because a genetic predisposition to schizophrenia is activated by the stress effects of childhood trauma. It is also possible, however, that the link between childhood abuse and a later diagnosis of schizophrenia does reflect, in some part, a neurodevelopmental interaction between the biology of posttraumatic stress (for example, alterations in the hypothalamic-pituitary-adrenergic axis and, more generally, the dopaminergic circuitry of the brain) and the presumed biological substrates of schizophrenia (J. Read, Perry, Moskowitz, & Connolly, 2001).

Drug and Alcohol Abuse/Dependence

Substance abuse and substance dependence (the latter occurring when there is also tolerance, withdrawal symptoms, and inability to sustain abstinence) are relatively common among those exposed to traumatic events, perhaps especially those who have experienced interpersonal violence (see review by Ouimette & Brown, 2003, and a comprehensive longitudinal study by Hedtke et al., 2008). Further, those with substance abuse problems are more likely than most other groups to report a history of trauma exposure and to present with symptoms of PTSD (Cisler et al., 2011; Najavits, 2002; Ouimette, Moos, & Brown, 2003). The comorbidity of trauma, PTSD, and substance abuse is widely discussed in both the substance abuse and trauma fields, primarily because such comorbidity can complicate assessment and interfere with treatment (P. J. Brown, Read, & Kahler, 2003; Najavits, 2002).

There are at least three major reasons why trauma, PTSD, and substance abuse may overlap (P. J. Brown & Wolfe, 1994): (1) trauma survivors seek out psychoactive substances as a way to "self-medicate" posttraumatic distress, (2) those who abuse substances are more easily victimized or otherwise prone to trauma exposure, and/or (3) substance abuse leads to more symptomatology (for example, PTSD) in those exposed to trauma. In general, of these three possibilities, it appears that self-medication is the most common explanation: Chilcoat and Breslau (1998), for example, found that individuals with PTSD were four times more likely to abuse alcohol or drugs than those without PTSD (irrespective of trauma history), whereas substance abuse was not a predictor of subsequent trauma exposure or PTSD. Nevertheless, some studies do suggest that substance abuse increases the likelihood of victimization (for example, Cottler, Compton, Mager, Spitznagel, & Janca, 1992; Resnick, Yehuda, & Acierno, 1997) and other trauma exposure, such as automobile accidents (Ursano et al., 1999). In fact, clinical experience with substance-abusing survivors suggests a "vicious circle":

- Early trauma exposure (for example, childhood sexual abuse) increases the likelihood of additional traumas later in life.
- The accumulation of these traumas leads to significant posttraumatic stress and dysphoria, and interferes with the development of affect regulation skills.
- Increased, insufficiently modulated distress motivates the use of drugs and alcohol as "self-medication."
- Drug and alcohol abuse leads to decreased environmental awareness and involvement in "risky" behaviors.
- These effects increase the likelihood of additional trauma and posttraumatic distress.
- Increased distress potentially leads to more substance abuse.

(See Allen, 2001; E. Becker, Rankin, & Rickel, 1998; Briere, 2004; Briere, Hodges, & Godbout, 2010; McFarlane, 1998.)

Complex Posttraumatic Presentations

Complex Posttraumatic Stress

Although not listed in *DSM-IV, complex posttraumatic stress,* also known as *complex PTSD* (Herman, 1992a), *disorder of extreme stress, not otherwise specified* (DESNOS; Pelcovitz et al., 1997), or *self-trauma disturbance* (Briere, 2002b), is frequently described in the clinical literature. Complex stress effects are thought to arise from severe, prolonged, and repeated trauma, almost always of an interpersonal nature, often beginning early in life (Briere & Spinazzola, 2009; Herman, 1992a, 1992b; van der Kolk, Roth, Pelcovitz, Sunday, & Spinazzola, 2005).

Reflecting its chronic and often developmental etiology, this more complex presentation includes the somatic and dissociative problems described previously, as well as chronic difficulties in identity, boundary awareness, interpersonal relatedness, and affect regulation (Briere & Spinazzola, 2009; Cook et al., 2005; Courtois, 2004; van der Kolk & d'Andrea, 2010). In the absence of sufficient affect regulation skills, for example, traumatized individuals may have to rely on external ways of reducing activated abuse-related distress, often referred to as *tension reduction behaviors* (Briere, 1996, 2002b). Such behaviors include compulsive or indiscriminant sexual behavior, binging and purging, self-mutilation, aggression, suicidality, and other "impulse control" problems (Brennan & Shaver, 1995; Briere et al., 2010; Briere & Rickards, 2007; Green et al., 2005; Herpertz et al., 1997; Kendler et al., 2000; Zlotnick, Donaldson, Spirito, & Pearlstein, 1997). Inadequate affect regulation may also lead to drug and alcohol abuse (for example, Grilo et al., 1997), dissociation (for example, Briere, 2006), and other dysfunctional avoidance strategies, which, as described previously, may decrease vigilance and thereby increase the likelihood of further trauma and other adverse events (for example, Acierno, Resnick, Kilpatrick, Saunders, & Best, 1999; Cottler et al., 1992).

The relational and identity disturbance subsumed under complex PTSD or DESNOS includes the tendency to be involved in chaotic and frequently maladaptive relationships, difficulty negotiating interpersonal boundaries, and reduced awareness of one's entitlements and needs in the presence of compelling others. This set of problems is often attributed to a history of inadequate or disrupted parent-child attachment (Cassidy & Shaver, 1999; Pearlman & Courtois, 2005; Sroufe, Carlson, Levy, & Egeland, 1999), typically as a result of childhood abuse or neglect (Cole & Putnam, 1992; Elliott, 1994; Ford, Connor, & Hawke, 2009).

Interestingly, despite the inclusion of "PTSD" in "complex PTSD"—as well as the frequent presence of comorbid PTSD in such cases—the reliving, avoidant, and hyperarousal symptoms of posttraumatic stress disorder are not included in this symptom cluster (Herman, 1992b; Pelcovitz et al., 1997). It has yet to be determined, in fact, whether complex posttraumatic stress represents (1) a discrete syndrome, (2) the associated features of PTSD, or (3) as we generally believe, a wide range of outcomes that vary from person to person as a function of neurobiology, age of trauma onset, type and duration of trauma, early attachment disruption, sociocultural phenomena, and many of the other variables described at the outset of this chapter (Briere & Spinazzola, 2005).

Borderline Personality Disorder

DSM-IV describes *borderline personality disorder* as a chronic disturbance in which there is "a pervasive pattern of instability of interpersonal relationship, self-image, and affects, and marked impulsivity beginning by early adulthood and present in a variety of contexts" (APA, 2000, p. 706). We include this disorder here because, as will be seen, borderline personality traits may be largely posttraumatic in nature. The *DSM-IV* criteria for borderline personality disorder are presented in Table 2.4.

Most traditional theories of borderline personality development (for example, Kernberg, 1976) trace the genesis of this disorder to dysfunctional parental (primarily maternal) behavior in the first several years of the child's

Table 2.4   *DSM-IV-TR* Criteria for Borderline Personality Disorder

A pervasive pattern of instability of interpersonal relationships, self-image, and affects and marked impulsivity beginning by early adulthood and present in a variety of contexts, as indicated by five (or more) of the following:

(1) frantic efforts to avoid real or imagined abandonment. **Note:** Do not include suicidal or self-mutilating behavior covered in Criterion 5.

(2) a pattern of unstable and intense interpersonal relationships characterized by alternating between extremes of idealization and devaluation

(3) identity disturbance: markedly and persistently unstable self-image or sense of self

(4) impulsivity in at least two areas that are potentially self-damaging (e.g., spending, sex, substance abuse, reckless driving, binge eating). **Note:** Do not include suicidal or self-mutilating behavior covered in Criterion 5.

(5) recurrent suicidal behavior, gestures, or threats, or self-mutilating behavior

(6) affective instability due to a marked reactivity of mood (e.g., intense episodic dysphoria, irritability, or anxiety usually lasting a few hours and only rarely more than a few days)

(7) chronic feelings of emptiness

(8) inappropriate, intense anger or difficulty controlling anger (e.g., frequent displays of temper, constant anger, recurrent physical fights)

(9) transient, stress-related paranoid ideation or severe dissociative symptoms

Source: Diagnostic and Statistical Manual of Mental Disorders, Fourth Edition, Text Revision (p. 710), 2000. Copyright 2000 by the American Psychiatric Association. Used with permission.

life. They assert that the soon-to-be-borderline child is rewarded for enmeshed dependency and punished (often through abandonment) for independence. There is limited empirical support for this specific model, although we agree that such treatment likely would be deleterious. Instead, a number of studies indicate that borderline personality disorder is generally (although not inevitably) associated with severe and extended childhood trauma and/ or neglect, perhaps especially sexual abuse (Afifi et al., 2011; Briere & Zaidi, 1989; Herman, Perry, & van der Kolk, 1989; S. N. Ogata et al., 1990; Sansone, Songer, & Miller, 2005; Van Dijke et al., 2012).

It is likely that severe, early trauma has both psychological and neurological impacts on some individuals, producing problems in identity, affect regulation, and relatedness (Briere & Hodges, 2010) as well as, in some cases, the orbitofrontal and hippocampal deficits that have been correlated with both borderline personality disorder (Berlin, Rolls, & Iversen, 2005; Schmahl & Bremner, 2006) and PTSD (Bremner et al., 2003). As might be expected, the symptoms of borderline personality disorder are markedly similar to those of complex posttraumatic disturbance (Courtois & Ford, 2009; Herman et al., 1989; van der Kolk et al., 2005). Unfortunately, the diagnosis has acquired a negative valence for many mental health practitioners, indicating someone who is difficult to work with, emotionally overreactive, and often manipulative, as opposed to someone who suffers deeply as a result of the impacts of, and adaptations to, negative life events.

Medical Sequelae of Trauma

Individuals with psychological disorders, especially PTSD, have also been shown to be at increased risk for physical health complications (Schnurr & Green, 2004; Zayfert, Dums, Ferguson, & Hegel, 2003). Although the nature of the relationship between trauma and physical illness has not been well elucidated, PTSD sufferers have been shown to have increased rates of back pain, hypertension, arthritis, lung disease, nervous system diseases, circulatory disease, cancer, stroke, digestive disorders, chronic pain, and endocrine disorders, among others (Abouzeid, Kelsall, Forbes, Sim, & Creamer, 2011; Dobie et al., 2004; Frayne et al., 2004; Phifer et al., 2011; Spitzer et al., 2009). PTSD also has been associated with lower overall physical health status, higher use of medical services, and higher health care costs (Frayne et al., 2004; Glaesmer, Braehler, Riedel-Heller, Freyberger, & Kuwert, 2011; Haskell et al., 2011; E. A. Walker et al., 1993). This association appears especially high in victims of chronic interpersonal violence. Surveys of people seeking medical care have shown that intimate partner violence, sexual abuse, and sexual assault are correlated with physical health outcomes such as musculoskeletal disorders, chronic pelvic pain, sexual dysfunction, neurological symptoms, and gastrointestinal complaints (Briere, 1992; Campbell, 2002; Pilver, Levy, Libby, & Desai, 2011). For this reason, as noted in Chapter 1, assessment of traumatized individuals should include evaluation of physical—as well as mental—health status. Similarly, those treating physical illness should routinely screen for child abuse and adult interpersonal trauma (see, for example, position papers by major medical associations, including Moracco & Cole, 2009, and Schulman, DePold, & Hohler, 2012).

Traumatic Brain Injury

Not all trauma-related outcomes are psychological in origin—in some cases, when the traumatic event results in physical damage to the brain, a neurological diagnosis, *traumatic brain injury (TBI)*, may be appropriate. As clinicians and researchers have developed increasingly sensitive assessments of central nervous system functioning, and as modern medicine's ability to preserve life following severe injuries (for example, in combat or following major motor vehicle accidents) results in more medically handicapped individuals, the rates of TBI identified in trauma survivors—especially war veterans—have escalated. In this regard, it is estimated that between 1.5 and 2 million Americans yearly suffer the effects of a traumatic brain injury (Kim et al., 2007; Thurman, Alverson, Dunn, Guerrero, & Sniezek, 1999).

The neurological effects of TBI often overlap with the psychological effects of trauma described earlier in this chapter, including reduced energy and motivation, poor attention and concentration, memory impairment, irritability, impulse control problems, mood disturbance, and personality changes (J. M. Silver, McAllister, & Arcineagas, 2009). Sleep disturbance, in particular, is common after head trauma, with almost half of TBI patients meeting criteria for either sleep apnea, posttraumatic hypersomnia, narcolepsy, or periodic limb movement disorder (Castriotta & Murthy, 2011). In addition, the experience of neurological injury and disability, themselves, can produce sustained helplessness, hopelessness, anxiety, decreased functioning at work, relationship problems, and impaired capacity for independent living (K. R. Gould, Ponsford, Johnston, & Schonberger, 2011). TBI and PTSD are frequently both present in head trauma survivors—often producing a more complicated and extended clinical presentation (Kennedy et al., 2007). As a result, it is often difficult to separate the neurological and psychological effects of physically traumatic injury in a given client, leading to potential misdiagnosis in either direction (McMillan, 2001).

Recently, research has focused on mild TBI (mTBI)—typically defined as involving less than 30 minutes of loss of consciousness, amnesia of 24 hours or less, and an initial Glasgow Coma Score (GSC) of 13–15[1] (American Congress of Rehabilitation Medicine, 1993). This is because, counter to what one might expect, mTBI has a greater association with PTSD, most particularly reexperiencing symptoms, than does moderate or severe TBI (Zatzick et al., 2010). Although the reasons for this finding are not entirely understood, more severe TBI is associated with greater brain damage and, consequently, more amnesia. As a result, the memory encoding and consolidation that would lead to PTSD is interrupted. At the same time, however, more severe TBI often leads to higher levels of cognitive and somatic disturbance.

DSM-IV does not have a TBI diagnosis; sequelae of head trauma are only included in research criteria as Postconcussional Disorder. These criteria are presented in Table 2.5.

The proposed revisions in *DSM-V* include two new categories: mild neurocognitive disorder associated with TBI, and major neurocognitive disorder associated with TBI.

---

[1]The GCS is a scoring system used to quantify consciousness after head injury, with 15 being the highest number possible and 3 indicating total unresponsiveness.

Table 2.5   *DSM-IV-TR* Criteria for Postconcussional Disorder

A. A history of head trauma that has caused significant cerebral concussion.

Note: The manifestations of concussion include loss of consciousness, posttraumatic amnesia, and, less commonly, posttraumatic onset of seizures. The specific method of defining this criterion needs to be established by further research.

B. Evidence from neuropsychological testing or quantified cognitive assessment of difficulty in attention (concentrating, shifting focus of attention, performing simultaneous cognitive tasks) or memory (learning or recalling information).

C. Three (or more) of the following occur shortly after the trauma and last at least 3 months:

   1. becoming fatigued easily

   2. disordered sleep

   3. headache

   4. vertigo or dizziness

   5. irritability or aggression on little or no provocation

   6. anxiety, depression, or affective lability

   7. changes in personality (e.g., social or sexual inappropriateness)

   8. apathy or lack of spontaneity

D. The symptoms in Criteria B and C have their onset following head trauma or else represent a substantial worsening of preexisting symptoms.

E. The disturbance causes significant impairment in social or occupational functioning and represents a significant decline from a previous level of functioning. In school-age children, the impairment may be manifested by a significant worsening in school or academic performance dating from the trauma.

F. The symptoms do not meet criteria for Dementia Due to Head Trauma and are not better accounted for by another mental disorder (e.g., Amnestic Disorder Due to Head Trauma, Personality Change Due to Head Trauma).

Source: Diagnostic and Statistical Manual of Mental Disorders, Fourth Edition, Text Revision, 2000. Copyright 2000 by the American Psychiatric Association. Used with permission.

Trauma Syndromes in Non-Western Cultures _____

As indicated at the beginning of this chapter, posttraumatic presentations are influenced by a variety of individual and environmental variables. People from different cultures or subcultures often experience trauma and express posttraumatic symptoms in ways that diverge from mainstream North American society (Friedman & Jaranson, 1994; Kohrt, & Hruschka, 2010; Lewis-Fernández et al., 2010; Marsella, Friedman, Gerrity, & Scurfield, 1996). For example, it appears that individuals from non-Anglo-Saxon cultures "often fail to meet PTSD diagnostic criteria because they lack avoidant/numbing symptoms despite the presence of reexperiencing and arousal symptoms" (Marsella et al., 1996, p. 533). Further, in some cultures, classic PTSD symptoms are often accompanied by more somatic and dissociative symptoms than are found in North American groups (Marsella et al., 1996).

Growing clinical awareness that not all posttraumatic stress responses are captured by the PTSD diagnosis, especially in non-Anglo cultures, has led to the concept of *culture-bound* stress responses. It should be noted, however, that PTSD itself should be considered partially culture bound, since it best describes the posttraumatic symptomatology of those born or raised in Anglo/European countries. Appendix I of *DSM-IV* lists several culture-bound syndromes that involve potentially trauma-related dissociation, somatization, and anxiety responses (for example, *attaques de nervios*, *nervios*, *dhat*, *latah*, *pibloktoq*, *shin-byung*, and *susto*). Also prevalent among some non-Western trauma survivors are complaints such as *khyal* attacks, *srog-rLung* imbalance, *djinnati*, and *khsaoy beh daung* (Benedict, Mancini, & Grodin, 2009; Hinton, Hinton, Um, Chea, & Sak, 2002; Hinton, Pich, Marques, Nickerson, & Pollack, 2010; Kianpoor & Rhoades, 2005).

This variation in the psychological impacts of trauma does not mean that individuals from other societies or cultures do not ever develop PTSD; symptoms of PTSD can be found among traumatized people to some extent regardless of geographic locale (Hinton & Lewis-Fernández, 2011). Rather, the existing literature suggests that cultural variables can impact trauma responses, and thus clinicians should be vigilant to the possibility of trauma syndromes above and beyond classic PTSD when clients originate from other cultures.

Suggested Reading

Brewin, C. R., Andrews, B., & Valentine, J. D. (2000). Meta-analysis of risk factors for posttraumatic stress disorder in trauma-exposed adults. *Journal of Consulting and Clinical Psychology, 68,* 748–766.

Briere, J. (2004). *Psychological assessment of adult posttraumatic states: Phenomenology, diagnosis, and measurement* (2nd ed.). Washington, DC: American Psychological Association.

Brown, L. S. (2008). *Cultural competence in trauma therapy: Beyond the flashback.* Washington, DC: American Psychological Association.

Bryant, R. A., Friedman, M. J., Spiegel, D., Ursano, R. J., & Strain, J. J. (2011). A review of acute stress disorder in DSM-5. *Depression and Anxiety, 28,* 802–817.

Herman, J. L. (1992). *Trauma and recovery: The aftermath of violence—From domestic abuse to political terror.* New York, NY: Basic Books.

Marsella, A. J., Friedman, M. J., Gerrity, E. T., & Scurfield, R. M. (Eds.). (1996). *Ethnocultural aspects of posttraumatic stress disorder: Issues, research, and clinical applications.* Washington, DC: American Psychological Association.

van der Kolk, B. A., McFarlane, A. C., & Weisaeth, L. (1996). *Traumatic stress: The effects of overwhelming experience on mind, body, and society.* New York, NY: Guilford.

3

Assessing Trauma and Posttraumatic Outcomes

Chapter 2 outlined the various symptoms, difficulties, and disorders that can arise from trauma exposure. The current chapter describes a number of ways in which these posttraumatic outcomes—and the events that produced them—can be assessed. We strongly encourage the use of empirically validated assessment instruments and structured diagnostic interviews. However, it is also true that most "real-world" clinical assessments occur in the context of less formal, relatively unstructured interchanges between the client and clinician during an intake session. Although more subjective, and thus potentially more prone to interpretative error, observation of client responses can yield important, sometimes unique, information that has direct implications for subsequent treatment. For this reason, we begin with the clinical interview and then move on to the application of more standardized methodologies.

Assessment in the Clinical Interview

Immediate Concerns

Most of this chapter describes assessment approaches that allow the clinician to evaluate specific trauma-related symptoms or dysfunction. Such assessment is necessary to ensure that whatever interventions occur are best suited to the client's specific needs. However, the evaluation of the client's immediate level of safety, psychological stability, and readiness for further assessment and treatment is even more critical.

Life Threat

The first focus of assessment in any trauma-related situation is whether the client is in imminent danger of loss of life or bodily integrity, or is at risk for hurting others (Briere & Lanktree, 2011). This includes—in the case of immediate accident, disaster, or physical attack—assessment of whether the client is medically stable. In cases of ongoing interpersonal violence, it is also very important to determine whether the client is in danger of victimization from others in the near future. Most generally, the hierarchy of assessment is as follows:

1. Is there danger of imminent death (for example, by bleeding, internal injuries, toxic or infectious agents) or immediate danger of loss of limb or other major physical functioning?

2. Is the client incapacitated (for example, through intoxication, brain injury or delirium, severe psychosis) to the extent that he or she cannot attend to his or her own safety (for example, wandering into streets or unable to access available food or shelter)?

3. Is the client acutely suicidal?

4. Is the client a danger to others (for example, homicidal or making credible threats to harm someone), especially when means are available (for example, a gun)?

[*Note:* No. 3 and No. 4 are of equal importance.]

5. Is the client's immediate psychosocial environment unsafe (for example, is he or she vulnerable to maltreatment or exploitation by others)?

The first goal of trauma intervention, when any of these issues are present, is to ensure the physical safety of the client or others, often through referral or triage to emergency medical or psychiatric services, law enforcement, or social services. It is also important, whenever possible, to involve supportive and less affected family members, friends, or others who can assist the client in this process.

Psychological Stability and Stress Tolerance

Psychological stability is also very important. A common clinical error is to immediately assess for psychological symptoms or disorders in a trauma survivor without first determining his or her overall level of psychological homeostasis. Individuals who have recently experienced a traumatic event, such as a rape or mass disaster, may still be in a state of crisis at the time of assessment—in some cases psychologically disorganized to the extent that they are unable to fully comprehend their current situation, let alone respond to a clinician's inquiries or interventions. In such instances, as is true with some cases of debilitating longer-term trauma impacts, psychological assessment may not only further challenge the survivor's fragile equilibrium, but it may also lead to compromised assessment results. For this reason, the first step in the mental health evaluation of trauma victims should be to determine the individual's relative level of psychological stability. When it appears that the client is overwhelmed or cognitively disorganized, stabilizing interventions (for example, reassurance, psychological support, or reduction in the level of environmental stimuli) should be provided before more detailed evaluation is pursued.

In some cases, although the trauma survivor may appear superficially stable following a traumatic event, he or she may suddenly display extreme distress, high anxiety, intrusive posttraumatic symptoms, or outbursts of anger when faced with even superficial inquiry about the event. As described later in this chapter, these reactions are referred to as *activation responses*—intense, often intrusive, trauma-specific psychological states that are triggered by reminders of the traumatic event. Although some level of activation is normal—even desirable—during treatment, and most survivors in research studies do not report significant negative effects of trauma evaluation, per se (E. B. Carlson et al., 1993; Griffin et al., 2003), assessment-related activation may be psychologically challenging if the individual does not have sufficient capacities to internally regulate his or her distress. As a result, it is important to determine the extent to which trauma issues can be discussed with a given survivor without unduly "retraumatizing" him or her. When excessive activation is likely, it is usually preferable to at least temporarily defer significant questions about or discussion of traumatic material (Najavits, 2002). The decision to avoid significant discussion of trauma with a trauma survivor should be made carefully, however, given the often helpful effects of talking about traumatic memories (see Chapter 4) and the sometimes immediate need for assessment.

At the risk of repetition, the usual components of assessment should be initiated only after the traumatized person's immediate safety, psychological stability, and capacity to discuss traumatic material have been verified. Failure to adequately evaluate these preconditions may result in unwanted outcomes, ranging from unnecessary client distress to, in more extreme cases, temporary emotional destabilization.

Assessing Trauma Exposure

Once the clinician has determined that the client is safe and reasonably stable, the specifics of trauma exposure and response can be investigated. In many cases, the clinician begins by asking about the traumatic event or events, including the nature of the trauma and its characteristics (for example, severity, duration, frequency, level of life threat). Because it is logical to start with events and then move on to outcomes, assessment of trauma exposure is presented here before the assessment of trauma effects. In some cases, however, the client's emergent psychological state is obviously of greater initial concern than how he or she got that way. For example, except in some forensic situations, the evaluation of an acute rape victim often will focus more immediately on her or his emotional functioning and psychological symptoms than on the specifics of the rape itself. In other cases, however, especially when the trauma is further in the past and the client is not currently acutely distressed, it is reasonable to begin with a trauma history.

Although one might assume that traumatized individuals easily disclose the events that bring them to therapy, this is not always the case. In fact, several studies indicate that trauma survivors are often reluctant to volunteer detailed (or any) information in this area unless directly asked, due to embarrassment, a desire to avoid reactivating traumatic memories, or the clinician's own avoidance of such information (Agar & Read, 2002). For example, Briere and Zaidi (1989) surveyed the admission charts of a randomly selected group of nonpsychotic women presenting to a psychiatric emergency room (PER) and found that only 6 percent documented a history of childhood sexual abuse. In a second phase of the study, PER clinicians were requested to routinely ask female patients about any history of childhood sexual victimization. When charts from this phase were examined, documentation of a sexual abuse history increased more than tenfold. Further, sexual abuse history assessed in the second phase was associated with a wide variety of presenting problems, including suicidality, substance abuse, multiple Axis I diagnoses, and an increased rate of borderline personality disorder.

We recommend that each client, whatever the presenting complaint, be assessed for trauma history as part of a complete mental health evaluation. When this occurs will vary according to the clinical situation. Often, as described previously, traumatized clients present with a chief complaint, such as depression, suicidality, generalized anxiety, or unexplained panic attacks, that does not obviously include the trauma. In such cases, it is advisable to explore with the individual the symptoms that bring him or her in for treatment before delving into the possibility of trauma exposure. This allows the client to develop an initial sense of trust and rapport with the evaluator, before answering what may be perceived as intrusive (if not irrelevant) questions about traumatic experiences.

Many individuals, especially those who have never before been evaluated by a mental health professional, respond to questions about trauma history, particularly child abuse and other forms of interpersonal victimization, with embarrassment and/or guardedness. It is not uncommon for clients to ask, "Why do you need to know that?" upon being queried about specifics of their trauma history. Victims of interpersonal violence who have been repeatedly hurt and betrayed by others may be especially reluctant to share intimate details with an evaluator who they have just met.

Even those clients whose chief complaints are related to a particular acute or past traumatic event may balk at being asked other questions about their past. The victim of an earthquake who complains of acute anxiety, for example, may not want to answer questions about child abuse, feeling that such details are not relevant to his or her current situation. Likewise, the recent rape victim may interpret questions about other sexual assaults and childhood sexual abuse as implicit criticism from the evaluator, or as a subtle message that he or she in some way "asks" to be victimized.

In light of such concerns, general guidelines for assessment of trauma exposure include the following:

- Establish an initial level of trust and rapport before assessing trauma.
- Spend some time at the beginning of the assessment interview exploring the client's overt reason for presenting for clinical services, whatever it may be.

- Ask questions in an empathic and nonjudgmental manner.
- Become comfortable talking about details of sexual abuse and violence experiences with clients; victims of interpersonal traumas may be especially sensitive to nuances in the clinician's voice and body language. For example, certain clients may avoid reporting disturbing experiences if they believe that the clinician will be too upset by such material or will make negative judgments.
- Use behavioral definitions. For example, a woman who was sexually assaulted and forced to perform oral sex on a man but was not vaginally penetrated may not believe that she was in fact raped. It is rarely sufficient to ask, "Were you ever raped?" Instead, a better question might be, "Did anyone ever do something sexual to you that you didn't want, or make you do something sexual to them?"
- Remember that trauma is deeply personal and that the client may fear being stigmatized. In the course of a trauma-focused interview, clients may disclose information that they have never told anyone before. The clinician should keep this possibility in mind and respond to such disclosures with visible support.
- Be aware that disclosure of trauma history may bring up intense feelings, including shame, embarrassment, and anger. Clients may respond in a variety of ways—some may cry, others may become agitated and anxious, and some may withdraw. Still others may become irritable and even hostile toward the interviewer. In such contexts, gentle support and validation of the client's feelings and reactions may be especially important.
- Repeat assessments as necessary—some clients may not disclose certain trauma-related information at the initial evaluation, but may do so later, when they feel more comfortable with the clinician and the treatment process.

Some evaluators find it helpful to preface questions about trauma exposure with an opening that frames assessment in a supportive and nonjudgmental context. Examples of such opening statements might include these:

- "If it is okay with you, I'd like to ask you some questions about your past. These are questions that I ask every client/patient I see, so I can get a better sense of what [he or she] has been through."
- "I'd like to ask you some questions about experiences you may have had in the past. If you feel uncomfortable at any time, please let me know. Okay?"
- "Sometimes people have experienced things in their pasts that affect how they are feeling now. If it is okay, I'd like to ask you some questions about things that may have happened to you."

Other clinicians prefer to integrate assessment of trauma history into the flow of the initial interview. What follows are two examples of how this might be accomplished with different clients. These examples are not intended to provide an exhaustive list of potential trauma exposures; rather, they illustrate ways of approaching traumatic material in a nonthreatening and organic way in the context of a mental health evaluation.

- For those clients who appear reluctant to discuss interpersonal information, a trauma history can be gathered at the same time as medical history is assessed. This formalizes the questioning and places it in the context of other, more routine questions that are generally experienced as both necessary and nonthreatening. The flow of questions in such a scenario might follow a pattern such as this:

  - "Do you have any medical problems?"
  - "Are you in any physical discomfort right now?"
  - "What medications are you currently taking?"
  - "Do you have any allergies to medications?"
  - "Have you ever had any surgeries?"
  - "Have you ever been in a car accident? Were you injured? Did you receive medical attention?"
  - "Have you ever been in a disaster such as a fire, earthquake, or flood? Were you injured? Did you receive medical attention?"
  - "Have you ever had a head injury? Did you lose consciousness? Did you receive medical attention?"
  - "Have you ever witnessed a violent event, such as a shooting?"
  - "Have you ever been assaulted by anyone? How old were you? Were you injured? Did you receive any medical attention afterward?"
  - "Has anyone ever forced you to do something sexual against your will? Has anyone ever touched you sexually in a way that made you feel uncomfortable? Did you receive medical attention for this?"

[Follow with childhood trauma exposure questions.]

- For those patients who are willing to discuss their family and relationships, an alternative scenario for questioning might follow a different pattern:

  - "Where did you grow up?"
  - "What was your childhood like?"
  - "Who did you grow up with?"
  - "When you were a child, what was home like?"
  - "Were both parents at home?"
  - "Did you witness any violence at home when you were a child?"
  - "How were you punished when you were a child?"
  - "When you were a child was anyone abusive to you in any way?" (In some cases, this question alone will prompt the client to report all of his or her childhood abuse experiences.)
  - "Did anyone ever do anything sexual to you when you were a child, or make you do something sexual to them?"

[Follow with more detailed childhood trauma questions.]

- "Have you ever been in a car accident? Were you injured? Did you receive any medical attention afterward?"
- "As an adult, were you ever attacked by anyone? How old were you? Were you injured? Did you receive any medical attention afterward?"

[Follow with other adult trauma questions.]

Given potential client reluctance in this area, and the likelihood that some traumas will be overlooked in an informal assessment interview, trauma assessment is probably best accomplished when the clinician refers to a pre-defined list of potential traumas during the evaluation interview. This structured approach ensures not only that trauma exposure will be formally assessed, but also that all relevant types of trauma will be explored. Included in Appendix 1 of this book is an instrument that can be used to evaluate the client's life history of traumatic events, the Initial Trauma Review-3 (ITR-3). This is a behaviorally anchored, semi-structured interview that allows the clinician to assess most major forms of trauma exposure. It also inquires about subjective distress in response to these traumas, as required by the *DSM-IV* A2 criterion for PTSD and ASD. The clinician should feel free to paraphrase the items of the ITR-3 in such a way that the process is supportive and nonstigmatizing, and to add any additional traumas that he or she thinks are relevant to the client's situation. There are also a number of other instruments available in the psychological literature (for example, the Stressful Life Events Screening Questionnaire, developed by Goodman, Corcoran, Turner, Yuan, & Green, 1998) that the clinician may use to review a client's trauma history. In addition, some psychological tests of traumatic stress include traumatic event reviews, as described later in this chapter.

Evaluating the Effects of Trauma

For the purposes of this book, the effects of trauma can be divided into two categories: *process* responses, involving trauma effects that are readily determined during the interview, and *symptom* responses, involving the more classic markers or forms of psychological disturbance.

Process Responses

Considerable information may be gained by observing the traumatized client's behavior during the clinical interview or therapy session. Because this form of assessment is based on the clinician's perceptions, and thus is influenced by both clinical experience and personal subjectivity, data gathered in this manner are not always as valid as the results of standardized testing. On the other hand, the alert and perceptive evaluator often can discern things that are rarely, if ever, tapped by psychometric tests. Such information can be divided into four areas: activation responses, avoidance responses, affect dysregulation, and relational difficulties.

Activation Responses. As described in greater detail in Chapter 8, activation responses are the sudden emergence of posttraumatic emotions, memories, and/or cognitions in response to some sort of triggering stimulus. Some of these responses may be sensory reexperiencing of the traumatic event; in other cases the response is less extreme, involving sudden emotional distress or anxiety. Although extreme activation is generally to be avoided, in most cases lower levels of such responses can provide information regarding both severity of the client's current posttraumatic stress and the degree to which his or her trauma memories can be readily activated by the external environment.

Typically, the clinician's intent is not to trigger activation, but rather to be alert to its emergence during the interview or during therapy. For example, the clinician interviewing a burn patient in his hospital room a week after a fire may watch carefully for changes in facial expression, tone of voice, verbal content, or even respirations when the patient is gently asked about his or her trauma experience. Or a child sexual abuse survivor may be observed for changes in emotion, body position, eye movement, or verbal syntax while he or she discusses a childhood molestation experience.

When the trauma is relatively recent, a moderate level of activation is often a good sign, indicating that the client is not in a highly avoidant or numbed state and that his or her traumatic material is available for internal processing. Especially easily triggered and intensely experienced activation, however, may suggest more severe posttraumatic stress and may indicate that unwanted intrusive symptoms can be triggered by a wide variety of stimuli in the environment. In a similar vein, easily triggered activation in chronic traumatic states (for example, tearfulness and distress in a combat veteran when discussing war experiences that occurred 30 years prior to the interview) may indicate inadequate processing, since, in the uncomplicated case, posttraumatic stress would be expected to resolve—or at least decrease—naturally over that time period.

The attuned examiner or therapist may find that consistent attention to an individual's emotional, verbal, and motor reactivity to trauma cues provides continuous information regarding (1) the level of posttraumatic stress the person is experiencing, and (2) the extent to which trauma reexperiencing is being blocked through dissociation or other avoidance responses. Information regarding the client's level of posttraumatic activation not only can assist in diagnosis and assessment, but it may also indicate his or her level and type of response to the exposure component of trauma therapy (see Chapter 8).

Avoidance Responses. Observational assessment of avoidance in trauma survivors generally involves attention to both inferred underactivation—the relative absence of expected activation—and the visible presence of avoidance activities. In the former case, avoidance can be hypothesized when activation would be expected (for example, in a recent sexual assault victim) but where little or no significant emotional reactivity is observed (for example, describing the event in an especially detached or overly matter-of-fact manner). In the latter, the clinician is able to detect direct evidence of dissociation or substance use, or the client informs the clinician of effortful avoidance (for example, no longer driving a car after a motor vehicle accident).

Underactivation can occur as a result of a number of different defensive responses that are not, by themselves, visible, although their effects may be inferred. They include the following:

- *Emotional numbing.* The client displays reduced emotional reactivity to trauma triggers as a result of severe posttraumatic stress (see Chapter 2).
- *Dissociative disengagement.* The client engages in subtle cognitive-emotional separation or disengagement from potentially upsetting stimuli (for example, by not understanding obvious questions at times or seeming somewhat distant interpersonally), but does so without exhibiting major signs of dissociation, per se.
- *Thought suppression.* The client cognitively blocks or suppresses emotionally upsetting thoughts or memories, often visible as sudden lapses in discourse or reports of inadequate memory.
- *Denial.* The client acknowledges the traumatic event, but develops a theory or perspective that reduces the perceived threat or seriousness associated with the trauma.
- *Anxiolysis without obvious intoxication.* The client uses a psychoactive substance (for example, alcohol or a benzodiazepine) prior to the session that is not evident during treatment or evaluation but that blocks anxious responses to trauma triggers.

Underactivation is often both difficult to identify and hard to pin down in terms of the specific mechanism involved. For example, when a trauma survivor presents as less upset than the circumstances might warrant (for example, a calm and nontraumatized demeanor one day after involvement in a major automobile accident with fatalities), potential mechanisms include those listed as well as the possibility that the client is not engaging in avoidance at all, but, instead, is especially resilient to stress. Despite this uncertainty, the experienced trauma clinician often learns to discriminate various types of defensive avoidance strategies from resilience, whether through increased sensitivity to subtle avoidance mechanisms or through a growing sense of when a posttraumatic response would logically occur.

Explicit signs of avoidance, on the other hand, usually involve the use of mechanisms that are visible to the clinician or are expressed directly. Most typically, these include the following:

- *Visible dissociative symptoms.* The client "spaces out," demonstrates obvious fixity of gaze (for example, the "thousand-mile stare"), moves in a disconnected manner, or seems to enter a different identity state.

- *Self-reported dissociation.* The client describes symptoms such as depersonalization (for example, out-of-body experiences) or derealization (for example, feeling like he or she is in a dream).
- *Intoxication.* The client comes to the session visibly intoxicated on drugs or alcohol.
- *Effortful avoidance.* The client describes behaviors consistent with the effortful avoidance cluster of PTSD symptoms, such as avoiding people, places, or situations that might trigger posttraumatic intrusions or distress. Effortful avoidance is also evidenced in the session by visible attempts to avoid discussing traumatic material. Missed sessions also may reflect effortful avoidance.

The excessive presence of emotional avoidance, in the evaluation or treatment session or elsewhere, typically signals a greater likelihood of posttraumatic stress (Pietrzak, Harpaz-Rotem, & Southwick, 2011; Plumb, Orsillo, Luterek, 2004), an increased chance of chronicity (Lawrence, Fauerbach, & Munster, 1996; Marshall et al., 2006), and potentially greater difficulties dealing with the exposure component of therapy (Jaycox, Foa, & Morral, 1998; Zoellner et al., 2011). In addition, client reports of effortful avoidance may indicate specific areas in which the client is having especially intrusive experiences (for example, avoidance of sexual activity because it triggers flashbacks to a rape). Such information may allow the clinician to explore Cluster B (reliving) PTSD symptoms that otherwise might not be identified or disclosed. It is important to note, however, that avoidance is typically a coping response that the survivor uses to maintain psychological stability in the face of potentially destabilizing trauma memories. As a result, although such responses typically indicate traumatic stress, they are not necessarily maladaptive at the moment they occur—especially early in the recovery process.

Affect Dysregulation. Some trauma survivors are prone to visible difficulties in affect regulation. Affect regulation refers to the individual's relative capacity to tolerate painful internal states (*affect tolerance*) and to internally reduce such distress without resorting to dissociation or other avoidance techniques (*affect modulation*). Affect regulation problems appear to arise from, among other phenomena, extreme and/or early trauma exposure (Briere & Rickards, 2007; Pynoos, Steinberg, & Piacentini, 1999; Schore, 2003) and, as noted earlier, are associated with subsequent distress-avoidance symptoms such as substance abuse, impulsivity, suicidality, self-injurious behavior, and other seemingly "personality disorder"–level responses (Briere et al., 2011; van der Kolk et al., 2005). Individuals with reduced affect regulation capacities may be less able to process traumatic memories in therapy without becoming overwhelmed by the associated painful emotions. The risk of overwhelming trauma survivors with too much therapeutic exposure is of sufficient concern that some clinicians (for example, Briere & Lanktree, 2011; Cloitre, Koenen, Cohen, & Han, 2002; Linehan, 1993a) consider affect dysregulation to be a central issue for those with more complex traumas. In other cases, typically

when the trauma is less severe and occurs later in life, affect regulation difficulties may be less relevant. In any case, however, a complete assessment of
the trauma victim should include such issues so that the treating clinician can
either address them in therapy (see Chapter 6) or be satisfied that otherwise
effective therapy is unlikely to retraumatize the client.

Problems with affect regulation may be identified in the assessment or
therapy session by any of the following signs:

- Mood swings that are not attributable to a bipolar or cyclothymic disorder
- Very short (for example, measured in hours), yet symptomatically
  intense depressive episodes that seem to resolve spontaneously
- Sudden, extreme, emotional distress during the session, with apparent
  difficulty calming down or shifting to a more positive emotional state
  thereafter
- A tendency to act out, self-mutilate, become aggressive, make suicide
  attempts or gestures, or otherwise engage in sudden tension reduction
  behaviors when upset or distressed
- Reports of long-term substance abuse or dependence
- Sudden dissociative responses in the context of strong emotionality

When such signs suggest affect regulation difficulties, the clinician should
evaluate the possibility that (1) the client has a history of severe or early
child abuse and neglect and/or (2) he or she has a personality disorder characterized by affective instability (although see Chapter 2 for cautions about
overgeneralizing from the borderline personality disorder diagnosis). In such
cases, as noted in Chapter 8, therapeutic intervention (especially exposure
activities) should be carefully titrated to the client's existing capacity to
regulate painful feelings.

Relational Disturbance. Relational information is obtained in the interview
by observing the client's responses to the clinician and to the therapy environment. Such information can also be extracted from the content of client
disclosures regarding important others in his or her life. In general, these
responses signal underlying cognitive schemas, assumptions, and beliefs (as
well as their associated affects) that the individual carries regarding important interpersonal figures and relationships.

Central relational issues (and their associated intra-interview signs) are
discussed next.

Alertness to interpersonal danger.

Because many trauma survivors have been hurt, betrayed, or otherwise maltreated in interpersonal relationships, they may respond to evaluation or treatment with hypervigilance to physical or emotional danger (Courtois, 2004;
Herman, 1992b). In extreme cases, this response may take on nearly paranoid
proportions: The recent victim of torture or rape may covertly examine the

clinical setting for possible weapons, spy holes, or hiding places for other people; the refugee from a totalitarian state may scrutinize the clinical process for evidence of governmental collusion; the stalking or battering victim may voice fears that he or she was followed to the session or that the clinician is in communication with his or her perpetrator; and the veteran of the war in Iraq may position himself or herself for ready access to the nearest doorway.

Although such responses are not always part of the clinical presentation of trauma survivors, even those less severely affected may display signs of hyperalertness to potential aggression, boundary violation, unfair criticism, or other potential dangers. The client may question the evaluator or therapist regarding his or her intentions, the appropriateness or relevance of various assessment questions, and the intended use of the information gathered from the session. Sexual trauma and trafficking victims may evidence special distrust of male interviewers, and those with highly punitive parents may be hypersensitive to the possibility of negative evaluation by the clinician.

Although the presence of such preoccupations may indicate a specific sensitivity to evaluation and interactions with authority figures (Briere & Lanktree, 2011), the fact that danger schemas are easily triggered in the survivor may signal a generalized expectation of potential injury in interpersonal situations and is, most basically, a reflection of posttraumatic stress.

Abandonment issues.

Individuals with histories of childhood neglect or rejection may signal abandonment concerns or sensitivity to rejection during assessment and treatment—both by their description of significant others in their lives and by their responses to the clinician. There may be a preoccupation with themes of needing people or relationships (sometimes regardless of the valence or health of those connections), fears or expectations of abandonment or loss in relationships, or historical renditions that seem excessively characterized by being left or rejected. In the session, clients with abandonment issues may become especially attached to the clinician, even over a very short period of time; they may be reluctant to allow termination of the interview and may seem especially "clingy" or dependent. On occasion, they may express anger or despair regarding the examiner's perceived insufficient caring or support and the brevity of the evaluation or therapy session, or concern that the clinician is not sufficiently attuned to their emotional experience. Also common is the tendency for clinician unavailability (for example, while on vacation or during personal emergencies) to trigger abandonment schemas and produce anger or despondency.

As might be expected, it is not always easy to detect abandonment fears in the evaluation interview or the first sessions of treatment—it may only be later in psychotherapy that the client's underlying preoccupation with relationships and avoiding abandonment or rejection becomes clear. As noted in Chapter 9, however, such issues are highly relevant in work with those who

were neglected or maltreated early in life. Not only do they represent potential sources of distress and conflict as the client encounters the constraints of
the treatment process, but the underlying dysfunctional schemas they reflect
are important targets for psychological intervention.

Need for self-protection through interpersonal control.

The experience of helplessness that arises from interpersonal victimization may lead to a later need for personal control in relation to others. Often,
this manifests as an insistence on autonomy, a tendency to micromanage
one's interactions with others so that one's own safety and self-determination
are intact, and negative responses to control, perceived manipulation, or
influence by other people. This interpersonal style may also manifest as difficulty with authority figures who, by definition, have some degree of
implicit control over the trauma survivor.

Those individuals with a high need for control may engage in behaviors
that seek to maximize their own autonomy during interpersonal interactions—including those that take place in the evaluation or treatment session.
For example, the trauma survivor may attempt to control the session by
speaking in a continuous manner, thereby keeping the clinician from exerting
verbal influence over the assessment or treatment process. In such instances,
interruptions by the therapist may be ignored or may prompt irritation or
anger. Similarly, the client may resist interview questions that lead away from
whatever topic he or she is discussing, often viewing the clinician's desire to
gain historical or psychological information as an attempt to overtake the
client's agenda or autonomy. Such behaviors arise from a fear of being revic-
timized by others and often reflect underlying relational anxiety—a posttraumatic state that leads to interpersonal rigidity and sometimes an almost
compulsive self-protectiveness.

Signs of a need for interpersonal control should be viewed as potential
evidence of a history of (1) highly controlling, intrusive, or abusive caretakers earlier in life; (2) early emotional neglect associated with a chaotic
childhood environment; and/or (3) later trauma experiences that were
especially characterized by extended helplessness, such as torture or forced
confinement.

The immediate implications of this interpersonal style are for the assessment process itself: It may be quite difficult to steer the control-focused
survivor into domains that the clinician (but not the client) feels are important to evaluate and treat, including current symptomatology, prior history,
and level of interpersonal functioning. Clinical experience suggests that the
clinician will be most effective in this regard to the extent that he or she does
not overly challenge the client's need for interpersonal control, but rather
works to reassure him or her—both verbally and nonverbally—of the benign
intent of the clinical process. In some cases, this will require considerable
patience on the part of the clinician.

Capacity to enter into and sustain a clinical relationship.

Psychological assessment and treatment typically require that the client enter into a working relationship with the clinician. Unfortunately, victims of interpersonal traumas such as child abuse, rape, torture, or partner violence may experience any sort of intimate connection to an authority figure as potentially dangerous—no matter how "safe" that figure is deemed by others (Briere & Lanktree, 2011; I. L. McCann & Pearlman, 1990). For example, during the normal process of therapy, the clinician may inadvertently activate victimization-related flashbacks, threat-related cognitions, or conditioned fears in the client that disrupt what otherwise might be a good working alliance. For this reason, one of the goals of assessment is to determine both the client's most obvious relational triggers and his or her overall capacity to form an ongoing relationship with the clinician. In cases where the relational capacities of the client are impaired, the therapist should be especially alert to potential difficulties with trust, boundaries, and safety—phenomena that may need to be addressed (or at least taken into account) before much overt trauma-related material can be processed.

To varying degrees, trauma survivors (especially those who were repeatedly victimized in childhood) may show evidence of some or all of the relational issues described here. On a practical level, such disturbances may result in responses and behaviors that are often labeled as "difficult," "manipulative," "demanding," or "attention seeking." Reframing such responses as the probable effects of trauma rather than as necessarily evidence of an underlying personality disorder may allow the clinician to approach the client in a more accepting, nonjudgmental, and therapeutically constructive manner.

These relational dynamics may also intrude upon the assessment process itself. The same trauma-related activations that discourage an effective therapeutic relationship may cause the client to produce test or interview responses that are compromised by extensive avoidance, fear, anger, or restimulated trauma memories (Briere, 2004). Although victimization-related hypervigilance, distrust, and traumatic reexperiencing are not easily addressed in the immediate context of psychological assessment, the clinician should do whatever he or she can to promote and communicate respect, safety, and freedom from judgment (Newman, Briere, & Kirlic, in press). Typically, this will involve the following:

- A positive, nonintrusive demeanor
- Good rapport
- Acknowledgment of the client's distress and immediate situation
- A clear explanation of the assessment process (including the goals of the evaluation and its intended use)
- Explicit boundaries regarding confidentiality and the limits of the assessment inquiry

It also may be helpful to avoid excessively direct or intrusive questions that might feel demeaning or interrogating, and, instead, work to facilitate the client's self-disclosure at his or her own pace and level of detail. When the assessment process communicates respect and appreciation for the victim's situation, he or she is more likely to be forthcoming about potentially upsetting, humiliating, or anxiety-producing traumas and symptoms.

Symptom Responses

Above and beyond the process signs of trauma response presented thus far, an obvious goal of trauma assessment is to determine the victim's current mental status and level of psychological functioning, and to inquire about the major symptoms known to be associated with trauma exposure. During a full psychological work-up, whether trauma focused or otherwise, the client should ideally be evaluated for the following forms of disturbance:

- Altered consciousness or mental functioning (for example, dementia, confusion, delirium, cognitive impairment, or other organic disturbance)
- Psychotic symptoms (for example, hallucinations, delusions, thought disorder, disorganized behavior, "negative" signs)
- Evidence of self-injurious or suicidal thoughts and behaviors
- Potential danger to others
- Mood disturbance (for example, depression, anxiety, anger)
- Substance abuse or addiction
- Personality dysfunction
- Reduced ability to care for self

In combination with other information (for example, from the client, significant others, and outside agencies or caregivers), these interview data provide the basis for diagnosis and an intervention plan in most clinical environments. However, when the presenting issue potentially includes posttraumatic disturbance, the classic mental status and symptom review is likely to miss important information. Individuals with significant trauma exposure—perhaps especially victims of violence—do not always disclose the full extent of their trauma history or their posttraumatic symptomatology unless directly asked, and thus require specific, concrete investigation in these areas.

When there is a possibility of trauma-related disturbance, the assessment interview should address as many (if not all) of the following additional components as is possible, many of which were outlined in the previous chapter:

- Symptoms of posttraumatic stress
  - Intrusive/reliving experiences such as flashbacks, nightmares, intrusive thoughts and memories
  - Avoidance symptoms such as behavioral or cognitive attempts to avoid trauma-reminiscent stimuli, as well as emotional numbing
  - Hyperarousal symptoms such as decreased or restless sleep, muscle tension, irritability, jumpiness, or attention/concentration difficulties

- Dissociative responses
  - Depersonalization or derealization experiences
  - Fugue states
  - "Spacing out" or cognitive-emotional disengagement
  - Amnesia or missing time
  - Identity alteration or confusion
- Substance abuse
- Somatic disturbance
  - Conversion reactions (for example, paralysis, anesthesia, blindness, deafness)
  - Somatization (excessive preoccupation with bodily dysfunction)
  - Psychogenic pain (for example, pelvic pain or chronic pain that cannot be explained medically)
- Sexual disturbance (especially in survivors of sexual abuse or assault)
  - Sexual distress (including sexual dysfunction and/or pain)
  - Sexual fears and conflicts
- Trauma-related cognitive disturbance
  - Low self-esteem
  - Helplessness
  - Hopelessness
  - Excessive or inappropriate guilt
  - Shame
  - Overvalued ideas regarding the level of danger in the environment
  - Idealization of the perpetrator or inaccurate rationalization or justification of the perpetrator's behavior
- Tension reduction activities
  - Self-mutilation
  - Bingeing/purging
  - Excessive or inappropriate sexual behavior
  - Compulsive stealing
  - Impulsive aggression
- Transient posttraumatic psychotic reactions
  - Trauma-induced cognitive slippage or loosened associations
  - Trauma-induced hallucinations (often trauma congruent)
  - Trauma-induced delusions (often trauma congruent, especially paranoia)
- Culture-specific trauma responses (for example, *attaques de nervios*), when assessing individuals from other countries or cultures

This list may be more comprehensive than necessary for certain posttraumatic presentations (for example, that of a motor vehicle accident survivor), although most of the components may be appropriate for chronic traumas (for example, extended child abuse or torture). Some review of these symptoms is usually indicated in a comprehensive evaluation, even if it is followed by a more structured diagnostic interview.

The assessment of the reexperiencing and dissociative symptoms associated with posttraumatic stress can be challenging, especially if the client has not described his or her symptoms to anyone before and views them as bizarre or even, perhaps, psychotic. Both reexperiencing and dissociation involve a change in level of consciousness and awareness of one's surroundings, which can be difficult to put into words. Suggested interview approaches and questions in this area are presented next.

- Posttraumatic nightmares. Some clients may not report nightmares that they only indirectly associate with the trauma in question—as a result, asking simply if they have nightmares about the event may not be sufficient. For example, a rape victim may not dream about the rape, but may have nightmares about being chased down a dark alley or about being attacked by animals or evil spirits. Clarifying questions may include these:
    - "Do you have bad or frightening dreams?"
    - "What are your dreams about?"
    - "Do you ever dream about bad things that have happened to you?"

- Flashbacks. Many clients will not know the meaning of the word *flashback* and may need a more descriptive explanation. More detailed questions include these:
    - "Do you ever have visions of the [trauma] that flash into your mind?"
    - "Do you ever see things in your mind that have happened to you?"
    - "Do you ever feel like the [trauma] is still happening to you?"
    - "Do you ever feel like you are reliving the [trauma]?"
    - "Do you ever hear the voice of the person who hurt you?"
    - "Do you ever hear the sound of the [gunshot/accident/war/other trauma]?"

- Intrusive thoughts. Some clients report intrusive or ego-dystonic thoughts that intrude "out of nowhere" and/or that are a major source of ongoing preoccupation. Questions that may assist in the exploration of such cognitive symptoms include these:
    - "Do you think about the [trauma] a lot? All the time?"
    - "Do you have times when you can't get the thought of the [trauma] out of your mind?"
    - "Does thinking about the [trauma] make it hard for you to concentrate on other things?"
    - *[For those with associated insomnia]* "When you can't sleep at night, are there thoughts that keep you awake?"

- Dissociation. Because dissociation is an internal process that may be difficult for the client to express to others, the clinician often can assist the clients by asking questions specific to the dissociative experience. Broken down by symptom type, these include the following:

- Depersonalization
  - "Do you ever feel like you are outside of your body?"
  - "Do you ever feel that you can't recognize parts of your body, or that they change size or shape?"
  - "Do you ever feel like you are watching things that happen to you from outside of yourself?"
- Derealization
  - "Do you ever feel like you are living in a dream or a movie?"
  - "Do you ever feel like people and things around you are not real?"
- Fugue states
  - "Have you ever found yourself somewhere far away and wondered how you got there?"
  - "Have you ever traveled a significant distance from home without realizing it?"
- Cognitive-emotional disengagement
  - "Do you find out that you 'space out' while at work or at home and lose track of what you are doing?"
  - "Do other people tell you that you sometimes seem 'a million miles away' or 'out of it'?"
- Amnesia or missing time
  - "Are there important things in your life that you can't remember very well or at all?"
  - "Do you ever have experiences where you 'zone out' for a few minutes and then find out that a much longer amount of time has passed?"
- Identity alteration
  - "Do people ever say that sometimes you act like a different person or use a different name?"
  - "Do you ever feel like there are different people inside you?"

Psychosis in the Context of Posttraumatic Response

Because dissociation and posttraumatic stress can sometimes involve reduced contact with—and altered perceptions of—the external environment, discriminating such responses from the symptoms of psychosis is not always easy. At times, the boundaries between posttraumatic reexperiencing and hallucinations; between reasonable posttraumatic fears, overvalued ideas, and paranoid delusions; and between anxiety-related cognitive fragmentation and frank thought disorganization may become blurred. In addition, severe trauma-related dissociation may appear nearly indistinguishable from withdrawn, internally preoccupied psychotic states. As reviewed in Chapter 2, there is a relationship between trauma and psychosis: Psychotic depression and PTSD are frequently comorbid, severe trauma can lead to brief psychotic reactions, and childhood trauma has been implicated in some instances of chronic psychosis. As well, those with underlying psychotic processes may be at increased risk for victimization due to decreased levels of vigilance or self-care. However, it is important to exercise caution before jumping to the conclusion that a trauma survivor is psychotic—not the least because some treatments for psychotic disorders are not typically effective for posttraumatic stress. In some instances, the clinical presentation may be so ambiguous as to make a definitive determination impossible; in such cases, clients should be carefully followed in treatment with frequent reassessments.

In differentiating psychosis from posttraumatic stress, the following, if present, may suggest a posttraumatic rather than psychotic process:

- Reexperiencing, as opposed to hallucinations
  - The content of the perceptions is trauma related (for example, hearing the voice of the perpetrator or another sound associated with the trauma). Note, however, that a prior trauma history can affect the content of psychotic hallucinations and delusions as well (Hardy et al., 2005; C. A. Ross, Anderson, & Clark, 1994; A. Thompson et al., 2010).
  - The perceptions occur in the context of a triggering experience or trauma-related anxiety.
  - The perceptions are not interactive: They do not, for example, "talk back" to the survivor.
  - The perceptions are not bizarre (for example, of God's face or demons).
- Posttraumatic expectations as opposed to delusions
  - The content of the ideas or fears is related to the traumatic event.
  - The client is able to express an understanding that such ideas or fears are not reasonable (for example, a woman who was raped may fear all men and may not want to be alone with men due to fears of being further victimized, although she may be able to cognitively express that not every man is a rapist).
- Trauma-induced fragmentation as opposed to loosened associations
  - The fragmentation or disorganization occurs only when the client is talking about upsetting or trauma-related subjects, and not throughout the client's discourse.
  - The level of disorganization decreases as the client becomes less anxious.

Conversely, the following, if present, may suggest a psychotic rather than posttraumatic process:

- Hallucinations as opposed to reexperiencing
  - At least some of the content of the perceptions is not trauma related (for example, hearing the voices of others not involved in the trauma).

- The perception is interactive, and/or the client is observed by others to be talking or laughing to himself or herself.

- Delusions as opposed to posttraumatic expectations

  - The content of the ideas/fears is not simply related to the traumatic event, but extends to other areas (for example, a woman who was raped not only states that all men will potentially hurt her, but believes that the CIA is wiretapping her home).

- Loosened associations as opposed to trauma-induced fragmentation

  - The cognitive slippage occurs throughout the client's discourse, whether the client is anxious or not, and irrespective of the topic of conversation.

The Structured Interview

Although an informal mental status examination and symptom review can reveal many forms of posttraumatic disturbance, the unstructured nature of such approaches often means that certain symptoms or syndromes may be overlooked or inadequately assessed. In fact, it is estimated that up to half of actual cases of PTSD are missed during unstructured clinical interviews (Zimmerman & Mattia, 1999). For this reason, some clinicians and most researchers use structured clinical measures when evaluating posttraumatic stress, especially PTSD. The most commonly used of these structured interviews are discussed next.

The Clinician-Administered PTSD Scale (CAPS)

The CAPS (Blake et al., 1995) is considered the "gold standard" of structured interviews for posttraumatic stress disorder. The CAPS has several helpful features, including standard prompt questions and explicit, behaviorally anchored rating scales, and assesses both frequency and intensity of symptoms. It generates both dichotomous and continuous scores for current (1 month) and lifetime ("worst ever") PTSD. In addition to the standard 17 PTSD items, the CAPS also contains items tapping posttraumatic impacts on social and occupational functioning, improvement in PTSD symptoms since a previous CAPS assessment, overall response validity, and overall PTSD severity, as well as items addressing guilt and dissociation. Unfortunately, the CAPS may require an hour or longer for complete administration, may sometimes provide more information than actually is needed clinically, and focuses only on PTSD. As *DSM-V* approaches, the CAPS authors have developed a new version that takes all criteria changes into account (F. W. Weathers, personal communication, May 22, 2012).

The Acute Stress Disorder Interview (ASDI)

When the diagnostic issue is ASD, as opposed to PTSD, the clinician may find the ASDI (Bryant, Harvey, Dang, & Sackville, 1998) useful. This interview consists of 19 items that evaluate dissociative, reexperiencing, effortful avoidance, and arousal symptoms. The ASDI has good reliability and validity and can be administered in a relatively short period of time (Bryant et al., 1998; Orsillo, 2001).

The Structured Interview for Disorders of Extreme Stress (SIDES)

The SIDES (Pelcovitz et al., 1997) was developed as a companion to existing interview-based rating scales for PTSD. The 45 items of the SIDES measure the current and lifetime presence of DESNOS and each of six symptom clusters: Affect Dysregulation, Somatization, Alterations in Attention or Consciousness, Self-Perception, Relationships with Others, and Systems of Meaning. Item descriptors contain concrete behavioral anchors in order to facilitate clinician ratings. The SIDES interview has good interrater reliability and internal consistency (Pelcovitz et al., 1997).

The Structured Clinical Interview for *DSM-IV* Dissociative Disorders-Revised (SCID-D)

The SCID-D (Steinberg, 1994, 2004) evaluates the existence and severity of five dissociative symptoms: amnesia, depersonalization, derealization, identity confusion, and identity alteration. This interview provides diagnoses for the five major *DSM-IV* dissociative disorders (presented in Chapter 2), along with acute stress disorder (although we recommend the ASDI for the latter). Also evaluated by the SCID-D are "intra-interview dissociative cues," such as alterations in demeanor, spontaneous age regression, and trancelike appearance, which are coded in a postinterview section.

The Brief Interview for Posttraumatic Disorders (BIPD)

Although the preceding (and other) diagnostic interviews are clearly helpful tools, we include the BIPD (Briere, 1998) in Appendix 2 (and at http://johnbriere.com) for those who desire a broader band, somewhat less structured interview. This measure, which can be photocopied or otherwise reproduced for general clinical use, is relatively easily and quickly administered. It reviews all those symptoms associated with a diagnosis of *DSM-IV* PTSD,

ASD, and brief psychotic disorder with marked stressors. On the other hand, the semi-structured format of the BIPD means that it is somewhat less objective than the CAPS or ASDI, and it does not provide as many detailed definitions regarding specific symptom criteria.

Psychological Tests

In contrast to clinical interviews, structured or otherwise, most psychological tests are self-administered, in the sense that the client completes a paper inventory using a pencil or pen. Standardized psychological tests have been normed on demographically representative samples of the general population, so that a specific score on such measures can be compared to what would be a "normal" value for that scale or test. We strongly recommend the use of such tests, since they provide objective, comparative data on psychological functioning (both trauma specific and general) in trauma survivors. A number of testing instruments are briefly described below. Not discussed are projective tests, although one (the Rorschach Ink Blot Test; Rorschach, 1921/1981) also can be helpful in the assessment of posttraumatic states (Armstrong & Kaser-Boyd, 2003; Luxenberg & Levin, 2004). The interested reader should consult the Suggested Reading list at the end of this chapter for books and articles that address in greater detail the psychometric evaluation of traumatized individuals.

Generic Tests

A variety of standardized psychological measures can be used to assess generic (that is, non-trauma-specific) psychological symptoms in adolescent and adult trauma survivors. Several of these assess anxiety, depression, somatization, psychosis, and other symptoms relevant to Axis I of *DSM-IV*. Because posttraumatic distress often includes such symptoms, a good psychological test battery should include at least one generic measure in addition to more trauma-specific tests.

Examples of often-used generic tests include the following:

- Minnesota Multiphasic Personality Inventory, 2nd edition (MMPI-2; Butcher, Dahlstrom, Graham, Tellegen, & Kaemmer, 1989)
- Minnesota Multiphasic Personality Inventory for Adolescents (MMPI-A; Butcher et al., 1992)
- Psychological Assessment Inventory (PAI; Morey, 1991)
- Millon Clinical Multiaxial Inventory, 3rd edition (MCMI-III; Millon, Davis, & Millon, 1997)
- Symptom Checklist-90-Revised (SCL-90-R; Derogatis, 1983)

Each of these tests (especially the PAI and MCMI-III) also provides some information on the personality-level (that is, Axis II) difficulties associated with the complex posttraumatic outcomes described in Chapter 2. In addition, three (the MMPI-2, PAI, and MCMI-III) include PTSD scales—although these scales are typically only moderately effective in identifying actual cases (and noncases) of posttraumatic stress disorder (Briere, 2004; E. B. Carlson, 1997). Most major generic instruments also include validity scales, used to detect client under- or overreporting of symptoms. Such scales can be helpful in identifying denial, exaggeration, and some cases of malingering. However, traumatized individuals—by virtue of the unusual quality of some posttraumatic symptoms—tend to score higher than others on negative impression (overreporting) scales, even when not attempting to malinger or otherwise distort their responses (for example, R. G. Jordan, Nunley, & Cook, 1992).

Trauma-Specific Tests

Although generic tests can detect many of the more nonspecific symptoms associated with trauma, as well as other comorbid disorders that might be present, psychologists often use more specific tests when assessing posttraumatic stress, dissociation, and trauma-related self-capacity disturbance (E. B. Carlson, 1997). The most common of these instruments are presented below. Non-normed/nonstandardized tests are listed only briefly, since measures without normative data cannot be easily interpreted relative to "normal"/less symptomatic individuals (see a brief discussion later in this chapter).

For Posttraumatic Stress and Associated Symptoms

- *Posttraumatic Stress Diagnostic Scale (PDS).* The PDS (Foa, 1995) evaluates exposure to potentially traumatic events, characteristics of the most traumatic event, 17 symptoms corresponding to *DSM-IV* PTSD criteria, and the extent of symptom interference in the individual's daily life. The PDS has high internal consistency (a .92 for the 17 symptom items) and good sensitivity and specificity with respect to a PTSD diagnosis (.82 and .77, respectively). PTSD symptom severity is estimated, based on extrapolation from a clinical sample of 248 women with trauma histories.
- *Davidson Trauma Scale (DTS).* The DTS (J. R. T. Davidson et al., 1997) is a 17-item scale measuring each *DSM-IV* symptom of PTSD on five-point frequency and severity scales. This measure yields a total score, as well as Intrusion, Avoidance/Numbing, and Hyperarousal scale scores, although there are no norms available for interpreting symptom severity on these scales. The DTS has good test-retest reliability and internal consistency, as well as concurrent validity. Criterion validity has been assessed vis-à-vis the SCID, where the DTS was found to have a sensitivity of .69 and a specificity of .95 in detecting PTSD.
- *Detailed Assessment of Posttraumatic Stress (DAPS).* The DAPS (Briere, 2001) yields *DSM-IV* diagnoses for PTSD and ASD, as well as

measuring a number of associated features of posttraumatic stress. Normed and standardized on general population individuals with a history of trauma exposure, the DAPS has validity scales (Positive Bias and Negative Bias) and clinical scales that evaluate lifetime exposure to traumatic events (Trauma Specification and Relative Trauma Exposure), immediate responses to a specified trauma (Peritraumatic Distress and Peritraumatic Dissociation), PTSD symptom clusters (Reexperiencing, Avoidance, and Hyperarousal), and three associated features of posttraumatic stress: Trauma-Specific Dissociation, Suicidality, and Substance Abuse. This measure has good sensitivity (.88) and specificity (.86) with respect to a CAPS diagnosis of PTSD.

- *Trauma Symptom Inventory-2 (TSI-2)*. The TSI-2 (Briere, 2011), a recent revision of the Trauma Symptom Inventory (TSI; Briere, 1995), is a 136-item standardized instrument that evaluates the overall level of posttraumatic symptomatology experienced over the previous 6 months. It has been normed on the general population and has been shown to have good reliability and validity. The TSI-2 has two validity scales (Response Level and Atypical Response), 12 clinical scales (Anxious Arousal, Depression, Anger, Intrusive Experiences, Defensive Avoidance, Dissociation, Sexual Disturbance, Impaired Self-Reference, Tension Reduction Behavior, Somatic Preoccupation, Suicidality, and Attachment Insecurity), and four summary scales (Posttraumatic Stress, Self-Disturbance, Externalization, and Somatization), determined by multiple groups confirmatory factor analysis.

For Affect Regulation, Interpersonal Relatedness, and Identity Problems

- *Trauma and Attachment Belief Scale (TABS)*. The TABS (Pearlman, 2003; formerly the Traumatic Stress Institute Belief Scale) is a normed and standardized instrument that measures disrupted cognitive schemas and need states associated with complex trauma exposure. It evaluates disturbance in five areas: Safety, Trust, Esteem, Intimacy, and Control. There are reliable subscales for each of these domains, rated both for "self" and "other." In contrast to more symptom-based tests, the TABS evaluates the self-reported needs and expectations of trauma survivors as they describe self in relation to others. For this reason, the TABS is helpful in understanding important assumptions that the client carries regarding his or her relationships to others, including the therapist.

- *Inventory of Altered Self Capacities (IASC)*. The IASC (Briere, 2000b) is a normed and standardized test of difficulties in the areas of relatedness, identity, and affect regulation. The scales of the IASC assess the following domains: Interpersonal Conflicts, Idealization-Disillusionment, Abandonment Concerns, Identity Impairment, Susceptibility to Influence,

Affect Dysregulation, and Tension Reduction Activities. Scores on the IASC have been shown to predict childhood trauma history, adult attachment style, interpersonal problems, suicidality, and substance abuse history in various samples. The Idealization-Disillusionment, Susceptibility to Influence, and Abandonment Concerns scales are useful in warning of potentially therapy-disrupting issues or dynamics that emerge in work with some survivors of more complex and severe trauma.

- *Bell Object Relations and Reality Testing Inventory (BORRTI)*. The only standardized test of what is generally referred to as object relations, the BORRTI (Bell, 1995) has scales that yield data on four constructs: Alienation, Insecure Attachment, Egocentricity, and Social Incompetence. These scales have been shown by the test author to predict and potentially explain relational dysfunction in individuals thought to have some form of personality disorder. Because the scales are linked to object relations theory, the results of this measure will be most directly applicable to clinicians who endorse that perspective.

For Dissociation

- *Dissociative Experiences Scale (DES)*. The DES (E. M. Bernstein & Putnam, 1986) is the most often used of the dissociation measures, although it is not normed on the general population. The DES taps "disturbance in identity, memory, awareness, and cognitions and feelings of derealization or depersonalization or associated phenomena such as déjà vu and absorption" (E. M. Bernstein & Putnam, 1986, p. 729). A score of 30 or higher on the DES correctly identified 74 percent of those with dissociative identity disorder (DID) and 80 percent of those without DID in a large sample of psychiatric outpatients (E. B. Carlson et al., 1993). Despite its nonstandardized/nonnormed psychometric status, it is included in this section because of its extremely wide use, and thus "quasi-normative" data.

- *Multiscale Dissociation Inventory (MDI)*. Based on data suggesting that dissociation is a multidimensional phenomenon, the MDI (Briere, 2002a) is a normed clinical test that consists of six scales (Disengagement, Depersonalization, Derealization, Memory Disturbance, Emotional Constriction, and Identity Dissociation), which, together, define an overall dissociation profile. The MDI is reliable and correlates as expected with child abuse history, adult trauma exposure, PTSD, and other measures of dissociation, including the DES. In one study, the Identity Dissociation scale had a specificity of .92 and a sensitivity of .93 with respect to a diagnosis of dissociative identity disorder (Briere, 2002a). At the time of this writing, the MDI is available without cost to qualified individuals (those licensed to perform psychological testing) at http://johnbriere.com.

Nonstandardized Tests

Because clinicians needed to evaluate posttraumatic disturbance well before there were standardized or validated tests available to them, a number of instruments were developed in research contexts that, as yet, have not been fully standardized and normed. The most common and potentially most useful of these, in addition to the DES, are the *Intrusive Experiences Scale* (IES; M. Horowitz, Wilner, & Alvarez, 1979), *Multidimensional Inventory of Dissociation* (MID; Dell, 2006), *Posttraumatic Cognitions Inventory* (Foa, Ehlers, Clark, Tolin, & Orsillo, 1999), *PTSD Checklist* (PCL; Weathers, Litz, Herman, Huska, & Keane, 1993), and the *Trauma Symptom Checklist-40* (TSC-40; Briere & Runtz, 1989; Elliott & Briere, 1992).

Some of these tests have been used in applied settings for years, and clinicians have developed cut-off scores for some in order to define normal versus clinical levels of distress (for example, the PCL). When deciding which of these measures to apply in a given clinical situation, we recommend that the clinician also consider any fully standardized and validated test that might be better (or additionally) employed, and consider any limitations of these tests that might constrain clinical interpretation. In general, psychometrically valid test interpretation (and modern psychological testing standards) requires that self-report clinical instruments demonstrate good internal consistency, convergent and discriminative validity, and statistical determination of symptom severity based on the relationship of a given score to the total distribution of scores in the general population (Anastasi & Urbina, 1997).

Health Status

A trauma evaluation is not complete without an assessment regarding the client's self-reported physical health status. At some point in the interview, the clinician (whether a medical or nonmedical practitioner) should ask if the client has any active medical conditions, whether he or she is in any current physical distress, and whether he or she takes any medications (including over-the-counter medications, vitamins, and herbal supplements). This part of the interview is especially relevant for traumatized individuals, because, as described in Chapter 2, those with PTSD are at increased risk for physical health problems. In addition, some medical conditions (such as endocrine problems, pain, neurological disorders, and traumatic brain injury) can mimic or overlap with the symptoms of PTSD (Asmundson & Taylor, 2006; Kudler & Davidson, 1995; McAllister & Stein, 2010).

Given this complexity, and the fact that somatization is more common in traumatized individuals, the determination of which symptoms are due to actual medical illness (and require medical intervention) often can be quite challenging. In health care settings that provide services to indigent, uninsured, or undocumented clients, or where, for various other reasons, clients have difficulty obtaining medical care, concerns about medical complications may be especially relevant. In such instances, the mental health clinician may be the client's primary point of contact with the health care system. We therefore recommend that therapists refer traumatized clients for full medical examinations and regular medical follow-ups.

Suggested Reading

Briere, J. (2004). *Psychological assessment of adult posttraumatic states: Phenomenology, diagnosis, and measurement* (2nd ed.). Washington, DC: American Psychological Association.

Briere, J., & Hodges, M. (2010). Assessing the effects of early and later childhood trauma in adults. In E. Vermetten, R. Lanius, & C. Pain (Eds.), *The impact of early life trauma on health and disease.* Cambridge, UK: Cambridge University Press.

Carlson, E. B. (1997). *Trauma assessments: A clinician's guide.* New York, NY: Guilford.

Simon, R. I. (Ed.). (1995). *Posttraumatic stress disorder in litigation: Guidelines for forensic assessment.* Washington, DC: American Psychiatric Press.

Weathers, F. W., Keane, T. M., & Foa, E. B. (2009). Assessment and diagnosis of adults. In E. B. Foa, T. M. Keane, M. J. Friedman, & J. A. Cohen (Eds.), *Effective treatments for PTSD: Practice guidelines from the International Society for Traumatic Stress Studies* (2nd ed., pp. 23–61). New York, NY: Guilford.

Wilson, J., & Keane, T. (Eds.). (2004). *Assessing psychological trauma and PTSD: A practitioner's handbook* (2nd ed.). New York, NY: Guilford.

PART II

Clinical Interventions

Once the client's trauma history and posttraumatic symptoms have been determined, trauma therapy can be initiated. We begin the treatment part of this book by outlining general issues relevant to trauma therapy; the more technical aspects of treatment follow.

We refer throughout these chapters to the integration of cognitive-behavioral, psychodynamic, mindfulness, and eclectic approaches in the treatment of trauma effects. It is our position that the various components of these methods can be combined into a single, broad therapeutic approach—one that can be adapted to the potentially wide range of symptoms and needs of each client. Nevertheless, these models are superficially quite different from one another, and some of their originators may disagree with the idea of combining their techniques with those of other clinicians. In our experience, however, effective therapy almost always consists of a variety of interventions and theoretical models—whether acknowledged by the clinician or not. For example, many good cognitive-behavioral therapists use relational techniques in their work with clients, and many psychodynamic interventions are, at their base, translatable into cognitive-behavioral principles.

A review of the existing literature on the treatment of posttraumatic states, in combination with clinical experience, suggests that effective therapy—irrespective of underlying theory—can usually be broken down into a number of broad components, the exact combination of which varies according to the client's specific clinical needs (Briere & Lanktree, 2011). These minimally consist of the following:

- An overall approach that is respectful, positive, and compassionate, and that provides support and validation in the context of an empathically attuned therapeutic relationship
- Psychoeducation on trauma and trauma symptoms

- Some form of stress reduction or affect regulation training
- Cognitive interventions that address harmful or debilitating trauma-related beliefs, assumptions, and perceptions
- Opportunities to develop a coherent narrative about the traumatic event
- Memory processing, usually involving guided self-exposure to trauma memories
- Processing of relational issues in the context of a positive therapeutic relationship
- Activities that increase self-awareness and self-acceptance, including opportunities to reflect on one's internal experience and change one's relationship to the effects of one's history

Many of these interventions may occur within the same therapy session and may be hard to distinguish from one another during the treatment process. Nevertheless, they represent, to some extent, separate processes and goals. For this reason, each receives detailed attention in the following chapters. We also include in Part II chapters on the treatment of more acute trauma presentations and the psychopharmacology of posttraumatic states.

4

Central Issues in
Trauma Treatment

A Basic Philosophy of Trauma,
Recovery, and Growth

Although much of this book is devoted to the technical aspects of treatment, we start this chapter with philosophical and, to some extent, theoretical issues associated with trauma therapy. This is because the way in which the clinician views trauma and trauma-related outcomes, and what he or she believes to be the overbridging goals and functions of treatment, have significant effects on the process and outcome of therapy.

Intrinsic Processing

Perspectives on trauma and its treatment vary among clinicians, and a variety of clinical models can inform effective psychotherapy. The approach that we advocate in this book emphasizes the probably innate tendency for humans to process trauma-related memories and, when possible, to move toward more adaptive psychological functioning. As discussed in more detail in Chapter 8, many of the "reexperiencing" symptoms of posttraumatic stress disorder can be conceptualized as recovery algorithms that humans have evolved over time as a response to trauma exposure (Briere, 1996, 2002b; see also a related perspective by M. J. Horowitz, 1978). The intrinsic function of these reliving experiences appears to be, at least in part, a way to process, desensitize, and integrate upsetting material. This implies that individuals who present with intrusive trauma-related symptoms are, in a sense, attempting to metabolize or internally resolve distressing thoughts, feelings, and memories. This perspective reframes many posttraumatic symptoms as, to some extent, adaptive and recovery-focused rather than as inherently pathological. It also suggests that therapeutic exposure (see Chapter 8) and other approaches to processing traumatic memories may work by optimizing those activities in which the client is already engaged, as opposed to imposing entirely new or alien techniques. Seen in this light, traumatized individuals are not collections of symptoms, but rather people who, at some level, are attempting to recover—albeit not always successfully. This view allows the therapist to more clearly understand expressed emotional pain as "just" emotional pain—not as intrinsically negative, nor as a trigger for countertransference, but rather as a process wherein the client can process her or his history and ultimately experience reduced emotional suffering.

A second, related notion offered here is that trauma can result in growth. Like many other therapists who work in this area, we have found that adversity and distress—beyond their capacity to disrupt and injure—often help people to develop in positive ways. As documented by various studies, this may involve new levels of psychological resilience, additional survival skills, greater self-knowledge and self-acceptance, a greater sense (and appreciation) of being alive, increased empathy, and a more broad and complex view of life in general (A. Brown, 2009; Joseph & Linley, 2008; V. E. O'Leary, 1998; K. Siegel & Schrimshaw, 2000; Updegraff & Taylor, 2000). The recently widowed person may learn new independence, the survivor of a heart attack may develop a more healthy perspective on life's priorities, and the person exposed to a catastrophic event may learn important things about his or her resilience in the face of tragedy. The implication is not that someone is lucky when bad things happen, but, rather, that not all outcomes associated with adversity are inevitably negative, and that the process of surmounting obstacles may lead to increased capacities, and perhaps even greater wisdom. The message is not that one should "look on the bright side," which can easily be seen as dismissive and unempathic, and may support avoidance. Instead, we suggest that the survivor's life, although perhaps irrevocably changed, is not over, and that future good things are possible.

Of course, some traumatic events are so overwhelming that they make growth extremely difficult; they may involve so much loss that it seems impossible (if not disrespectful) to suggest any eventual positive outcomes to the client. Survivors of traumas such as severe childhood abuse, torture, or disfiguring fire may feel that they have been permanently injured, if not ruined for life. In other cases, life experiences may have pushed some survivors so far into withdrawal and defense that they cannot easily see beyond the immediate goals of pain avoidance and psychological survival. Even in these instances, however, treatment should not be limited to symptom reduction; it may also include the possibility of new awareness, insights, and skills. In less tragic circumstances, it may even be possible to suggest that adversity can make the survivor more, as opposed to less.

This philosophy may appear to be a distraction from the technical job of trauma treatment. Clearly, an injured person first needs attention to immediate safety and life support, and help with painful symptoms; it is often only later that the more complicated and subtle aspects of recovery and growth become salient. Yet, ultimately, some of the best interventions in posttraumatic psychological injury are implicitly existential and hopeful. This perspective can also be beneficial for the therapist—the possibility that the client not only can recover, but also may grow from traumatic experience, brings tremendous richness and optimism to the job of helping hurt people.

Respect, Positive Regard, and Compassion

One of the implications of this philosophy is that the traumatized client should be seen as someone who, despite being confronted with potentially overwhelming psychic pain and disability, is struggling to come to terms with his or her history—and, perhaps, to develop beyond it. It is often hard to be in therapy, especially when (as is outlined in the next few chapters) such treatment requires one to feel things that one would rather not feel and think about things that one would rather not consider. The easy choice, in many cases, is to block awareness of the pain and avoid the thought—to "let sleeping dogs lie." It is a harder choice, when the option is available, to directly engage one's memories and their attendant psychological distress and attempt to integrate them into the fabric of one's life. As noted at various points in this book, it may be that—in order to survive pain—the client must engage in some level of avoidance in order to deal with otherwise overwhelmed memories, thoughts, and/or feelings during treatment. These responses are logical, even helpful, and should be understood as such by the clinician. Although sometimes problematic, such "resistance" does not contradict the fact that the client deserves considerable respect for being willing to revisit painful events and to choose some level of awareness over the apparent (although typically false) benefits of complete denial and avoidance.

Continuous appreciation of the client's bravery is a central task for the trauma-specialized clinician—acknowledging the courage associated with the client's mere physical presence during the therapy hour, and taking note of the strength that is required to confront painful memories when avoidance is so obviously the less challenging option. When the therapist can accomplish a respectful and positive attitude, imbued with the notion that the client is doing the best he or she can with the circumstances that confront him or her, the therapy process almost always benefits. Although the client may not completely believe the therapist's nonjudgmental, positive appraisal of him or her (in C. R. Rogers's [1957] lexicon, his or her *unconditional positive regard*), visible therapist respect and appreciation assists greatly in establishing a therapeutic rapport, increasing the likelihood that the client will make himself or herself psychologically available to the therapeutic process.

Related to positive regard, but extending beyond it, is the notion of *compassion*. Considered at various points in this book, compassion can be defined as nonjudgmental, nonegocentric awareness and appreciation of the predicament and suffering of another (in this case, the client), with the directly experienced desire to relieve that person's distress and to increase his or her well-being. Compassion involves a positive emotional state in the clinician—unconditional caring that is directed to the client regardless of his or her actual or presumed good or bad qualities (see Briere, 2012a; Germer, 2009; as well as Chapter 10, for discussions of compassion and its various definitions).

Importantly, compassion is not equivalent to pity, which implies a power imbalance and clinician sympathy regarding the diminished state or status of the client. Rather, it reflects the clinician's awareness that he or she and the client share a common human predicament—the impermanence and fragility of life and well-being—and the fact that all humans, including the clinician, will suffer at various points in their lives. It also involves the natural caring feelings that tend to arise when we see, without distortion, the struggle and vulnerability of others.

From this perspective, the clinician communicates nonjudgmental caring in a way that is not clinically detached, pathologizing, or superior. In the presence of such valuation, the traumatized client may be more able to fully inhabit, accept, and process his or her distress, while incorporating a sense of loving acceptance in relationship to another. As we note in Chapters 8 and 9, this positive state may activate attachment-related neurobiological phenomena that, in turn, serve to countercondition the client's negative emotional responses associated with past relational traumas.

Compassion is probably a normal human state, but it can be further developed in the clinician in various ways. These include clinical training and supervision that emphasizes nonegocentric attention and mindfulness, specific didactic and experiential exercises that teach compassion (Gilbert, 2009), and, for those interested in this path, contemplative activities such as *metta* and mindfulness meditation (for example, Salzberg, 1995).

Hope

Hope is critically important to effective trauma treatment. Repeated experience of painful things (including symptoms) may cause the client to expect continuing despair as an inevitable part of the future. In this light, part of the task of therapy is to reframe trauma as challenge, pain as (at least in part) awareness and growth, and the future as opportunity. This in no way means that the clinician should be Pollyanna-ish about the client's experiences and current distress; it is very important that the client's perceptions be acknowledged and understood. However, it is rarely a good idea for the therapist to accept and therefore inadvertently reinforce the helplessness, hopelessness, and demoralization that the client may infer from life experiences; to do so is, to some extent, to share in the client's injury. Instead, the challenge is to acknowledge the sometimes incredible hurt that the client has experienced, while, at the same time, gently suggesting that his or her presence in treatment signals implicit strength, adaptive capacity, and hopefulness for the future.

Instilling hope does not mean that the therapist promises anything. For a variety of reasons (for example, genetic or biological influences, the possibility of premature termination, treatment interference through substance abuse, especially complex and severe symptomatology, new traumas, and so on), not every client experiences complete symptom remission. Because we cannot predict the future, we cannot guarantee that things will go well for any given person. Yet an overall positive view of the client and his or her future is often justified and helpful. Even when not treated, many of those individuals exposed to major trauma will experience significant symptom reduction over time (Freedman & Shalev, 2000), probably as a function of the intrinsic self-healing processes described earlier in this chapter and in Chapter 3. Even more important, having completed trauma-focused treatment is associated with greater symptom reduction than not having done so (see Foa, Keane, Friedman, & Cohen, 2008, for a review of most current therapies and their effectiveness for trauma). For such reasons, it is generally appropriate to communicate guarded optimism regarding the client's future clinical course and to note signs of improvement whenever they occur.

Ultimately, hope is a powerful antidote to the helplessness and despair associated with many major traumas and losses. Although not typically described as a therapeutic goal, the instillation of hope is a powerful therapeutic action (Meichenbaum, 1994; Najavits, 2002). It takes advantage of the ascribed power and knowledge of the clinician to communicate, with some credibility, that things are likely to get better. The impact of this message for many trauma survivors should not be underestimated.

The Pain Paradox

Implicit in various aspects of this discussion is something we can call the *pain paradox*. It is referred to as a paradox because traumatized or otherwise suffering people sometimes inadvertently engage in pain-enhancing or sustaining behaviors while trying to reduce painful or upsetting states. In an effort to remediate distress and suffering, survivors may do things that specifically increase, not decrease, posttraumatic distress, and that often make them more chronic.

The paradox lies in how we are socialized to address emotional pain and discomfort. It is not uncommon to receive advice from friends or others to "just get over it," "put your past behind you," or "snap out of it." Similarly, media advertising campaigns counsel the viewer or listener to take pills for all varieties of discomfort, buy things to feel better, and address self-perceived inadequacies with purportedly ego-boosting products, ranging from make-up to automobiles. The message is often that pain, distress, and dissatisfaction are bad things. Because they are bad, they should be removed, medicated, distracted from, or otherwise avoided. Once a person is no longer in pain, or his or her pain has been numbed, once he or she is not aware of bad feelings, then he or she will feel good and will experience happiness. In this context, in fact, feeling good often arises when one has done things to stop from feeling bad.

However, although a common approach to distress in our culture is to do whatever possible to end it, modern psychology (and, as it turns out, philosophies such as Buddhism) suggests that avoiding unwanted thoughts, feelings, and memories actually increases or sustains pain, symptoms, and distress—whereas directly experiencing and engaging pain ultimately reduces it. For example, numerous studies indicate that those who use drugs or alcohol, dissociate, avoid discussing what has happened to them, and/or engage in other avoidance behaviors such as denial or thought suppression are more likely to develop intrusive and chronic posttraumatic problems and syndromes (Briere, Scott, & Weathers, 2005; Cioffi & Holloway, 1993; D. M. Clark, Ball, & Pape, 1991; Gold & Wegner, 1995; Morina, 2007; Pietrzak, Harpaz-Rotem, & Southwick, 2011). In contrast, those who are able to more directly experience distress, or engage in psychotherapy, mindfulness training, therapeutic exposure, or other ways of accessing traumatic memory, are likely to have improved and less chronic outcomes (Foa, Huppert, & Cahill, 2006; Hayes, Strosahl, & Wilson, 2011; Kimbrough, Magyari, Langenberg, Chesney, & Berman, 2010; Palm & Follette, 2011; B. L. Thompson & Waltz, 2010). As Bobrow (2011) notes, "what we cannot hold, we cannot process. What we cannot process, we cannot transform. What we cannot transform haunts us" (para. 5; also see Bobrow, 2007).

The pain paradox thus suggests that people who have been hurt do best if—to the extent possible—they can stay present in their pain, avoid less, and experience more. From this perspective, pain is not "bad," nor are anxiety or sadness "bad" feelings; in fact, the experience of pain, distress, or even flashbacks may be "good": It represents access to experiences that can be cognitively and emotionally processed and, once addressed, may then lessen or fall away.

Of course, it is easy to say that people in pain should try not to block, suppress, or deny. As noted at various points in this book, trauma-related problems in affect regulation and tolerance, especially in the context of overwhelming memories, and/or a lack of sufficient social support, may mean that the survivor essentially has no choice but to avoid, in order to maintain some degree of internal homeostasis. Asking a homeless war veteran, hospitalized burn victim, or torture survivor to "stay with the pain" can be a harsh, perhaps impossible, request. Yet even the very beleaguered person may have moments when he or she could tolerate more direct access to internal distress, painful memories, or potentially difficult realization. Further, the titrated exposure activities described in Chapter 8 are designed to provide the otherwise avoidant survivor with the opportunity to experience and process small increments of nonoverwhelming traumatic memory. Thus, the suggestion to allow emotional pain rather than avoid it is a general one—not a demand that the overwhelmed trauma survivor open the floodgates of previously suppressed trauma, but rather an invitation to engage when it is safe and appropriate to do so, and only to the extent possible.

The implications of the pain paradox for trauma therapy are significant. They suggest that approaches that encourage awareness of one's ongoing experience, that allow access to nonoverwhelming amounts of painful memory, and that encourage deeper insight into the basis for ongoing suffering, will be helpful—whereas medications that only numb or mask unwanted emotional states, or therapies that distract, focus merely on support, or even teach avoidance, may be less efficacious.

In general, concepts such as the pain paradox and intrinsic processing are depathologizing: Painful posttraumatic states such as flashbacks, grief, anxiety, or depression are not necessarily evidence of a disorder, per se. In many cases, they represent a healthy condition: access to immediate awareness, even if that awareness carries with it things that cause distress, make one sad, or bring one fear. As the client is more able to hold, tolerate, and process these states and their etiologies, without unnecessary interference through avoidance, the emotional mechanisms described in Chapter 8 will more easily take place and recovery will be more likely.

Central Treatment Principles

Beyond a philosophy of trauma and recovery, there are a number of basic principles of effective trauma-focused treatment. Although these principles apply most directly to psychotherapy, some are also relevant to other treatment methodologies, including trauma psychopharmacology.

Provide and Ensure Safety

Because trauma is about vulnerability to danger, safety is a critical issue for trauma survivors (Cook et al., 2005; Herman, 1992b; Najavits, 2002). It is often only in perceived safe environments that those who have been exposed to danger can let down their guard and experience the relative luxury of introspection and connection. In therapy, safety involves, at a minimum, the absence of physical danger, psychological maltreatment, exploitation, or rejection. Physical safety means that the survivor perceives, and comes to expect, that there is little likelihood of physical or sexual assault at the hands of the clinician or others, and that the building is not likely to collapse or burn during the session. Psychological safety, which is sometimes more difficult to provide, means that the client will not be criticized, humiliated, rejected, dramatically misunderstood, needlessly interrupted, or laughed at during the treatment process, and that psychological boundaries and therapist-client confidentiality will not be violated. It is often only when such conditions are reliably met that the client can begin to reduce his or her defenses and more openly process the thoughts, feelings, and memories associated with traumatic events. In fact, as discussed in Chapter 8, it is critical that the client experience safety while remembering danger; only under this circumstance will the fear and distress associated with trauma in the past lose its capacity to be evoked by the present.

Unfortunately, in order to feel safe, not only must there be safety; the client must be able to perceive it. This is often a problem because, as noted earlier, trauma exposure can result in hypervigilance; many traumatized people come to expect danger, devote considerable resources to detecting impending harm, and have a tendency to misperceive even safe environments and interactions as potentially dangerous (Janoff-Bulman, 1992; Pearlman & Courtois, 2005). As a result, even a safe therapeutic environment may appear unsafe to some clients. For this reason, among others, treatment may take considerably longer—and call more on the clinician's patience and sustained capacity for caring—than is allowed for by shorter-term therapies. Some multiply traumatized individuals—former child abuse victims, torture survivors, victims of sustained political oppression, adolescent gang members, "street kids," or battered women, for example—may need to attend therapy sessions for relatively long periods of time before they can fully perceive and accept the fact that they will not be hurt if they become vulnerable in treatment. For such people, interventions such as therapeutic exposure or psychodynamic interpretation may not be appropriate until therapy has been in place for a long enough time to allow an expectation of safety and stability (Courtois, 2010). Given these concerns, it is obviously important that the therapist be able to determine the client's relative *experience* of therapeutic safety, since many clinical interventions involve the activation and processing of upsetting memory material. To the extent that such memories trigger fear and pain, those who are not aware that they are safe may become more distressed by such activations.

As noted earlier in this chapter, providing safety also means working to ensure that the client will be relatively free of danger outside of the therapeutic setting. Highly fearful or endangered survivors are unlikely to have sufficient psychological resources to participate in psychotherapy without being emotionally overwhelmed and/or especially avoidant. The battered woman should be as safe as possible from further battery, and the sexual abuse victim must be out of danger from his or her perpetrator, before psychological processing of symptoms is attempted. Otherwise, the client's life and physical integrity may be risked in the service of symptom relief. Although this may seem an obvious fact, many therapists fall into the trap of attempting to process traumatic memories with acutely traumatized individuals who continue to live in obviously dangerous circumstances.

This does not mean that all psychological interventions are ruled out in work with the still-at-risk—only those having as their exclusive focus the direct processing of traumatic memories and feelings, or those that prize insight over safety. For example, the acutely battered woman may easily gain from psychoeducational activities or cognitive interventions that provide information on increasing personal safety or that support the often daunting task of leaving an abusive partner (C. E. Jordan, Nietzel, Walker, & Logan, 2004). On the other hand, she may be placed at continued risk if the immediate focus of therapy is to emotionally process her last battery experience or to analyze what childhood issues are involved in her attraction to authoritarian men in the first place. Of course, some chronic life-endangering phenomena, such as unsafe sexual practices or intravenous substance abuse, are not threats that can be easily terminated—the individual may need some level of symptom reduction, increased coping, or psychoeducation before these behaviors can be significantly reduced or terminated. Nevertheless, when the danger is acute and potentially avoidable, the clinician's first focus must be on ensuring immediate safety.

Provide and Ensure Stability

Stability refers to an ongoing psychological and physical state whereby one is not overwhelmed by disruptive internal or external stimuli. It also implies some degree of capacity to resist the effects of such stimuli in the near future. Stability concerns are highly relevant to work with trauma survivors, since adverse events are often destabilizing and can produce conditions (for example, chaotic interpersonal or physical environments, posttraumatic stress, depression) that further increase susceptibility to stress. In addition, some trauma-related responses (for example, substance abuse, problematic personality traits, or reactive psychosis) can contribute to unstable lifestyles, such as homelessness, recurrent involvement in chaotic and intense relationships, or chronic self-destructiveness.

Life Stability

Life stability refers to generally stable living conditions. For example, those living in extreme poverty, chaotic environments, or chronically risky occupations (for example, prostitution) may have difficulty tolerating the additional distress sometimes activated by trauma therapy. Such conditions may involve hunger, fear, racial or sexual oppression, and the insecurity associated with inadequate or absent housing—none of which support emotional resilience in the face of activated distress. In fact, without sufficient security, food, and shelter, avoidance of traumatic material (for example, through numbing or substance abuse) may appear more useful to the trauma survivor than the seemingly counterintuitive notion of reliving painful memories. Trauma therapy is most helpful to those who have the social and physical resources necessary to experience safety and the option of trust. As a result, the first intervention with traumatized people who have few resources is often social casework: arranging adequate and reliable food, shelter, and physical safety.

Emotional Stability

In addition to physical stability, trauma survivors should have some level of psychological homeostasis before certain aspects of trauma therapy can be initiated (Cloitre et al., 2010; Ford, Courtois, Steele, van der Hart, & Nijenhuis, 2005; Herman, 1992a). In general, this means that those with acute psychotic symptoms, high suicidality, extremely high levels of posttraumatic stress, or debilitating anxiety or depression may require other interventions before exposure-based aspects of trauma therapy can be initiated. These include the appropriate use of medication (see Chapter 12), crisis intervention, development of affect tolerance and regulation skills, and, in some cases, simple supportive psychotherapy. In the absence of such pretreatment, activation of trauma-related material not only may result in an exacerbation of existing symptoms (for example, renewed psychosis or posttraumatic stress) but also may overwhelm the survivor's existing capacity to regulate his or her emotional state, producing new distress and dysfunction (Briere, 2002b). Exacerbated or newly activated symptoms, in turn, may result in increased avoidance behaviors, such as substance abuse or suicidality, as well as increasing the likelihood that the client will drop out of therapy.

It is not always easy to determine when symptoms are too intense to warrant immediate trauma-specific interventions, as opposed to being worthy targets of treatment. For example, when is posttraumatic stress or anxiety too severe to support therapeutic exposure to traumatic memory, and when are these symptoms in the range that would be appropriate for such treatment? Specific assessment approaches that may shed some light on these issues were presented in Chapter 3. Most generally, the issue is whether the symptoms in question have significantly reduced the client's capacity to "handle" or regulate the almost inevitable upsurge of emotion that follows therapeutic exposure to unresolved trauma memories. If the increased activation is not overwhelming, classic trauma treatment is usually indicated. If the response to treatment would be to become flooded with negative affects, more grounding, skills-development, and/or supportive psychotherapy will be required until greater psychological stability is present.

Interestingly, some forms of disorder traditionally assumed to be synonymous with psychological instability may not always be contraindications for therapeutic exposure. For example, some traumatized individuals with "borderline personality disorder" or low-level chronic psychosis may be sufficiently stable to tolerate trauma treatment, whereas others with less diagnostic severity may not. Clinicians often have appropriate concerns when working with psychotic, or Axis II, disorders because such disturbance is frequently associated with affect regulation problems and more extreme dysphoria. However, the critical issue is less the type of disorder, per se, than the client's relative capacity to tolerate the emotions associated with exposure to traumatic memories.

Maintain a Positive and Consistent Therapeutic Relationship

One of the most important components of successful trauma therapy appears to be a good working relationship between client and therapist

(Courtois & Ford, in press; Kudler, Krupnick, Blank, Herman, & Horowitz, 2009; Pearlman & Courtois, 2005). In fact, a number of studies indicate that therapeutic outcome is best predicted by the quality of the treatment relationship, as opposed to the specific techniques used (M. J. Lambert & Barley, 2001; Martin et al., 2000; Orlinski, Grawe, & Parks, 1994). Although some therapeutic approaches stress relationship dynamics more than others, it is probably true that all forms of trauma therapy work better if the clinician is compassionate and attuned, and the client feels accepted, liked, and taken seriously. Even in short-term, highly structured treatment approaches (for example, some forms of cognitive-behavioral therapy), clients with good relationships with their helpers are more likely to persevere in treatment, adhere to whatever regimen is in place, and, as a result, experience a more positive clinical outcome (Rau & Goldfried, 1994). Longer-term and more interpersonal treatment approaches, in which relational issues are more prominent, are even more likely to benefit from a strong therapeutic relationship.

Because trauma therapy often involves revisiting and processing painful memories, as well as potentially reactivating feelings of danger and vulnerability, successful treatment is especially contingent on therapeutic support and connection. Distant, uninvolved, or emotionally disconnected client-therapist relationships are, in our experience, quite often associated with less positive therapeutic outcomes (see Dalenberg, 2000, for an empirically based discussion of this issue). At a minimum, a positive therapeutic relationship provides a variety of benefits. These potentially include decreased treatment dropout and more reliable session attendance, less avoidance and greater disclosure of personal material, greater treatment adherence and medication compliance, greater openness to—and acceptance of—therapist suggestions and support, and more capacity to tolerate painful thoughts and feelings during therapeutic exposure to trauma memories (American Psychiatric Association, 2001; Cloitre et al., 2002; Farber & Hall, 2002; A. F. Frank & Gunderson, 1990; Horvath, 2007; McGregor, Thomas, & Read, 2006; Rau & Goldfried, 1994).

In addition to supporting effective treatment, the therapeutic relationship is more likely to be helpful to the extent that it both (1) gently triggers memories and schemas associated with prior relational traumas and (2) provides the opportunity to process these activations in the context of therapeutic caring, safety, and support (Briere, 2002b). As is described in more detail in Chapter 9, even the most benign client-therapist relationship may trigger at least some rejection or abandonment fears, misperception of danger, or authority issues in survivors of extended or severe trauma. When these intrusions occur at the same time that the client is feeling respect, compassion, and empathy from the therapist, they may gradually lose their generalizability to current relationships and become counterconditioned by positive relational feelings. In this sense, a good therapeutic relationship is not only supportive of effective treatment, but it is virtually integral to the resolution of major relational traumas.

Tailor the Therapy to the Client

Although a review of some currently available treatment manuals might suggest that clinical interventions are applied more or less equally to all mental health clients with similar complaints, this is almost never the case in actual clinical practice. In fact, the highly structured, sometimes manualized nature of some empirically validated therapies more directly reflects the requirements of treatment outcome research (that is, the need for treatment to be highly similar and equally applied for each client in a given study) than any clinically based intent to provide equivalent interventions for all presenting clients (Westen et al., 2004). In the real world of clinical practice, clients vary significantly with regard to their presenting issues, comorbid symptoms, and the extent to which they can utilize and tolerate psychological interventions. For this reason, therapy is likely to be most effective when it is tailored to the specific characteristics and concerns of the individual person (Briere & Lanktree, 2011; Cloitre et al., 2002). We next describe several of the more important individual variables that should be taken into account when providing mental health interventions, including trauma therapy.

Affect Regulation and Memory Intensity Issues

As noted previously, *affect regulation* refers to an individual's relative capacity to tolerate and internally reduce painful emotional states. People with limited affect regulation abilities are more likely to be overwhelmed and destabilized by negative emotional experiences—both those associated with current negative events and those triggered by painful memories. Since trauma therapy often involves activating and processing traumatic memories, individuals with less ability to internally regulate painful states are more likely to become highly distressed, if not emotionally overwhelmed, during treatment (Cloitre et al., 2002; Cloitre et al., 2010; Courtois, 2010).

The affect regulation construct can be oversimplified, however. For example, some people are better at tolerating or regulating one type of feeling (for example, anxiety) than another (for example, anger), despite the common implication that any given person has a generalized capacity to regulate emotions. As well, some people's emotional responses may be more intense than others', as a function of having been exposed to more painful experiences. In this regard, it may take more affect regulation capacity to down-regulate emotions associated with some very painful memories (for example, of prolonged torture) than those associated with less intense memories (for example, of an automobile accident). It is rarely enough to decide that someone has "affect regulation difficulties" without also determining the affective load that requires regulating.

Variability in affect regulation capacity—and the severity of the memory-triggered affect to be regulated—has significant clinical implications. Most generally, individuals with impaired affect regulation—especially in the context of easily triggered, highly painful memories—are more likely to experience overwhelming emotionality when exposed to upsetting memories during treatment and to respond with increased avoidance, including "resistance" and/or dissociation. Such responses, in turn, reduce the client's exposure to traumatic material and to the healing aspects of the therapeutic relationship. As described in Chapter 8, treatment of those with impaired affect regulation capacities and/or a heavy trauma load should proceed especially carefully, such that traumatic memories are activated and processed in smaller increments than otherwise might be necessary. Often described as "titrated exposure" or "working within the therapeutic window" (Briere, 1996, 2002b), this usually involves adjusting treatment so that trauma processing that occurs within a given session does not exceed the capacities of the survivor to tolerate that level of distress—while, at the same time, providing as much processing as can reasonably occur (see Chapter 8). In individuals with substantially reduced affect regulation capacities (and/or especially distressing memories), this level of exposure and processing may be quite limited at any given moment. Nevertheless, over time, even seemingly small amounts of trauma processing tend to add up, ultimately leading to potentially significant symptom relief and greater emotional capacity without the negative side effect of overwhelming affect.

Preponderant Schemas

As noted in Chapter 2, trauma exposure often has effects on cognition. Depending on the type of trauma and when in development it occurred, this may include easily triggered perceptions of oneself as inadequate, bad, or helpless; expectations of others as dangerous, rejecting, or unloving; and a view of the future as hopeless. Such distortions inevitably affect the client's perception of the therapist and of therapy. For example, the survivor may expect the therapist to be critical, unloving, or even hostile or abusive.

Early child abuse and neglect may result in latent gestalts of preverbal negative cognitions (Baldwin, Fehr, Keedian, Seidel, & Thompson, 1993; DePrince, Combs, & Shanahan, 2009; Dutra, Callahan, Forman, Mendelsohn, & Herman, 2008) and feelings that are easily evoked by reminiscent stimuli in the immediate interpersonal environment. These relational schemas, when triggered, may result in sudden, intense thoughts and feelings that were initially encoded during childhood maltreatment and that are hard for the survivor to discriminate from current, real-time perceptions. As a result, the adult abuse survivor may experience sudden feelings of abandonment, rejection, or betrayal during psychotherapy and attribute them to the therapist.

Because the cognitive effects of trauma vary from client to client, as a function of the individual's specific history, therapy must be adjusted to take into account each client's preponderant schemas of self and others (Pearlman & Courtois, 2005). In general, this means that the clinician should do as much as possible to (1) respond in ways that specifically do not reinforce the client's negative expectations and (2) avoid (to the extent possible) triggering underlying cognitive-emotional gestalts related to broader themes such as interpersonal danger or rejection. The individual with a tendency to view important interpersonal figures with distrust, for example, may require a therapist who is especially supportive and validating and who is careful not to trigger too many relational memories of maltreatment. This does not simply involve statements to the client that he or she is safe or positively valued—more important, the therapist should act and respond in such a manner that safety and caring is demonstrated and can be inferred. Because the distrustful client will be predisposed to miss such signs, and perhaps even actively misinterpret them, therapeutic interventions must be even more explicit and obvious in these areas than is the case for those without (or with less of) this cognitive set.

It is important to note here that tailoring one's treatment approach to a given person's major cognitive issues does not mean that these distortions or disruptive schemas are no longer evoked in therapy. As noted in Chapter 9, no matter how hard the clinician tries, the survivor who has been substantially maltreated in the past is likely to view some of the therapist's behaviors as punitive, critical, or abusive, and thus issues in this area almost unavoidably become a topic of discussion during therapy. However, because the therapist is working hard to minimize the extent of these misattributions and triggered schemas, whatever emerges over time in therapy is likely to be less intense and more easily demonstrable as contextually inaccurate. The repetitive experience of fearing that one's therapist is cold and rejecting, for example, and yet finding, over time, that these perceptions are manifestly untrue, often can be extremely helpful.

Significantly, although the clinician works hard to communicate an absence of criticism or rejection, this does not mean that he or she discourages the client's discussion and processing of these perceptions and feelings as they relate to subtle client-therapist dynamics or to others in the client's environment. Ultimately, the goal is to make treatment possible for those who are especially sensitive and suspicious of the vulnerability, connection, and intimacy that are part of the normal operating conditions of treatment. Knowledge that client X has "abandonment issues," client Y tends to perceive caring as intrusive or sexual in nature, or that client Z responds to authority figures with expectations of hostility or domination can allow the therapist to adjust his or her approach so that it does not unnecessarily trigger these issues and thereby unduly interfere with the process of treatment.

Take Gender Issues Into Account

Although there is little doubt that men and women undergo many of the same traumatic events and suffer in many of the same ways, it is also clear that (1) some traumas are more common in one sex than the other and (2) sex role socialization often affects how such injuries are experienced and expressed. These differences, in turn, have significant impacts on the content and process of trauma-focused therapy.

As noted in Chapter 1, women are more at risk for victimization in close relationships than are men, and both girls and women are especially more likely to be sexually victimized than their male counterparts. In contrast, boys are at greater risk than girls of childhood physical abuse, and boys and men are more likely to experience nonintimate physical assaults than girls and women. In addition to trauma exposure differences, men and women tend to experience, communicate, and process the distress associated with traumatic events in different ways. Although there is major variation among people within each sex, and across cultures and sexual orientations, women are generally socialized to express more directly certain feelings, such as fear or sadness, but are taught to dampen or avoid others, such as anger, whereas men are often more permitted the expression of anger, but may be socially discouraged from communicating "softer" feelings, such as sadness or fear (Cochrane, 2005; Krause, DeRosa, & Roth, 2002; Levant & Pollack, 1995; Renzetti & Curran, 2002). Men and women may also differ in how they act upon feelings and needs. Men are to some extent taught to externalize or cognitively suppress unpleasant feelings, and to act on the environment in order to reduce pain or distress, whereas women are generally socialized to express their distress to trusted others, and are, overall, less prone to externalizing their pain through acting on the environment (Bem, 1976; Briere, 1996; Feuer, Jefferson, & Resick, 2002; Renzetti & Curran, 2002). These sex-role-related differences in symptom expression and behavioral response often manifest themselves during trauma-focused psychotherapy. All things being equal, for example, male trauma survivors in treatment may be more prone to expressions of anger—or to denying posttraumatic distress entirely—than female survivors, whereas traumatized women may be more open to emotional expression, especially of feelings of sadness, fear, or helplessness.

Given these sociocultural influences, the therapist should be alert to ways in which trauma survivors express or inhibit their emotional reactions based on sex-role-based expectations. Often, this will involve supporting the client to express the full range of feelings and thoughts associated with a traumatic event, as opposed to only those considered socially appropriate to his or her gender. In fact, to the extent that (as described in Chapter 8) feelings and thoughts are more easily processed when fully expressed during treatment, unaddressed sex role constraints are likely to inhibit full psychological recovery.

The therapist also should be aware of sex differences in how trauma is cognitively processed. Because boys and men are often socialized to present themselves as strong and able to defend themselves, victimization may be more of a sex role violation for them than it is for girls and women (Mendelsohn & Sewell, 2004). Such social expectations can result in different responses to trauma. Victimized men, for example, may struggle with feelings of inadequacy, shame, and low self-esteem associated with the social implication that an inability to fight off maltreatment reflects lesser masculinity or competence (Mendel, 1995). In addition, many sexually assaulted or abused males have sexual orientation concerns related to their trauma. In the case of childhood sexual abuse, for example, heterosexual boys and men may fear that molestation by another male has caused them to be (or be seen as) latently homosexual (Alaggiaa, 2005)—a response that, in a homophobic culture, may result in compensatory hypermasculinity or overinvolvement in heterosexual activity (Briere, 1996). Conversely, homosexual or bisexual men who were sexually abused by males as children may incorrectly believe that their sexual orientation somehow caused them to be abused by men, or that their abuse caused them to be paradoxically attracted to men, conclusions that, in many cultures, may lead to feelings of guilt, shame, and self-hatred (Briere, 1996).

Sex role expectations also affect, to some extent, how traumatized women view their victimization. Women who have been sexually assaulted may believe that they in some way enticed their perpetrators into raping them—a concern that reflects the traditional stereotype of females as sexual objects who are intentionally or unintentionally seductive (Baugher, Elhai, Monroe, & Gray, 2010; M. R. Burt, 1980). Similarly, women battered or otherwise abused by their partners may believe that their supposed lack of subservience or failure to perform as an adequate mate means that they deserved to be maltreated (Barnett, 2001; L. E. Walker, 1984).

Given these gender-specific influences on trauma-related cognitions, the clinician is likely to be more helpful if he or she closely attends to concerns about unacceptability, self-blame, low self-esteem, shame, and sexual orientation as they are expressed in survivors' cognitive reactions to trauma. Traumatized men may require additional reassurance that they are not less masculine (regardless of sexual orientation) by virtue of having been victimized, and may gain from interventions that support the full range of emotional and cognitive expression without fear of stigmatization. Especially relevant, in this regard, is the need for many victimized men to process feelings of shame associated with viewing themselves as deviant and socially unacceptable. Women survivors, on the other hand, may gain especially from interventions that support self-determination and that help them to reject feelings of responsibility for their abuse, including the unwarranted notion that they somehow sought out or otherwise deserved maltreatment.

Be Aware of—and Sensitive to—Sociocultural Issues

Social Maltreatment

One of the more overlooked issues in the treatment of trauma survivors is that people with lesser social status are more likely than others to be victimized (Bassuk et al., 2001; Breslau, Wilcox, Storr, Lucia, & Anthony, 2004; Carter, 2007). Traumas common among those with lower socioeconomic status, in addition to child abuse, neglect, and exposure to domestic violence (Bergner, Delgado, & Graybill, 1994; Finkelhor, Ormrod, Turner, & Hambry, 2005; Kyriacou et al., 1999; Sedlak & Broadhurst, 1996), are sexual and physical assaults by peers, community violence, shootings, robbery, sexual exploitation through prostitution, trauma associated with refugee status, and loss associated with the murder of a family member or friend (for example, Berthold, 2000; Breslau, Davis, Andreski & Peterson, 1991; Farley, 2003; Giaconia, Reinherz, Silverman, & Pakiz, 1995; Schwab-Stone et al., 1995; Singer et al., 1995).

Social, sexual, and racial discrimination also have direct negative psychological effects that are, in a sense, posttraumatic (Berg, 2006; Carter & Forsyth, 2010; Loo et al., 2001; Root, 1996) and typically are associated with environmental conditions in which further trauma is common (Breslau et al., 1998; North, Smith, & Spitznager, 1994; Sells, Rowe, Fisk, & Davidson, 2003). Some groups in North America suffer from multigenerational trauma, including African Americans, whose ancestors were held in slavery (Mattis, Bell, Jagers, & Jenkins, 1999), and American Indians, who, as a group, have experienced extended maltreatment and cultural near-annihilation (Duran & Duran, 1995; Manson et al., 1996). Social marginalization also means that many traumatized people have reduced access to appropriate mental health services (for example, McKay, Lynn, & Bannon, 2005; Perez & Fortuna, 2005; Rayburn et al., 2005). Combined with the discrimination often experienced by other racial/ethnic minority groups, and the relatively dangerous living environments in which many are forced to live, social inequality provides a vast depot of trauma and trauma impacts in North America.

Refugees

Beyond North America, individuals from certain regions of the world are especially likely to be maltreated. When these people immigrate to North America or other places, they often carry with them the trauma experienced in their countries of origin. Mental health centers specializing in refugee or immigrant issues regularly deal with the effects of holocausts or mass murder (for example, "ethnic cleansing"), political imprisonment, war, extended torture, trafficking, "honor" killings, sexual violence, and extreme ethnic or gender discrimination (Allden, Poole, Chantavanich, & Ohmar, 1996; Basoglu, 1992; Marsella, Bornemann, Ekblad, & Orley, 1994; K. E. Miller & Rasco, 2004; Steel et al., 2009). The effects of such experiences tend to be especially long-lasting; in one sample of 80 Vietnamese refugees resettled to Norway, the majority still had very high symptom scores on a standardized measure 23 years later (Vaage et al., 2010). The concatenation of social adversity and ethnic variation means that cultural and historical issues are often highly relevant to the process and content of trauma-focused psychotherapy and should not be overlooked (Marsella et al., 1996; Nickerson, Bryant, Silove, & Steel, 2011).

Cultural Variation

Partially because ethnic and racial minorities are more likely to be traumatized, and partially due to the general multicultural mix present in many modern societies, individuals presenting for trauma services are likely to reflect a wide range of cultures and ethnic groups. Such cultural differences are not merely a function of race: People of low socioeconomic status often have different worldviews and experiences than those of the same race or ethnicity who have more economic and social opportunities. Similarly, merely knowing that someone is, for example, "African American," "Hispanic," "Asian," or "American Indian" says little about his or her cultural context. An individual from Vietnam, for example, may be quite different in perspective, language, and emotional style from a person raised in Japan. The Surgeon General's (2001) last report on the cultural aspects of mental health services noted:

> Asian Americans and Pacific Islanders . . . include 43 ethnic groups speaking over 100 languages and dialects. For American Indians and Alaska Natives, the Bureau of Indian Affairs currently recognizes 561 tribes. African Americans are also becoming more diverse, especially with the influx of refugees and immigrants from many countries of Africa and the Caribbean.

These wide cultural differences often translate into different trauma presentations and idioms of distress, as described in Chapter 2. In addition, above and beyond their social status in North America, people from the various cultures and subcultures of the world have widely different expectations of how clinical intervention should occur, and of the ways in which clinicians and clients should interact (Marsella et al., 1996; Nader, Dubrow, & Stamm, 1999; Van der Veer, 1995). In one culture, for example, eye contact between clinician and client is a sign of respect; in another, it may be the complete opposite. Similarly, in some cultures, certain topics (for example, sexual issues, visible loss of dignity) are considered to be more embarrassing or shameful than in others, and thus should be raised only when relevant to treatment, and then with great sensitivity.

Although the focus of this book precludes a detailed discussion of this issue, a central point must be made: Cultural awareness and sensitivity are an important part of any psychotherapeutic process—including trauma therapy. Clinicians who find themselves, for example, regularly working with Cambodian refugees, Hmong clients, or Mexican immigrants have a responsibility to learn the primary rules of clinical engagement with people from these cultures, as well as, if possible, something of their culture, history, and language.

Monitor and Control Counteractivation

An additional important concept in trauma-focused therapy is what is commonly referred to as *countertransference* (described as *counteractivation* in self-trauma theory [Briere, 2006]; see Chapter 8). Although this phenomenon has many different definitions, we use it here to refer to occasions when the therapist responds to the client with cognitive-emotional processes (for example, expectations, beliefs, or emotions) that are strongly influenced by prior personal experiences. In many of these cases, these experiences involve childhood maltreatment, adult traumas, or other upsetting events. Of course, all behavior is influenced by past experience, and not all counteractivation responses are negative (Dalenberg, 2000; Pearlman & Saakvitne, 1995). Even positive countertransference, however, must be monitored by the therapist, since it may produce unhelpful responses such as idealization of the client, the need to normalize what are actually problematic client behaviors or symptoms, or even sexual or romantic feelings. Ultimately, the concern is that counteractivation can interfere with treatment by leading to either (1) a deleterious clinical experience for the client or (2) processes that disrupt the treatment process.

For example:

- Therapist A was raised by a critical, psychologically punitive parent. She now finds that she tends to experience angry or guilty feelings when her client complains about any aspect of the therapy.
- Clinician B experienced a traumatic miscarriage a month ago. Upon hearing her client's excitement about a new pregnancy, she experiences unexpected anger and distress.
- Therapist C, who is dealing with a recent traumatic death of a loved one, finds that he is prone to feelings of extreme sadness and emptiness while treating a client whose son was killed in a fire.
- Clinician D grew up in a violent, chaotic family atmosphere, where safety and predictability were rarely in evidence; her supervisor notices that she has a strong need to control the process of therapy and tends to see certain clients as especially manipulative, malingering, or engaging in therapeutic "resistance."
- As a child, Clinician E was often protected by a supportive aunt when his mother would go into angry, abusive tirades. He is now treating an older, kindly woman whom he has a difficult time seeing as psychologically disabled, despite her obvious symptomatology.

An additional form of counteractivation involves therapist denial or cognitive avoidance of certain subjects or themes during the treatment process. A clinician who tends to avoid thinking about unresolved traumatic material in his or her own life may unconsciously work to prevent the client from exploring his or her own trauma-related memories and feelings. In such instances, the clinician may even become resentful of the client for restimulating his or her own avoided memories or feelings, or may reinterpret appropriate client attempts to confront the past as hysteria, self-indulgence, or attention seeking.

The primary manifestations of an unconscious desire to distance oneself from the client's distress are attempts to avoid discussion of the client's trauma history and generally decreased emotional attunement to the client. In each instance, the underlying strategy is the same: reduced therapeutic contact as a way to reduce the likelihood of triggered emotional pain. When this response is especially powerful, the clinician may slow or neutralize therapy by decreasing the client's exposure to traumatic material to such a point that it is not processed. At the same time, therapist distance or lack of attunement may activate client abandonment issues, further impeding treatment.

Reducing the Negative Effects of Therapist Counteractivation

As noted earlier, not all counteractivation is necessarily problematic, and, in fact, all therapists experience some level of counteractivation in their work. When it interferes with treatment, however, steps must be taken to reduce its influence.

One of the best preventive measures against countertransference problems is regular consultation with a seasoned clinician who is familiar with trauma issues and, hopefully, the therapist (Briere, 2006; Pearlman & Courtois, 2005). Another option is to form a consultation group with one's peers. However structured, such meetings should allow the clinician to share the burden of his or her daily exposure to others' pain as well as to explore ways in which his or her own issues can negatively affect therapeutic outcome. In many instances, inappropriate identification or misattribution can be prevented or remedied by the consistent availability of an objective consultant who is alert to countertransference issues in general, and the clinician's vulnerabilities in specific.

An additional intervention, for clinicians who acknowledge the impacts of trauma in their own lives, is psychotherapy. It is an ironic fact that, at least in some environments, clinicians endorse the power of psychological treatment for others yet eschew it for themselves as somehow shameful or unlikely to help. This double standard is unfortunate, since having experienced psychotherapy is usually a good thing for therapists. Therapy is not only likely to reduce the clinician's trauma-related difficulties; it can also increase the richness of his or her appreciation for human complexity and can dramatically decrease the intrusion of his or her issues into the therapeutic process.

Practice Ethically and Within the Standard of Care

A final topic in this chapter is that of ethical and professional practice. Because the trauma client is often in a vulnerable state, and psychotherapy generally involves a power imbalance between client and therapist, it is very important that the clinician attend to any issues or dynamics that might even remotely result in maltreatment, exploitation, or inadequate care.

In many cases, ethical and risk-reducing activities correspond to what would be good therapeutic practice in any event. For example, honoring the client's boundaries, refraining from any form of exploitation or maltreatment, reporting and (when appropriate) intervening in potential danger to the client and others, and guarding the client's confidentiality all reflect activities that increase safety (Chapter 4), support identity development and functioning (Chapter 9), and/or encourge a positive therapeutic relationship (Chapter 4). Similarly, the therapist should take care to not overdisclose his or her personal history, relationships, preferences, or ideas about things unrelated to the client, as well as constraining the extent to which the client and therapist interact outside of the treatment. This not only allows him or her to manage the client's trauma activations, but it also addresses professional and ethical issues around dual relationships, clinical boundaries, and professional standards of care. Finally, professional requirements regarding documentation and charting allow the clinician to monitor the client's progress in therapy, such that treatment interventions correctly address the client's current needs, as well as to provide relevant information to other professionals when warranted.

As noted earlier in this chapter, because the form of treatment outlined in this book emphasizes relational connection with—and positive regard toward—the trauma survivor, issues associated with counteractivation are especially salient. For example, although compassion—requiring nonegocentric caring and the need for the therapist to be interpersonally "present"—is an important part of trauma-focused psychotherapy, these issues occasionally can be challenging for the clinician. For example, when are one's caring feelings for the client based on compassion and appreciation of his or her suffering, and when do they potentially represent the clinician's own needs for intimacy or connection, or unprocessed sexual or romantic issues? Similarly, how is the therapist to discriminate understandable anger at the client's trauma perpetrator, or sadness at his or her irrevocable losses, from counteractivation of the clinician's own childhood memories? What is the exact boundary point that must be reinforced when the client requests additional attention, caring, or self-disclosure from the therapist? In some cases, responsivity and slightly increased connection or attunement can be helpful, if it is appropriate to the situation and monitored for counteractivational distortions. In other cases, the therapist's over-response to such demands or requests may reflect co-transferential dynamics and produce problems.

Although this is obviously a complex topic, we offer several suggestions:

• Therapy boundary violations, including voyeurism, emotional gratification, exploitation, dual relationships (inside or outside of the therapy environment), romanticization, or any sexual behavior are unethical and potentially very harmful to the client. If the clinician is concerned that any of these phenomena are occurring, he or she should proceed under the assumption that the concern is valid. Under such circumstances, outside help, consultation, or (in the case of actual and significant behavior) intervention should be sought.

• Authoritarian or overly directive treatment can have negative impacts. A corollary of this is that the therapist should not be definitive when, in fact, the issues are complex; the client is, in some ways, unknowable to the therapist; and absolute truth is hard to find. Interventions that involve lecturing or heavy-handed declarations of fact are likely to go awry, and may be bad practice. Examples include

- o Telling the client that he or she has or has not been abused, despite his or her protestations to the contrary or a lack of evidence one way or the other;
- o Making definitive interpretations about the meaning or etiology of the client's current behavior when, in fact, such hypotheses are largely speculative;
- o Validating or supporting unfair or prejudicial social messages about sex, race, age, ethnicity, sexual orientation, gender identity, or socio-economic status;
- o Reinforcing dependency or acquiescence in someone who needs to become more entitled, self-referenced, and independent; and
- o Making value judgments about things that are best seen nonjudg-mentally, such as many forms of "bad" or "immoral" behavior.

- • Duty to report trumps confidentiality. If the therapist becomes aware—or has reasonable suspicion—of child, elder, or dependent adult abuse, or of the client's danger to himself or herself or others, the clinician must do whatever is required by law and professional ethics to ensure safety. This may involve the child welfare system, law enforcement, or involuntary hospitalization. Issues in this area are sometimes hard for clinicians to confront, especially when the correct action goes against the wishes of the client. There are no easy answers to the breach of trust that the client may feel in such circumstances. We suggest, however, that clients be informed at the onset of therapy about what the law or professional ethics require the therapist to report or intervene in, so that such actions at a later date are less surprising (see Briere and Lanktree, 2011, for a more detailed discussion of this topic).

- • Clinician counteractivational responses are, in our experience, typically triggered ones. If the therapist notes a significant change in his or her internal state or perspective, or intrusive phenomena similar to those outlined for *trigger identification* in Chapters 6 and 7, he or she should entertain a strong hypothesis that such responses are at least partially a function of his or her own history, as opposed to solely client-level stimuli. Although this is not always true—sometimes sudden affective or cognitive shifts reflect insight or compassion—we generally recommend the psychoanalytic dictum that if the therapist suddenly wants to make an exception to the relational rules in therapy, the best advice is not to do so and to reflect on the impetus.

- • As a correlate to the above, be wary of very strong feelings or reactions during therapy, even if they seem to be about social justice, the client's entitlements, or things that have been done to him or her. It is entirely appropriate to be on the client's "side," even to be his or her advocate, when necessary and therapeutically appropriate. And social injustice should be confronted whenever possible. However, if the therapist detects strong anger, outrage, overidentification with the client, or an intrusive need to protect or parent, it is at least possible that he or she is being triggered and is responding to his or her own needs rather than those of the client. Such instances violate a significant principle of relational treatment: The central unit of analysis in psychotherapy is the client, not the therapist. All of this is difficult to parse in some instances, and we do not mean that the therapist should be distant or uninvolved. Rather, we suggest that the attuned and helpful clinician is someone who carefully scrutinizes his or her therapeutic behaviors to make as sure as possible that they are dedicated to the client's safety and well-being, as opposed to reflecting his or her own history, needs, or inappropriate expectations.

• This work is sometimes very difficult, albeit important and meaningful. As noted earlier, we strongly recommend that the trauma-focused clinician (as well as other helpers) access resources that can provide the support necessary to sustain this process—whether in consultation, supervision, or one's own psychotherapy. The clinician's willingness to hear painful things, connect with people who may have difficulty with interpersonal connections, and do this work rather than something else, is a tremendous gift to the traumatized client. But such work should not be done alone.

The reader is referred to the following sources for more detailed information on ethical practice, counteractivation/countertransference issues, and professional standards of care related to trauma treatment: Cloitre et al., (2011); Courtois and Ford (in press); Courtois, Ford, and Cloitre (2009); Dalenberg (2000); Kinsler, Courtois, and Frankel (2009); and Pearlman and Saakvitne (1995).

Suggested Reading

Bassuk, E. L., Melnick, S., & Browne, A. (1998). Responding to the needs of low-income and homeless women who are survivors of family violence. *Journal of the American Medical Women's Association, 53,* 57–64.

Courtois, C. A., & Ford, J. D. (in press). *Relational integrated treatment of complex trauma: A practical guide for therapists.* New York, NY: Guilford.

Dalenberg, C. J. (2000). *Countertransference and the treatment of trauma.* Washington, DC: American Psychological Association.

Marsella, A. J., Friedman, M. J., Gerrity, E. T., & Scurfield, R. M. (Eds.). (1996). *Ethnocultural aspects of posttraumatic stress disorder: Issues, research, and clinical applications.* Washington, DC: American Psychological Association.

Pearlman, L. A., & Saakvitne, K. W. (1995). *Trauma and the therapist: Countertransference and vicarious traumatization in psychotherapy with incest survivors.* New York, NY: Norton.

Rees, S., Silove, D. M., Chey, T., Ivancic, L., Steel, Z., Creamer, M. C., . . . Forbes, D. (2011). Lifetime prevalence of gender-based violence in women and the relationship with mental disorders and psychosocial function. *Journal of the American Medical Association, 306,* 513–521.

5

Psychoeducation

Although much attention is paid in the treatment literature to the cognitive and emotional processing of traumatic memories, psychoeducation also can be an important aspect of trauma therapy (Friedman, 2000a; Hien et al., 2009; Mueser, Rosenberg, & Rosenberg, 2009; Najavits, 2002; although, see Wessely et al., 2008). Many survivors of interpersonal violence were victimized in the context of overwhelming emotion, narrowed or dissociated attention, and, in some cases, a relatively early stage of cognitive development—all of which can reduce the accuracy and coherence of the survivor's understanding of these traumatic events. In addition, interpersonal violence frequently involves a more powerful figure who justifies his or her aggression by distorting objective reality—for example, by blaming victimization on the victim or endorsing social messages that support violence or maltreatment of those with lesser social power. These fragmented, incomplete, or inaccurate explanations of traumatic events are often carried by the survivor into adulthood, with predictable negative results.

Therapists can be helpful in this area by providing, when indicated, accurate information on the nature of trauma and its effects, and by working with the survivor to integrate this new information and its implications into his or her overall perspective. Although often presented relatively early in treatment (for example, Talbot et al., 1998), psychoeducational activities are helpful throughout the therapy process. For example, as the client addresses traumatic material later in treatment, he or she may gain from additional information that normalizes or provides a new perspective on traumatic memory.

Although psychoeducation is usually provided during ongoing individual treatment, it also can occur in the context of separate, clinician-led support groups, wherein a small number of people with similar trauma histories compare stories, give each other advice, and discuss interpersonal violence and its effects. An advantage of group interventions is that the survivor can learn from the similar experiences of others, a process that may be more powerful and enduring than when similar material is delivered solely by the therapist. On the other hand, by their very nature, support groups may be less efficient than face-to-face psychotherapy, in terms of the client's own processing, integration, and personal application of whatever he or she learns from such information.

Handouts

Whether it occurs in individual therapy or in a guided support group, psychoeducation sometimes may include the use of printed handouts. These materials typically present easily understood information on topics such as the prevalence and impacts of interpersonal violence, common myths about victimization, and social resources available to the survivor. However, the therapist should keep at least four issues in mind when deciding what (if any) written material to make available and how it should be used:

1. *The quality of the materials.* Some handouts contain misinformation; may advocate religious or social perspectives that may indirectly blame, proselytize, or exclude; or may be written at a level that is not easily understood by the survivor.

2. *The language of the materials.* For example, a person whose primary language is Spanish may gain little from a pamphlet written in English.

3. *The cultural appropriateness of the information or depictions.* For example, materials may reflect more middle-class concerns, or visual depictions may be limited to White figures (Lanktree & Briere, 2008).

4. *The risk of insufficient cognitive-emotional integration.* Merely offering educational materials is not the same as providing effective psychoeducation, especially if the materials are distributed without sufficient discussion or application to the client's own history or current situation (E. Becker et al., 1998).

Most important, handouts should be considered tools in the psychoeducation process, not stand-alone sources of information. The public health literature, for example, suggests that didactic material alone may not be especially effective in changing the beliefs or behaviors of victimized individuals (E. Becker et al., 1998; Briere, 2003). Instead, the clinician should ensure that the information is as personally relevant to the survivor as possible, so that whatever is contained in the handout or media is directly applicable to his or her life, and thus has greater implicit meaning.

Client-oriented brochures and information sheets can be obtained from a number of organizations, especially via the Internet. At the time of this writing, several sites include useful consumer information:

David Baldwin's Trauma Information Pages
(http://www.trauma-pages.com/pg4.htm)

International Society for Traumatic Stress Studies
(http://www.istss.org/resources/index.htm)

Jim Hopper's website
(http://www.jimhopper.com/)

National Center for PTSD
(http://www.ptsd.va.gov/)

National Child Traumatic Stress Network
(http://www.nctsnet.org/nccts/nav.do?pid=lgn_main)

Office for Victims of Crime (U.S. Department of Justice)
(http://www.ojp.usdoj.gov/ovc/help/welcome.html)

Books

Clinicians may also refer clients to readily available books that are "survivor friendly," such as Judith Herman's (1992b) *Trauma and Recovery: The Aftermath of Violence—From Domestic Abuse to Political Terror.* Although obviously limited to individuals with adequate reading skills, such books allow clients to "read up" on traumas similar to their own. Other books are specifically written for the survivor or interested layperson (for example, Allen's [2005] *Coping With Trauma: Hope Through Understanding* and Follette and Pistorello's (2007) *Finding Life Beyond Trauma*) and contain advice as well as information. Some occasionally may be too emotionally activating for some survivors with unresolved posttraumatic difficulties, however—especially those individuals early in their recovery or treatment process. Other books may contain erroneous information or suggest self-help strategies that are not, in fact, helpful. For these reasons, we recommend that the clinician personally read any book before recommending it to a client, not only to make sure that it is appropriate to the client's needs and is factually accurate but to gauge its potential to activate significant posttraumatic distress in those unprepared for such emotional exposure.

Verbal Information During Therapy

Although written psychoeducational materials can be helpful, more typically information is provided verbally by the clinician during the ongoing process of psychotherapy. Because the educational process is directly embedded in the therapeutic context, it is often more directly relevant to the client's experience, and thus more easily integrated into his or her ongoing understanding (Briere, 2003). Additionally, psychoeducation provided in this manner allows the therapist to more easily monitor the client's responses to the material and to clear up any misunderstandings that might be present. As noted at the end of this chapter, however, over- or misapplication of psychoeducation during treatment can also impede therapy progress; as with many aspects of good therapy, the issue is often the correct balance of content versus process and sufficient attunement to the client's clinical response.

General Focus

Whether through written or verbal means, clinicians in the trauma field often focus on several major topics during psychoeducation.

- *The prevalence of the trauma.* Information on the prevalence of interpersonal violence tends to contradict the common belief that the client was specifically selected by the perpetrator by virtue of weakness, badness, or unconscious provocation, or that the client is virtually alone in having experienced the trauma. For example, knowing that approximately one in five women in the general population have been raped at some point in their lives, or that 10 to 20 percent of men have been sexually abused as children (Briere, 2004), may be a meaningful antidote to the survivor's fear that he or she alone has experienced such events and that something specific to him or her caused the event to occur.
- *Common myths associated with the trauma.* As noted at various points in this book, interpersonal violence often occurs within a broader social context that, to some extent, blames victims for their experiences and/or supports perpetrators for their behaviors. For example, rape victims are often believed to have been seductive or otherwise to have "asked for" their victimization, domestic violence may be normalized as appropriate and rightful dominance of wives by husbands under certain circumstances, childhood physical abuse may be justified in terms of parental rights or appropriate discipline, and it may be assumed that individuals, in general, frequently lie about having been abused or assaulted in the service of manipulation or retribution (Anderson & Huesmann, 2003; Briere, 1987; Briere, Henschel, & Smiljanich, 1992; M. R. Burt, 1980; Petrak, 2002; L. E. Walker, 1984). When the client subscribes to these myths, he or she is more likely to, in fact, blame himself or herself for the victimization or explain away the trauma as something not worthy of treatment (Resick & Schnicke, 1993). For this reason, it can be helpful to discuss "rape myths" or "common myths about partner abuse" in a way that makes it clear that such beliefs are not accurate (for example, Moor, 2007).
- *The usual reasons why perpetrators engage in interpersonal violence.* This may include describing the often compulsive, multivictim nature of many perpetrator behaviors, and the psychology driving the perpetrator's actions—including the offender's frequent need for power and

dominance in the face of insecurity and feelings of inadequacy. Such information can reduce the client's self-focused explanations for the assault and increase his or her awareness of the perpetrator's dysfunctional or malignant characteristics. This shift in attribution may make self-blame appear less logical to the survivor. In addition, knowledge that the client was "one of many" for the perpetrator may further decrease his or her tendency to take personal responsibility for what was done to him or her.

- *Typical immediate responses to trauma.* Among other victim reactions to adverse events, this may include peritraumatic dissociation (for example, "spacing out," out-of-body experiences, or experiencing time distortion at the time of the trauma), occasional sexual responses associated with sexual traumas (as opposed to positive psychological feelings), relief at not being injured or killed when others have been, and "Stockholm effects," wherein the victim becomes attached or somehow bonded with the perpetrator. Because these are all relatively normal responses to trauma, despite their apparent negative qualities, the client may eventually experience relief, as well as decreased guilt and self-blame, upon receiving and integrating such information.

- *The lasting posttraumatic responses to victimization.* Information on the commonness and logical nature of posttraumatic stress symptoms (for example, flashbacks, numbing, or hyperarousal responses) and other trauma-related responses (for example, substance abuse, self-injury, panic attacks, or intimacy fears)—as described in Chapter 2—are an important part of most good trauma therapy. As the client comes to understand that posttraumatic symptoms are normal (in the sense that such symptoms are logical and relatively common) responses to abnormal or toxic circumstances, he or she is less likely to experience himself or herself as damaged or mentally ill and may feel less out of control. Similarly, it is almost always preferable to view oneself as suffering from a well-understood cluster of typical responses to traumatic events (for example, posttraumatic stress disorder [PTSD]) than it is to see oneself as besieged by a variety of bizarre, unrelated symptoms. In addition, psychoeducation may prepare the client for symptoms that arise in the future. By describing symptoms before they occur, the clinician can provide a sense of predictability. This, in itself, may significantly reduce posttrauma anxiety. And successfully predicting potential symptoms enhances the overall credibility of the therapist, especially in terms of his or her nonpathologizing analysis of what symptoms mean and do not mean.

- *Reframing symptoms as trauma processing.* Psychoeducation can involve reframing certain posttraumatic symptoms more positively, even as evidence that recovery is occurring. This is a somewhat more active process than the normalization of symptoms described earlier. Not all symptoms can be reframed, of course. Depression, panic attacks, suicidality, or psychosis, for example, are generally what they appear to be: evidence of psychological disturbance or dysregulation of some form or another. On the other hand, as described in Chapter 8, posttraumatic reliving symptoms can be evidence of attempted psychological processing (even when unsuccessful), and posttraumatic avoidance is frequently an adaptive attempt to reduce the overwhelming aspects of reactivated distress, and thus may represent an attempt to increase safety. By reframing posttraumatic symptoms as potentially adaptive, the clinician may counter some of the helplessness, perceived loss of control, and stigmatization that can accompany flashbacks, activated trauma memories, or psychological numbing. In fact, clients who accept reframing of flashbacks as trauma processing may even come to welcome some reexperiencing responses as evidence of movement toward recovery.

- *Safety plans.* Women or men who are at risk for ongoing domestic violence or are victims of crimes such as sex trafficking, prostitution, continuing abuse from childhood, or stalking may need to learn about "safety plans" that others have used successfully in similar circumstances. Typically, this involves developing a detailed strategy for exiting a dangerous environment (for example, involving prepacked suitcases, escape routes) and finding a new, safer, location, whether it be a friend's home, a shelter, or a local women's refuge (Briere & Lanktree, 2011; C. E. Jordan et al., 2004). Other clients may benefit from concrete information on how to access medical or social services, a child protection worker, or police assistance. The goal of such interventions is to increase the power of victims to ensure their own safety, and thus to decrease not only the likelihood of continued victimization, but also some of the helplessness often associated with exposure to chronic interpersonal violence.

Constraints

Despite its potentially positive effect, psychoeducation can backfire if not carefully adapted for the individual client, or if the conclusions that the client draws from the process are not monitored. For example, while information on the commonness of interpersonal violence may reduce the client's sense of being the only one who has been victimized, it may also reinforce the client's overestimation of the amount of danger in the interpersonal environment, leading to increased fear and avoidance of others. Similarly, too much focus on perpetrator dynamics may reinforce the client's need to excuse his or her victimizer, and information on standard posttraumatic reactions may inadvertently cause the client to feel disordered or dysfunctional or to take on a trauma "sick" role.

Ultimately, psychoeducation should not occur in a vacuum. Information is often helpful, and may be antidotal to distorted beliefs and maladaptive responses, but it must occur in the context of ongoing therapeutic discussion and evaluation (Najavits, 2002). Specifically, the clinician should attend carefully to how clients integrate new information into their worldviews and how they apply such information in their daily lives. Simply teaching (let alone lecturing) clients about what to do or not do, or suggesting how they should think about trauma and its effects, is rarely helpful in and of itself (Briere & Lanktree, 2011; Neuner, Schauer, Klaschik, Karunakara, & Ebert, 2004). Instead, psychoeducation is most useful when it is integrated into the ongoing therapeutic process.

Suggested Reading

Allen, J. G. (2005). *Coping with trauma: Hope through understanding*. Washington, DC: American Psychiatric Press.

Briere, J. (2003). Integrating HIV/AIDS prevention activities into psychotherapy for child sexual abuse survivors. In L. Koenig, A. O'Leary, L. Doll, & W. Pequenat (Eds.), *From child sexual abuse to adult sexual risk: Trauma, revictimization, and intervention* (pp. 219–232). Washington, DC: American Psychological Association.

Herman, J. L. (1992). *Trauma and recovery: The aftermath of violence—from domestic abuse to political terror*. New York, NY: Basic Books.

Najavits, L. M. (2002). *Seeking safety: A treatment manual for PTSD and substance abuse*. New York, NY: Guilford.

Resick, P. A., & Schnicke, M. K. (1993). *Cognitive processing therapy for rape victims: A treatment manual*. Newbury Park, CA: Sage.

6 Distress Reduction and Affect Regulation Training

As described in Chapter 2, treatment-seeking trauma survivors often experience chronic levels of anxiety, dysphoria, and posttraumatic arousal. Many also describe extremely negative emotional responses to trauma-related stimuli and memories—feeling states that are easily triggered and hard to accommodate internally. When faced with overwhelming arousal, distress, and/or emotionally laden memories, the survivor is often forced to rely on emotional avoidance strategies such as dissociation, substance abuse, or external tension reduction activities. Unfortunately, as described in Chapter 8, excessive avoidance often inhibits psychological recovery from the effects of traumatic events. In the worst case, the need to avoid additional posttraumatic distress may lead the hyperaroused or emotionally dysregulated client to avoid trauma-related material during therapy, or to drop out of treatment altogether. As well, emotional states that are aversive enough to overwhelm available affect regulation resources may negatively affect the client's perception of the treatment process and the psychotherapist.

This chapter describes two sets of interventions: those intended to reduce acute, destabilizing emotions and symptoms that emerge during the treatment process, and those focused on the client's more general capacity to regulate negative emotional states. This material is presented early in the treatment part of the book because, in some cases, high anxiety and/or low affect regulation capacity should be addressed before more classic trauma therapy (for example, emotional processing) can be fully accomplished (Chu, 2011; Cloitre et al., 2011; Courtois, 2010; Ford et al., 2005). The interventions outlined here can be used at any point during therapy, however. For example, although the relaxation techniques described in this chapter may be initiated early in treatment, these and other approaches to affect regulation may be relevant whenever the survivor experiences escalating or intrusive negative internal states. In addition, the intrinsic development of affect regulation skills usually occurs in the context of repeated exposure to—and processing of—trauma-related emotions, a phenomenon that progressively unfolds as treatment continues.

The techniques presented here are variously described in the trauma and anxiety literature as forms of "grounding," relaxation training, cognitive therapy, stress inoculation, meditation, and anxiety management. However labeled, these approaches all focus on the client's increased capacity to tolerate and down-regulate painful emotional states, both during treatment and in his or her ongoing life.

Dealing With Acute Intrusion: Grounding

Although much of this chapter is devoted to increasing trauma survivors' affect regulation skills, there are occasions when the clinician may have to intervene more directly in a client's emotional dysregulation. For example, in response to some triggering stimulus or memory, the client may experience sudden panic, flashbacks, intrusive negative thoughts, dissociative states, or even transient psychotic symptoms during therapy. These internal processes can be frightening—if not destabilizing—to the client and can diminish his or her moment-to-moment psychological contact with the therapist. At such times, it may be necessary to refocus the survivor's attention onto the immediate therapeutic environment (with its implicit safety and predictability) and the therapist-client connection.

This intervention, often referred to as *grounding,* can be quite helpful in acute situations. It is also, however, by its very nature, potentially disruptive to the treatment process. Grounding techniques tend to alter the immediate narrative/relational stream of psychotherapy, and run the risk of implying that something is going awry, such that a sudden, "emergency" procedure is required. For this reason, grounding should only be used when clearly indicated, should be adjusted to the minimal level necessary to reduce the client's internal escalation, and should be framed in such a way that it does not stigmatize the client or overdramatize the experience. In some cases, other therapeutic interventions may be just as effective, such as gently moving the client's narrative into more cognitive or less emotionally intense aspects of whatever is under discussion (see Chapter 8), or by engaging in some other intervention that does not involve an obvious change in focus.

If, despite these concerns, grounding is indicated (that is, the client is acutely overwhelmed by intrusive symptoms or escalating trauma memories, and psychological contact with the therapist is diminishing), we suggest the following general steps.

1. *Attempt to focus the client's attention onto the therapist and therapy,* as opposed to whatever internal processes are occurring. This may involve—to the extent that it does not trigger the client—shifting one's chair slightly closer to him or her, unobtrusively moving into his or her visual field, or slightly changing one's voice so that it compels more attention. This does not mean, of course, that the therapist yells at the client or behaves in an unduly intrusive manner. In addition, it usually does not suggest that one should touch the client, since physical contact can intensify the client's fear or sense of invasion, or trigger memories.

Whether to touch or not is contingent on the specifics of the situation, including, for example, the nature of the trauma and whether the therapist is well known to the client and trusted by him or her.

2. *Ask the client to* briefly *describe his or her internal experience.* For example, "Susan, is something going on/upsetting you/happening right now?" If the client is clearly frightened or responding to distressing internal stimuli, but can't or won't describe them, go to Step 3. If the client is able to talk about the internal experience, however, it is often helpful for him or her to generally label or broadly describe it. This does not mean the survivor should necessarily go into great detail—detailed description of the flashback or memory may increase its intensity, thereby reinforcing the response rather than lessening it.

3. *Orient the client to the immediate, external environment.* This often involves two, related messages: (a) that the client is safe and is not, in fact, in danger, and (b) that he or she is *here* (in the room, in the session, with the therapist) and *now* (not in the past, undergoing the trauma). In some cases, the client can be oriented by reassuring statements, typically using the client's name as an additional orienting device (for example, "Susan, you're okay. You're here in the room with me. You're safe."). In other, more extreme cases, grounding may involve asking the client to describe the room or other aspects of the immediate environment (for example, "Susan, let's try to bring you back to the room, okay? Where are we?/What time is it?/Can you describe the room?"). The client might be asked to focus his or her attention on the feeling of the chair or couch underneath him or her, or of his or her feet on the floor. However accomplished, the client's reorientation to the here and now may occur relatively quickly (for example, in a few seconds) or may take longer (for example, a number of minutes).

4. *If indicated, focus on breathing or other methods of relaxation.* This is an example of when breath or relaxation training (as described later in this chapter) can be especially helpful. Take the client through the relaxation or breathing exercise for as long as is necessary (typically for several minutes or longer), reminding the client of his or her safety and presence in the here-and-now.

5. Repeat Step 2, and assess the client's ability and willingness to return to the therapeutic process. Repeat Steps 3 and 4 as needed.

If it is possible for therapy to return to its earlier focus, normalize the traumatic intrusion (for example, as a not-unexpected part of trauma processing) and the grounding activity (for example, as a simple procedure for focusing attention away from intrusive events), and continue trauma treatment. It is important that the client's temporary reexperiencing or symptom exacerbation be neither stigmatized nor given greater meaning than appropriate. The overall message should be that trauma processing sometimes involves the intrusion of (and distraction by) potentially upsetting memories, thoughts, and/or feelings, but that such events are part of the healing process, as opposed to evidence of psychopathology or loss of control.

Intervening in Chronic Affect Dysregulation

In contrast to grounding, which addresses relatively acute emotional intrusions or activations, this section describes psychological interventions in the sustained hyperarousal and anxiety experienced by many survivors of major, chronic trauma.

Medication

When dysphoria or posttraumatic arousal is of sufficient intensity that it interferes with treatment and recovery, psychoactive medications may be indicated. As described in Chapter 12, pharmacologic agents that target anxiety and/or hyperarousal, or stabilize mood, sometimes may be helpful in reducing such symptoms during trauma-focused psychotherapy. As also noted, however, such medications are not a cure-all for dysregulated emotional states; their efficacy is variable from case to case and may be counterindicated in some instances because of significant side effects. Often, the best approach to high pretreatment arousal and anxiety is to use psychiatric medication, if necessary, but also to apply psychological interventions that reduce anxiety and increase affect regulation skills, as described in this chapter.

Relaxation and Breath Control

One of the most basic forms of arousal reduction during therapy is learned relaxation. Strategically induced relaxation can facilitate the processing of traumatic material during the therapy session by reducing the client's overall level of anxiety. Reduced anxiety during trauma processing both lessens the likelihood the client will feel overwhelmed by trauma-related distress and probably serves to countercondition traumatic material, as described in Chapter 8. In addition, relaxation can be used by the survivor outside of treatment as a way to reduce the effects of triggered traumatic memories. For individuals with especially easily activated anxiety or intrusive reexperiencing, the benefits of calling upon an internal relaxation mechanism cannot be overstated.

There are two general approaches to relaxation training, *breath training* and *progressive relaxation*, both of which are described only briefly here. For more detailed information, the reader should consult the Suggested Reading list at the end of this chapter.

Progressive Relaxation

This technique involves clenching and then releasing muscles, sequentially from head to toe, until the entire body reaches a relaxed state (Jacobson, 1938; Rimm & Masters, 1979). As clients practice progressive relaxation on a regular basis, most are eventually able to enter a relaxed state relatively quickly, if not automatically. Some practitioners begin each session with relaxation exercises; others teach it initially in treatment, then utilize it only when specifically indicated, for example, when discussion of traumatic material results in a high state of anxiety. Two points should be made about the use of relaxation training in the treatment of posttraumatic stress: (1) use of this technique alone (that is, in the absence of coexisting trauma-processing activities) is unlikely to significantly reduce trauma-related symptoms, per se (Rothbaum, Meadows, Resick, & Foy, 2000), and (2) clinical experience suggests that a minority of traumatized individuals may have unexpected anxious or dissociative reactions to induced relaxation (for example, Allen, 2001; Fitzgerald & Gonzalez, 1994) or may not be able to successfully self-induce a relaxed state. Those who are chronically flooded with flashbacks and other reexperiencing symptoms may be less likely to gain from relaxation training (S. Taylor, 2003). In our experience, progressive relaxation can be quite helpful, when indicated, but the client should be monitored for possible, seemingly paradoxical, increases in anxiety or arousal during this procedure.

Breath Training

Although progressive relaxation is successfully used by some clinicians, our preference—all other things being equal—is to teach breathing techniques. When stressed, many people breath in a more shallow manner, hyperventilate, or, in some cases, temporarily stop breathing altogether. Teaching the client "how to breathe" during stress can help restore more normal respiration, and thus adequate oxygenation of the brain. Equally important, as the client learns to breathe in ways that are more efficient and more aligned with normal, nonstressed inhalation and exhalation, there is usually a calming effect on the body and the autonomic nervous system.

Breath training generally involves guided breathing exercises that teach the client to be more aware of his or her breathing—especially the ways in which it is inadvertently constrained by tension and adaptation to trauma— and to adjust his or her musculature, posture, and thinking so that more effective and calming respiration can occur (Best & Ribbe, 1995). There are a number of manuals that include information on breath training during trauma treatment (for example, Foa & Rothbaum, 1998; Rimm & Masters, 1979). Presented in Appendix 3 is a simple version of this protocol.

Learned relaxation—however initiated—can be employed by the client to down-regulate stress responses as they occur. In many cases, relaxation can be cued by repetitively associating it with a calming word during relaxation training, so that later use of the word releases a conditioned relaxation response (Best & Ribbe, 2000). For example, the emotionally activated trauma survivor might say the word *relax* to himself or herself during progressive relaxation activities. Similarly, as presented in Appendix 3, counting during inhalation and exhalation can both focus awareness and produce a cue (counting) that eventually may trigger a relaxation response.

Once the client is able to induce relaxation, the therapist can call on this skill during the processing of traumatic memories. As described in Chapter 8, for example, the therapist may either ask the client to induce relaxation prior to memory exposure activities or suggest relaxation when the client specifically appears to need it, for example, when major anxiety or fear emerges during the session. In many instances, the client may only have to focus on breathing, or relaxing muscle groups for a short while, using the cue word (or counting breaths), before relaxation is sufficient to allow further trauma processing. In some cases, of course, it may take longer.

It should be reiterated that although relaxation training is often a helpful component of trauma therapy, it is not always necessary or indicated. Some clients are neither so hyperaroused nor so anxious that they require special intervention in this area. Other clients (and therapists) find relaxation training too mechanistic, or a distraction from the relational process of psychotherapy. Like some other techniques presented in this book, relaxation training is an option, not a requirement, for trauma treatment.

Meditation and Yoga

Another approach to affect de-escalation and regulation involves (1) dispassionately noting negative, repetitive, and habitual thoughts and feelings, and then moving one's attention toward certain, other processes (for example, the breath), and/or (2) engaging in activities (for example, specific movements or physical positions) that produce positive states and preclude or lessen negative ones. The former is often referred to as *mindfulness meditation,* whereas the latter is best represented by *yoga.* Both approaches recently have been embraced as methods not only of affect regulation, but also potentially as interventions for trauma-related distress. Although these methodologies will be reviewed briefly below, the reader is referred to Briere (2012a); Emerson and Hopper (2011); Waelde (2004), and Chapter 10 for more detailed discussion.

Meditation

Meditation represents a broad category of inwardly directed practices, typically involving sitting or lying in a specific position, or walking in a certain way, while focusing on one's breath or some other internal sensation or process. In most instances, the meditator learns to maintain this attention for

relatively long periods of time, noting inevitable distracting thoughts and feelings without judgment, then returning to his or her ongoing focus of attention.
As described in Chapter 10, a number of studies indicate that meditation has
positive effects on both physical and psychological well-being, generally by
reducing stress, increasing equanimity, and, sometimes, prompting existential
insights about the basis of suffering. Among the positive impacts noted in the
literature are improved blood pressure and other cardiovascular functions,
and reduced psychological or physiological problems, ranging from fibromyalgia and chronic pain to anxiety, depression, substance abuse, eating disorders, aggression, and posttraumatic distress (Bormann, Liu, Thorp, & Lang,
2011; Hofmann, Sawyer, Witt, & Oh, 2010; Rosenthal, Grosswald, Ross, &
Rosenthal, 2011; T. L. Simpson et al., 2007; see, also, Chapter 10). Although
it is not entirely clear exactly how meditation impacts stress, it seems likely
that it decreases arousal of the autonomic nervous system, reduces preoccupation with negative or upsetting thoughts, lessens psychological reactivity, and
broadens psychological perspective. For these and related reasons, meditation
is increasingly suggested by clinicians—empirically oriented and otherwise—
for those suffering from trauma-related symptoms, although not without
some cautions and contraindications, as described in Chapter 10.

Yoga

Like meditation, yoga is a contemplative exercise that, over time, appears
to improve psychological and physical functioning (Emerson & Hopper,
2011). Involving careful stretching, and specific movements, postures, and
positions in specific sequences, it also includes attention to breath, meditation, relaxation, diet, and a specific philosophical perspective. Yoga not only
appears to calm the mind, but it also may increase physical strength, flexibility, and capacity, with associated reductions in psychophysiological stress
(R. P. Brown & Gerbarg, 2009; Harvard Mental Health Letter, 2009).
Recent research suggests that regular involvement in yoga practice may be
associated with improvements in posttraumatic stress, anxiety, and depression (R. P. Brown & Gerbarg, 2009; Descilo et al., 2009; Janakiramaiah
et al., 2000), although some studies have significant methodological flaws.

Obviously, meditation and/or yoga is not for everyone, and many trauma
survivors do not begin such practices solely as a method of stress reduction
or affect regulation. However, many trauma-exposed people find themselves
drawn to such contemplative practices and gain significantly from them.

Increasing General Affect Regulation Capacity

Above and beyond immediate methods of distress reduction, such as
grounding, relaxation, and meditation or yoga, there are a number of suggestions in the literature for increasing the general affect regulation abilities

of trauma clients. All are focused on increasing the survivor's overall capacity to tolerate and down-regulate negative feeling states, thereby reducing the likelihood that he or she will be overwhelmed by activated emotionality. In some cases, such affect regulation "training" may be necessary before any significant memory processing can be accomplished (Cloitre et al., 2011; Courtois, 2010).

Identifying and Discriminating Emotions

One of the most important components of successful affect regulation is the ability to correctly perceive and label emotions as they are experienced (Linehan, 1993a). Many survivors of early, chronic trauma have trouble knowing exactly what they feel when activated into an emotional state, beyond, perhaps, a sense of feeling "bad" or "upset" (Briere, 1996; Luterek, Orsillo, & Marx, 2005). In a similar vein, some individuals may not be able to accurately differentiate feelings of anger, for example, from anxiety or sadness. Although this sometimes reflects dissociative disconnection from emotion, in other cases it appears to represent a basic inability to "know about" one's emotions. As a result, the survivor may perceive his or her internal state as consisting of chaotic, intense, but undifferentiated emotionality that is not logical or predictable. For example, the survivor triggered into a seemingly undifferentiated negative emotional state will not be able to say, "I am anxious," let alone infer that "I am anxious because I feel threatened." Instead, the experience may be of overwhelming and unexplainable negative emotion that comes "out of the blue."

The clinician can assist the client in this area by regularly facilitating exploration and discussion of the client's emotional experience. Often, the client will become more able to identify feelings just by being asked about them on an ongoing basis. On other occasions, the therapist can encourage the client to do "emotional detective work," involving attempts to hypothesize an experienced emotional state based on the events surrounding it (for example, the client guessing that a feeling is anxiety because it follows a frightening stimulus, or anger because it is associated with resentful cognitions or angry behaviors). Affect identification and discrimination sometimes can be fostered by the therapist's direct feedback, such as "It looks like you're feeling angry. Are you?" or "You look scared." This option should be approached with care, however. There is a certain risk of labeling a client's affect as feeling *A* when, in fact, the client is experiencing feeling *B*—thereby fostering confusion rather than effective emotional identification. For this reason, we recommend that, in all but the most obvious instances, the therapist facilitate the client's exploration and hypothesis testing of his or her feeling state, rather than telling the client what he or she is feeling. The critical issue here is not, in most cases, whether the client (or therapist) correctly identifies a particular emotional state, but rather that the client explores and attempts to label his or her feelings on a regular basis. In our experience, the more this is done as a general part of therapy, the better the survivor eventually becomes at accurate feeling identification and discrimination.

Identifying and Countering Thoughts That Antecede Intrusive Emotions

It is not only feelings that should be identified—in many cases, it is also thoughts. This is most relevant when a given cognition triggers a strong emotional reaction, but the thought is somehow unknown to the survivor. As suggested by some clinicians (for example, Cloitre et al., 2002; Linehan, 1993a), affect regulation capacities often can be improved by encouraging the client to identify and counter the cognitions that exacerbate or trigger trauma-related emotions. Beyond the more general cognitive interventions described in Chapter 7, this involves the client monitoring whatever thoughts mediate between a triggered traumatic memory and a subsequent negative emotional reaction. For example, upon having child abuse memories triggered by an authority figure, the survivor may have the unconscious or partially suppressed thought, "He is going to hurt me," and may then react with extreme anxiety or distress. Or the survivor of sexual abuse might think, "She wants to have sex with me," when interacting with an older woman, and then may experience revulsion, rage, or terror. In such cases, although the memory itself is likely to produce negative emotionality (conditioned emotional responses, or CERs; see Chapter 8), the associated cognitions often exacerbate these responses to produce more extreme emotional states. In other instances, thoughts may be less directly trauma related, yet still increase the intensity of the client's emotional response. For example, in a stressful situation the client may have thoughts such as "I'm out of control" or "I'm making a fool of myself" that produce panic or fears of being overwhelmed or inundated.

Unfortunately, because triggered thoughts may be out of superficial awareness, their role in subsequent emotionality may not be observed by the survivor (Beck, 1995). As the client is made more aware of the cognitive antecedents to overwhelming emotionality, he or she can learn to lessen the impact of such thoughts. In many cases, this is done by explicitly disagreeing with the cognition (for example, "Nobody's out to get me," or "I can handle this"), or merely by labeling such cognitions as "old tapes" rather than accurate perceptions (Briere, 1996; see also Chapter 10). In this regard, one of the benefits of what is referred to as *insight* in psychodynamic therapy is often the self-developed realization that one is acting in a certain way by virtue of erroneous, "old" (for example, trauma- or abuse-related) beliefs or perceptions—an understanding that often reduces the power of those cognitions to produce distress or motivate dysfunctional behavior (see Chapter 7).

When the thoughts that underlie extremely powerful and overwhelming emotional states are triggered by trauma-related memories, the therapist can focus on these intermediate responses by asking questions such as "What happened just before you got scared/angry/upset?" or "Did you have a thought or memory?" If the client reports that, for example, a given strong emotion was triggered by a trauma memory, the therapist may ask him or her to describe the memory (if that is tolerable) and to discuss what thoughts the memory triggered. Ultimately, this may involve exploration and discussion of four separate phenomena:

1. The environmental stimulus that triggered the memory (for example, one's lover's angry expression)

2. The memory itself (for example, of maltreatment by an angry parent)

3. The current thought associated with the memory (for example, "He/She hates me," "I must have done something wrong," or "He/She is blaming me for something I didn't do")

4. The current feeling (for example, anger or fear)

These triggered, often catastrophizing cognitions (that is, expectations or assumptions of extremely negative outcomes) can then be discussed as to their relevance to the current situation. In such instances, the client is generally asked to explore the accuracy of such thoughts, their possible etiology (often involving childhood abuse, neglect, or other maltreatment), and what he or she could do to address such thoughts (for example, remind himself or herself that the thought is not accurate or that it is "just my childhood talking"). As the client becomes better able to identify these cognitions, place them in some realistic context, and counter them with other, more positive thoughts, he or she often develops greater capacity to forestall extreme emotional reactivity, and thereby better regulate the emotional experience.

Trigger Awareness and Intervention

There is another cognitive intervention that can help the survivor maintain emotional equilibrium in his or her daily life: The clinician can help the survivor learn to identify and address triggers in the environment that activate intrusive negative feelings. Although, as noted in Chapter 2, activated memories of trauma are not intrinsically negative phenomena, they can motivate behaviors that—although sometimes effective in reducing triggered distress—may be maladaptive or even self-destructive in contexts where attention and adaptive strategies would be more helpful. Successful trigger identification can facilitate a greater sense of control and better interpersonal functioning by allowing the client to alter situations in which these triggers might occur and problem-solve emerging negative states before they produce behavioral problems. Ultimately, as noted later, trigger interventions help increase affect regulation and tolerance.

Trigger identification and intervention is generally learned as a regular component of therapy, so that it can be called upon later when the survivor encounters a trigger in his or her environment. Importantly, it is often hard to figure out exactly what to do when one has been triggered; it is better to have previously identified the trigger (among others), its etiology, and its solutions, in the context of therapeutic guidance and support.

As described by one survivor, the development of intervention strategies prior to being triggered is like creating a "message in a bottle": preplanning about what to do when triggered (the "message") can be developed for later use (placed in a "bottle") and called upon once the individual is triggered (the bottle "floats" to the triggered circumstance, allowing a more measured and thought-out approach to what otherwise might be a crisis situation).[1]

In this regard, trigger identification can be taught as a series of tasks:

1. *Identify a given thought, feeling, or intrusive sensation as posttraumatic.* This is relatively easy in some cases. For example, it may not be difficult to recognize an intrusive sensory flashback of a gunshot as trauma related. In others, however, the reexperiencing may be more subtle, such as feelings of anger or fear, or intrusive feelings of helplessness that emerge during relational interaction. Typical questions the client can learn to ask himself or herself include the following:

   o Does this thought/feeling/sensation "make sense" in terms of what is happening around me right now?
   o Are these thoughts or feelings too intense, based on the current context?
   o Does this thought or feeling carry with it memories of a past trauma?
   o Am I experiencing any unexpected alteration in awareness (for example, depersonalization or derealization) as these thoughts/feelings/sensations occur?
   o Is this a situation in which I usually get triggered?

2. *Evaluate stimuli present in the immediate environment, and identify which are trauma reminiscent* (that is, "find the trigger"). This typically involves a certain level of detective work, as the client learns to objectively evaluate the environment to see what might be trauma reminiscent, and thus potentially a trigger. Examples of triggers the client might learn to recognize, depending on his or her trauma history, include these:

   o Interpersonal conflict
   o Criticism or rejection
   o Sexual situations or stimuli
   o Interactions with an authority figure
   o People with physical or psychological characteristics that are in some way similar to the client's past perpetrator(s)
   o Boundary violations
   o Sirens, helicopters, gunshots
   o The sound of crying

---

[1]Another, more structured version of trigger identification and intervention, specifically targeted at adolescents and young adults, involving a "trigger grid" worksheet, can be found in Briere and Lanktree (2011) and at http://johnbriere.com.

In some cases, the trigger will be obvious and easily recognized. In others, the client may have to work hard to identify what may be triggering him or her.

3. *Employ an adaptive strategy.* This usually involves some version of "improving the moment" (Linehan, 1993a, p. 148), whereby the survivor reduces the likelihood of an extreme emotional response. Examples include the following:

   o Intentional behavioral avoidance or "time outs" during especially stressful moments (for example, leaving a party when others become intoxicated, intentionally minimizing arguments with authority figures, learning how to discourage unwanted flirtatious behavior from others)

   o Analyzing the triggering stimulus or situation until a greater understanding changes one's perception and thus terminates the trigger (for example, carefully examining the behavior of an individual who is triggering posttraumatic fear, and eventually becoming more aware of the fact that he or she is not acting in a threatening manner; or coming to understand that a given individual's seemingly dismissive style does not indicate a desire to reject or ignore as much as it does interpersonal awkwardness)

   o Increasing support systems (for example, bringing a friend to a party where one might feel threatened, or calling a friend to "debrief" an upsetting situation)

   o Positive self-talk (for example, working out beforehand what to say to oneself when triggered, such as "I am safe," "I don't have to do anything I don't want to do," or "This is just my past talking, this isn't really what I think it is")

   o Relaxation induction or breath control, as described earlier in this chapter

   o Strategic distraction, such as starting a conversation with a safe person, reading a book, or going for a walk, as a way to pulling attention away from escalating internal responses such as panic, flashbacks, or catastrophizing cognitions

   o Delaying tension reduction behaviors (TRBs; see Chapter 2) and "urge surfing" (see Chapter 10). These strategies can be especially helpful for the triggered survivor, and thus are described in detail below

Delaying Tension Reduction Behavior

Triggered phenomena can be reduced by intentionally forestalling TRBs until they become less probable or lose some of their power. In general, this involves encouraging the client to "hold off," as long as possible, on behaviors that he or she normally would use to reduce distress when triggered (for example, self-mutilation, impulsive sexual behavior, or binging/purging) and then, if the behavior must be engaged in, doing so to the minimal extent possible (Briere & Lanktree, 2011).

There are probably at least two important aspects of this strategy. First, many survivors learn that their TRB responses are to some extent reflexive:

Given sufficient attention and thought, such behaviors could be delayed or avoided without too much difficulty. For example, a person whose immediate response upon being triggered into a negative state is to self-injure might discover that, in fact, the upsetting feeling was ultimately tolerable, and that his or her threshold for self-mutilation was, in that instance, unnecessarily low. Second, as noted by Marlatt and Gordon (1985) and others, many triggered emotional states that otherwise would motivate a TRB or episode of substance abuse have a relatively short half-life: If the individual can sit out the activated emotional state, it will often pass in a matter of minutes, thereby obviating the need for maladaptive behavior.

Urge Surfing

Regarding the limits of activated distress, the client may be taught to "urge surf" (Bowen, Chawla, & Marlatt, 2011), as described in greater detail in Chapter 10. When triggered into a state in which a TRB is likely (for example, rage associated with a memory of childhood abuse), the client can attempt to enter a mindful perspective (as presented in Chapter 10) and then, rather than act, "ride out" or "surf" the emotion and associated urge to tension reduce, until it peaks and then fades away. Notably, in both delaying and urge surfing, the survivor does not try to suppress triggered thoughts or feelings, but rather changes his or her relationship to them.

Although the therapist should take a clear stand on the harmfulness of most TRB responses to triggering, and work with the client to terminate or at least decrease their frequency and injuriousness, he or she should not appear to judge the client regarding TRBs: Value judgments about the wrongness or immorality of a given behavior—other than activities that harm others—are rarely helpful. Such statements not only increase guilt and shame, but they often "drive the therapy underground" by forcing the client to keep things (in this case, continued tension reduction) from the therapist.

Because TRBs ultimately serve to reduce distress, client attempts to delay their use (or "surf" them) provide opportunities to develop affect tolerance. For example, in the delay approach, if a survivor is able to try to not binge eat or act on a sexual compulsion following a triggering situation, if only for a few minutes beyond when he or she would otherwise engage in such activity, two things may happen:

1. The client may be exposed to a brief period of sustained (but temporarily manageable) distress, during which time he or she can learn a small amount of distress tolerance.

2. The impulse to engage in the TRB may fade, because the emotionality associated with the urge to engage in the TRB often lessens if not immediately acted upon.

With continued practice, the period between the initial triggered experience and the actual TRB may be lengthened, the TRB itself may be decreased in severity, and affect tolerance may be increased. An added benefit of this approach is that the goal of decreasing (and then ending)

TRBs is seen as not stopping "bad" behavior, but rather as a way for the client to learn affect regulation and to get his or her behavior under greater personal control.

Importantly, inherent in either of these approaches is the possibility that it will not be entirely successful. It is an unavoidable fact of clinical life that tension reduction and other avoidance behaviors are survival based and are therefore not easily given up by the client. Nevertheless, by empowering the survivor to engage ("allow") the aversive state and consciously attempt to change his or her normal response to it, the circumstance is also changed and new behavior is often possible.

Affect Regulation Learning During Trauma Processing

In addition to the above, it appears that affect regulation and tolerance can be learned implicitly during the ongoing process of longer-term, exposure-based trauma therapy. Because, as discussed in later chapters, trauma-focused interventions involve the repeated activation, processing, and resolution of distressing but nonoverwhelming distress, such treatment slowly teaches the survivor to become more "at home" with some level of painful emotional experience and to develop whatever skills are necessary to deescalate moderate levels of emotional arousal. As the client repetitively experiences titrated (that is, not overwhelming or destabilizing) levels of distress during exposure to trauma memories (Chapter 8), he or she may slowly develop the ability to self-soothe, reframe upsetting thoughts, and call upon relational support. In addition, by working with the client to deescalate distress associated with activated CERs, the therapist often models affect regulation strategies, especially those involving normalization, soothing, and validation. However developed, this growing ability to move in and out of strong affective states, in turn, fosters an increased sense of emotional control and reduced fear of negative affect.

Suggested Reading

Bowen, S., Chawla, N., & Marlatt, G. A. (2011). *Mindfulness-based relapse prevention for addictive behaviors: A clinician's guide.* New York, NY: Guilford.

Cloitre, M., Cohen, L. R., & Karestan, K. C. (2006). *Treating survivors of childhood abuse: Psychotherapy for the interrupted life.* New York, NY: Guilford.

Cloitre, M., Koenen, K. C., Cohen, L. R., & Han, H. (2002). Skills training in affective and interpersonal regulation followed by exposure: A phase-based treatment for PTSD related to childhood abuse. *Journal of Consulting and Clinical Psychology, 70,* 1067–1074.

Jacobson, E. (1938). *Progressive relaxation.* Chicago, IL: University of Chicago Press.

Linehan, M. M. (1993). *Cognitive-behavioral treatment of borderline personality disorder.* New York, NY: Guilford.

Schore, A. N. (2003). *Affect regulation and the repair of the self.* New York, NY: Norton.

7

Cognitive Interventions

As noted in Chapter 2, trauma survivors—especially victims of interpersonal violence—are prone to self-blame, guilt, shame, low self-esteem, overestimation of danger, and other negative beliefs and perceptions. The rape victim may believe he or she somehow "asked for it" or otherwise caused or contributed to the assault, and the battered woman may assume that she deserved to be beaten. Individuals who have been repeatedly exposed to situations in which they were helpless to escape or otherwise reduce their trauma exposure often develop a sense of having little power to affect future potentially negative events. Some survivors view their posttraumatic symptoms as evidence of being defective or "crazy." Victims of sexual trauma often feel ashamed and isolated by their experiences.

In general, cognitive therapy of posttraumatic disturbance involves the guided reconsideration of negative perceptions and beliefs about self, others, and the environment that arose from the trauma. As these negative assumptions are reevaluated, a more affirming and empowering model of self and others can take its place. At the same time, the client may develop a more detailed and coherent understanding of the traumatic event, a process that is associated with clinical improvement (Foa, Molnar, & Cashman, 1995; Shipherd, Street, & Resick, 2006).

Cognitive Processing

In most cases, trauma-related cognitive disturbance is addressed through detailed verbal exploration of the traumatic event and its surrounding circumstances. As the client repeatedly describes the trauma in the context of treatment, he or she, in a sense, relives the past while viewing it from the perspective of the present. By verbally recounting the traumatic event, the client (often with the assistance of the therapist) has the opportunity to "hear" the assumptions, beliefs, and perceptions that were encoded at the time of the trauma; consider the reasons they may have arisen; and compare them with what he or she now knows. Together, the client and therapist can then work to create a more accurate cognitive model of what occurred.

This interactive process frequently fosters more positive self-perceptions as the client comes to reinterpret former "bad" behaviors, deservingness of maltreatment, and presumed inadequacies in a more accurate light. For example, the client who has always interpreted her behavior just prior to a rape as "sluttish" may gain from the opportunity to relive and review what actually happened, and to see for her (current) self if her judgments about herself appear valid. Exploration of the events prior to the rape may reveal that she was not behaving in a seductive manner, nor is she likely to recall wanting to be abused or otherwise hurt. Importantly, such insights do not suggest that these early perceptions were irrational, but rather that they logically arose from the original context of the trauma.

A growing awareness of what one could reasonably have done at the time of the trauma—that is, what one's options actually were—can be antidotal to inappropriate feelings of responsibility, self-blame, or self-criticism. For example, describing memories of childhood abuse—while simultaneously listening to them from the perspective of an adult in a safe context—may lead to the realization that one had few options other than subservience or accommodation at the time of the abuse. The notion that "I should have done something to stop it," for example, might be countered by a greater experiential appreciation of the size and power differentials inherent in an adult forcing his or her will (and body) on a 7-year-old child.

Finally, blaming or shaming statements made by an assailant may gradually lose their power when examined in the context of a temporally distant, nondangerous environment. Many victims of interpersonal violence internalize or otherwise accept rationalizations used by the perpetrator at the time of the assault (Salter, 1995). These include batterer statements that the victim deserved violence for failing to be a good spouse, rapist statements that the victim was asking to be sexually assaulted, and child abuser statements that physical abuse was merely appropriate punishment for bad behavior. In a recent example, a refugee may have partially accepted statements made by his torturers that he was responsible for the slaughter of his family by virtue of escaping forced induction into the army, when, in fact, he did nothing to justify such horrible events. The childhood trauma survivor may internalize more general perpetrator comments that he or she is bad, fat, ugly, or worthless. As the client and therapist discuss the circumstances of the event and consider perpetrator statements in the absence of danger or coercion, the objective lack of support for these statements may become more apparent to the client.

Because the clinician is often more able to see these cognitive distortions than is the client, he or she may feel pressed to voice an opinion regarding the lack of culpability of the victim or the obvious cruelty of the perpetrator. This is understandable, and, in small doses, is usually appropriate. But such statements should be presented as a form of "going on the record" regarding the therapist's clear understanding that the victim was, in fact, victimized. Rarely will such statements, in and of themselves, actually change the client's opinion. In fact, clinical experience suggests that cognitive therapy is rarely helpful when the clinician merely disagrees (or argues) with the client about his or her cognitions or memories, or makes definitive statements about what reality actually is or was. Rather, cognitive interventions are most effective when they provide opportunities for the client to experience the original trauma-related thoughts and self-perceptions (for example, feelings of responsibility and guilt when recalling being beaten by a spouse), while at the same time considering a more contemporary, positive, hopefully self-generated perspective (for example, that the beatings were, ultimately, about the spouse's chronic anger, alcoholism, and feelings of inadequacy, and not due to the client's failure to wash the dishes or provide sex on demand).

As suggested by Resick and Schnicke (1992), the reworking of trauma-related assumptions or perceptions is probably most effective when it occurs while the client is actively remembering the trauma and reexperiencing the thoughts and feelings he or she had at the time. In other words, merely discussing a traumatic event without some level of emotional memory activation is less likely to allow the client to change the cognitions related to the memory. In contrast, active recall and description of a traumatic event probably trigger two parallel processes: (1) observation of one's own trauma-related attributions regarding the specifics of the event and (2) activation of the emotions associated with the event. The second component of this response is covered in more detail in the next chapter. However, it is important to acknowledge it here because emotional activation allows the client to more directly relive the traumatic event, such that any cognitive interventions are more directly linked to specific memories of the trauma.

There are two major ways that the client can remember and, to some extent, reexperience traumatic events during the process of treatment: (1) by describing them in detail and (2) by writing about them. In the first instance, the therapist encourages the client to describe the traumatic event or events in as much verbal detail as is tolerable, including feelings he or she experienced during and after the victimization experience. As noted in the next chapter, this is an important component of emotional processing. It also facilitates cognitive processing to the extent that it includes discussion of conclusions or beliefs the survivor formed from the experience.

In response to the client's description, the therapist will generally ask open-ended questions that are intended to make apparent any cognitive distortions that might be present regarding blame, deservingness, or responsibility. As the client responds to these questions, the therapist provides support and encouragement, and, when appropriate, offers titrated (that is, careful, limited) information that counters the negative implications or self-perceptions that emerge in the client's responses. The client might then have responses that lead to further questions from the therapist. Or the topic might shift to the client's emotional processing of the implications of any new information, insights, or feelings that arose from the discussion process.

The second major form of cognitive processing involves the use of homework, wherein the client is asked to write about a specific topic related to the trauma, bring it to the next session, and read it aloud in the presence of the clinician (see Briere & Lanktree, 2011, for a specific, more structured version of cognitive homework for adolescents and young adults). In this way, the client has the opportunity to continue therapeutic activities outside of the session, including desensitization of traumatic memories (see Chapter 8) and continued cognitive reconsideration of trauma-related assumptions and perceptions. In addition, research suggests that the mere act of writing about an upsetting event, especially if done on multiple occasions, can, in some cases, reduce psychological distress over time (Pennebaker & Campbell, 2000; although also see Batten, Follette, Rasmussen Hall, & Palm, 2002) and potentially increase posttraumatic growth (Smyth, Hockemeyer, & Tulloch, 2008). See Chapter 8 for an example of trauma processing homework, adapted from Resick and Schnicke (1992).

The goal of such activities, whether verbal or written, is to activate the client's memories of the traumatic event and to cognitively process them in subsequent discussions. In verbal processing, the initiation and maintenance of such discussions often center on what is referred to as the *Socratic method*: a series of gentle, often open-ended inquiries that allow the client to progressively examine the assumptions and interpretations he or she has made about the victimization experience.

Typical questions, in this regard, include (but are not limited to) these:

- "Did you have any thoughts while it was happening? What were they?"
- "Given the situation, do you think there was anything else you could have done?"
- "So, that made you feel that you were to blame/responsible/bad/stupid/seductive. Can we go over what happened and see why you thought that?"
- "Do you think you actually wanted him/her/them to rape/beat/abuse/hurt you? Do you remember wanting that?"
- "You say that you were hurt/raped/beaten because you asked for it/were seductive/didn't lock the door/were out late. Can we go over what made you come to that conclusion?"
- "If this happened to someone else, would you think the same things about them?"
- "It sounds like you believe what he/she said about that. Was/is he/she the kind of person you would believe when he/she said something?"
- "Why do you think he/she said/did that?

The goal here is for the client to update his or her trauma-based understanding—not merely to incorporate the therapist's statements or analyze the client's "thinking errors." In this regard, although therapist statements about the presumed reality of things sometimes may be helpful, much of the knowledge the client acquires in therapy is best learned from himself or herself. By repeatedly comparing "old" trauma-based versions of reality with newer understandings that arise in the context of a detailed examination of past events, the client can often revise his or her personal history—not in the sense of making things up, but by updating assumptions and beliefs that were made under duress and were never revisited in detail.

This approach also can be used to examine distorted beliefs about future events, not just feelings of responsibility or self-blame. Most typically, these thoughts involve beliefs such as the following:

- I am broken/intrinsically bad and will never get better/be loved/get what I want.
- The world is dangerous and I will be hurt again.
- I am helpless to avoid additional traumas.
- People/men/women/authority figures are predatory and can't be trusted.
- The future is hopeless.

Cognitive interventions for such trauma-related assumptions are much like those used to address self-blame, except that they focus more on an analysis of future outcomes. Among the general questions the therapist might ask, rephrased for better attunement, as necessary, are the following:

- "What are the chances that something like that would happen to you again in the future?"
- "What would it take for something like that to happen again?"
- "Can you think of any examples that wouldn't fit your belief? Could there be any exceptions to the rule?" (For example, any men who probably wouldn't rape you, any places where you would be safe, any things you could do to avoid potential exposure to the trauma, at least one person you can probably trust)
- "Is there any way in which you might be underestimating your abilities when you say that?"
- "Can you think of something you might be able to do if that happened/looked like it might happen again?"

The therapist may ask such questions, which obviously will vary from client to client and session to session, as the description of the trauma unfolds or after the client's rendition is completed. We tend to favor the latter approach: encouraging the client to describe the trauma in detail, and then following up with questions. In doing so, the client is more able to more fully expose herself or himself to the story, with its attendant emotional triggers, and the therapist has a better chance of determining what the client thinks about the trauma without the rendition being affected by therapist responses.

However accomplished, the central goal of cognitive therapy in this area is to assist the client to more fully and accurately explore his or her beliefs or assumptions, and the context in which they arose, without the clinician lecturing, arguing, or labeling such beliefs as "wrong." Instead, such cognitions should be viewed (and reflected back to the client) as entirely understandable conclusions regarding overwhelming events that involved extreme anxiety and distress, incomplete information, coercion, confusion, and, in many cases, the need for survival defenses. Trauma-related cognitions should be treated not as the product of client error or of inherent neurosis, but rather as initial perceptions and assumptions that require updating in the context of safety, support, and new information. The reader is referred to Resick and Schnicke (1992); Chard, Weaver, and Resick (1997); Monson et al. (2006); and Briere and Lanktree (2011) for more detailed and programmatic discussions of the cognitive processing of traumatic experiences, both conversational and written.

While addressing misunderstandings about the event and their implications for the client, the clinician also may encounter distortions the client has formed regarding the meaning of symptoms he or she is experiencing. In general, these involve beliefs that the intrusive-reliving, numbing/avoidance, and hyperarousal components of traumatic stress represent loss of control and/or major psychopathology. The therapist can facilitate cognitive processing of these perceptions or beliefs by asking the client—especially after some level of psychoeducation has transpired—about

1. what might be a nonpathologizing explanation for the symptom (for example, the survival value of hypervigilance, or the self-medicating aspects of substance abuse);

2. whether the symptoms actually indicate psychosis or mental illness (for example, whether flashbacks are the same thing as hallucinations, or whether it is really "paranoid" to be fearful about trauma-reminiscent situations); and

3. whether it is better to actively experience posttraumatic stress (especially reexperiencing) than to shut down or otherwise avoid trauma memories.

Each of these (and similar) questions may stimulate lively and clinically useful conversations, the goal of which is not for the clinician's view to prevail, but for the client to explore the basis for (and meaning of) his or her internal experience.

Developing a Coherent Narrative

In addition to the cognitive processing of traumatic memories, therapy can provide broader meaning and context. Clinical experience suggests that client descriptions of past traumatic events often become more detailed, organized, and causally structured as they are repeatedly discussed and explored in therapy. Research (for example, Amir, Stafford, Freshman, & Foa, 1998) indicates that such increased coherence is directly associated with a reduction in posttraumatic symptoms. Although it is likely that narrative coherence is a sign of clinical improvement, it also appears that the development of an integrated version of one's trauma has a positive effect on recovery (Pennebaker, 1993). As the client is increasingly able to describe chronologically and analytically what happened, and to place it in a larger context, he or she often experiences an increased sense of perspective, reduced feelings of chaos, and a greater sense that the universe is predictable and orderly, if not entirely benign (Meichenbaum & Fong, 1993). Further, creating meaning out of one's experiences (including conclusions about cause and effect) may provide some degree of closure, in that the experiences "make sense" and thus may require less rumination or preoccupation. Finally, a more coherent trauma narrative, by virtue of its organization and complexity, may support more efficient and complete emotional and cognitive processing (Amir et al., 1998). In contrast, fragmented recollections of traumatic events that do not have an explicit chronological order and do not have obvious cause-effect linkages can easily lead to additional anxiety, insecurity, and confusion—phenomena that inhibit effective trauma processing.

The development of a coherent narrative usually emerges naturally during effective trauma-focused therapy. As the traumatic event (or events) is discussed repetitively and in detail, a process sometimes referred to as *context reinstatement* (J. R. Anderson & Bower, 1972) may occur. Specifically, a detailed trauma description may increase the survivor's access to more aspects of the memory that, in turn, may trigger recall of additional details. For example, a client might initially report that "he hit me on the head, and there was yelling and blood." In the moment of making this statement, the reference to blood might activate more specific memories of blood on the carpet, which, in turn, might trigger additional recollection of the location or, perhaps, the feeling of pain associated with a scalp laceration. Further discussion might then provide the context for a chronological sequence. For example:

> Okay, he was yelling at me, saying I was lazy, and then he hit me with an ashtray, a green metal one. It cut my head bad. I bled all over the carpet in the living room; I remember thinking I'd never get that stain out. [Followed by obscene attribution of perpetrator responsibility]

As the sequence and details of the event become clearer, there is more material to cognitively process and a greater sense of stability associated with "knowing what happened." Further, as described earlier, greater detail often provides information that is antidotal to cognitive distortions. For example, a client might state:

> I've just been thinking, I told him to stop. I did. When it started getting too heavy. I tried to stop him, but he wouldn't stop. It's not like I wanted it to happen. Kissing, maybe. But not what happened.

Although a more coherent narrative often arises naturally from repeatedly revisiting the trauma in therapy, the clinician can work to further increase the likelihood of this happening. This generally involves gentle, nonintrusive questions regarding the details of the trauma, and support for the client's general exploration of his or her thoughts and feelings regarding the event—in the same manner described earlier for cognitive processing. In this way, narrative interventions support the development of broader explanations and an overbridging "story" of the traumatic event, its antecedents, and its effects. In addition to its obviously clinical effects, an integrated version of adverse experiences may lead to a broader overall perspective on life and, perhaps, greater personal wisdom, as described in Chapter 4.

Cognitive Changes Arising From Nonoverwhelming Emotional Activation

As emphasized by Foa and Rothbaum (1998), not all cognitive effects of trauma therapy involve verbal reconsideration or "restructuring" of traumatically altered thinking patterns—it is also possible for the survivor's beliefs to change during the process of remembering and processing upsetting memories during treatment. Summarizing a cognitive component of Foa and Kozak's (1986) emotional processing model, S. Rogers and Silver (2002) note that

> individuals with anxiety disorders also have erroneous beliefs about the nature of anxiety. They tend to see anxiety as something that will persist until they escape the feared situation, that anxiety is physically or psychologically damaging, and that the consequences of being anxious are very aversive. (p. 45)

In the context of processing traumatic memories in therapy, the client repetitively experiences three things: (1) anxiety that is conditioned to the trauma memory (that is, as a conditioned emotional response, or CER), (2) the expectation that such anxiety signals danger and/or is, itself, a dangerous state and must be avoided, and yet (3) an absence of actual negative outcome—he or she does not actually experience physical or psychological harm from anxiety or what it might presage. This repetitive *disparity* (a technical term that is discussed in greater detail in Chapter 8) between the expectation of anxiety as signaling danger and yet, the subsequent experience of nondanger probably changes the expectation over time (in Foa and Kozak's [1986] parlance, it modifies the attendant "fear structure"). Beyond its cognitive effects on beliefs and assumptions associated with the specific trauma memory, the repetitive experience of feeling anxious during trauma therapy—in the context of therapeutic safety—probably lessens the negative valence of anxiety, per se. In many cases, this means that the client becomes less anxious about anxiety, coming to see it as merely an emotion and not necessarily as a harbinger of danger, loss of control, or psychological disability. Viewed in this context, the interconnection between trauma processing and affect regulation training, as described in the previous chapter, becomes clear: Increased ability to experience negative affect without the associated catastrophizing cognitions reduces the likelihood that such emotion will be overwhelming.

Supporting Metacognitive Awareness of Thoughts, Emotions, and Memories

Cognitive interventions also can help the client to develop *metacognitive awareness* (Teasdale, Segal, & Williams, 1995): the relative capacity to dispassionately observe and reflect upon one's thoughts and feelings, and to learn that such internal processes are, most immediately, products of the mind and not necessarily evidence about the true state of reality. As metacognitive awareness grows, the individual is more able to discern the potentially insubstantial and limited nature of many beliefs and perceptions about self and others, and discover that such cognitions are not necessarily "real": they may be more relevant to the past than the present (Briere, 2012a).

Typically, metacognitive awareness manifests as insights into the subjectivity of one's cognitive world—the realization that, in the words of one abuse survivor, "just because I think it, doesn't mean it's real." Metacognitive awareness may allow, for example, a client to understand that self-hating thoughts are not proof that he or she is hateful, triggered expectations of danger do not necessarily signal the presence of actual threat, and reexperienced sensory/emotional memories are only that—not necessarily input regarding the current state of things. This learning to take internal experience "with a grain of salt"—not necessarily rejecting its counsel, but also not necessarily accepting it—can lead to decreased emotional reactivity and more balanced appraisals when the trauma survivor is triggered or experiences cognitive distortions based on prior maltreatment.

Interestingly, the process of developing metacognitive awareness does not involve changing one's thoughts as much as changing one's relationship to them. For example, as described earlier, the usual cognitive approach to low self-esteem might be to help the client identify distorted/inaccurate thoughts or assumptions about oneself, then work to counter these cognitions with more accurate information. A metacognitive shift, on the other hand, would attend less to the content of what one is thinking about oneself, and more to the fact that such thoughts are only that—internal productions of the mind that may, in fact, reflect historical events, such as abuse by a parent. Once seen as intrusions from the past, these thoughts may lose some of their credibility in the present.

Developing Metacognition

There are several ways in which the trauma client can increase his or her metacognitive awareness during therapy. First, as outlined in Chapter 10, exercises that increase mindfulness, including meditation, tend to increase insight into the difference between thoughts about things and the actual things themselves. In meditation, for example, the process of devoting a small amount of time, on a regular basis, to nonjudgmental awareness of one's ongoing internal activities, including thinking, feeling, and remembering, often leads to a growing awareness that such internal processes are constantly being generated, almost independent of what is happening in the outside world (sometimes referred to as "monkey mind," based on the notion that such self-talk is similar to the seemingly mindless chattering of primates in the jungle). Over time, such exercises can teach a nonjudgmental acceptance of thoughts, feelings, and related phenomena, such that self-criticisms, triggered abandonment issues, or expectations of maltreatment are viewed with greater equanimity and have fewer psychological impacts. In a similar vein, dialectical behavior therapy (Linehan, 1993a), which incorporates aspects of Buddhist psychology but does not involve as much formal meditation, teaches the client various skills to increase mindful attention to thoughts and feelings as merely thoughts and feelings.

Metacognitive awareness also can be increased by explicit therapeutic discussions that more directly interpret intrusive self-thoughts as "tapes" or automatic cognitions that were learned in the past but that are triggered in the present, at which time they appear to be perceptions of reality. For example, during the process of trauma-focused therapy, the client—with the assistance of the therapist—may become able to recognize (a) certain negative thoughts as replicas of what he or she heard as an abused child (for example, "you are bad," "you are lazy") or (b) more global self-appraisals (for example, that he or she is helpless, inadequate, or unworthy) that were inferred in the context of early maltreatment. In each instance, these cognitions or thought patterns eventually can be understood as "tapes" of the past that, although often compelling, are not necessarily accurate perceptions of self or others in the present (Briere, 1996). As they emerge, the survivor can learn to discount them as "just my past talking," "an old movie," or "there goes Maple Street [where the individual was maltreated as a child] again"—thereby decreasing their ability to upset, destabilize, or contribute to negative mood states.

Cognitive Interventions and Insight

As noted earlier in this chapter, one of the major goals of cognitive interventions is to change how the client views himself or herself, his or her prior life experiences, and others in his or her interpersonal environment. Such cognitive reconsideration is often equivalent to the psychodynamic notion of *insight*. For example, when the client understands (has insight into the fact) that there really wasn't much that he or she could do in the face of one or more uncontrollable traumatic events, self-blame for having experienced or deserved the trauma—or for not having avoided it—is actively contradicted. Although such newer cognitive understanding may not have immediate salutary effects, over time (and upon repeatedly revisiting this fact, in treatment and out) the disparity between old assumptions and perceptions versus more recent, more accurate appraisals can serve to neutralize or update inaccurate trauma-related cognitions.

In addition, a greater understanding of the past—and insight into the various ways in which it differs from the present—may reduce the capacity of stimuli in the current environment to trigger posttraumatic responses. For example, "realizing" (that is, through cognitive reconsideration and/or ongoing interactions with a benign therapist) that interpersonal closeness is not always dangerous may reduce the amount of distrust, fear, or anger triggered by relationships in one's adult environment. In this way, what would otherwise be a trigger for memories of previous interpersonal violence can be changed. An understanding that one can be vulnerable around some people and not be hurt means that, on average, fewer directly reminiscent or trauma-similar stimuli are likely to be experienced during current intimate interactions. In other words, if people, as a group, are not immediately equated with one's abusive parent, batterer, or rapist, close relations with people—in general—are less likely to trigger trauma-related memories and associated distress. Similarly, the experience that one can be anxious without being annihilated or victimized may result in an increased sense of security and, in some cases, better interpersonal functioning.

There are, of course, theoretical differences in how psychodynamic and cognitive clinicians seek to change cognitive distortions. Whereas the cognitive therapist generally works to identify irrational thinking and to supplant it with more accurate perceptions and beliefs, the psychodynamic clinician is especially invested in helping the client understand the original basis for such distortions. As Goin (1997) notes, "The cognitive therapist battles the illogic with logic, while the psychodynamic therapist searches for the logic in the illogical" (p. 308). In trauma therapy (and some forms of modern cognitive-behavioral therapy), both phenomena ideally occur: The client is provided with opportunities to identify prior inaccurate thoughts about self, others, and the future (that is, through cognitive reconsideration), and is supported in finding more accurate models of reality, but also learns the logical basis for these distortions, given the parameters of the trauma and the client's initial need to adapt to them. In the latter instance, this greater understanding of the "whys" of cognitive distortion allows a more coherent narrative of the past, its logical effects on the survivor, and, ultimately, the greater validity of more recent (that is, less trauma-influenced) understandings.

The similarity between the notion of insight and cognitive interventions is emblematic of the hidden commonalities across many supposedly different therapeutic approaches. In this regard, most of the best therapies provide new information, new experiences, and the opportunity for new learning, often in the context of a supportive therapeutic relationship. Frequently, the issue is less what specific treatment is involved in this process than it is how well the client's access to—and integration of—new information is accomplished. The heavy-handed confrontation of thinking errors is probably as likely to be unsuccessful as is the ill-timed or disattuned use of depth interpretation in psychodynamic treatment. On the other hand, a therapeutic approach that facilitates the client's growing knowledge (and coherent narrative) of himself or herself, both now and in the past, can have substantial impacts on his or her psychological recovery.

Suggested Reading

Beck, J. S., & Beck, A.T. (2011). *Cognitive behavior therapy: Basics and beyond* (2nd ed.). New York, NY: Guilford.

Chard, K. M., Weaver, T. L., & Resick, P. A. (1997). Adapting cognitive processing therapy for child sexual abuse survivors. *Cognitive and Behavioral Practice, 4,* 31–52.

Follette, V. M., & Ruzek, J. I. (Eds.). (2006). *Cognitive-behavioral therapies for trauma* (2nd ed.). New York, NY: Guilford.

Janoff-Bulman, B. (1992). *Shattered assumptions: Towards a new psychology of trauma.* New York, NY: Free Press.

Resick, P. A., & Schnicke, M. K. (1993). *Cognitive processing therapy for rape victims: A treatment manual.* Newbury Park, CA: Sage.

8

Emotional Processing

In addition to the cognitive interventions described in the previous chapter, most trauma therapies include some form of emotional processing. The perspective used in this book (the self-trauma model; Briere, 1996, 2002b) holds that emotional processing occurs when exposure to trauma-reminiscent stimuli (either in the environment or as a result of thinking about or describing a traumatic event):

- triggers associated implicit and/or explicit memories, which then
- activate emotional and/or cognitive responses initially co-encoded with (and conditioned to) these memories, and yet,
- the activated responses are not reinforced in the external environment, or they are, in fact,
- counterconditioned by opposite emotional experiences, leading to
- extinction or alteration of the original memory-emotion association.

For example, talking about a trauma in treatment requires access to explicit (narrative) trauma memories that—through context reinstatement and the cuing aspects of reminiscent stimuli—often activate conditioned emotional responses (CERs; for example, fear, horror) or implicit schemas (for example, self-hatred or fear of abandonment) that are conspicuously not reinforced within the safety of good psychotherapy and that may be counterconditioned, over time, by the positive feelings engendered by the therapeutic relationship. As a result, after sufficient trauma processing, exposure to trauma triggers and memories no longer activates posttraumatic distress. This model further assumes, however, that things are not always this simple—any given "trauma memory" is likely to encompass a collection of many separate and discrete memories of that traumatic event. Further, evocation of these memories (and associated conditioned responses, which, themselves, are memories of a sort) may trigger recollections of other traumas and other conditioned responses— leading to a highly complicated cascade of internal associations and activated states or experiences. In contrast to some perspectives, this model holds that thoughts and expectations also may be activated by trauma memories. Specifically, we suggest that—similar to CERs—triggered trauma memories may activate simple cognitive material (for example, negative assumptions or expectations) that was encoded at the time of the event and became conditioned to the memory (see Olsen & Fazio, 2002, for a discussion of implicit, classically conditioned "attitudes"). Such activated cognitions do not necessarily represent "fear structures," however, because they do not inevitably produce fear (for example, they may be associated with anger or shame) and they may not, in fact, always lead to distressing emotions at all.

Importantly, this perspective does not necessarily require that cognitions be verbally addressed or altered in order for memories to be processed. For example, a reminiscent event in the environment (for example, a critical comment by a loved one) may trigger a memory or cluster of memories of earlier, traumatic experiences (for example, physical and verbal abuse by a parent), which may directly activate emotional or cognitive responses (for example, expectations of danger, intrusive fear, or anger) without the contribution of cortical processes (that is, "thinking" about what happened). If these responses are not reinforced in the environment (for example, the loved one is reliably not abusive or dangerous), or a similar process occurs in therapy (for example, the therapist's appearance or behavior repeatedly triggers memories of abuse, though he or she is not abusive), these responses may diminish without ever being discussed or even explicitly "thought about."

In this regard, LeDoux (1998) and others suggest that emotional (and perhaps simple cognitive) responses can be triggered "without the involvement of the higher processing systems of the brain, systems believed to be involved in thinking, reasoning, and consciousness" (p. 161). LeDoux has demonstrated that this subcortical route transmits sensory information directly from the thalamus to the amygdala, as opposed to the slower, bifurcated route that transmits from the thalamus to both the cortex and the hippocampus—where it is integrated with more contextual and often verbal information—and then sent to the amygdala.

In other words, trauma memories may be processed on noncognitive as well as cognitive levels, and thus may not inevitably require the modification of fear structures in order to reduce their emotional properties. On the other hand, similar to Foa and Kozak's view of habituation as partially cognitive (for example, the client learns that sustained fear is not intrinsically dangerous), extinction can involve nonverbal learning that certain responses are no longer relevant to formerly triggering stimuli. This may be a "cognitive" conclusion, but it is not a verbal (or even necessarily conscious) one. As is seen throughout this book, although much emphasis is placed on the verbalizable cognitions of trauma survivors as they seek to understand and resolve traumatic experiences, it is also true that much of trauma activation and processing occurs at implicit, nonverbal, often relational, levels.

Reexperiencing as Trauma Processing

Before we can proceed with a description of how trauma memories can be addressed during treatment, we must reintroduce the notion of *intrinsic processing*, described in Chapter 4. We, like some others, suggest that intrusive reexperiencing can be an inherent form of trauma processing, wherein the mind's repeated presentation of upsetting memories to itself (through flashbacks, nightmares, or other intrusive memories) represents an evolutionarily derived attempt to prompt cognitive accommodation to the reality of the traumatic event (M. J. Horowitz, 1978) and to systematically desensitize or extinguish emotions (CERs) and conditioned expectations associated with trauma memories (Briere, 1996, 2002b). This mechanism may, in part, explain why some people recover from posttraumatic stress within months of the trauma (Bryant & Harvey, 2000; Norris et al., 2002; Norris, Tracy, & Galea, 2009; Rothbaum, Foa, Riggs, Murdock, & Walsh, 1992), even in the absence of therapy. In fact, many early traumatic stress responses may represent attempts at self-healing as much as symptoms of an emerging stress disorder.

Some traumatic memories are so upsetting (for example, those associated with extended abuse, torture, rape, or concentration camp experiences), however, that they cannot be easily accommodated or desensitized. In addition, some traumatized people are sufficiently compromised by other psychological phenomena (for example, psychosis, comorbid depression or anxiety, or preexisting posttraumatic stress), neurological dysregulation (for example, traumatic brain injury or an altered hypothalamic-pituitary-adrenal axis; see Chapters 11 and 12), distressing cognitions (for example, guilt or shame), or insufficient affect regulation skills (see Chapter 6), that they are unable to experience "normal" trauma reliving without being overwhelmed by the attendant emotionality. The resultant distress may motivate the various avoidance responses described in Chapter 2, which then interfere with exposure to traumatic memory and reduce further processing. For example, the individual whose negative emotional responses (CERs) to a triggered trauma memory exceed his or her capacities to tolerate such feelings may be forced to use dissociation, substance abuse, thought suppression, distraction, and other avoidance responses to maintain internal equilibrium. In such a case, the intrusion-disparity-extinction process is likely to be ineffective, resulting in continuing reexperiencing without recovery.

The self-trauma model has significant implications for the process of trauma therapy. It suggests that avoidance may be adaptive, even necessary, for individuals who have especially aversive trauma memories or significant difficulties in regulating the associated negative emotions. It also implies that overly enthusiastic or excessive attempts by the therapist to prematurely remove such avoidance, resistance, denial, or dissociative symptoms may represent a threat to the client's internal equilibrium.

This presents a therapeutic conundrum: Some individuals (especially chronic trauma survivors) have difficulty tolerating the cognitive-emotional activation associated with remembering trauma in therapy, and thus cannot easily process such material (Ford et al., 2005). The solution lies in finding a way to monitor and control the level of the client's emotional and cognitive activation yet still provide sufficient exposure to trauma memories—to provide enough therapeutic exposure that extinction or counterconditioning can eventually occur, but not so much that the client becomes overwhelmed and has to invoke avoidance strategies that block processing. In this regard, part of the therapist's role in treatment may be to take on the "job" of intrinsic trauma exposure, to some extent replacing intrusive reexperiencing with careful therapeutic exploration of trauma memories. In contrast to naturally occurring trauma processing, however, therapy provides a relatively controlled environment in which the therapist can adjust or *titrate* the level of memory exposure (and subsequent activation) within the session in order to accommodate the reduced emotional capacities or excessively upsetting memories of some trauma survivors.

It should be noted that not all trauma specialists accept the validity of titrated exposure as it is described here. Clinician-researchers such as Foa and Rothbaum (1998; Foa, Hembree, & Rothbaum, 2007) advocate, instead, *prolonged exposure*, wherein the client is encouraged to experience the full extent of trauma-related emotionality while recounting the experiences in the first person, present tense, for extended periods of time. Although we do not deny the effectiveness and efficiency of prolonged exposure in some cases, the current model reflects concerns that such activities can exceed the affect regulation capacities of some individuals with more severe or complex posttraumatic symptomatology. Instead, we suggest that treatment generally occur within the *therapeutic window* (Briere, 1996, 2002b), as described in the next section.

The Therapeutic Window

The therapeutic window refers to a psychological midpoint between inadequate and overwhelming activation of trauma-related emotions and cognitions during treatment: It is a hypothetical "place" where therapeutic interventions are thought to be most helpful. Interventions within the therapeutic window are neither so trivial or nonevocative that they provide inadequate memory exposure and processing, nor so intense that the client's balance between acceptable memory activation and overwhelming emotion is tipped toward the latter. In other words, interventions that take the therapeutic window into account are those that trigger trauma memories and promote processing but do not overwhelm internal protective systems and thereby motivate unwanted avoidance responses.

Interventions that *undershoot* the therapeutic window are those that either completely and consistently avoid traumatic material or are focused primarily on support and validation with a client who could tolerate greater exposure and processing. Undershooting is rarely dangerous; it can, however, waste time and resources in instances when more effective therapeutic interventions are possible. *Overshooting* the window, on the other hand, occurs when the clinician inadvertently provides too much memory exposure and cognitive-emotional activation relative to the client's existing affect regulation resources or is unable to prevent the client from flooding himself or herself with overwhelming traumatic distress. Interventions that are too fast-paced may overshoot the window because they do not allow the client to adequately accommodate and desensitize previously activated material before triggering new memories. When therapy consistently overshoots the window, the survivor must engage in avoidance maneuvers in order to keep from being overwhelmed by the therapy process. Most often, the client will increase his or her level of dissociation (for example, through disengagement or "spacing out") during the session, or will interrupt the focus or pace of therapy by arguing, "not getting" obvious therapeutic points, distracting the therapist with various behaviors, or changing the subject to something less threatening. In the worst case, he or she may drop out of treatment. Although therapists may interpret these behaviors as "resistance," such avoidance often represents appropriate protective responses to therapist process errors. Unfortunately, the need for avoidance can easily impede treatment by decreasing the client's exposure to memory material and the ameliorative aspects of therapy.

In contrast, effective trauma therapy provides titrated exposure to traumatic material while maintaining the safety necessary to eventually extinguish conditioned emotional and cognitive responses. By carefully adjusting the amount of therapeutic exposure so that the associated activation does not exceed the survivor's capacities, treatment within the therapeutic window allows the client to slowly process trauma memories without being retraumatized and needing to terminate the process.

Intensity Control

Intensity control refers to the therapist's awareness and relative control of the level of cognitive-emotional activation occurring within the session. We recommend that—especially for those clients with impaired affect regulation capacities—emotional intensity be highest at around (or slightly before) mid-session, whereas the beginning and end of the session should be at the lowest intensity (see Figure 8.1). Ideally, at the beginning of the session, the client gradually enters the process of psychotherapy; by the middle of the session, the focus has shifted to relatively more intense processing and activation; at the end of the session the client is sufficiently dearoused that she or he can reenter the outside world without needing later avoidance activities. Importantly, the relative safety of psychotherapy sessions may allow some clients to become more affectively aroused than they would outside of the therapeutic environment. As a result, it should be the therapist's goal to leave the client in as calm an affective state as is possible—ideally no more emotionally aroused than he or she was at the beginning of the session.

The need for the client to experience upsetting feelings and thoughts during trauma-focused treatment requires the therapist to carefully titrate the

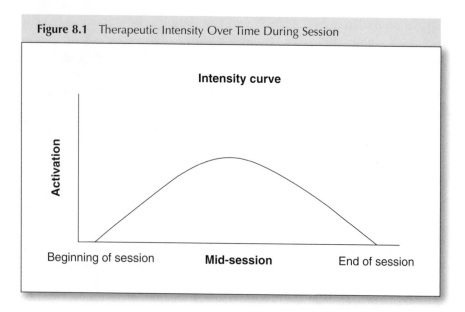

Figure 8.1   Therapeutic Intensity Over Time During Session

level of emotional activation the client experiences, at least to the extent that this is under the therapist's control. From the therapeutic window perspective, intense affect during treatment pushes the client toward the outer edge of the window (that is, toward an increased possibility of being overwhelmed), whereas less intensity moves the client toward the inner edge (that is, toward reduced exposure and processing). The goal is to keep the client near the "middle" of the window—to feel neither too little (for example, to dissociate or otherwise avoid to the point that abuse-related CERs and cognitions cannot be processed) nor too much (for example, to become flooded with previously avoided emotionality that overwhelms available affect regulation resources and is retraumatizing).

Constraints on Trauma Processing

As noted throughout this book, exposure to trauma memories and the attendant distress can be quite challenging. In most instances, trauma processing is tolerable to the extent that it occurs within the therapeutic window. In some relatively rare cases, however, almost any level of memory processing "overshoots the window," irrespective of the clinician's efforts. When this occurs, it is usually because (1) the trauma is so recent or severe that CER activation is inherently overwhelming, (2) the client has insufficient affect regulation capacities, and/or (3) he or she generally suffers from such high levels of comorbid emotional distress or negative cognitive preoccupation that the additional (especially trauma-related) distress is incapacitating.

For these reasons, exploration of traumatic material is not always appropriate. As noted by various authors (for example, Bryant & Harvey, 2000; Cloitre et al., 2002; Najavits, 2002; Pitman et al., 1991), therapeutic exposure to trauma memories may be contraindicated for clients experiencing the following:

- Very high anxiety (including easily triggered panic attacks)
- Severe depression
- Acute psychosis
- Major suicidality (that is, moderate or high risk of suicide attempts)
- Overwhelming guilt and shame associated with the traumatic event
- Especially impaired affect regulation capacity
- Very recent and substantial trauma exposure
- Substance intoxication or some instances of substance dependence (specific recommendations regarding exposure-based treatment of substance-addicted trauma survivors are presented later in this chapter)

When these conditions preclude exposure therapy, the clinician is advised to focus on the various other interventions outlined in this book, including the development of affect regulation skills (Chapter 6), cognitive (as opposed to emotion-based) therapy (Chapter 7), or psychiatric medication (Chapter 12). In many cases, repeated use of these other interventions will eventually set the stage for more classic emotional processing and thus more efficient trauma desensitization.

The Components of Trauma Processing

Assuming that none of the constraining conditions presented here are in force, or that they have been sufficiently diminished, formal trauma processing can be initiated. For the purposes of this book, the processing of traumatic memory within the therapeutic window will be divided into five components: *exposure, activation, disparity, counterconditioning,* and *desensitization/resolution* (Briere, 2002b). These components do not always follow a linear progression. In fact, in some cases, interventions at a "later" stage may lead to further work at an "earlier" stage. In other instances, certain components (for example, counterconditioning) may be less important than others (for example, disparity). And, finally, as described in Chapter 6, the therapy process may require the client to learn (or invoke previously learned) affect regulation techniques to down-regulate distress when emotional responses inadvertently become overwhelming.

Exposure

In the current context, *exposure* refers to any activity engaged in by the therapist or the client that provokes or triggers client memories of traumatic events. Therapeutic exposure has been described, for example, as "repeated or extended exposure, either in vivo or in imagination, to objectively

harmless but feared stimuli for the purpose of reducing anxiety" (Abueg &
Fairbank, 1992, p. 127). From the trauma perspective, the "objectively
harmless" stimuli are memories of prior trauma that are, by definition, not
currently occurring; the "anxiety" is the triggered emotional response to
these trauma memories.

Several types of exposure-based therapies are used to treat traumatic
stress, one of which—prolonged exposure—has been shown to be effective
in treating adult traumas (Powers, Halpern, Ferenschak, Gillihan, & Foa,
2010). As noted earlier, this approach typically eschews titrated or graduated access to traumatic memories and, instead, involves extended exposure
to the full force of a traumatic memory (for example, the moment-to-
moment experience of a rape) until the associated anxiety is habituated. In
contrast, the exposure approach we suggest here is a variant of *systematic
desensitization* (Wolpe, 1958), wherein the client is asked to recall nonoverwhelming but moderately distressing traumatic experiences in the context of
a safe therapeutic environment. The exposure is generally (but not inevitably) graduated according to the intensity of the recalled material, with less
upsetting memories being recalled and verbalized before more upsetting
ones. However, this approach usually does not adhere to a strict, preplanned
(that is, hierarchical) series of extended exposure activities. This is because
the client's ability to tolerate exposure may be quite compromised and may
vary considerably as a function of outside life stressors; level of support from
friends, relatives, and others; and, most important, the extent of affect regulation capacities available to him or her at any given point in time. In self-
trauma parlance, the "size" of the therapeutic window may change within
and across sessions.

In general, exposure involves the client recalling and discussing traumatic
events with the therapist, or writing about them and then reading them to
the therapist. Although some forms of trauma therapy focus on memories of
a single trauma (for example, of a motor vehicle accident, war event, or
physical assault) and discourage much discussion of other traumas, the
approach we advocate is considerably more permissive. It is quite common
for trauma survivors to "jump" from one memory to another, often making
associations that are not immediately apparent to the therapist—or even, in
some cases, to the client. Especially for survivors of multiple, complex, and
extended traumas, the focus of a given session may move from a rape experience to earlier childhood maltreatment, and then, perhaps, to an experience of domestic violence. For example, a war veteran may begin the session
with a memory of hand-to-hand combat and find himself, 20 minutes later,
describing being physically abused by his father when he was a child.

The broader exposure activities of the therapy described here reflect the
complexity of many trauma presentations. Although a client may come to
treatment in order to address a recent assault experience, it may soon become
apparent that either (1) an earlier trauma is actually more relevant to his or
her ongoing distress or (2) the extent of the distress is partially due to the

cumulative or interacting effects of multiple traumas. A woman enmeshed in prostitution, for example, might seek treatment for the effects of a violent rape by a customer and soon discover that this rape activates memories of the vast collection of other distressing experiences she undergoes on a regular basis, as well as the childhood incest experiences that partially determined her involvement in prostitution in the first place (Farley, 2003). In such instances, insisting that the client focus exclusively on a single trauma during therapy, or even on just one trauma at a time, may be contraindicated and not well appreciated by the client. As well, recollections of early trauma are often fragmented and incomplete (Elliott & Briere, 1995), and, in many cases, preverbal (Berliner & Briere, 1998), precluding the client's exposure to a discrete, coherent, describable memory.

Instead of being constrained to a single trauma, we suggest that the trauma survivor be allowed to discuss—and thereby expose himself or herself to—whatever trauma seems important at a given time, or whatever memory or part of a memory is triggered by any other memory. Although, in a minority of cases, the clinician may encourage the client to "stay with" a certain, obviously important memory, he or she should not insist on this, but rather should prize the client's right (and perhaps need) to process whatever he or she chooses to, at whatever level of emotional activation he or she believes is tolerable and acceptable. There is little doubt that this approach is less efficient, in terms of addressing any given single trauma. It is, however, more appropriate when the multitrauma client presents for treatment and when the client's self-determination and entitlements are in need of support.

Explaining the Value of Therapeutic Exposure

Although therapeutic exposure is widely understood by clinicians to be a powerful treatment methodology, the trauma survivor may be less enthusiastic about the process. Prior to therapy, the survivor may have devoted considerable time and effort to controlling his or her symptoms by avoiding people, places, and conversations that trigger posttraumatic intrusion. In fact, avoidance of reminders of the trauma is a central aspect of posttraumatic stress disorder (PTSD) and other stress responses (American Psychiatric Association, 2000). As a result, exposure techniques, wherein the client is asked to intentionally experience events that he or she has been avoiding, may seem—at best—counterintuitive.

For this reason, an important aspect of trauma therapy is *prebriefing*: explaining the rationale for exposure, and its general methodology, prior to the onset of formal treatment. Without sufficient explanation, the process and immediate effects of exposure may seem so illogical and stressful that the client will automatically resist and avoid. On the other hand, if exposure can be explained so that the client understands the reasons for this sometimes distressing procedure, it usually is not hard to form a positive client-therapist alliance and a shared appreciation for the process.

Although the way in which exposure is introduced may vary from instance to instance, the clinician should generally make the following points when preparing clients for exposure interventions:

- Reexperiencing is not only a source of upsetting experiences but, also, potential evidence of the mind's attempt to heal itself.
- Unresolved memories of the trauma usually have to be talked about and reexperienced, or else they may not be processed and keep coming back as symptoms.
- Although the client understandably would like to not think about what happened, and may have been avoiding upsetting feelings about the trauma, such avoidance often serves to keep the symptoms alive.
- If the client can talk enough about what happened, the pain and fear associated with the trauma is likely to decrease. Do not, however, promise recovery.
- By its nature, exposure is associated with some level of distress. Some people who undergo exposure experience a slight increase in flashbacks, nightmares, and distressing feelings between sessions, but this is normal and usually not a bad sign. Ask the client to tell you if and when this occurs, so that you can monitor whether exposure has been too intense.
- You will work to keep the discussion of these memories from overwhelming the client, and he or she can stop talking about any given memory if it becomes too upsetting. Reassure the client that he or she only needs to talk about as much as he or she is comfortable with. But stress that the more the client can remember, think, feel, and talk about the memories, the more likely it will be that significant improvement will occur.

This last point, explicitly supporting the client's right to control the level of exposure in treatment, is in relatively stark contrast to classic prolonged exposure methodologies (for example, Foa & Rothbaum, 1998). As noted earlier, those advocating prolonged exposure emphasize the need to focus on a single trauma, and encourage the client to stay present in strong memory-activated emotions until they habituate and the activation fades. From this perspective, our suggestion—that the client determine how much memory exposure and emotional activation should occur in the session—may be seen as supporting resistance or avoidance. It is our experience, however, that the reverse often occurs: By being empowered to determine the focus, rate, and intensity of treatment, the client feels more in control of the process, and thus may be more willing to experiment with higher levels of exposure than he or she might otherwise. This process tends to reinforce the collaborative aspects of good trauma therapy: The therapist encourages exposure and awareness, and may suggest a processing target, but the client, in the end, gets to decide what memories he or she exposes himself or herself to, and how much activation he or she is willing to undergo. This approach not only reduces the likelihood that the client will be overwhelmed (for example, when the therapist miscalculates how much exposure is appropriate), but also, ironically, reduces "resistance" in those survivors whose automatic response to authority or seeming coercion is to shut down or avoid. As well, encouraging the client to be an equal partner in determining the type and extent of memory exposure is likely to support the client's growing sense of self-efficacy and self-reference, as described in Chapter 9.

Homework

As noted in the previous chapter, trauma therapy sometimes includes homework assignments. This typically involves the client writing about the traumatic event outside of therapy and then reading aloud what he or she has written in the next session. Along with providing additional opportunities to examine and process cognitions initially associated with the event (see Chapter 7), this activity requires that the client access the original trauma memory in order to write about it, and thus provides significant therapeutic exposure. This exposure is then repeated when the client reads the narrative aloud to the therapist.

In general, we recommend that the therapist say something like this:

> Try to write a page or two about [the trauma]. Include as much detail about it as you can remember, and be as specific as possible—for instance, what happened, what feelings you had, what you thought when it happened, what anyone else said, and what you did right afterward. You don't have to do all of this at once; sometimes people take several tries to get it all down. And you only have to write about as much as you feel comfortable with—but, remember, the more you can write, the better. After you're done writing, read it to yourself at least once before our next session. If it is too upsetting to read all at once, try reading as much as you can, and then read the rest when you are able to, or in our next session.[1]

Typically, the client is asked to repeat this writing exercise on several different occasions over the course of treatment, and to read his or her writing each time to the therapist. The specific timing of these writing and reading exercises may vary according to (1) the client's current capacity for written expression, (2) his or her readiness to directly confront the trauma, and (3) his or her immediate stability and affect regulation capacity. The therapist's response to hearing the client's story should be characterized by support,

---

[1]Because written homework is often helpful for younger trauma clients, a more structured version of this exercise has been developed for adolescents, including worksheets for written trauma descriptions and other components. These materials are also appropriate for many adult trauma survivors. See the *About My Trauma* worksheet in Briere and Lanktree (2011) or download it at http://johnbriere.com.

validation, and appreciation for the client's willingness to engage in such a potentially difficult task.

Obviously, this approach is not possible for those who are unable to read and write fluently or who are too cognitively debilitated (for example, by psychosis or severe depression) to accomplish such activities. In some instances, there may be no safe home, in fact, in which to do homework—the client may be homeless or may live in an environment where safety or confidentiality cannot be assured, for example, where the perpetrator or unsupportive family members still live or can gain access to the client's writing. In such circumstances, we recommend that homework not be part of treatment or that it occur only within the therapy session.

In cases where literacy, comorbidity, and safety are not issues, however, writing exercises can be initiated at some point after the first few sessions and then repeated several times at intervals. The total number of times this is done may increase if there are several different traumas in need of emotional processing. In general, the clinician will find that these written renditions become more detailed and emotionally descriptive upon repetition and that the client's emotional responses when reading the assignment aloud become less extreme over time.

Activation

If treatment is to be effective, some degree of activation must take place during exposure. *Activation* refers to conditioned emotional responses (such as fear, sadness, or anger) and/or trauma-specific cognitions (such as intrusive negative self-perceptions or sudden feelings of helplessness) that are triggered by trauma memories. Other, related memories and their associated affects and cognitions may be triggered as well. A woman who is asked to describe a childhood sexual abuse experience, for example, undergoes therapeutic exposure to the extent that she recalls aspects of that event during the therapy session. If these memories trigger emotional responses conditioned to the original abuse stimuli (for example, fear or disgust), or associated cognitive intrusions (for example, "I asked for it"), or stimulate further memories (for example, of other traumas or other aspects of the abuse triggered by remembering certain parts of it), therapeutic activation can be said to have taken place.

Activation is usually critical to trauma processing; in order to extinguish emotional-cognitive associations to a given traumatic memory, they must be (1) activated, (2) not reinforced, and, ideally, (3) counterconditioned. As a result, therapeutic interventions that consist solely of the narration of trauma-related memories without emotional activation will not necessarily produce symptom relief (Foa & Kozak, 1986; Samoilov & Goldfried, 2000). In order for optimal activation to occur, there should be as little avoidance as is reasonably possible during the exposure process. The dissociated client, for example, may experience very little activation during treatment, despite giving what may be a quite detailed rendition of a specific trauma memory.

On the other hand, as noted throughout this book, too much activation is also problematic, because it generates high levels of distress (thereby linking memory to emotional pain rather than to safety or positive feelings) and motivates avoidance (thereby reducing further exposure and processing).

Because activated cognitive-emotional responses are, to some extent, the crux of trauma work, we describe in the following sections several interventions aimed at controlling the level of activation during treatment. The goal, in each case, is to work within the therapeutic window—to support emotional and cognitive activation that is neither too little nor too much for optimal processing.

Increasing Activation

The therapist typically seeks to increase activation in instances when, despite available affect regulation capacity, the client unnecessarily blocks some portion of his or her emotional responses to the traumatic material. It is not uncommon for avoidance responses to become so overlearned or conditioned to stress that they automatically, but unnecessarily, emerge during exposure to trauma memories and/or emotions. In other instances, gender roles, cultural influences, or occupational socialization may discourage emotional expression in an individual who could otherwise tolerate it, as described in Chapter 4. In such cases, reduced avoidance during treatment is not only likely to be reasonably safe, but it may be necessary for significant desensitization to occur. When avoidance is not required for continued emotional homeostasis, yet appears to be blocking trauma processing, several interventions may be appropriate.

First, the therapist may ask questions that can only be answered in a relatively less avoidant state. These include, for example:

- "What were you feeling/how did it feel when that happened?"
- "What are you feeling now?"
- "Are you aware of any thoughts or feelings when you describe [the trauma]?"

In such cases, the avoidance may decrease, yet never be acknowledged—an outcome that is entirely appropriate, since the primary intent is to keep activation at a reasonable level, not to label the client's reaction as problematic.

Second, the clinician can indirectly draw attention to the avoidance, without stigmatizing it, and ask the client to increase his or her level of contact during the process of activation. This is often most effective when the client's avoidance, or the power of the CERs to overwhelm, has previously been identified as an issue in therapy. This may involve encouraging suggestions such as these:

- "You're doing well. Try to stay with the feelings."
- "Don't go away, now. You're doing great. Stay with it."
- "I can see it's upsetting. Can you stay with the memory for just a few more minutes? We can always stop if you need to."

In other instances, however, for example, when dissociation may or may not be present, or when the client is more prone to a defensive response, the therapist may intervene with a question-statement combination, such as these:

- "How are you doing? It looks like maybe you're spacing out a little bit."
- "It looks like you're going away a little bit, right now. Are you?"

Although calling direct attention to avoidance is sometimes appropriate, it tends to break the process of exposure/activation and probably should be used only when less direct methods of encouraging activation (and thus reducing avoidance) have not been effective.

The clinician can increase activation not only by discouraging cognitive or emotional avoidance but also by increasing the emotional experience. Often this involves requesting more details about the traumatic event and responding in ways that focus the client on emotional issues. As the client provides more details, the opportunity for greater activation increases—both because greater details often include more emotionally arousing material and because they reinstate more of the original context in the client's mind, thereby increasing access to emotions and thoughts that occurred at the time of the trauma. The following is an example of a discussion that evoked greater levels of emotional activation in the client without specifically addressing avoidance.

THERAPIST: Can you tell me what happened?

CLIENT: [*flattened voice*] A drive-by.

THERAPIST: A shooting? Did anyone get hurt?

CLIENT: [*pause*] Yeah. A neighbor got shot.

THERAPIST: A neighbor? Who was it?

CLIENT: A lady I sorta knew. She was nice.

THERAPIST: *Was* nice? Is she okay?

CLIENT: [*slight increase in volume, face slightly reddened*] She's dead.

THERAPIST: [*pause*] Man . . . what happened? It sounds bad.

CLIENT: Yeah, it was [*voice lower, looking away*].

THERAPIST: So, she was shot. Were you there? When she got hit?

CLIENT: Yeah, she got shot in the chest [*voice wavering, throat sounding constricted*]. She was bleeding all over the place. . . . I couldn't help her. I had to protect myself [*hand covering eyes*].

In this case, the client is reluctant to describe the event, but does not indicate dramatic signs of emotional dysregulation. His avoidance responses (initially reduced emotionality, looking away, covering his eyes with his hand) are not extreme, suggesting that he can tolerate some further emotional activation and processing without becoming overwhelmed. Cognitive intervention is probably also indicated, at some point, to address what appears to be guilt or shame at not being able to help the woman.

Decreasing Activation

In general, the intensity of activation is determined by (1) the level of exposure, (2) the aversiveness of the trauma memory (typically, the extent of negative emotionality conditioned to it), and (3) the amount of affect regulation capacity available to the client. If the therapist encourages too much activation, or is unsuccessful in keeping the client's activation at a tolerable level, the therapeutic window will be exceeded. For this reason, those with reduced affect regulation capacities typically should not be exposed to especially upsetting memories until their ability to regulate negative emotions improves (Chu, 2011; Cloitre et al., 2010). This may mean that the therapist redirects the client to less upsetting material when the client becomes too activated, focuses the client on relaxation, or directs the conversation to less emotionally charged aspects of the event. In such cases, affect skill development (see Chapter 6) may receive priority over especially intense trauma processing, and supportive interventions and responses may predominate over exploratory ones. When avoidance is more extreme, for example, when the client becomes highly dissociated in the session, the therapist will typically stop the exposure/activation process entirely and focus stabilizing interventions on whatever is producing the avoidance.

This general approach might appear to deprive the client of the opportunity to efficiently address major traumas. We believe, however, that such restraint is one of the responsibilities of the therapist. If the clinician suspects—based on observation of the client—that activation is likely to exceed the therapeutic window in any given circumstance, it is important that he or she ensure client safety by reducing the intensity and pace of the therapeutic process. This does not mean that the clinician necessarily avoids trauma processing altogether in such circumstances, only that processing should proceed slowly and carefully, or be temporarily delayed. Fortunately, the need for such a conservative approach is usually transient. As the traumatic material is slowly and carefully processed, progressively fewer trauma memories will have the potential to activate overwhelming affect, and, as described in Chapter 6, the client's overall capacity to tolerate distress will grow. The primary issue, overall, is one of time: The individual with good affect regulation capacities, less than extremely distressing trauma memories, and no interfering comorbidities may be able to tolerate higher levels of activation without exceeding the therapeutic window, and thus may respond relatively quickly to treatment. Those with difficulties in one or more of these areas, however, may require titration to lower levels of exposure and activation during trauma processing, and thus may have to be in therapy for a considerably longer period of time before major symptom improvement occurs.

Unfortunately, not all activation is visible to the therapist. There may be occasions when the client "overshoots" the therapeutic window during treatment yet does not appear to be especially overwhelmed. This may occur because (1) the client feels relatively safe in the controlled environment of the therapist's office and does not fully experience the overwhelming nature of the exposure until he or she leaves the session; (2) he or she is concerned about therapist approval and does not show distress in the session so as to appear strong, healthy, or in control; or (3) the client is dissociating or cognitively suppressing upsetting internal processes. Such unapparent exceeding of the therapeutic window, whether or not it is acknowledged by the client, may cause elevated anxiety, despondence, or shame after the session ends—distress that may then result in tension reduction behaviors (for example, self-injurious or impulsive behavior), substance abuse, or other avoidance activities. In some cases, the client may make emergency calls to the therapist, may miss the next therapy session, or may arrive late to it.

In trauma work, missed sessions and lateness sometimes represent avoidance of the distress associated with therapeutic exposure to specific traumatic material, rather than a response to the therapy or the therapist, per se. In such instances, the client's behavior may reflect his or her fear of further emotional activation in subsequent sessions. Once a session is missed, further missed sessions may follow. When a client repeatedly misses appointments, we recommend that the therapist explore this issue with him or her in a nonjudgmental, collaborative manner: assessing what aspects of the therapeutic process or content are motivating avoidance, assuring the client that the therapist is not angry and will not be punitive, and problem solving whatever miscommunication, disattunement, or therapy dynamics are contributing to the problem. Often, a permissive, exploratory attitude toward "no-shows" is more necessary in trauma work than in other psychotherapy contexts. By accepting and discussing the underlying motivation for nonattendance—as opposed to confronting and criticizing it—the therapist has a better chance of decreasing the likelihood of future missed sessions.

Remediating Window Errors

Obviously, it is important to avoid exceeding the therapeutic window whenever possible. Given the delicate nature of exposure work, however, and the sometimes obscuring effects of client emotional avoidance, it is often impossible to entirely avoid overactivation. As a result, part of the clinician's job in therapy is to intervene when overactivation occurs and to work to address the effects of such experiences.

When it is apparent that the therapeutic window has been significantly exceeded, the therapist is advised to consider the following:

- Reducing the duration and intensity of the current activation, through relaxation or breathing exercises, cognitive (as opposed to emotional) interventions, and, generally, a shift in focus away from overly activating topics
- Taking some responsibility for the client's overactivation while, at the same time, not disparaging one's own work or abilities
- Supporting and validating the client's expression of distress, including suggesting that emotional reactivity is indicative of doing "good work" (as opposed to engaging in avoidance)
- Discussing and reframing major activation after it occurs, so that the client understands his or her reactions as a normal response to the power of the triggering memory and does not pathologize them
- Problem solving with the client to identify ways in which (1) the therapist can better detect the client's escalating distress (this is especially relevant if the client habitually uses emotional avoidance defenses in the session), (2) the client can more directly communicate distress at the time it occurs, and (3) the therapist and client can work to bring the activation level back into the therapeutic window
- Making nondefensive, supportive, and validating statements that convey cautious optimism that the "emotional rollercoaster" of early trauma sessions may gradually abate over time

Disparity

Exposure and activation are not, in and of themselves, sufficient in trauma treatment. There also must be a disparity between what the client is feeling (for example, activated fear associated with a trauma memory) and the current state of reality (for example, the manifest absence of immediate danger). For CERs to traumatic memories to be diminished or extinguished over time, they must consistently not be reinforced by similar danger (physical or emotional) in the current environment.

As we described earlier, safety can be manifest in at least two ways. First, the client should have the opportunity to realize that he or she is safe in the presence of the therapist. This means safety not only from physical injury and sexual exploitation, but also from harsh criticism, punitiveness, boundary violation, or underappreciation of the client's experience. Because the survivor of interpersonal violence, maltreatment, or exploitation tends to overidentify danger in interpersonal situations, the absence of danger in the session must be experienced directly, not just promised. In other words, for the client's anxious associations to trauma memories to lose their power, they must consistently not be reinforced by current danger or maltreatment in the session, however subtle.

Second, safety in treatment includes protection from overwhelming internal experience. The client whose trauma memories produce destabilizing emotions during treatment may not find therapy to be substantially disparate from the original experience. As noted earlier, this may occur because one or both of two things are present: (1) the memory is so traumatic and has so much painful affect (for example, anxiety, rage) or cognitions (for example, guilt or shame) associated with it that untitrated exposure produces considerable psychic pain, or (2) the survivor's affect regulation capacities are sufficiently compromised that any major reexperiencing is overwhelming. In each instance, safety—and therefore disparity—can only be provided within the context of the therapeutic window. Because processing within the window means, by definition, that exposure to memories does not exceed the client's ability to tolerate those memories, reexperiencing trauma in this context is less associated with overwhelming negative affect, identity fragmentation, shame, or feelings of loss of control.

The processing of CERs and implicit cognitions to trauma memories operates in a manner similar to the processing of fear in behavioral treatments for phobias. The ongoing activation of fear and other negative emotional responses during the repetitive recounting of traumatic material in the absence of any discernable, "real" reason for such responses in the session means that such emotionality goes unreinforced. Eventually, responses that are not reinforced tend to fade. Possible reasons for this phenomenon range from traditional extinction theories (Wolpe, 1958) to cognitive models involving the experience-based modification of cognitive fear structures (Foa & Kozak, 1986). Regardless of the underlying mechanisms, the role of disparity in trauma recovery is clear: The environment in which trauma activation occurs must reliably not reinforce the original danger-fear association. Otherwise, the client's fear response to the memory will remain strong, if not increase.

Counterconditioning

Not only is it important that there be a manifest absence of danger during trauma processing, but in the best circumstances there also should be *counterconditioning*—the presence of positive phenomena that are antithetic to triggered negative emotions and cognitions. Thus, for example, a woman in therapy for problems related to long-standing domestic violence may expect her therapist to be critical or rejecting. When her fears not only are met with the absence of those things in treatment (the disparity associated with therapeutic safety), but occur in fact in the presence of acceptance, validation, and nurturing, the activated distress may diminish in intensity because it is incompatible with the positive feelings that arise in therapy. As a result, the emotional associations to memories of being battered are not only not reinforced, but weakened by contradictory, positive feeling states.

In some cases, especially when therapy is of a longer duration, counter-conditioning arises when positive aspects of the therapeutic relationship (for example, the therapist's steady attunement and compassion) trigger inborn positive states associated with the neurobiology of attachment (Briere, 2012a). As noted by various authors (for example, Schore, 2002; D. J. Siegel, 2012), it is likely that humans have evolved a biological reinforcement system, probably involving, among other things, dopamine and oxytocin release, that rewards close interpersonal relationships. By reinforcing interpersonal relatedness, this neurochemical response increases the likelihood that the parent and child will stay in close proximity for extended periods of time (since both parties would be rewarded for doing so) and that the parents experience positive dyadic states that encourage pair bonding—both of which are likely to increase the young child's safety, continued supervision, and, therefore, survival. The self-trauma model suggests that this biological process also is evoked in the context of a stable, positive, and ongoing therapeutic relationship, wherein some of what have been described as "transferential feelings" by the client may, in fact, represent neurobiological support for attachment in intimate relationships (Briere, 2002b).

In trauma therapy, the presence of these positive neurobiological states, at the same time that the client is being exposed to traumatic memories and associated cognitive-emotional activations, is likely to weaken the connection between memory and emotional distress. We suggest that this occurs through a multi-step process: The therapist's visible, sustained, noncontingent caring and compassion (a) engages the client's inborn attachment system, which is sensitive to, and triggered by, loving attention from important relational figures (Bowlby, 1988), which (b) activates biological self-soothing circuitry that down-regulates the activity of threat recognition and response systems (Gilbert, 2009) and triggers the release of pleasurable neurohormones, leading to (c) greater client openness to the therapy experience and the eventual counterconditioning and extinction of classically conditioned distress associated with trauma-reminiscent stimuli. A similar (although often less powerful) process may ensue for the client in shorter-term therapy who recounts traumatic material in the presence of therapist support, understanding, and caring without the neurobiological effects of activated attachment circuitry—the negative emotions associated with trauma activation are countered by simultaneous positive feelings associated with the treatment environment.

Like many aspects of cognitive-behavioral therapy, the contribution of counterconditioning to trauma resolution is debated, with some arguing that it is probably not an active ingredient of treatment. However, the primary counterconditioning state examined thus far in the empirical literature has been relaxation during exposure therapy (Foa, Keane, & Friedman, 2000)—a considerably less powerful experience, we believe, than the sustained positive emotions stimulated by a positive therapeutic relationship.

A second form of counterconditioning may be the experience of emotional release. Crying or other forms of emotional expression in response to upsetting events typically produce relatively positive emotional states (for example, relief) that can countercondition the fear and related affects initially associated with the traumatic memory. In other words, the common suggestion that someone "have a good cry" or "get it off of your chest" may reflect cultural support for emotional activities that naturally countercondition trauma-related CERs. From this perspective, just as traditional systematic desensitization often pairs a formerly distressing stimulus to a relaxed, anxiety-incompatible state in an attempt to neutralize the anxious response over time, repeated emotional release during exposure to painful memories may pair the traumatic stimuli to the relatively positive internal states associated with emotional expression. For this reason, optimal trauma therapy typically provides gentle support for—and reinforcement of—expressed emotionality during exposure activities. The level of emotional response in such circumstances will vary from person to person, partially as a function of the client's affect regulation capacity, personal history, and socialization. As a result, the therapist should not "push" for emotional expression when the client is unable or unwilling to engage in such activity but should support it when it occurs.

Desensitization/Resolution

Together, the process of remembering painful (but not overwhelming) events in the context of safety, positive relatedness, emotional expression, and minimal avoidance can serve to break the connection between traumatic memories and associated negative emotional responses. As this desensitization occurs, environmental and internal events that trigger memories of traumatic experiences no longer produce the same level of negative emotion. Once they are processed, traumatic memories become, simply, memories; their ability to produce great distress is significantly diminished. In the case of the multiply trauma-exposed person, however, the process does not end with the resolution of a given memory or set of memories. Instead, other memories, often those that are associated with even greater distress, tend to become more available for discussion as avoidance responses to previously upsetting material wane—at which point the process continues anew. In our experience, however, memories addressed later in treatment often desensitize more quickly than those addressed earlier. This may be due to the increased affect regulation abilities associated with the successful processing of traumatic material (see Chapter 6), as well as the possibility that the extinction of CERs to one traumatic memory may partially generalize to CERs related to other trauma memories.

Processing "Hot Spots"

It may become apparent during a given session that certain memories are especially powerful activators of negative CERs and intrusive cognitions. These memories may respond less well to the titrated exposure methodologies that have been presented thus far in this chapter. Such "hot spots" (Foa & Rothbaum, 1998) may require more concentrated attention in order to produce significant symptom relief. Examples of hot spots include the following:

- A client describes a rape in which she was forced to engage in an especially abhorrent act. Whenever she recalls this aspect of her assault, she becomes increasingly upset and cognitively disorganized. In addition, although other memories of the rape experience are becoming desensitized over time, this memory continues to produce the same level of distress.
- A survivor of the attacks of September 11, 2001, "can't get one thing out of my mind," despite otherwise successful treatment for what he experienced and witnessed on that day. He continues to have intrusive flashbacks of people jumping out of the windows of the World Trade Center and perseverates on these images whenever discussing the attacks.
- A woman who accidentally ran over a homeless man on a crowded city street becomes especially upset when describing the sound of her tires running over his body. This specific memory produces obsessional thoughts and repetitive nightmares, and she continues to hear her tires making a bumping sound whenever she drives.

In cases when such intrusive memory fragments are part of a general presentation of multiple traumatic events and reduced affect regulation capacities, the therapist may find it helpful to focus on less evocative and distressing memories with the client, at least until he or she builds a more effective affect regulation repertoire. In other instances, however, such hot spots may occur in someone who could reasonably be expected to tolerate more direct processing of aversive memories. In the latter case, the clinician may choose to induce—with the client's permission—more highly focused and circumscribed exposure and activation. As opposed to the general approach outlined in this volume, this therapeutic activity more directly parallels the "prolonged exposure" methodology advocated by Foa and her colleagues (Foa & Rothbaum, 1998), except that the entire process is usually limited to a shorter period of time.

We suggest the following general procedure with regard to hot spot processing:

- *Thoroughly explain the procedure, and gain consent before initiating it.* Indicate that some memories occasionally need more concentrated attention than others if they are to lose their painful qualities. Describe the procedure, especially the idea that the client will be asked to describe the "hot spot" in greater detail, perhaps repetitively, and that the process is likely to be somewhat more challenging emotionally. Note that the client can always stop the process at any time if it becomes overwhelming. Nevertheless, note that the longer he or she can tolerate the exposure, the more benefits may accrue.

- *Encourage the client to become as relaxed as possible.* If the client appears especially anxious, suggest slow, even breathing and/or some level of focused muscle relaxation, as described in Chapter 6, or mindfulness exercises if these have been previously learned (see Chapter 10). When the client indicates that he or she is in a less activated state, move on to the next step. Repeat this step whenever needed during the process in order to keep the experience within the therapeutic window.

- *Ask the client to close his or her eyes, if tolerable,*[2] and to describe the upsetting memory slowly and in detail, using the present tense. Tell him or her to try to "go back" to the event and relive it as much as possible while talking about it. Present tense processing involves statements like "The car is coming right at me, it's not going to stop," as opposed to "The car was coming right at me, I was thinking it wasn't going to stop." This grammatical shift tends to increase activation, since it frames the event as though it were happening at the present moment. If present tense processing appears to be too stressful, allow the client to use past tense for a time, until using the present tense becomes possible again. When appropriate, ask (in the present tense) about how he or she felt when the trauma happened; what it looked, smelled, or sounded like; what other objects or people were present at the time; and what his or her specific thoughts were at the time. Generally, the greater the detail, the more effective the processing—but only if it occurs within the therapeutic window.

- *Encourage emotional expression whenever it appears to emerge* (for example, tears or anger), but do not put pressure on the client to express emotion if he or she appears resistant to it. The more emotional access the client has to the CERs, the more direct and potentially effective the eventual extinction of this response may be. Note, again, that emotional activation should not exceed the therapeutic window. If there is significant evidence of

---

[2]Although some clients will be able to close their eyes, others (for example, some survivors of interpersonal violence) may feel safer with their eyes open. In such cases, normalize and validate this choice.

affect dysregulation, such as emotional lability, cognitive disorganization, dramatically increased dissociation, or seemingly overwhelming distress, hot spot processing should be carefully discontinued—while congratulating the client on how far he or she was able to go in the process. Early termination of hot spot processing should not be framed as a failure, but rather as partial completion of a task that can be taken up again at a later time or dropped altogether in favor of another approach.

• *Feel free to interrupt,* gently, to focus the client on the topic, to keep him or her in the present tense (if indicated), to invite him or her to relax or focus on breathing, or to move his or her attention away from overwhelming material.

• *Whenever necessary, orient the client to the here-and-now.* If the client appears to be experiencing potentially overwhelming activation, remind the client that, although he or she is remembering the past, it is just a memory—he or she is actually safe in the room with the therapist. For example, the clinician might say, "Even though you are remembering the [trauma] in your mind, it is not really happening right now. This is very important: The [trauma] is in the past. You are here, safe with me. These are just memories." If further orientation is needed, consider using the grounding techniques described in Chapter 6.

• *Repeat these steps* over as many sessions as indicated and well tolerated. Hot spot processing is typically limited to one episode per session, however, and generally should not exceed 20 minutes in duration. This time limit is based on clinical experience with survivors of more complex trauma, who typically require significant time after hot spot processing for relational support and deescalation of potential trauma-related distress. Proponents of prolonged exposure, however, typically prescribe considerably longer exposure/activation periods.

Hot spot processing can be an efficient way of addressing especially symptom-producing material while still providing ongoing, relational psychotherapy. The extent to which such processing is needed—and tolerable to the client—varies from case to case. When trauma memories are especially upsetting, or affect regulation capacity is notably low, this procedure is rarely appropriate until later in treatment, if ever. On the other hand, hot spot processing may be a regular part of trauma therapy for relatively uncomplicated traumatic material in a client who has reasonably good affect regulation skills.

An Example of Hot Spot Processing

We present a brief, composite example of this technique here. The client, badly hurt in a multicar automobile accident two months prior, is recounting part of the trauma in the present tense, with eyes closed. He is approximately 10 minutes into a 20-minute processing period.

CLIENT: I just kept spinning around, out of control. It was just flying, really fast, hitting things.

THERAPIST: OK, good. Try to say it in the present tense, like we talked about. The car keeps spinning around . . .

CLIENT: I'm trying to turn the wheel, but it's stronger than I am, pulls my arms, like they're gonna pull out of their sockets if I don't let go. Nothing I can do, can't fight it. It's like "bang," and then everything goes crazy, the car's totally crashing into things.

THERAPIST: That's good. You're doing well. What are you feeling while this is happening?

CLIENT: I'm scared. I'm trying to steer, but I know I'm screwed. Everything's going so fast. It starts to tip, it's going to roll over. . . . Which it did, it skids over on the roof. And then I'm upside down, with the seat belt, can't move [Pause, rubbing face]. I think I'm going to die. I don't want to die. I want to go back to where I was before it happened. We're going sideways, the car's sliding sideways upside-down, where is it going? I can't do anything. [Speech volume and rate increasing]

THERAPIST: OK, very good, Tim. Stay with it. You're doing fine. What happens next?

CLIENT: It keeps sliding, then it hits that light post, but I didn't know what it was. Then my head hits the thing. The side metal thing. [Stops speaking]

THERAPIST: You're doing well, Tim. Is this OK? Can we keep going?

CLIENT: Yeah, I'm alright.

THERAPIST: Good. OK, what's happening now?

CLIENT: I hit it hard. It feels crushed, smashed, this pain going through my head like a knife. I can feel it. And all the noise. I thought that was it. I thought I was history. I thought I was gonna die. [Starts to hyperventilate]

THERAPIST: You're doing really well, Tim. Good job. Why don't you try the breathing exercise for a minute. Like we talked about before, OK? . . .

CLIENT: [spends approximately 30 seconds breathing as described in Chapter 6] OK. OK.

THERAPIST: That's good. Alright? Ready to go back?

CLIENT: Yeah, OK. Freaks me out.

THERAPIST:	I know. But you are doing a great job. Stay with it. Remember, stay with the present tense as much as you can.
CLIENT:	It hurts everywhere, like something really bad has happened to my head, my back. I can't move. [Voice volume rising] I can't move. I'm trying to move my arms, but I can't move. I'm paralyzed, hanging down, blood's dripping. What the [expletive]'s happened? I'm so scared about what's happening to me. What's happening to me? And I . . . [tears form, eyes move back and forth]. Oh, God. I want to get away, get out, but I can't.
THERAPIST:	You're OK, Tim. You are doing really well. Can you stay with the feelings? Can we keep going?
CLIENT:	Yeah.
THERAPIST:	OK. What's happening now?
CLIENT:	I'm dying, I'm sure I'm dying. All that blood everywhere. Oh, man. I'm all broken up. Where is everybody? I'm gonna die. [Inaudible]
	[Five second pause]
	Jesus. It's like it's all right there, waiting for me. At least you're here this time.
THERAPIST:	Yes, I am. [smiles] That's good that you are able to do this. I know it's hard.
	[CLIENT nods]
THERAPIST:	So let's take it from there. There's blood everywhere and you think you are going to die. What happens now?
	[CLIENT continues hot spot processing for several more minutes, then is slowly returned to the here-and-now of the therapy room]
THERAPIST:	That was excellent, Tim. Very good. How are you doing?
CLIENT:	I'm OK. That was intense.
THERAPIST:	But you handled it really well.
	[Session continues, with debriefing of processing, normalization of the client's reactions]

_____ Emotional Processing and Substance Dependence

Most of the cognitive-behavioral principles called upon in modern trauma therapy were developed in the context of treatment-outcome research that excluded substance abusing or dependent participants (Bradley et al., 2005; Spinazzola et al., 2005). As a result, there is less known about using exposure and other emotional processing approaches with those who suffer from both posttraumatic stress and involvement in substance abuse (Ouimette et al., 2003). This is unfortunate, since, as described in Chapter 2, a substantial number of substance abusers have trauma histories, and many experience significant posttraumatic stress.

The usual suggestion for treating comorbid trauma symptoms and substance use disorders (SUDs) is to first treat the chemical dependency and then, after abstinence has occurred, treat trauma-related symptoms (Chu, 1988; Keane, 1995). The primary rationale for this treatment sequence is that premature exposure to trauma memories may intensify substance abuse, trigger relapses, or otherwise challenge the diminished affect regulation capacities and coping skills of many substance-abusing trauma survivors. Perhaps apropos of these reasonable concerns, one of the best known and most effective treatment approaches to comorbid PTSD and SUD (*Seeking Safety: A Treatment Manual for PTSD and Substance Abuse;* Najavits, 2002) eschews any form of therapeutic exposure to, or exploration of, trauma memories.

Despite these issues, however, there are several problems with using an "abstinence first" approach in general clinical practice. These include the fact that (1) a high proportion of those presenting for trauma treatment have significant substance abuse issues—blocking their access to treatment would mean underserving many treatment-seeking trauma survivors; (2) in most urban mental health contexts, competent and readily available chemical dependency services are rarely immediately available— waiting lists are often many months long, and specialized programs for substance abusing trauma survivors are exceedingly rare; and (3) research indicates that SUD treatment is considerably less effective for those who also experience major trauma-related difficulties (Grella & Joshi, 2003; McCann & Roy-Byrne, 1998; Ouimette et al., 2003). In other words, successful SUD "pretreatment" or abstinence requirements before trauma treatment may in some cases be empirically, if not logically, inconsistent.

Given these problems, some clinicians and researchers advocate combined trauma and SUD treatment (for example, Abueg & Fairbank, 1992; Expert Consensus Guideline Series, 1999; Watkins, Hunter, Burnam, Pincus, & Nicholson, 2005). Further, several studies suggest that classic trauma therapy, including cognitive-behavioral components, can be effective with some substance dependent trauma survivors (for example, Coffey, Dansky, & Brady, 2003; L. R. Cohen & Hien, 2006). In basic agreement with this perspective, we suggest that the most useful and inclusive approach to trauma-SUD comorbidity is to treat posttraumatic stress in abusing or addicted survivors generally as outlined for others in this book. Given what is known about PTSD-SUD comorbidity, however, and the problems associated with substance abuse in general, we suggest several potential modifications to regular trauma processing:

1. Many substance abusing trauma survivors are noteworthy for their diminished affect regulation skills and coping capacities (Briere et al., 2010; Khantzian, 1997). For this reason, the clinician should consider delaying emotional (or even cognitive) processing of trauma memories until the emotionally unstable client has benefited from the stress reduction and affect regulation interventions outlined in Chapter 6.

2. If some level of trauma processing is possible, either because affect regulation is adequate or as a result of successful intervention in this area, therapeutic exposure and activation should be approached with caution. Specifically, the clinician should especially ensure that processing occurs within the therapeutic window when SUD is present. Most important, exposure to traumatic memory should follow the dictum, "Start low and go slow." Traumatic material should be explored and processed in small increments, and exposure should be terminated if it appears to overly challenge existing affect regulation capacities (that is, if it exceeds the therapeutic window).

3. Trauma therapy generally should not take place if the survivor comes to treatment in an intoxicated state. Instead, the focus should be on client safety (for example, did he or she drive to the session, and can he or she get home safely?) and on managing any clinical issues that might be present (for example, suicidality, aggression, intoxication-related lability). Further, the next session should include nonjudgmental discussion of the client's reason for previously coming to treatment intoxicated, reiteration that intoxication automatically means that therapy is not possible, and exploration of ways in which the client can regain abstinence or at least ensure sobriety at the time of future sessions. Although therapists may vary on this point, typically we do not require substance abstinence in trauma clients (although we recommend it). We do, however, require that the client not abuse substances close enough to his or her session that he or she arrives in an altered state.

4. Whenever possible, the client should be involved in some sort of outside group, self-help or clinician-guided, that focuses on substance abuse issues. Alcoholics Anonymous or other "12-step" programs may serve this purpose, to the extent that their precepts are psychologically and spiritually acceptable to the client.

5. Trauma treatment, as outlined in this book, should be augmented, when possible, with effective substance abuse treatment techniques. The reader is referred to Najavits's (2002) treatment manual and Ouimette and Brown's (2003) edited volume for excellent coverage of specific PTSD-SUD approaches.

Emotional Processing From
Another Perspective: EMDR

In addition to classic cognitive-behavioral and psychodynamic approaches to emotional processing, a number of therapists use an additional model, Eye Movement Desensitization and Reprocessing (EMDR). This approach, developed by Francine Shapiro (1995, 2002), involves asking the client to recall a traumatic event, and then to focus on visual images, negative beliefs, bodily sensations, and emotional responses associated with the memory. At the same time, the client visually tracks the therapist's finger as it moves back and forth across his or her visual field, or the client is exposed to tapping, auditory tones, or moving or flashing lights.

The phases or components of EMDR generally involve the following:

- Treatment planning and target identification
- Ensuring stability, teaching stress reduction skills
- Identification of a negative and opposing positive cognition
- Focus on a disturbing image, negative and positive cognitions, and negative emotions and/or bodily sensations, followed by eye movements (this process may be repeated multiple times in a session) and intermittent assessment of client distress
- Exposure to both the distressing image and the former (or a new) positive cognition
- "Body scans"
- Closure, debriefing, and journaling
- Reevaluation

Several meta-analyses suggest that EMDR is relatively effective, generally reducing posttraumatic stress symptoms to the same degree demonstrated for therapeutic exposure methods (for example, Bradley et al., 2005; Seidler & Wagner, 2006; Van Etten & Taylor, 1998; see EMDR Institute, 2011a, for a list of the many studies validating this intervention). As noted by Spates, Koch, Cusak, Pagoto, and Waller's (2008) chapter in the International Society for Traumatic Stress Studies practice guidelines, "A review of seven meta-analyses revealed that EMDR is an effective treatment for PTSD, and equally effective as exposure-based therapies" (p. 298). Interestingly, another oft-cited meta-analysis concludes that the specific eye movement or "bilateral stimulation" component of EMDR has little effect on outcome and may be superfluous (P. R. Davidson & Parker, 2001), although not all clinicians agree with this interpretation, and the EMDR website vigorously rejects it.

Our own conclusion is that EMDR is a form of cognitive-behavioral therapy that can be as effective as other brief therapies, including exposure therapy, in treating PTSD. EMDR may be most helpful in addressing relatively discrete, less complex trauma effects, or in providing hot spot processing during more long-term, relational therapy. As noted by the EMDR Institute (2011b), this procedure, like other exposure therapies, is not recommended unless "the client has adequate methods of handling emotional distress and good coping skills, and . . . the client is in a relatively stable state. If further stabilization is required, or if additional skills are needed, therapy focuses on providing these" (para. 4).

Working With Those With Unavailable Narrative Memory: "Date Rape" Drugs, Alcohol Intoxication, and Trauma-Related Loss of Consciousness

A not-uncommon scenario in trauma centers and rape crisis programs is a client who presents with incomplete or absent memories of his or her trauma, either due to the covert administration of a drug or because he or she was very intoxicated at the time of the event. In a typical example, a woman (or, less commonly, a man) describes awakening to a sense that she has been sexually assaulted, but has no memory of it because she had been drugged. Although often referred to as "date rape" drugs, the substances used in these assaults are often administered by someone the victim may not know, for example in a bar or club, at a rave, or at a party.

In almost all cases, date rape drugs are delivered through doctored drinks or food. They are typically sedatives, hypnotics, or dissociative compounds that lead to unconsciousness or, when this does not occur, extreme intoxication, confusion, passivity, "blank" periods, and, in some cases, paralysis (U.S. Department of Health and Human Services, Office on Women's Health, 2008). They include benzodiazepines (especially flunitrazepam [Rohypnol], midazolam [Versed], and temazepam [Restoril]), gamma-hydroxybutyric acid (GHB), and ketamine hydrochloride. Many authorities add alcohol to this list, since it appears to be the most commonly used drug in the commission of rape (Du Mont et al., 2009).

Although a small number of studies indicate that date rape drugging may be overreported (for example, Hurley and Parker, 2006), there are several problems with existing research that make it difficult to specifically refute any given claim, or estimate the actual incidence or prevalence of drug-assisted sexual assaults. These include (a) lack of agreement on which drugs, in fact, are considered to be "date rape" compounds; (b) whether all drugs were screened for following a complaint, as opposed to, for example, solely Rohypnol or Versed; (c) the time lapse between reported ingestion and laboratory testing, since many of these drugs are rapidly metabolized; and (d) since date rape drugs typically produce amnesia, and rape often goes unreported in any event, a large proportion of victims may not seek out law enforcement or medical assistance, making incidence estimates based on complaints highly questionable (U.S. Drug Enforcement Administration, n.d.; U.S. Department of Health and Human Services, Office on Women's Health, 2008).

Following ingestion of the drug, the victim may experience partial or complete amnesia about what transpired or who was involved, an outcome that often protects the perpetrator from detection or prosecution. Unfortunately, although explicit/narrative memory is commonly impaired by these drugs, fragments of implicit/sensory/emotional memories may persist (see, for example, Verba, Bering, & Fischer, 2007). As a result, the victim may not verbally recall what happened to him or her, yet he or she may have intrusive sensory or emotional memories in the form of flashbacks, nightmares, intrusive sensations or emotions, or brief periods of triggered dissociation. In addition to the already traumatic effects of sexual assault, victims of drug-assisted crimes also must deal with the implications of amnesia for the event: Upon awakening, the victim may be confused about whether he or she even has been victimized, let alone when, by whom, or in what way. This lack of certainty can interfere with recovery, in part because the victim has no narrative or closure on the details of the event, and thus has fewer options for cognitively processing it. Further, not knowing the identity of the perpetrator can lead to broadly generalized fear, distrust, and hypervigilance in social or dating situations, in the presence of men, and so on.

The amnesiogenic aspects of many date rape drugs, as well as similar effects associated with severe alcohol intoxication or traumatic brain injury, mean that emotional processing of the trauma can be very difficult or impossible, potentially leading to a more chronic course of posttraumatic stress. As described earlier in this chapter, in order for most traumatic memories to be habituated or desensitized, the survivor typically must recall and verbalize the event, reexperience the associated distress, and, in the context of disparity (safety), slowly break the connection between the memory and the emotions and cognitions conditioned to it. However, since the amnestic victim often does not have explicit memories of the assault, this cannot occur—there is no simple way for him or her to verbalize what happened and have this discussion trigger processable material.

The unavailability of verbalizable, conscious memory following date rape drug administration, alcohol intoxication, or events that produce memory loss (for example, severe motor vehicle accidents or combat injury) can be addressed in at least two different ways, although these methods are rarely as effective as emotional processing of verbal memories. These are (1) processing of peripheral, but more available memory and (2) description and processing of flashbacks, nightmares, and activated implicit emotional material.

Processing of peripheral memories involves discussing in detail the last memories the client has prior to the trauma and the first ones following it. Although not always successful, in some cases specific description of proximal, intact memories can trigger implicit material (that is, through context reinstatement) that then emerges into the session and can be addressed, as described below. As well, for reasons that can only be hypothesized, it is our experience that some clients appear to recover more narrative memory at the "edges" of previously recalled material—in other words, a small amount of additional explicit memory material may become available—in effect "shrinking" the amnestic portion. It is important, however, that the clinician refrain from pressuring the client, in any way, to remember new things. Otherwise, the suggestible client may seek to recover memory fragments that, in fact, are not available, thereby increasing the risk of false memories and complicating treatment. For this reason, the clinician would not say "Try to remember anything else you can," but rather "What is the last thing you remember before [the trauma]?" and "What is the first thing you remember after [the trauma]?" As the client describes these memories, it is not uncommon for him or her to remember additional details unprompted, which then become part of the trauma narrative and can be processed to whatever extent possible.

Another route into narratively amnestic, but sensorily available, memories is to encourage the client to describe in detail any flashbacks, nightmares, or triggered emotions he or she has experienced associated with the trauma. In some instances, repeated description of a flashback, for example, will trigger additional implicit material, such as suddenly reexperienced fear or helplessness, that, in the presence of the safety (disparity) of the session, can be at least partially counterconditioned or extinguished. Consider the following example:

THERAPIST: What is the last thing you can remember?

CLIENT: I started feeling dizzy, for no reason, and the room was spinning around. I was, like, what's happening? I felt really woozy, like I was drunk. But I wasn't drinking. And then I guess I passed out.

THERAPIST: OK, Sarah, that's good. See if you can stay with what happened. Tell me what it feels like.

CLIENT: It was embarrassing. I started getting scared because I didn't know what was happening.

People were looking at me, probably laughing, thinking I was drunk. . . . I was scared that it might be what it was, like a rape drug or something. And then, maybe . . . [a pause], I think I remember a little later . . .

THERAPIST: You remember something else?

CLIENT: I'm like fading in and out. Something's happening. I'm being grabbed. Oh my God, something bad happened, I can feel it. Like maybe the guy sitting next to me?

THERAPIST: I'm not sure if we can know exactly what's happening. But stay with the feeling. What's going on?

CLIENT: I don't know! But it feels bad. Scary.

THERAPIST: That's good, Sarah. Can you tell me the feelings?

CLIENT: Like gross, scared. Being grabbed and pushed around. Wanting to throw up. Scared!

THERAPIST: You are doing really well. Remember, it's only a memory, you are here, and you are safe. Can you stay with those feelings just a little longer?

It is important to note, as implied in this example and in other chapters, that memory need not be present in solely narrative form in order to be processed; in fact, the self-trauma model suggests that it is implicit, sensory or affective states, conditioned to the trauma memory, that are actually diminished by exposure-based methodologies (Briere, 2002b). As a result, to the extent that the amnestic trauma survivor can repetitively reexperience implicit trauma memories in the presence of therapeutic safety and support, trauma-related emotions and cognitions may become less salient, resulting in decreased emotional distress.

Sequence and Session-Level Structure of Memory Processing

The current and previous chapters have described various techniques and approaches for the cognitive and emotional processing of traumatic memory. Although the actual processing and desensitization of traumatic memory will vary in degree from session to session, generally all such sessions should adhere to a basic structure. This framework allows the therapist to assess the client's current needs, provide relevant processing activities as needed, reassess the client's current state, deescalate session-level arousal if needed, and provide end-of-session closure. We suggest some version of the following in a 50-minute session:

- Opening (5–15 minutes):

  1. Inquire about any changes in the client's life since the last session.
     - Have there been any new traumas or victimizations?
     - Has the client engaged in dysfunctional or self-destructive behaviors?
     - If any of the foregoing is of concern, work to assure or increase the client's ongoing physical safety. Do this before (or instead of) formal trauma processing.

2. Check with the client regarding his or her internal experience since the last session. Have intrusive or avoidance symptoms increased significantly since the last meeting? If yes, normalize the experience and validate symptoms as intrinsic trauma processing. If the intrusions or avoidance responses are substantial, consider decreasing the intensity of exposure and activation in the current session.

3. If appropriate, have client spend 5 minutes or so in a relaxation/breathing exercise (see Chapter 6) or, if he or she has learned this approach, mindfulness meditation (Chapter 10).

- Mid-session (20–40 minutes):

1. Provide emotional and cognitive memory processing, staying within the therapeutic window whenever possible.

2. If significant processing is contraindicated, revert to psychoeducation, general discussion, affect skills development, or a focus on less upsetting events in the client's life.

- Later in session (15–20 minutes):

1. Debrief, normalize, and validate any memory processing that occurred, as necessary.

2. Inquire about the client's subjective experience during processing, as well as any thoughts or feeling he or she had while it was occurring.

3. Provide cognitive therapy as needed for additional cognitive distortions that emerged during processing (see Chapter 7).

4. If the client's level of activation remains high, work to deescalate his or her emotional arousal. This may include an increasing focus on nonemotional issues, further cognitive (but not emotional) processing, and/or grounding per Chapter 6.

- Ending (final 5–15 minutes):

1. Remind the client (as necessary) of the potential delayed effects of trauma processing, including occasionally increased flashbacks, nightmares, and a desire to engage in avoidance activities such as substance abuse or tension reduction behaviors.

2. Provide safety planning (if necessary) regarding dangers identified in the session, or any possible self- (or other) destructive behavior.

3. Provide closure statements (for example, summing up the session) and encouragement.

4. Explicitly refer to the time and date of the next session.

5. If appropriate, have the client spend 5 minutes or so in a relaxation exercise or in mindfulness meditation.

Suggested Reading

Briere, J. (2002). Treating adult survivors of severe childhood abuse and neglect: Further development of an integrative model. In J. E. B. Myers, L. Berliner, J. Briere, C. T. Hendrix, T. Reid, & C. Jenny (Eds.), *The APSAC handbook on child maltreatment* (2nd ed., pp. 175–202). Thousand Oaks, CA: Sage.

Cloitre, M., Cohen, L. R., & Koenen, K. C. (2006). *Treating survivors of childhood abuse: Psychotherapy for the interrupted life*. New York, NY: Guilford.

Foa, E. B., & Rothbaum, B. O. (1998). *Treating the trauma of rape: Cognitive-behavioral therapy for PTSD*. New York, NY: Guilford.

Follette, V. M., & Ruzek, J. I. (Eds.). (2006). *Cognitive-behavioral therapy for trauma* (2nd ed.). New York, NY: Guilford.

Ouimette, P., & Brown, P. J. (2003). *Trauma and substance abuse: Causes, consequences, and treatment of comorbid disorders*. Washington, DC: American Psychological Association.

Shapiro, F. (2001). *Eye movement desensitization and reprocessing: Basic principles, protocols, and procedures* (2nd ed.). New York, NY: Guilford.

9 Increasing Identity and Relational Functioning

As noted in Chapter 2, trauma can produce ongoing problems in identity and interpersonal relatedness, above and beyond posttraumatic stress, cognitive distortions, and affect dysregulation. Most typically associated with a history of ongoing and severe childhood abuse and/or neglect (Briere & Rickards, 2007; Pearlman & Courtois, 2005; Schore, 2003), identity and relational disturbance is often viewed by clinicians as evidence of a personality (especially "borderline") disorder. Although there is a significant link between trauma and some forms of enduring psychological disturbance, not all problems in this area necessarily relate to a dysfunctional personality, per se. In many cases, they represent reactions, accommodations, or coping strategies developed in the face of chronic childhood maltreatment.

With the exception of models developed by Cloitre et al. (2002), Linehan (1993a), Najavits (2002), and a few others, most cognitive-behavioral trauma therapies focus primarily on treating cognitive or posttraumatic stress symptoms. However, many survivors of multiple, complex traumas present with significant—often highly distressing—difficulties in identity and interpersonal functioning. As a result, we recommend interventions that address these areas as well.

Identity Problems

Survivors of early and severe childhood trauma often complain of problems associated with an inability to access, and gain from, a stable sense of self. This may present, for example, as problems in the following areas:

- Determining one's own needs or entitlements
- Maintaining a consistent sense of self in the context of strong emotions or the presence of compelling others
- Having an internal reference point at times of stress
- Predicting one's own reactions or behavior in various situations
- Being one's "own best friend," that is, having direct access to a positive sense of self

Many of these difficulties are thought to develop in the first years of life, when the parent-child attachment relationship is disrupted by care-taker aggression or, somewhat paradoxically, neglect (Allen, 2001; Hesse, Main, Abrams, & Rifkin, 2003). In addition to possible negative impacts on the developing child's psychobiology (for example, reducing or disrupting the orbitofrontal cortex's capacity to regulate cortical and autonomic processes; Schore, 1994, 1996; D. J. Siegel, 1999), childhood abuse and neglect can motivate the development of adaptations and defenses that, in turn, reduce the child's development of a coherent sense of self.

Although the reasons for identity disturbance in survivors of childhood trauma are no doubt complex, probable etiologies include early dissocia-tion, other-directedness, and the absence of benign interactions with others (Briere, 2002b). Dissociating or otherwise avoiding trauma-related distress early in life is likely to block the survivor's awareness of his or her internal state at the very time that a sense of self is thought to develop in children. Further, the hypervigilance needed by the endangered child in order to ensure survival means that much of his or her attention is directed out-ward, a process that detracts from internal awareness. In this context, when introspection (which is probably necessary for the development of an internal model of self; Stern, 1985) occurs, it is often punished, since (1) such inward focus takes attention away from the environment and, therefore, increases danger, and (2) greater internal awareness means—in the context of ongoing trauma—greater emotional pain. Finally, most theories of self-capacities stress the role of benign others in the child's development of an internal model of self (Bowlby, 1988). One may have to interact with positive others in order to form a coherent and positive sense of oneself. This is thought to occur when the loving and attuned parent or caretaker reflects back to the child what the child appears to be feeling or experiencing (for example, smiling when the infant smiles or appearing concerned when the infant cries), responds to the child's needs in a way that reinforces the child's legitimacy, and treats the child in such a manner that he or she can infer positive self-characteristics. As the child develops into an adolescent, and then an adult, the growing complexity of his or her interactions with the social environment ideally bestows a growing sense of self in the context of others. Unfortunately, this progression into increas-ingly coherent identity may be less possible for those who were deprived of positive parenting.

Interestingly, the Western notion of the importance of a "self" is not rep-licated to the same extent in some other cultures (Walsh, 1988); in fact, in some societies it may be seen as contrary to the more prized notion of inter-dependence and relatedness. Yet some of this disagreement may be semantic in nature, revolving around not the notion of a self, per se, but rather whether any one person can be truly separate from, or independent of, oth-ers or the surrounding world, and whether "self" is a concrete, stable entity, or an ongoing process that is constructed from the past and the present on a moment-to-moment basis.

Even in environments where individuality and independence are less prized, however, some level of self-esteem, self-efficacy, self-confidence, and boundary awareness is usually acknowledged to be both important and healthy.

Intervention

Because much of self-development appears to involve interactions with caring others, the therapeutic relationship can be a powerful environment in which the client's sense of identity self-reference may evolve. In this context, the clinician can work to provide safety, support self-validity, and encourage self-exploration.

Providing Safety

Introspection is, ultimately, a luxury that can only occur when the external environment does not require hypervigilance. For this reason, the clinical setting should promulgate those aspects of safety previously outlined in this book. Not only should the client feel physically safe, that is, from the therapist and (at least temporarily) from the world, but he or she also should experience psychological safety—the clinician should be psychologically noninvasive, careful to honor the client's boundaries (regardless of whether the client is yet aware of them), and reliable enough to communicate stability and security. When these conditions are met, the client is more likely to trust the environment enough to explore his or her internal thoughts, feelings, and experiences and, as noted later in this chapter, form a more positive attachment to the therapist. The process of actually discovering that one is safe in treatment, however, may be protracted—as noted earlier, many survivors of severe childhood or adult trauma experiences may have to be in treatment for some time before they are able to accurately perceive the safety inherent in the session (Allen, 2001). Even then, this sense of relative safety may wax and wane throughout therapy.

Supporting Self-Validity

Also helpful is the therapist's visible acceptance of the client's needs and views as intrinsically valid. To some extent, this might appear to contradict the need to challenge the client's trauma-based self-perceptions and other cognitive distortions. However, the approach advocated in this book is not to argue with the client regarding his or her "thinking errors" about self, but rather to work with the client in such a way that he or she is able to perceive incorrect assumptions and reconsider them in light of his or her current (therapy-based) relational experience. Not only will the therapist not validate the client's self-rejection (for example, the belief that one does not have entitlement to respectful and caring treatment by others), he or she will provide a therapeutic experience in which such thoughts are contradicted. This is, in some ways, a form of the disparity described in Chapter 8: Although the client may view himself or herself as not having rights to self-determination, these self-perceptions will be contrary to the experience of acceptance and positive regard experienced in the session. Such cognitions, when not reinforced by the clinician, are likely to decrease over time. Equally important, as the message of self-as-valid is repeatedly communicated to the client by the therapist's behavior, client notions of undeservingness and unacceptability are relationally contradicted.

This general focus on the client's entitlements can help to reverse the other-directness the survivor learned in the context of abuse or neglect (Briere, 1996). During most childhood abuse, attention is typically focused on the abuser's needs, the likelihood that he or she will be violent, and, ultimately, the abuser's view of reality. In such a context, the child's needs or reality is irrelevant, if not dangerous when asserted. In a client-focused environment, however, reality becomes more what the client needs or perceives than what the therapist demands or expects. In such an environment, the client is more able to identify internal states, perceptions, and needs, and discover how to "hang on to" these aspects of self even when in the presence of meaningful others (initially, the therapist). By stressing to the client that his or her experience is the ultimate focus, and by helping the client to identify and label his or her internal feelings and needs, the therapist helps the client to build a coherent and positive model of self—much in the way parents would have, had the client's childhood been more safe, attuned, and supportive.

Self-actualization versus socially based devaluation. The therapist's support for the client's self-validity also may include exploration of how he or she may have been maltreated based on gender, race, ethnicity, sexual orientation, or gender identity. For example, gay, lesbian, or transgendered clients may have conflicting experiences of self, reflecting, in part, socially transmitted messages about the unacceptability of any sexual orientation not classically heterosexual. Similarly, those whose ethnicity or race has been devalued may have internalized what are essentially self-hating perspectives. Women who have been repeatedly sexually harassed or victimized may need to address not only trauma-related symptoms but also the impacts of a sexually exploitive, and sometimes sexually violent, culture on self-perception and identity. In such cases, an important goal of therapy may be to work to assist the survivor in developing self-perceptions that are positive, efficacious, and empowering, despite the social context in which he or she may be embedded (L. S. Brown, 2008).

Encouraging Self-Exploration

By facilitating self-exploration and self-reference (as opposed to defining self primarily in terms of others'—including the therapist's—expectations or reactions), therapy can allow the survivor to gain a greater sense of his or her internal topography. Increased self-awareness may be fostered particularly when the client is repeatedly asked about his or her ongoing internal experience throughout the course of treatment. This may include (as described in Chapter 7) multiple, gentle inquiries about the client's early perceptions and experiences, his or her feelings and reactions during and after victimization experiences, and what his or her thoughts and conclusions are regarding the ongoing process of treatment. Equally important, however, is the need for the client to discover, quite literally, what he or she thinks and feels about current things, both trauma related and otherwise. Because the external-directedness necessary to survive victimization generally works against self-understanding and identity, the survivor should be encouraged to explore his or her own likes and dislikes, views regarding self and others, entitlements and obligations, and related phenomena in the context of therapeutic support and acceptance. This more broad, less specifically trauma-focused intervention is, to some extent, "identity training": providing the survivor with the opportunity to discover what he or she thinks and feels, as distinct from what others think and feel.

The therapist's consistent and ongoing support for introspection, self-exploration, and self-identification allows the client to develop a more articulated and accessible internal sense of self. Ultimately, the therapist takes on the role of the supportive, engaged, helpful attachment figure whose primary interest—beyond symptom resolution—is the development of the client's internal life and self-determinism. This process, although less anchored in specific therapeutic techniques or protocols, can be one of the more important aspects of treatment.

Relational Disturbance

The perspective offered in this book is that many of the relationship problems experienced by traumatized people arise from early learning about—and accommodation to—a harsh interpersonal world. Although such difficulties may occur as a result of chronic interpersonal traumas in adulthood (for example, ongoing domestic violence, torture, or living in a chronically dangerous environment), they are seen far more often in the context of earlier childhood maltreatment (Briere & Rickards, 2007; Pearlman & Courtois, 2005). One of the earliest impacts of abuse and neglect is thought to be on the child's internal representations of self and others (Allen, 2001; Bowlby, 1982), based on how he or she is treated by his or her caretakers. In the case of abuse or neglect, these inferences are likely to be especially negative.

For example, the child who is being maltreated may conclude that he or she must be intrinsically unacceptable or malignant to deserve such punishment or disregard, or may come to see himself or herself as helpless, inadequate, or weak. As well, this negative context may mean that the abused or neglected child comes to view others as inherently dangerous, rejecting, or unavailable.

These early inferences about self and others often form a generalized set of expectations and assumptions, sometimes described as *internal working models* (Bowlby, 1982) or *relational schemas* (Baldwin et al., 1993). Such core understandings are often relatively nonresponsive to verbal information or the expressed views of others later in life, since they are encoded in the first years of life and thus are preverbal in nature. For example, the individual who believes, based on early learning, that he or she is unlikable or unattractive to others, or that others are not to be trusted, will not easily change such views based on other people's declarations that the person is valued by them or that they can be relied upon.

Such memory is often referred to as *implicit,* involving largely nonverbal and nonautobiographical memories that cannot be recalled, per se, but can be triggered by reminiscent stimuli in the current environment (see D. J. Siegel, 1999, for a discussion). As a result, most people have "infantile amnesia" for these early relational memories—although such memories can trigger cognitions and conditioned emotional responses (CERs), they cannot be consciously recalled as part of the past.

The quality and valence of these core schemas are thought to affect the individual's later capacity to form and maintain meaningful connections and attachments with other people (Bowlby, 1988). As a result, formerly abused or neglected individuals may find themselves in conflictual or chaotic relationships later in life, may have problems with forming intimate adult attachments, and may engage in behaviors that are likely to threaten or disrupt close relationships (Allen, 2001; Pearlman & Courtois, 2005). These core schemas are often referred to as *attachment styles*. The reader is referred to modern texts on attachment theory (for example, Cassidy & Shaver, 2010; Rholes & Simpson, 2004; M. F. Solomon & Siegel, 2003), since the lessons learned by the child during early parent-child attachment are clearly relevant to dysfunctional interpersonal behavior in traumatized adolescents and adults (P. C. Alexander, 1992; E. A. Carlson, 1998; Coe, Dalenberg, Aransky, & Reto, 1995).

Because relational schema (or internal working models) are typically encoded at the implicit, nonverbal level, and are primarily based in safety and attachment needs, they may not be evident except in situations where the survivor perceives interpersonal threats similar to the abuse, such as rejection, abandonment, criticism, or physical danger. When this occurs, these underlying cognitions may be triggered with resultant negative affect and interpersonal difficulties (J. A. Simpson & Rholes, 1994). For example, an individual who experienced early separation or abandonment may relate relatively well in a given occupational or intimate context until he or she encounters stimuli that suggest (or are in some way reminiscent of) rejection, empathic disattunement, or abandonment. These perceived experiences, by virtue of their similarity to early trauma, may then trigger memories, emotions (CERs), and cognitions that, although excessive or out of proportion in the immediate context, are appropriate to the feelings and thoughts of an abused or neglected child (Briere, 2002b). This activation may then motivate behavior that, although intended to ensure proximity and to maintain the relationship, is so characterized by "primitive" (that is, child-level) responses and demands, and so affectively laden, that it challenges or even destroys that relationship.

The most dramatic example of chronic relational trauma activations may be what is referred to as borderline personality disorder. As noted in Chapter 2, those individuals with borderline personality features are often described as prone to (1) sudden emotional outbursts in response to minor or imagined interpersonal provocation, (2) self-defeating cognitions, (3) feelings of emptiness and intense dysphoria, and (4) impulsive, tension-reducing behaviors that are triggered by perceptions of having been abandoned, rejected, or maltreated by another person (American Psychiatric Association, 2000). A fair portion of such behavior and symptomatology can be seen as arising from triggered relational memories and CERs associated with early abuse, abandonment, rejection, or lack of parental responsiveness, generally in the context of reduced affect regulation capacities. The "borderline" individual, upon having abuse memories triggered by stimuli in adult relational contexts, may then attempt to avoid the associated distress by engaging in activities such as substance abuse, inappropriate proximity seeking (for example, neediness or attempts to forestall abandonment), or involvement in distracting, tension-reducing behaviors.

Intervention

The interventions for relational disturbance parallel, to some extent, those outlined in Chapters 7 and 8. In the relational context, however, the various components of trauma processing occur more directly as a function of the therapeutic relationship. Because most disturbed relatedness appears to arise from maltreatment early in life, and is often triggered by later interpersonal stimuli, it is not surprising that the most effective interventions for relational problems are, in fact, relational as well. Far from being the nonspecific placebo effect or inert ingredient suggested by some advocates of short-term therapy, the relationship between client and therapist can be seen as directly and specifically curative.

Among other things, as we have noted, the therapeutic relationship is a powerful source of interpersonal triggers. As the connection between client and therapist grows, the client's increasing attachment to the therapist can trigger implicit (nonverbal, sensory, or experiential) memories of attachment experiences in childhood. For many clients, these early attachment memories include considerable abuse or neglect, which may be reexperienced in the form of maltreatment-related thoughts and feelings during therapy. Such emergent, largely implicit "relational flashbacks" do not contain contextual information signaling that they represent the past (D. J. Siegel, 1999), and thus are often misperceived as being feelings related to the current therapist-client relationship (what cognitive theorists sometimes call a *source attribution error*). Once activated and expressed, such cognitions and emotions can be discussed and processed in the context of the safety, soothing, compassion, and support associated with a positive therapeutic relationship.

As in work with more "simple" traumatic memories, the therapeutic processing of relational memories and their associations (for example, CERs and attachment-level cognitions) can be seen as involving the exposure, activation, disparity, and counterconditioning described in the previous chapter.

Exposure

In the session, the client reexperiences implicit memories of earlier interpersonal traumas in response to therapeutic stimuli that are in some way similar to those early experiences.

Therapy stimuli that can trigger exposure to relational memories, by virtue of their similarity to the original trauma, include the clinician's physical appearance; his or her age, sex, race, and quasi-parental behaviors; and the power differential between client and therapist that may engender feelings of vulnerability and diminished status. Even positive feelings associated with the therapeutic relationship can trigger distress—the client's loving feelings toward the therapist (or perception of similar feelings from the clinician) can activate sexual feelings or fears, and perceptions of therapist caring and acceptance can trigger fears of losing such experiences (that is, of abandonment by an attachment figure). As well, therapists are inevitably prey to the vagaries of normal human experience, including momentary lapses in empathic attunement, distraction by personal problems, fatigue, or, as described in Chapter 4, the triggering of their own issues by some aspect of the client's presentation—any of which may inadvertently expose the client to memories of earlier maltreatment or neglect.

Beyond these discrete triggers, the therapeutic relationship itself—by virtue of its ongoing nature and importance to the client—may replicate stimulus conditions similar to those of early important relationships, including the client's childhood need for attachment. To the extent that the earlier relationship was characterized by trauma, disattunement, or neglect, the current therapeutic relationship is likely to trigger negative relational memories.

Just as noted in previous chapters for more simple trauma processing, exposure must occur within the context of the therapeutic window. In this regard, the clinician may have to work actively, and pay careful attention, to ensure that his or her stimulus value or the characteristics of the therapeutic relationship do not produce so much exposure to negative relational memories that the client becomes overwhelmed. Just as the therapist treating PTSD may titrate the amount of exposure the client undergoes regarding a traumatic memory, the clinician treating relational traumas ideally seeks to ensure that reminiscent aspects of the therapeutic environment are not overwhelming. For example, as noted in Chapter 4, clients with easily accessible schemas arising from punitive parenting may require treatment that especially avoids any sense of therapist judgment. Similarly, the client who has been physically or sexually assaulted may require (1) special, visible attention to safety issues, (2) therapist responses that stress boundary awareness and respect, or even (3) a greater-than-normal physical distance between the client's chair and the therapist's. A client with abandonment issues arising from early psychological neglect, on the other hand, may be more comfortable when the clinician is especially attuned and psychologically available to the client. On a more general level, therapists of chronically traumatized clients may need to devote even greater attention than usual to avoiding behaviors that in some way appear to involve intrusion, control, or narcissism.

Unfortunately, some characteristics of the therapist may be such powerful triggers that useful therapy is not always possible. Probably the best example of this is therapist gender. Many women who have been recently sexually assaulted by a man or men have considerable difficulty working in therapy with a male clinician. In some cases, regardless of the therapist's personal qualities and best intentions, his masculine stimulus value may trigger overwhelming exposure to trauma memories of assault by a male, thereby exceeding the therapeutic window and negating the possibility of meaningful intervention (Briere, 1996). In such cases, the best solution is usually to refer the client to a woman therapist. Similar scenarios may occur when the therapist's ethnic or racial identity is the same as the client's perpetrator, or where the therapy location (for example, a hospital) overwhelmingly triggers trauma memories in the client (for example, of being tortured in a governmental facility in his or her country of origin).

More typically, however, therapeutic stimuli are titratable, and therefore the relationship is more able to be helpful. Such adjustment does not mean that the therapist generally undershoots the therapeutic window with regard to interpersonal trauma. It is almost inevitable that the therapeutic relationship will trigger the client's relational memories, if only because of the importance that therapy has for him or her, and because such treatment regularly involves themes of shared experience, attachment, intimacy, and vulnerability.

Activation

As a result of therapeutic exposure, the client experiences emotions and thoughts that were encoded at the time of the relational trauma.

Activated emotional responses to early relational memories are often notable for the suddenness of their emergence, their intensity, and their seeming contextual inappropriateness. Intrusive negative cognitions about self or the therapist may be activated, or attachment-related schema involving submission, childlike perceptions, or dependency may suddenly appear. In some cases, such activation may also trigger sensory flashbacks and dissociative responses.

Cognitive-emotional activation can be easily understood by both client and therapist when it occurs in the context of discrete trauma memories, such as those of an assault or disaster. When activation occurs in the context of triggered relational stimuli, however, the actual "reason" behind the client's thoughts and feelings may be far less clear. Because the original trauma memory may have been formed in the first years of life, and therefore is not available to conscious (explicit) awareness, neither client nor therapist may know why the client is feeling especially anxious or angry, or why he or she is suddenly so distrustful of the clinician. In fact, in instances where such activations are dramatic, they may appear so irrational and contextually inappropriate that they are seen by some as evidence of significant psychopathology, perhaps even psychosis. Ultimately, however, these activations are logical, in the sense that they represent conditioned responses to triggered relational memories.

Cognitive-emotional activation is especially relevant in longer-term, more intensive psychotherapy, where the triggering of client attachment responses (both positive and negative) is more likely. An example of the activation of relational trauma memories and associated negative schema is presented by Briere (2002b):

> [A] 24-year-old woman with a long history of emotional abuse by her narcissistic father . . . enters therapy with an older male clinician. Although the client initially views her therapist as supportive and caring, she soon comes to feel increasing distrust toward [him], begins to see subtle "put-downs" in his remarks, and eventually finds herself angry at the therapist's perceived lack of empathy, lapses in attunement and caring, and judgmental behavior. (p. 194)

In this instance, the seemingly benign relationship between client and clinician contains stimuli (for example, the growing feeling of emotional intimacy as treatment progresses) that trigger childhood abuse memories and activate trauma-specific cognitive-emotional responses. In agreement with many psychodynamic theorists, we suggest that such activation of relational memories and feelings should be expected when treating those with childhood (and extended adult) traumas and is, in fact, often necessary for the successful resolution of chronic interpersonal problems. Absent such relational activation, therapy might be easier to conduct but would be unlikely to release the very material that has to be processed before the client's relational life can significantly improve.

Disparity

Although the client thinks and feels as if maltreatment or abandonment is either happening or about to happen during treatment, in reality, the session is safe and the therapist is not abusive, rejecting, or otherwise dangerous.

Although this component is often critical to trauma processing, those who have been victimized interpersonally—especially if that victimization was chronic—may find disparity difficult to fully accept, let alone trust. There are a number of reasons for this. First, those exposed to chronic danger often come to assume that such danger is inevitable. The battered woman, combat veteran, or prostitute, for example, may find it very difficult to accept that the rules have suddenly changed and that he or she is safe—especially in situations that bear some similarity to the original (dangerous) context. Second, in many cases, the original perpetrator(s) of violence promised safety, caring, or support as a way to gain access to the victim. As a result, reassurance or declarations of safety may seem like just "more of the same," if not a warning of impending danger. Finally, therapy implicitly requires some level of intimacy, or at least vulnerability from the client, a requirement that—from the survivor's perspective—can be a recapitulation of past experience of intimate demands and subsequent injuries.

For these and related reasons, not only must disparity/safety be present, but the client must be able to perceive it. Although occasionally frustrating for the therapist, this sometimes means that considerable time in therapy is necessary before sufficient trust is present to allow true relational processing. For example, the survivor of extended political torture, warfare, or gang violence may require months of weekly therapy before "letting down his or her guard" enough to fully participate in trauma therapy. Similarly, the therapist should be prepared in such cases for client disbelief or immediate rejection of statements like "You are safe here" or "I won't go away." This does not mean that the clinician shouldn't make such statements (when they are accurate and expressed in a nonintrusive, nondemanding way), only that he or she should understand that such declarations rarely alter cognitions that have been repeatedly reinforced by prior adversity and may be nonverbally encoded.

In fact, for those hypervigilant to danger in interpersonal situations, disparity cannot be communicated; it must be demonstrated. As noted earlier, therapist statements that he or she should be trusted can have the opposite effect on traumatized clients—because they have heard similar promises or protestations from ill-meaning or profoundly ambivalent people in the past, such statements may make them feel less safe, not more. Instead, when working with chronic relational trauma survivors, the therapist must behave in a reliably safe and nonexploitive way, over time, until the client can truly extrapolate safety into the future and imagine disparity.

The exposure/activation/disparity process may proceed in a stepwise fashion for the relational trauma survivor. Early in therapy, he or she may occasionally (and often inadvertently) reveal some small degree of vulnerability or suffering to the therapist and then reflexively expect a negative consequence. When this vulnerability is not, in fact, punished by the therapist and (as noted in the next section) is met with support and some carefully titrated level of visible caring, the client may slowly lower his or her psychological barriers (including his or her avoidance strategies) and express more thoughts or feelings. As these responses are likewise supported, and not exploited or punished, the client's willingness to process pain in "real time" (that is, directly, in the presence of the therapist) generally increases. It should be stressed that this may take time, and therapist expressions of impatience may, ironically, subvert the process by communicating criticism, rejection, or even narcissism.

In other cases—for example, when the client has experienced less extreme or less chronic relational trauma, when the conditions surrounding the victimization are clearly quite different (and perceivable as such by the client) than the current ones in therapy, or when there were supportive people in the client's environment in addition to the perpetrator(s)—disparity may be considerably easier to establish and trauma processing may be more immediately possible. In any case, however, this is an assessment issue, as opposed to something that can be automatically assumed. In the worst-case scenario, the hypervigilant or otherwise overly fearful client will not gain from full exposure-activation activities; in fact, exposure may be contraindicated until disparity has been reliably demonstrated.

Counterconditioning

Not only is the client able to perceive safety in the therapy session, but he or she experiences fear-diminishing emotional states in the context of the therapist's positive regard, compassion, and caring attention.

When counterconditioning was introduced in Chapter 8, the healing aspect of this phenomenon was described as the simultaneous presence of both (1) the activated distress associated with traumatic memory exposure and (2) the positive feelings engendered by a supportive, caring therapy environment. In this regard, activated negative relational cognitions (for example, "He/she doesn't like me," "He/she will hurt/abandon me," or "I'll be taken advantage of if I become vulnerable") and feelings (for example, associated fear of authority figures or intimacy) are directly—and, therefore, potentially more efficiently—contradicted by the therapist's sustained empathic attunement, visible warmth, and compassionate caring for the client. In other words, there may be something especially helpful about having fears and expectations of maltreatment in the specific context of—as C. R. Rogers (1957, 1961) described long ago—the therapist's empathy and unconditional positive regard for the client. In the language of earlier psychodynamic theory, such real-time contradiction of activated schemas and feelings may provide a *corrective emotional experience* (F. Alexander et al., 1946).

As Rogers also noted, it is important that the clinician's unconditional caring for the client be as authentic as possible. If the clinician projects a demeanor of support and acceptance, and yet, in actuality, is harboring judgmental thoughts and feelings, this discrepancy is often detected by the client who is likely to have long experience with people who misrepresent themselves as caring. For this reason, we recommend that the clinician work hard to marshal authentic positive feelings during therapy, essentially regardless of the client's perceived likeability. Among the ways that unconditional positive regard can be engaged by the therapist are (a) working with a supervisor, consultant, or one's own therapist to process countertransferential feelings associated with the therapist's relational history that produce negative reactions to the client; (b) seeking training in methodologies that specifically teach compassion skills (for example, compassion-focused therapy; Gilbert, 2009); or (c) if of interest to the clinician, engaging in spiritual or meditational activities that engender noncontingent caring toward others, including the client (Briere, 2012a; Chapter 10).

Although the juxtaposition of negative client emotions and cognitions with therapist caring and nonjudgment can be very helpful, it is also true that activated, negative relational cognitions can sometimes prevent the client from identifying and accessing these positive phenomena. Fortunately, this is rarely an all-or-none experience; in most cases, even distrustful or hypervigilant clients will slowly come to reevaluate negative relational cognitions when therapist support and validation are visibly and reliably present. As is the case for client difficulties in perceiving therapeutic safety, the incremental process of "letting in" therapeutic caring and positive regard (and, thereby, positive attachment experiences) may require considerable time in treatment.

As noted in Chapter 8, clients involved in longer-term psychotherapy may experience an even more powerful form of counterconditioning than therapist support and caring. This is often described as a sense of deeper warmth and connectedness between client and therapist: an affective state that seems to be especially supportive of trauma processing. Although this phenomenon is difficult to quantify or identify empirically, we, like others (for example, D. J. Siegel, 2007), suspect that such responses represent the activation of inborn, attachment-level emotions and cognitions.

Beginning relatively soon after the birth of a child—in the absence of intervening problems—both parent and infant typically experience very positive emotions toward one another. These feelings and their associated cognitions are likely to constitute an evolutionarily derived survival function

(Bowlby, 1982). The child seeks proximity to the parent in order to not only avoid the pain of separation, but also, we suggest, to activate biologically based positive feelings triggered by parent-child relatedness and intimacy. Similarly, the parent maintains attachment to the child because, among other reasons, separation from the child hurts, while proximity to the child produces positive emotions. This mutual desire for parent-child proximity maximizes the likelihood that the child will be fed and protected, thereby supporting the ongoing survival of the species.

Although the notion of an inborn reward system for attachment is somewhat speculative, recent research indicates that positive attachment experiences appear to activate reward system neurochemistry, involving dopamine, beta-endorphins, and oxytocin (Schore, 2003), that, in turn, may attenuate emotional distress and reactivity (Simeon et al., 2011). It is likely that these physiologic systems of reward for intimacy and connectedness are available to humans throughout their lives and can be triggered in contexts where there is sustained proximity to a caring and nurturing person. When activated in parent-child dyads, major friendships, or sexual relationships, this phenomenon is usually referred to as *love*. A similar feeling may be present when such activation occurs in nurturing, longer-term psychotherapy—something that psychoanalysts consider a form of transference and that we will refer to, for lack of a better phrase, as *attachment activation*.

To the extent that attachment activation occurs during the process of ongoing psychotherapy, several outcomes are likely. First, the positive feelings and distress reduction engendered by triggered inborn attachment responses are likely to be especially effective in counterconditioning negative thoughts and feelings associated with previous traumatic experiences, as described in Chapter 8. Second, attachment activation may produce other kinds of child-parent thoughts, feelings, and behaviors in the client—responses that must be monitored carefully for their impacts on treatment. For example, the client may become more dependent and "childlike" as the therapeutic relationship continues and deepens. He or she may begin to request more contact with the therapist, make more phone calls to him or her, and in other ways seek greater proximity. Third, those clients whose early attachment experiences were especially insecure or otherwise problematic may find that the therapeutic relationship becomes a powerful trigger for reliving of these early relational traumas.

In some cases, this type of transformation may appear problematic, as the client "regresses" to a more basic level of relational functioning with the therapist. However, it may be helpful for the therapist to understand this as attachment-level reliving, in the same way as emotionally processing an assault in the session is reliving. As described earlier, the goal is to work within the therapeutic window—providing sufficient relational contact, support, and positive regard that the client has the opportunity to reexperience implicit childhood memories in the context of a distress-diminishing, nurturing state. At the same time, however, the clinician must not provide so much quasi-parental support that early trauma-related distress is too strongly activated or the client's dependency needs are reinforced in a way that is detrimental to growth. The latter is probably best prevented by the therapist's continuous examination of his or her own needs to protect and/or rescue the client. In addition, obviously, the possible emergence of attachment-level feelings in the therapist requires special vigilance to the possibility of inappropriate sexualization or romanticization of the client, or exploitation of the client to meet the therapist's unmet attachment (including parenting) needs (Chu, 2011; Herman, 1992b). Any such countertransference (referred to as *counteractivation* in the self-trauma model), if acted upon, both destroys disparity (that is, eliminates safety) and reinforces or augments trauma-related CERs and cognitions.

Desensitization

The client's repeated exposure to relational trauma memories, triggered by his or her relationship with the therapist, in combination with the reliable nonreinforcement and counterconditioning of his or her negative expectation and feelings by the therapeutic relationship, leads to a disruption of the learned connection between relatedness and danger.

As described in Chapter 8, the process of exposure, activation, disparity, and counterconditioning, when repeated sufficiently in the context of the therapeutic window, often leads to the desensitization of trauma memories. This probably involves a series of processes, including (1) extinction of nonreinforced emotional responses (for example, CERs), via disparity; (2) counterconditioning effects, involving some form of "overwriting" the association between memory and emotional pain with new connections between memory and more positive feelings (for example, those associated with therapist support and caring); and (3) an alteration in the capacity of relational stimuli to trigger trauma memories (that is, insight or new information that changes the client's interpretation of interpersonal events). Regarding the last point, positive therapeutic experiences may change the ability of relationships or interpersonal intimacy to automatically trigger early abuse memories, since relationship, per se, is no longer perceived as necessarily dangerous and therefore is less reminiscent of childhood abuse or neglect.

However this occurs, the overall effect of the progressive activation and processing of implicit relational memories and their cognitive and emotional associations is to change the client's reaction to his or her interpersonal world. Successful therapy, in this regard, means that the client is more able to enter into and sustain positive interpersonal relationships, because connection with others no longer triggers the same levels of fear, anger, distrust, and negative or avoidant behaviors. As a result, the client's interpersonal life can become more fulfilling and less chaotic—a source of support rather than of continuing stress or pain.

Suggested Reading

Allen, J. (2001). *Traumatic relationships and serious mental disorder.* Chichester, UK: Wiley.

Courtois, C. A. (2010). *Healing the incest wound: Adult survivors in therapy* (2nd ed.). New York, NY: Norton.

Courtois, C. A., & Ford, J. D. (Eds.). (2009). *Treating complex traumatic stress disorders: An evidence-based guide.* New York, NY: Guilford.

Linehan, M. M. (1993). *Cognitive-behavioral treatment of borderline personality disorder.* New York, NY: Guilford.

McCann, I. L., & Pearlman, L. A. (1990). *Psychological trauma and the adult survivor: Theory, therapy, and transformation.* New York, NY: Brunner/Mazel.

Pearlman, L. A., & Courtois, C. A. (2005). Clinical application of the attachment framework: Relational treatment of complex trauma. *Journal of Traumatic Stress, 18,* 449–459.

Rholes, W. S., & Simpson, J. A. (Eds.). (2004). *Adult attachment: Theory, research, and clinical implications.* New York, NY: Guilford.

Solomon, M. F., & Siegel, D. (2003). *Healing trauma: Attachment, mind, body, and brain.* New York, NY: Norton.

10 Mindfulness in Trauma Treatment

Meditation and mindfulness have been described at various points in this book as potentially helpful for trauma survivors. We explore this component more directly in this chapter, outlining the research, goals, and methodology of mindfulness-relevant trauma treatment. Most intriguing is the possibility that such interventions do not just duplicate the effects of standard therapy, but they also provide "new"[1] or incremental technologies and perspectives that are especially suited to those who have had adverse experiences.

A rapidly growing number of researchers and clinicians have come to integrate mindfulness approaches into their therapies, both cognitive-behavioral (for example, Hayes, Follette, & Linehan, 2004; Segal, Williams, & Teasdale, 2002) and psychodynamic (for example, Bobrow, 2010; M. Epstein, 2008). In fact, even when mindfulness-based interventions are not specifically employed, various other aspects of Buddhist psychology or practice (for example, compassion, metacognitive awareness, and appreciation of dependent origination, each discussed in this chapter) can be helpful in work with traumatized people (Germer & Siegel, 2012).

What Is Mindfulness?

Mindfulness can be defined as the capacity to maintain awareness of—and openness to—current experience, including internal mental states and impinging aspects of the external world, without judgment and with acceptance (for a range of definitions, see Bishop et al., 2004; Germer, 2005; Kabat-Zinn, 2003; D. J. Siegel, 2007). The ability to attend to the present moment and view oneself and the world nonjudgmentally—as opposed to being preoccupied with (and affected by) negative aspects of the past, or worry about the future—is thought to decrease psychological suffering

---

[1]Constructs such as mindfulness and nonegocentric compassion are thousands of years old, most associated with Buddhism, but also found in Christianity, Judaism, and other contemplative traditions.

(Kabat-Zinn, 2003) as well as, we will suggest, allow certain helpful psychological processes to occur.

In Buddhism, mindfulness is one of a variety of activities whose ultimate purpose is to increase existential insight, reduce suffering associated with unnecessary attachments, and, ultimately, provide spiritual enlightenment. Although not without controversy in the Buddhist community (see, for example, Kearney, n.d.; Wallace, 2006), the last several decades have witnessed a more secular application of mindfulness: as a component of psychological treatment to reduce psychological symptoms and problems (Baer, 2003; Hofmann et al., 2010). As we will see, mindfulness-based clinical interventions have been shown in research studies to be helpful for a wide range of psychological issues and complaints. Mindfulness is more than psychotechnology, however; we encourage the reader to view the therapeutic applications of mindfulness as a relatively small and excised part of the much broader domain of Buddhist psychology, which, we believe, can offer rich existential lessons and insights for traumatized and nontraumatized people alike.

An important component of mindfulness is the notion of acceptance, which involves acknowledgment of and openness to current experience of oneself and of one's situation, without defining it as "good" or "bad." In an online interview (Goldstein, 2009), Brach described this as "an honest acknowledgment of what is going on inside you, and a courageous willingness to be with life in the present moment, just as it is" (para. 10). Similarly, Germer (2009) refers to this process as "a conscious choice to experience our sensations, feelings, and thoughts, just as they are, moment to moment" (p. 32).

In his discussion of acceptance, Steven Hayes, the originator of Acceptance and Commitment Therapy (ACT; Hayes, Strosahl, & Wilson, 2011), suggests that a major basis of human suffering is the attempt to avoid or control unwanted thoughts and feelings ("experiential avoidance"), whereas mindful acceptance involves an active attempt to embrace one's self and one's experience, including unwanted states, in the here-and-now, without judgment. As evidenced by the success of ACT in the treatment of a range of symptoms and disorders (see reviews by Hayes, Luoma, Bond, Masuda, & Lillis, 2006; Ruiz, 2010), the acceptance component of mindfulness may be important, above and beyond the development of attention and awareness skills also found in mindfulness training models. The implicit contradiction involved in embracing acceptance as a way to change one's thoughts or feelings was articulated in another context, long ago, by Carl Rogers (1961), who said, "The curious paradox is that when I accept myself just as I am, then I can change" (p. 17).

The first part of this chapter describes the applications of mindfulness to psychological distress from a science perspective, summarizing research on empirically evaluated mindfulness-based treatments. The second part attempts to apply those aspects of mindfulness most relevant to trauma as well as some of the existential/philosophical lessons of Buddhist psychology.

Research

Empirically based, structured mindfulness interventions have been shown to significantly reduce a variety of psychological symptoms and disorders, including many associated with trauma exposure:

- Anxiety and panic
- Depression, or prevention of relapse into depression
- Substance abuse
- Disordered eating
- Attention deficit disorder
- Self-injurious behavior
- Aggression
- Low self-esteem and other cognitive distortions
- Chronic pain
- The psychological effects of cancer and other life-threatening medical conditions
- Symptoms of fibromyalgia
- Chronic affect dysregulation
- Borderline personality disorder
- Aspects of bipolar affective disorder

(See the following reviews or meta-analyses of studies on the clinical efficacy of mindfulness for these and other difficulties: Baer, 2003; Coelho, Canter, & Ernst, 2007; Grossman, Neimann, Schmidt, & Walach, 2004; Hayes et al., 2006; Hofmann et al., 2010; Lynch, Trost, Salsman, & Linehan, 2007.)

Current Mindfulness-Based Therapies

A number of different empirically validated mindfulness interventions have been developed over the last several decades, all of which are relevant to trauma-related distress. These include *Mindfulness-Based Stress Reduction* (MBSR; Kabat-Zinn, 1982), *Mindfulness-Based Cognitive Therapy* (MBCT; Segal et al., 2002), *Mindfulness-Based Relapse Prevention* (MBRP; Bowen et al., 2011; Marlatt & Gordon, 1985), *ACT* (Hayes et al., 2011), and *Dialectical Behavior Therapy* (DBT; Linehan, 1993a). Two of the most popular of these, MBSR and MBCT, are described below as examples of how mindfulness can be taught to clients with good effect.

MBSR

Developed at the University of Massachusetts Medical Center by Jon Kabat-Zinn, PhD, MBSR is the best known and most commonly employed mindfulness intervention in the West. It typically involves eight weekly group sessions, each lasting approximately two and a half hours, as well as one day-long session during the sixth week. In addition to homework assignments, participants are asked to meditate 6 days a week for 45 minutes each day. CDs and books on MBSR-related topics are also often employed. A central component of MBSR is instruction on how to do mindfulness meditation, including (a) specific sitting and lying positions, (b) focusing one's attention on a single target (for example, the breath, or sensations in the body), and (c) when, inevitably, the mind is distracted by emergent thoughts, emotions, or sensations, noting these intrusions in a nonjudgmental way and then returning to the target of attention. In a related activity, the *body scan*, participants are led through a guided exploration of sensations arising from the body, starting at the feet and eventually ending at the head. Other exercises include gentle stretching and Hatha yoga positions, and teaching and group discussions on mindfulness, meditation, and mind-related contributions to stress. MBSR has been shown to be effective in many studies of chronic pain and other health conditions, as well as anxiety, depression, sleep disturbance, binge eating, and overall psychological distress (see reviews by Baer, 2003; Grossman, et al., 2004).

MBCT

MBCT is an adaptation of MBSR, specifically targeted to preventing relapse in individuals with a past history of major depressive episodes, although now being applied to other domains as well, including anxiety (for example, Evans et al., 2008; Semple & Lee, 2011). This intervention typically involves eight 2-hour sessions and teaches many of the same skills as MBSR, such as mindful, nonjudgmental attention to thoughts, feelings, and sensations, and the development of meditation skills. However, MBCT focuses to a much greater extent on participants' thought processes, based on the well-established fact that cognitive distortions and negative preoccupations may become self-perpetuating and contribute significantly to the development of depression (Beck, 1995). Participants are especially taught to develop a "decentered" or "metacognitive" perspective on their thoughts, whereby negative cognitions or depressive thinking patterns are recognized as merely thoughts—not necessarily as evidence of the true state of reality. When they occur, such cognitive intrusions (for example, "I am a bad person," "things are hopeless," or "I can't do this") are not suppressed, but rather they are noted dispassionately and considered mindfully—that is, as emergent processes of the mind that inevitably come and go, but that do not have intrinsic meaning or truth. Typically prescribed for individuals who have had at least three bouts of major depression in the past, MBCT has been shown to be helpful in preventing or reducing the severity of future depressive episodes in many studies (see Piet & Hougaard, 2011). Although MBCT was developed to prevent depression relapse, it also appears to be helpful in the treatment of ongoing depression as well (Hofmann et al., 2010).

Applications to Traumatized Individuals

Surprisingly, despite considerable discussion in the literature regarding applications of mindfulness in the treatment of PTSD (for example, Cloitre et al., 2011; Follette, Palm, & Hall, 2004; Germer, 2005; Orsillo & Batten, 2005; Vujanovic, Niles, Pietrefesa, Schmertz, & Potter, 2011; Wagner & Linehan, 2006; Walser & Westrup, 2007), there are relatively few empirical studies of mindfulness interventions for trauma survivors (Follette & Vijay, 2009). It is not clear why this is true, although possibilities include (a) the notion that trauma and PTSD are somehow more severe clinical presentations, such that current mindfulness-based treatment models might be overwhelming to clients, or (b) the dominance of classic cognitive-behavioral approaches to PTSD, such that mindfulness researchers have avoided this area.

The first concern has some circumscribed merit. As described in Chapter 2, those with severe trauma-related difficulties may suffer from significant intrusive symptomatology, comorbidity, and reduced affect regulation capacities, and are sometimes involved in problematic avoidance activities (for example, substance abuse and suicidality). These issues and problems mean that some traumatized people are more easily overwhelmed than others, and possibly more vulnerable to interventions that increase access to negative internal states. For this reason, we outline possible contraindications for mindfulness-based interventions for traumatized people later in this chapter. This issue is not restricted to mindfulness, however; asking anyone who is in significant psychological pain to be more aware of their feelings, thoughts, and memories is asking a lot—whether in the context of exposure therapy, psychoanalysis, or mindfulness-based treatment.

The second possibility, that cognitive-behavioral therapy for trauma-related symptoms somehow precludes the use of mindfulness-based components, is no longer a compelling argument. Various writers describe a "third wave" of cognitive-behavioral theories and therapies, involving the explicit compatibility of mindfulness with CBT (for example, Hayes, 2004; Hayes, Follette, & Linehan, 2004). Further, as we describe later in this chapter, some of the primary active ingredients of mindfulness are seemingly cognitive-behavioral in nature, involving, for example, exposure, cognitive restructuring, and affect regulation training.

Despite such research impediments, at least one mindfulness-based treatment, DBT, has a long track record of success with client populations in which trauma is overrepresented, especially borderline personality disorder (Kliem, Kröger, & Kosfelder, 2010; Öst, 2008), and several research-clinicians have developed mindfulness interventions for child abuse survivors (Kimbrough et al., 2010; Smith, 2009; Steil, Dyer, Priebe, Kleindienst, & Bohus, 2011). Further, the empirically oriented National Center for PTSD, of the U.S. Department of Veteran Affairs, notes that "research findings show that mindfulness can help with problems and symptoms often experienced by survivors. Mindfulness could be used by itself or together with standard treatments proven effective for PTSD" (U.S. Department of Veterans Affairs, 2011, para. 9). We anticipate that applications of mindfulness training to trauma will increase substantially in the future as the power of such interventions become more obvious.

Mindfulness and Trauma Therapy

Although the mindfulness-based interventions described above have been shown to be helpful for a range of symptoms and concerns, many of which can arise from adverse experience, they have a singular limitation for classic trauma treatment: They are generally not implemented in the context of individual psychotherapy, which is a central modality in work with seriously impacted trauma survivors. In fact, empirically based mindfulness interventions, almost without exception, occur in group settings and tend to be relatively nonclinically oriented, focusing more on the development of skills (for example, mindfulness, metacognitive awareness, capacity to meditate) than on individual psychological symptoms, per se (Baer, 2003). This is entirely appropriate, and skill development groups such as MBSR or MBCT (as well as ACT and DBT) can be very helpful adjuncts in work with traumatized persons, assuming there are no obvious contraindications. At the same time, it is unlikely that a person suffering from some combination of the various issues and problems listed in Chapter 2 would have all or even most of their clinical needs addressed by mindfulness-based groups, or a meditation practice, alone (see a paper by Buddhist teacher and psychologist Jack Kornfield, n.d., that addressed this issue with prescience). Finally, because mindfulness is often best learned through meditation, which can be contraindicated for some trauma survivors, the potential impacts of the client's trauma history—including trauma symptomatology—must be taken into account and monitored on an individual basis, so that the survivor is not adversely affected.

In this context, we suggest a hybrid approach:

1. *Screening for the appropriateness of mindfulness (typically meditation) training.* Experience suggests that clients who are subject to acutely overwhelmingly intrusive flashbacks, rumination, or easily triggered trauma memories are sometimes more likely to experience distress or destabilization when meditating (Germer, 2005; D. H. Shapiro, 1992; Williams & Swales, 2004), probably because meditation and mindfulness reduce

experiential avoidance and provide greater exposure to internal experience, including memories and painful emotional states (Baer, 2003; Germer, 2005; Hayes et al., 2011; Treanor, 2011). Furthermore, as described in Chapter 2, some survivors suffer from reduced affect regulation/tolerance capacities, meaning that triggered sensory or emotional material may be more overwhelming once activated in meditation. More obviously, trauma survivors experiencing psychosis, severe depression, bipolar mania, significant suicidality, or some instances of substance dependence should typically avoid meditation-based mindfulness training until these symptoms or conditions are resolved or are under better control. Interestingly, research suggests that even these higher risk groups may sometimes gain from carefully administered mindfulness training (for example, Deckersbach et al., 2011; Langer, Cangas, Salcedo, & Fuentes, 2011; Williams & Swales, 2004). Even in such controlled circumstances, of course, the decision to employ mindfulness training must be made on a case-by-case basis. See Germer (2005) for common-sense suggestions regarding the use and adaptation of mindfulness practice with symptomatic trauma survivors.

Given these concerns, we recommend that clients considering meditation in the context of trauma issues be assessed for possible risk factors beforehand. In most cases, there will not be any psychological impediment to undergoing meditation/mindfulness training, and multiple benefits may accrue. In the remaining instances, the issue may be less that the client cannot ever attempt meditation, but rather that he or she only do so when he or she is more stable and/or less debilitated.

2. *For those who can tolerate it, and wish to learn mindfulness, referral to an MBSR or MBCT group, or a qualified meditation training center, where basic meditation skills can be learned.*[2] Mindfulness training during psychotherapy sessions can be inefficient in some cases, since such skills development usually requires a significant investment of time, during which, presumably, trauma-focused therapy would have to take a back seat. In addition, qualified meditation teachers typically have devoted years of training and experience to acquiring meditation and mindfulness skills, as well as knowledge of how to teach them to others—a background that may not be fully available to the average therapist.

In some lucky circumstances, the clinician will, in fact, be sufficiently experienced in both domains—a situation that may allow the client to receive both therapy and meditation/mindfulness training from the same source (see, for example, Brach, 2003, in press; Germer, 2005). In other contexts, the clinician may introduce elementary mediation instruction to increase relaxation or metacognitive awareness, but not spend an inordinate

---

[2]As specific mindfulness training groups for trauma survivors (for example, Kimbrough et al., 2010) become more routinely available, they will obviously be the best referral option.

amount of time doing so. In either instance, the therapist should make sure that standard trauma-focused psychotherapy is not receiving short shrift by virtue of too much attention given to the development of meditation or mindfulness skills.

Although the clinician is unlikely to be the client's primary meditation teacher, his or her personal experience with meditation nevertheless can be important. During the period when the client is simultaneously attending psychotherapy and mindfulness training, the meditation-experienced therapist can monitor and inform the process—helping the client to understand and integrate what he or she is learning and experiencing in both domains, and continuing to assess the appropriateness of mindfulness training over time.

3. *As the client gains meditation and mindfulness skills, these capacities can be called upon during trauma-focused psychotherapy.* Minimally, this may involve the following:

- The use of *settling skills* learned in meditation. The individual who is able to decrease his or her anxiety or hyperarousal through meditation (Baer, 2003; Ogden, Minton, & Pain, 2000)—for example, by attending to his or her breath, engaging the here-and-now, and occupying a less self-identified cognitive perspective—can use these skills at points when therapy involves painful memories and triggered emotional states. Similarly, mindfulness skills involving the ability to "let go" of intrusive or persistent mental content may be helpful when the client encounters upsetting thoughts, feelings, or memories that dominate his or her experience during trauma treatment.

- *Exposure,* as described in Chapter 8. Multiple writers (for example, Baer, 2003; Germer, 2005; Kabat-Zinn, 2003; Treanor, 2011) note that the decreased avoidance associated with mindfulness can expose the individual to emotionally laden memories in the context of a relatively relaxed state and a less involved, nonjudgmental, and accepting cognitive perspective—a process that is likely to desensitize and countercondition such material and decrease its power to produce distress (Briere, 2012). In the therapy session, this process (described by Zen Buddhist writers as "inviting your fears to tea" [unknown original author] or "leaning into fear" [Brach, 2003]) may be engaged by asking the client to recall traumatic events, and feel the attendant emotions, while intentionally engaged in as mindful a state as possible.

- *Metacognitive awareness,* as described in Chapter 7. During trauma therapy, the client can be invited to consider his or her trauma-related negative cognitions, feelings, and memories as "just" products of the mind that are not especially real in the current context, but rather vividly reexperienced history. Although the intent is not to convince the survivor that his or her memories are irrelevant or, worse yet, delusive, he or she may be able to gain from increased awareness that such phenomena represent the reflexive actions of the mind or brain, and are not necessarily accurate feedback on the current state of reality.

• *Reduced reactivity and need to engage in tension reduction activities or other avoidance behaviors.* The client's meditation experiences and mindfulness training may also increase his or her affect regulation capacity, by essentially changing his or her relationship to thoughts, memories, and feelings. For example, as the survivor engages metacognitive awareness during therapeutically activated trauma memories and in the outside world, there may be less need for him or her to act on (or emotionally respond to) catastrophic, trauma-related cognitions such as "he's disrespecting me," "I'm in danger," or "I deserve this." Instead of seeing these intrusions as data about reality, the survivor may come to interpret them as "old tapes" or "movies from my past," at which point their perceived acuity and overwhelming nature may diminish, requiring less emotional regulation and need for avoidance strategies.

Another option, derived from Mindfulness-Based Relapse Prevention, is "urge surfing" (Marlatt & Gordon, 1985; Bowen et al., 2011; see also Chapter 6), wherein the client learns to apply mindfulness skills to sudden, often trauma-related cravings or urges to engage in substance abuse or a tension reduction activity. Reflecting Kabat-Zinn's (1994) reminder that "you can't stop the waves, but you can learn to surf" (p. 32), the survivor is encouraged to see the need to tension-reduce as similar to riding a wave: The need starts small, builds in size, peaks (often at around 20–30 minutes), and then falls away. If the client can view triggered feelings as temporary intrusions that can be ridden like a surfboard—neither fought against nor acted upon—he or she may be able to avoid problematic or self-destructive behavior, whether taking a drink, using a drug, bingeing or purging, or engaging in self-mutilation.

4. *In the context of ongoing treatment, the therapist can encourage existential insight,* potentially changing the client's perspective on situations and events that otherwise might produce greater distress. Such insight does not involve the development of a skill, as is true for mindfulness, but rather tends to occur as the client explores basic life assumptions in conversations with the clinician or, when relevant, in the context of meditation. Among these notions are *attachment, impermanence,* and *dependent origination.*

In Buddhist psychology, *attachment* refers to "grasping" or "clinging," involving the desire to hang on to or overly invest in things that, ultimately, are impermanent.[3] *Impermanence* refers to the fact that all things are in a

---

[3]Note that this Buddhist construct does not correspond to what is described as attachment in developmental psychology. The latter refers to a positive, interactive psychobiological function in humans that allows close and intimate relationships.

state of flux, and that no thing or event lasts forever. The ubiquitous need for things that do not last, or may not even exist, is thought in Buddhism to increase human suffering. As a result, this perspective counsels against preoccupation with material possessions, wealth, or prestige, as well as rigid ideas or perceptions about oneself or others, since these things and ideas are inevitably unsustainable and unreliable, resulting in loss, disappointment, and unhappiness (Bhikkhu Bodhi, 2005).

Importantly, the proscription against undue attachment does not mean that one should not possess anything, maintain self-esteem, or enjoy various activities—only that one should not be preoccupied with them, nor deceived that such things will last indefinitely. In a similar vein, there is nothing "wrong" with (and much that is good about) loving or caring for others and wanting to be cared for; on the other hand, it is probably helpful to acknowledge and accommodate the fragility of the lives and phenomena involved, the inevitability, at some point, of loss, and the not necessarily accurate expectations and perceptions that one can bring to close relationships. In fact, the appreciation of such transience and insubstantiality, given our need for succor and connection, may easily make our relationships more precious, not less so.

Trauma is a powerful threat to attachment, since it often involves the loss of people, possessions, social status, beliefs, hopes, self-esteem, and well-being. The burn survivor may have to grapple with disfigurement or diminished functioning; the disaster victim may have lost possessions, property, and perhaps loved ones; someone who has been raped or tortured may suffer the loss of belief in personal safety, justice, or the beneficence of others; and the heart attack survivor may have to confront previously unexamined assumptions about personal immortality. Thus, there may be two sources of distress associated with any given trauma—the event itself, and the interpretations and loss that follow from it.

One of the earliest Buddhist teachings describes this binary aspect of pain and reaction to pain in the parable of a person shot with two arrows, one immediately following the other. The first arrow is the objective pain felt when encountering an adverse event, such as a trauma or loss. The second arrow is the extent to which the pain is exacerbated by needs and responses that increase suffering—especially those involving nonacceptance (Thanissaro Bhikkhu, 1997). Although the original parable (at least in translation) appears somewhat judgmental of those afflicted by the second arrow, this is, of course, the human condition—it is unlikely that any person can entirely avoid triggered states or resistance when exposed to very hurtful events. Nevertheless, to the extent that treatment can reduce this second source of suffering by (a) loosening the survivor's grip on beliefs, needs, and expectations that have been challenged or proven false and (b) redirecting his or her attention to more realistic, nourishing, and accepting ways of being, the survivor may be able to change what is possible to change—his or her perspective and understanding—as opposed to what cannot be changed—the trauma or its concrete impacts.

Finally, *dependent origination* holds that all things arise from concrete conditions and sustaining causes, which, themselves, arise from other causes and conditions (Bhikkhu Bodhi, 2005). In other words, all events occur because of the effects of previous events: No event occurs independently or in isolation. This view is in agreement with the basic principles of behavioral science—that people do things because of the influence of other things. Dependent origination and Western psychology both suggest that attributions of badness, inadequacy, or even pathology to self or others may be due to insufficient information: If we could know about the logical *why* of a given person's (or our own) problematic behavior or painful history, we would be less likely to judge or blame him, her, or ourselves (Briere, 2012b).

In the typical instance, the clinician might encourage the client to explore his or her thoughts, feelings, and reactions, and provide nondirective opportunities for the *whats* of the traumatic event: What did the client believe about him- or herself before the trauma? What hurts the most now, after the trauma has passed? What is the client resisting that is nevertheless true? What was the first arrow? What was the second? When this process occurs in the absence of pressure from the clinician to decide on one version versus another, in the context of noncontingent acceptance and support, the client's detailed analysis may lead to a slow transition (a) from a view of self as weak or pathological to that of someone who was not responsible for what happened and whose responses (then and now) may be the logical effects of traumatization, and, in some cases, (b) from a view of the perpetrator or abuser as intrinsically evil to that of someone whose behavior arose from of his or her own problematic predispositions and adverse history. Importantly, this second notion does not mean that the victim should immediately or necessarily "forgive" the perpetrator, especially to the extent that doing so implies that the survivor is not entitled to negative feelings and thoughts (Briere, 2012b). In fact, as noted at various points in this book, social or personal pressure to block or avoid painful internal states (including anger) may inhibit the normal psychological processing necessary for recovery. Yet it is likely that the unabated experience of hate and deep resentment is bad for people, whereas being less involved in such states can improve mental well-being (Dalai Lama & Goleman, 2003). From this perspective, embracing dependent origination is not necessarily in the service of redeeming the perpetrator, but, rather, is for the benefit of the survivor (Kornfield, 2008).

The Mindful Therapist

Not only can it be helpful for the trauma client to increase his or her mindfulness and existential appreciation, as described above, the clinician's level of functioning in these areas is also important. A therapist who is able to focus his or her attention on the client in an alert, accepting, and compassionate way will almost inevitably increase the quality of the therapeutic relationship (Bruce, Shapiro, Constantino, & Manber, 2010). A positive client-therapist relationship, in turn, as described in Chapter 4, appears to be the most helpful general component of treatment— often exceeding the effects of specific therapeutic interventions (M. J. Lambert & Barley, 2001; M. J. Lambert & Okishi, 1997; Martin et al., 2000). This is especially true for the trauma survivor in therapy, where a positive relationship can be both a minimal requirement and a powerful intervention (Cloitre, Stovall-McClough, Miranda, & Chemtob, 2004; Pearlman & Courtois, 2005).

Several aspects of therapist mindfulness may contribute to the positive therapeutic conditions that assist and comprise trauma therapy, as outlined in Chapter 4. These potentially include *empathic attunement, compassion, unconditional positive regard,* and *reduced transference-related reactivity.*

Because mindfulness involves the learned capacity to pay close and non-judgmental attention to internal and external phenomena, it can assist the clinician in maintaining a significant degree of attunement to the client (Germer, 2005; W. D. Morgan & Morgan, 2005; S. L. Shapiro & Carlson, 2009). In fact, D. J. Siegel (2007) suggests that mindfulness is, ultimately, a form of self-attunement that, in turn, allows the practitioner to attune to the internal experience of others. In their helpful discussion of the role of therapist mindfulness in the psychotherapeutic relationship, Bruce et al. (2010, p. 83) note that "through mindfulness practice, a psychotherapist comes to increasingly know and befriend himself or herself, fostering his or her ability to know and befriend the patient." Not only does this state increase the capacity of the therapist to understand and "diagnose" the client's ongoing experience, but it may help the client to process negative interpersonal schemas and emotional responses.

As described earlier, when attunement is continuously experienced by the client, especially if the clinician's compassion is also evident, the client may enter a form of attachment activation, engaging psychological and neurobiological systems that encourage openness and connection, reduce expectations of interpersonal danger (and, therefore, defensiveness), and increase well-being. These positive feelings, elicited in an interpersonal context that might otherwise trigger fear in the trauma survivor, tend to countercondition relational distress, producing an increased likelihood of trust and interpersonal connection (Briere, 2012a).

The therapist's mindfulness not only allows him or her to foster attunement and compassion toward the client, but it also serves as a partial protection from his or her own excessive or inappropriate reactivity during psychotherapy. By facilitating greater awareness of his or her internal processes, mindfulness helps the clinician to better understand the subjective and multidetermined nature of his or her own thoughts, feelings, memories, and reactions—a form of the metacognitive awareness described in Chapter 7. As he or she is more able to recognize specific emotional and cognitive responses to the client as potentially triggered phenomena—as opposed to arising solely from the client's clinical presentation—the therapist can place them in proper perspective before they result in significant countertransferential behaviors or, potentially, vicarious traumatization.

Developing Mindfulness in the Therapist

If clinician mindfulness and compassion has positive effects, the obvious question is how this capacity can be developed or enhanced. In general, the best answer—as for the trauma client—appears to be a regular meditation practice. Although there are many books available to the clinician that teach *about* mindfulness, regular meditation provides the structure, repetitive opportunity for skills development, and, eventually, existential insights usually necessary to meaningfully increase mindfulness. Furthermore, most authorities on the clinical application of mindfulness (for example, Kabat-Zinn, 2003; Semple & Lee, 2011; S. L. Shapiro & Carlson, 2009) require that the therapist already have a regular meditation practice before attempting to teach mindfulness to others. This does not mean, of course, that important understanding of mindfulness and compassion cannot be gained by attending lectures or workshops, or by reading books by teachers such as Batchelor (1997, 2010), Boorstein (2002), Brach (in press), Chödrön, (2000), Hahn (1987), Kornfield (2008), or Salzberg (1995); in our experience, this information can be quite helpful. However, as various teachers suggest, mindfulness, in particular, is probably best learned experientially, in the same way that reading about riding a bicycle is usually insufficient for being able to actually ride one.

In Western cultures, there are generally two related ways in which clinicians can learn to meditate and cultivate mindfulness: by attending classes or trainings at an established meditation or retreat center, or by participating in a formal MBSR or MBCT training. In either case, we recommend the clinician attend a center that provides classes or trainings with experienced, accredited teachers. In the United States, there are high-quality retreat centers on both the West and East Coasts (for example, Spirit Rock [http://www.spiritrock.org] and the Insight Meditation Society [http://www.dharma.org], respectively), as well as city-based retreat and training centers (for example, InsightLA [http://www.insightla.org] in Los Angeles and the Zen Center of New York City [http://mro.org/firelotus]). The reader is referred to http://www.dharmanet.org/listings for other training locations in North America and beyond.

Suggested Reading

Baer, R. A. (2003). Mindfulness training as a clinical intervention: A conceptual and empirical review. *Clinical Psychology: Science and Practice, 10,* 125–143.

Batchelor, S. (1997). *Buddhism without belief: A contemporary guide to awakening.* New York, NY: Riverhead Books.

Briere, J. (2012). Working with trauma: Mindfulness and compassion. In C. K. Germer & R. D. Siegel (Eds.), *Wisdom and compassion in psychotherapy* (pp. 265–279). New York, NY: Guilford.

Bruce, N., Shapiro, S. L., Constantino, M. J., & Manber, R. (2010). Psychotherapist mindfulness and the psychotherapy process. *Psychotherapy: Theory, Research, Practice, Training, 47,* 83–97.

Germer, C. J., Siegel, R. D., & Fulton, P. R. (2005). *Mindfulness and psychotherapy.* New York, NY: Guilford.

Kabat-Zinn, J. (2003). Mindfulness-based interventions in context: Past, present, and future. *Clinical Psychology: Science and Practice, 10,* 144–156.

Segal, Z. V., Williams, J. M. G., & Teasdale, J. D. (2002). *Mindfulness-based cognitive therapy for depression: A new approach to preventing relapse.* New York, NY: Guilford.

11

Treating the Effects of Acute Trauma

Janelle Jones, Heidi Ardern, John Briere, and Catherine Scott

Much of this book has been concerned with the treatment of chronic trauma-related distress. However, the needs of those who have been exposed to more recent adverse events are also important. Unfortunately, there are fewer well-validated treatment strategies for acute stress disorder (ASD), for example, than for chronic posttraumatic presentations. Most current interventions for acute traumatic stress are modifications of treatments for posttraumatic stress disorder (PTSD), based on the assumption that what is helpful when posttraumatic stress has become chronic will also be helpful for more acute responses. Although this approach is generally valid, there are significant differences in how most people experience acute, as opposed to more chronic, traumatic stress. These differences often require somewhat different intervention approaches.

This chapter reviews the literature on acute stress and provides an overview of how treatment can be modified to take into account the special needs of the acute trauma victim. In the context of PTSD, the term *acute* generally refers to symptoms emerging in the first 3 months following a traumatic event. With the addition of ASD to the diagnostic nomenclature, however, it is also used to describe reactions within the first month. In this chapter, we use the term in its broadest sense, to refer to responses that occur within the first weeks or months following trauma exposure.

Research on Acute Traumatic Stress

Since the introduction of the diagnosis of ASD to the *Diagnostic and Statistical Manual of Mental Disorders* (DSM-IV-TR; American Psychiatric Association, 2000), and following the events of September 11, 2001, there has been a groundswell of research and clinical interest in acute traumatic stress. Most published articles in this area limit their discussion to the phenomenology of ASD and risk factors associated with the development of PTSD, however, rather than focusing on intervention strategies or approaches.

Acute Symptoms and Risk for PTSD

As noted in earlier chapters, a significant proportion of acute trauma victims recover naturally from trauma exposure; their posttraumatic symptoms decrease (but do not necessarily entirely resolve) over time, even in the absence of treatment (for example, Briere & Elliott, 2000; Norris et al., 2002; Rothbaum et al., 1992). On the other hand, when initial symptoms are of sufficient severity, lasting posttraumatic stress—including PTSD—may ensue. For example, early research suggests that most trauma victims whose initial symptoms are of sufficient severity to warrant a diagnosis of ASD will, as time passes, develop PTSD (Bryant & Harvey, 2000).

Interestingly, however, recent research indicates that it may be specific PTSD symptoms, more than those of ASD, that predict chronic PTSD (see Bryant, 2011, for a systematic review). In this regard, while dissociative symptoms are required for a diagnosis of ASD, and have been associated with the later emergence of PTSD (Briere, Scott, & Weathers, 2005; Sugar & Ford, 2012), other studies suggest that they may not be as important in the development of later PTSD as are early-onset hypervigilance, sleep disturbance, irritability, and reexperiencing (Dalgleish et al., 2008; Halpern et al., 2011).

Research also suggests that, in addition to initial symptoms of posttraumatic stress, the victim's age, education, and injury severity predict later PTSD (Schonenberg, Jusyte, Hautzinger, & Badke, 2011), as do a host of additional variables. These include disrupted work and social life, reduced social support, initial panic reactions, mild traumatic brain injury, pain, and maladaptive emotional coping (Bryant et al., 2011; Schnyder, Wittman, Friedrich-Perez, Hepp, & Moergeli, 2008; Yasan, Guzel, Tamam, & Ozkan, 2009).

The high risk of lasting distress for those trauma survivors who develop ASD and/or early symptoms of PTSD—as well as the psychosocial dysfunction associated with most acute trauma presentations—underscores the potential benefit of early intervention in posttraumatic symptomatology. Unfortunately, despite ongoing research, the specific nature of these interventions, as well as their ideal timing, is not entirely clear. For example, as noted in Chapter 12, the few studies of medications used in the initial days and hours after a trauma to prevent PTSD have been equivocal. Similarly, as discussed next, the widespread use of psychological "debriefing" techniques has not been shown to be especially helpful in treating acute stress or preventing PTSD. Fortunately, a growing body of literature suggests that other approaches may be beneficial in the treatment of ASD, as well as decreasing the likelihood of later PTSD.

...s for Acute Stress

...ially developed as a way to intervene ...vors in circumstances where individual ...ible, such as during war or after terror- ...early as World War II, debriefing was ...ldiers to "purge" themselves of the dis- ...sson, McFarlane, & Rose, 2000).

...ing approach has been Critical Incident ...ed protocol developed by J. T. Mitchell ...cuers, first responders, and law enforce- ...c events. For example, after the terrorist ...was widely applied to groups of people ...saster, who lived or worked nearby, or ...ttacks but did not witness or experience

...a group setting with 10 to 20 people, ...individual debriefing. Sessions last any- ...usually conducted within a week of the ...escribe in detail their experiences of the ...raisal and interpretation of the event, and ...Group sharing is encouraged, with the intention of normalizing stress reactions as well as providing social support. Sessions end with a discussion of coping strategies and psychoeducation regarding possible future consequences of the event (J. T. Mitchell, 1983).

Despite early anecdotal reports of its effectiveness in providing education and assistance to survivors it is unclear whether CISD offers any clear benefits in reducing current distress or preventing the development of PTSD symptoms. Although Boscarino, Adams, and Figley's (2005) study of employer-sponsored crisis interventions indicated that two to three brief sessions had beneficial impacts in several areas, including PTSD, two meta-analyses (Rose, Bisson, & Wesley, 2002; van Emmerik, Kamphuis, Hulsbosch, & Emmelkamp, 2002) and a more recent randomized trial (Adler et al., 2008) indicate that single-session debriefing does not protect against the development of PTSD, nor does it hasten recovery from already-present symptoms. Non-CISD interventions—and no intervention at all—have sometimes been associated with better outcomes than CISD. In fact, in several studies, debriefing has been found to have a potentially detrimental effect, with higher rates of PTSD at long-term follow-up (Mayou, Ehlers, & Hobbs, 2000). On the other hand Adler et al. (2008) found that CISD did not cause undue distress, and was actually preferred over stress management groups by the peacekeeping soldiers to whom it was administered, despite the fact that it was no more effective.

There are several possible reasons why CISD might occasionally have deleterious effects. First, CISD in group settings often involves individuals with different trauma exposure histories, levels of distress, symptomatology, and risk for PTSD. In such situations, some individuals may be retraumatized or additionally distressed by hearing the experiences of others before they have processed and integrated their own reactions. Second, CISD is sometimes used with primary victims of trauma (for example, accident victims), a purpose for which it was not developed. A review of the CISD literature suggests that CISD is more apt to be effective in reducing PTSD risk in the populations for which it was initially intended—such as, emergency services personnel and first responders (Jacobs, Horne-Moyer, & Jones, 2004). Third, although CISD is intended to normalize and validate emotional responses, in some cases it may lead to stigmatization; for example, certain individuals may have visibly more extreme reactions to the traumatic event than others, and, as a result, perceive themselves (or are perceived by others in the group) as psychologically disturbed. Fourth, in some group settings—especially those in which members work closely together or depend upon each other for safety (such as in law enforcement)—expressing one's feelings and demonstrating fear and vulnerability may lead to group rejection and other interpersonal difficulties that decrease social support and lead to future job-related difficulties. Finally, to the extent that CISD is administered to all individuals in a unit or squad who were exposed to a potentially traumatic event, there are likely to be individuals who were not traumatized by the event and who may therefore have negative responses to being treated.

Notably, from a systematic perspective, it may be more useful to view CISD (now referred to as Critical Incident Stress Management [CISM]); as part of a larger, policy-driven prevention program, as opposed to a treatment. However, given the relative lack of information, to date, on the actual preventative utility of CISD/CISM, this suggestion awaits further research.

Proximity, Immediacy, and Expectancy

Another form of debriefing—Proximity, Immediacy, and Expectancy (PIE, also referred to as Frontline Treatment; Ritchie, Watson, & Friedman, 2006)—is used in military settings, with the goal of returning injured soldiers to the front lines of war. PIE emphasizes the need to intervene with injured survivors as close to the front lines as possible (proximity), as promptly as possible (immediacy), and with the expectation of recovery upon return to the military unit (expectancy; E. Jones & Wessely, 2003; Z. Solomon & Benbenishty, 1986). This intervention also includes attention to basic needs and medical care, along with the opportunity for emotional ventilation and expression. The PIE model was used with Israeli soldiers in the 1982 Lebanon War, with some apparent short-term and long-term success (Z. Solomon & Benbenishty, 1986; Z. Solomon, Shklar, Mikulincer, 2005). A more recent study by Potter, Baker, Sanders, and Peterson (2009) also provided some evidence for the effectiveness of the PIES (the additional S refers to simplicity) model in treating stress reactions during deployment.

Regardless of its possible efficacy, the concept of return to duty, which implies a return to the situation and circumstances of the original trauma—as well as to the possibility of further trauma exposure—is somewhat controversial. In the Vietnam War, for example, rapid return to duty was not associated with better mental health outcomes (Shalev, 2002). For some individuals, particularly those who are less traumatized, who have a more resilient underlying biology, or who are otherwise at low risk for posttraumatic symptomatology, it may be true that immediate reexposure hastens psychological recovery. However, for those who are overwhelmed by events, who lack sufficient affect regulation skills, or who have a biological vulnerability to stress, such reexposure may in fact be retraumatizing and harmful. The reader is referred to E. Jones and Wessely (2003) for a detailed and, ultimately, negative review of PIE in combat environments, including the suggestion that early estimates of its effectiveness were significantly overstated.

Other Acute Interventions

Defusing

Another, less common form of acute trauma intervention is referred to as "defusing." Defusing is a brief (typically 10–30 minutes) "conversational" intervention, intended to provide support, reassurance, and information to trauma-exposed individuals in informal contexts (Ritchie et al., 2006; Young, Ford, Ruzek, Friedman, & Gusman, 1998). Although little research data are available on this approach, one study of Swedish peacekeepers in Bosnia found that, in combination with peer support, defusing was associated with greater postservice mental health (Larsson, Michel, & Lundin, 2000). This improvement did not occur, however, for those with the worst preservice psychological functioning. Although the results of this study are encouraging, further research is required to evaluate the efficacy of defusing, especially independent of the effects of peer support.

Psychological First Aid

Psychological First Aid (PFA) was developed by the Terrorism Disaster Branch of the National Child Traumatic Stress Network and the National Center for PTSD. The *PFA Field Operations Manual, 2nd Edition*—a working document published in response to the need for written materials for those providing assistance after Hurricane Katrina in the Gulf of Mexico region—can be downloaded from http://www.nctsnet.org/content/psychological-first-aid. In contrast to debriefing techniques and defusing,

PFA is not a specific therapeutic intervention. Instead, it outlines a modular framework for mental health professionals who provide individualized assistance to victims of natural disasters, terrorism, and other mass traumas.

PFA can be delivered in the field in diverse settings (such as shelters, hospitals, and mobile response units) and can be used with children, adolescents, and adults. Although modular, it is intended to be flexible, and the different components can be tailored to fit the specific needs of the individuals involved. The main goals of the intervention are to decrease the initial distress associated with exposure to trauma and to improve longer-term adaptive functioning.

The model emphasizes a nonintrusive, compassionate attitude on the part of clinicians. Notably, PFA discourages trauma debriefing in any form. Clinicians are encouraged to allow traumatized individuals to talk about their experiences as little or as much as they wish, but never to push for information or processing. The core components of PFA focus on giving practical assistance with immediate needs, providing safety and comfort, and establishing connections with primary support networks and social resources. Additionally, the operations manual provides a variety of resources and handouts for several specialized populations, such as homeless populations.

Cognitive-Behavioral Interventions

Generally in contrast to the approaches outlined previously, there is empirical evidence from several trials that a course of cognitive-behavioral therapy (CBT) in the weeks following a trauma can reduce the likelihood of subsequent PTSD—immediately posttreatment, at 5 months, 6 months, 9 months, and in one study, at 4 years posttrauma (Bryant, Moulds, & Nixon, 2003; Bryant, Sackville, Dang, Moulds, & Guthrie, 1999; Echeburúa, De Corral, Sarasua, & Zubizarreta, 1996; Foa, Hearst-Ikeda, & Perry, 1995; Roberts, Kitchiner, Kenardy, & Bisson, 2010; Shalev et al., 2012).

The first investigations of CBT for acute trauma survivors were conducted before the introduction of ASD as a diagnosis and, as a result, included individuals who met symptomatic criteria for PTSD soon after trauma exposure. Initial results were not especially encouraging; interventions involving psychoeducation, anxiety management, cognitive techniques, and therapeutic exposure generally did not result in major, sustained symptom reduction relative to controls (Bryant & Harvey, 2000). However, many of these studies were limited by small sample sizes and widely varying degrees of impairment and symptomatology.

Later studies of CBT have shown more promise. In the first of two studies, Bryant et al. (1998) provided victims of motor vehicle or industrial accidents with five sessions of psychoeducation, anxiety management, prolonged exposure, *in vivo* exposure, and cognitive therapy. A control group received supportive counseling. Immediately posttreatment, as well as 6 months later, a significantly lower percentage of those who received CBT met PTSD diagnostic criteria as compared to controls. Bryant et al. (1999) next studied victims of more varied nonsexual traumas, who received cognitive and behavioral therapy, or supportive counseling. A similar pattern emerged, with a lower percentage of those who received prolonged exposure and cognitive interventions meeting PTSD criteria as compared to those receiving supportive treatment. Again, a significant difference remained between the two groups at a 6-month follow-up. However, 20 percent of the treatment group dropped out of the study, and the dropouts were noted to have more severe ASD than therapy completers. Four years later, Bryant et al. (2003) reevaluated 41 of the participants from both of these studies and found that those who received supportive counseling were three times more likely to meet criteria for PTSD than those receiving CBT; they also reported more intense and frequent posttraumatic symptoms overall. In a similar study, Ehlers et al. (2003) compared up to 12 sessions of CBT, use of a self-help booklet, and repeated clinician assessment in recent survivors of motor vehicle accidents who met criteria for PTSD. At 6 months follow-up, 11 percent of those who received CBT met criteria for PTSD, compared to 61 percent of the self-help group and 55 percent of those who received repeated assessments.

Two recent reviews also support the effectiveness of CBT interventions with acute stress symptoms. In a comprehensive meta-analysis of CBT for anxiety disorders, Hofmann and Smits (2008) found a strong effect size for the treatment of acute stress disorder utilizing CBT strategies, compared to other anxiety disorders. Similarly, a systematic review by Roberts et al. (2010) of the effectiveness of early psychological interventions in treating acute stress symptoms found that brief, trauma-focused CBT was more effective than waiting list interventions and supportive counseling; these effects were maintained 6 months later.

Finally, a clinical trial conducted by Shalev et al. (2011) has taken psychotherapy research in this domain a step further, comparing early versus delayed CBT for PTSD, as well as examining the effects of a selective serotonin reuptake inhibitor (SSRI) medication (escitalopram) in the prevention of PTSD. Participants were adult survivors of recent single-episode traumatic events, recruited via the emergency service of a large hospital in Jerusalem, and randomly assigned to one of four experimental groups: prolonged exposure treatment, cognitive treatment, treatment with SSRI versus placebo, or waiting list and subsequent delayed prolonged exposure treatment. Outcome data collected 5 months and 9 months posttreatment revealed fewer PTSD symptoms in the prolonged exposure and cognitive therapy groups, compared to the SSRI and placebo groups. At the 9-month mark, the waiting list group also demonstrated fewer PTSD symptoms than the SSRI and placebo groups. Overall, prolonged exposure and cognitive therapy were found to be equally effective in preventing PTSD over a

9-month period, and delaying prolonged exposure treatment did not affect the 9-month outcome. These data are important, suggesting that if it is not feasible to provide treatment for ASD/PTSD shortly after a traumatic event or disaster, survivors will still benefit from treatment if it is delayed, and may not be at any higher risk for developing chronic PTSD should this occur. This study also supports targeting for treatment those individuals who meet full diagnostic criteria, as opposed to partial PTSD, since the latter fared well whether or not they participated in treatment. Notably, the escitalopram group fared the worst after 9 months, with no apparent preventative effect.

Overall, this literature suggests that CBT approaches can be effective in reducing symptoms and the risk of later PTSD in at least some of those suffering from ASD. Whether this effect is specific to classic CBT or would occur with any treatment that involved careful therapeutic exposure to trauma memories is unclear. It also should be noted that the strongest studies with the largest samples have focused on survivors of motor vehicle accidents, disasters, and other noninterpersonal traumas. This makes it harder to generalize the results of such studies to the larger clinical environment, since sexual and physical interpersonal traumas are often more common in clinical caseloads than are noninterpersonal events, can cause particularly severe symptoms, and generally lead to higher rates of PTSD.

Intervening in Acute Posttraumatic Stress: An Overview

The literature reviewed above, although generally limited to the treatment of screened samples of noninterpersonal trauma survivors in specialty clinics or, in some cases, battleground environments, provides important guidance for clinicians working with the acutely traumatized—both in terms of what one should and should not do. At the same time, these studies are similar to the cognitive-behavioral literature on treating more chronic posttraumatic disturbance in that they shed less light on the actual conduct of acute trauma therapy as it occurs in (and is constrained by) general clinical practice. The originators of the most effective interventions described in this chapter are highly trained and specialized clinicians who devote much of their time to the study and treatment of acute trauma, often with relatively "pure" cases of ASD, in the context of relatively academic environments.

In contrast, most clinicians in the "real world" do not necessarily have such specialized training and often deal with clients who (1) present with multiple old and new traumas and (2) frequently suffer from a broad range of comorbid psychiatric conditions. In other words, the acute trauma survivor presenting to the average community mental health clinic is often someone who has a variety of needs—psychosocial, psychological, and sometimes physical or medical—for whom intervention ideally involves considerable assessment and carefully monitored treatment.

Given this complexity, and issues related to generalizability, the rest of this chapter is based on our clinical experience with acute trauma survivors in community mental health, emergency, and trauma clinic settings, as informed by the existing psychological literature. The suggestions we offer, therefore, represent an attempt to balance empiricism with practicality.

Fortunately, once certain preconditions are met, much of the treatment of acute trauma parallels the intervention approach described in earlier chapters for more chronic posttraumatic reactions. For example, therapy tends to involve the steps of trauma processing outlined previously, that is, exposure, activation, disparity, counterconditioning, and extinction/resolution, as well as other cognitive-behavioral components, such as psychoeducation. However, when the client is an acute trauma survivor, assessment of readiness for treatment is a considerably larger issue, and the process of therapy requires even more attention to the appropriate focus, intensity, and pace of treatment.

Immediate Assessment

The evaluation of acutely traumatized individuals follows the general principles of assessment as presented in Chapter 3. It is especially important to remember that individual responses to acute trauma can differ dramatically and that there is no single, typical response—some survivors appear to be relatively unaffected, whereas others may have extreme and dramatic responses characterized by anger, tearfulness, erratic behavior, and tension reduction activities. Even seemingly asymptomatic responses can be deceiving, however, because an expressionless exterior may reflect dissociation, numbing, and significant internal distress. As a result, a common mistake made by evaluators is to assume that all of those who appear to be "in control" or otherwise euthymic soon after a trauma are necessarily coping well.

At the same time, however, the avoidant trauma survivor should not be forced or coerced into treatment, regardless of his or her inferred needs. High levels of dissociation or cognitive avoidance soon after a trauma may signal overwhelming distress and/or reduced affect regulation capacities. As noted in other chapters, too much (or sometimes any) exposure to traumatic memory in such cases may "overshoot the window" and retraumatize.

In general, we recommend that clinicians let acutely traumatized individuals talk as little or as much as they wish to during the assessment process. Pushing for details about the trauma, or encouraging victims to talk when they are reluctant to do so, should be avoided when possible. Obviously, however, certain issues are a critical part of assessment in the acute phase and may require some potentially intrusive questioning. The goal is to find a balance between providing gentle support while eliciting necessary information in a nonthreatening manner.

Critical issues to be assessed initially are among those described in Chapter 3:

- *Physical safety.* Is there injury requiring medical attention? Does the individual have adequate access to shelter, clothing, and food? Does the victim of rape or domestic violence have a safe place to go, where he or she cannot be found by the perpetrator?

- *Suicidality.* Has the acute experience of personal loss, overwhelming shame, betrayal by an attachment figure, massively reduced functioning, or physical disfiguration resulted in suicidal thoughts and impulses? Is there a suicide plan? Are there methods (for example, pills, knives, guns) easily available? This is particularly pertinent in light of a recent study showing that individuals with acute stress reactions have a much higher rate of completed suicides (10 times higher than those who do not exhibit such reactions; Gradus et al., 2010). This risk is greatly increased by comorbid substance abuse or depressive symptoms.

- *Homicidality/potential for violence.* Has the trauma increased the likelihood of aggressive behavior, that is, in the service of revenge or punishment? Does the victim have access to a gun or other weapon? Is he or she making a credible threat? Does he or she have a history of violent behavior?

- *Psychosis.* Has the trauma resulted in psychotic symptoms? If so, do these symptoms interfere with the client's access to resources by impairing cognitive capacities and goal directedness? Do the symptoms place the individual at immediate risk for additional harm by impairing his or her judgment or understanding?

- *Other psychological debilitation.* Is the victim experiencing severe anxiety, depression, or dissociation, such that the client's ability to behave in an appropriate, goal-directed manner is impaired? Is he or she overwhelmed or dramatically destabilized, by either extreme emotional distress or highly intrusive or debilitating posttraumatic stress symptoms?

- *Cognitive symptoms.* Is there evidence of deficits in attention, memory, and/or executive functioning? Such deficits, related to dysregulated fronto-temporal brain functioning, have been found in individuals with acute PTSD (LaGarde, Doyon, & Brunet, 2010) and may interfere with the course of treatment.

- *Family or other sources of social support.* Are there relational or social resources available to the survivor that he or she can access in the acute aftermath of the trauma?

- *Trauma status.* Is the trauma over? The clinician may assume that a given trauma is now in the past and thus is not a continuing threat. Unfortunately, many forms of interpersonal violence are repetitive and ongoing, resulting in both continuing danger to the victim and survival responses that may make psychotherapy difficult. Immediate assessment questions should include the following:

- Does the perpetrator still have physical access to the victim?
- Is the victim emotionally connected to the assailant in a way that will allow the assailant continuing access to him or her?
- If the perpetrator was arrested, was he or she incarcerated? If incarcerated, how long will he or she be imprisoned? Does the perpetrator have access to outside contacts who could still harm the victim?

Referral

Based on answers to these questions, immediate intervention may or may not be appropriate. When it is indicated, in many cases the clinician's first function is that of referral agent. If there are signs of significant psychological, medical, or psychosocial difficulties, the clinician will typically act on assessment by triaging to appropriate resources. For example:

- Injured or otherwise medically ill trauma victims should be referred for immediate medical attention or transported to the nearest emergency room.
- Those needing shelter, clothing, or food should be given information about social service agencies and/or shelters, and/or relevant caseworkers should be alerted to the clients' needs.
- Victims of rape and domestic violence should be referred to a local emergency room, crisis center, shelter, or appropriate service agency. If necessary, reports should be made to law enforcement, adult protection services, and/or child abuse agencies.
- Individuals who are psychotic or otherwise impaired by psychiatric symptoms to the extent that they cannot care for themselves, are at risk of harming themselves or others, or have become suicidal should be referred for psychiatric hospitalization.
- To the extent possible, and within the constraints of any confidentiality issues, attempts should be made to contact family and friends who may be able to assist the traumatized individual.

Treatment

Although some form of referral is often indicated for symptomatic individuals who have been exposed to acute trauma, the need for formal psychological treatment (as well as the client's perception of this need) varies from person to person. The reasons for this include the following:

- The time frame may not support psychological interventions. The first days, and sometimes weeks, after a traumatic event often involve emotional responses and symptoms that spontaneously resolve after a period of cognitive adjustment and consolidation—a process that can be interrupted or diverted by ill-timed psychological treatment (Bisson, 2003).

• As noted earlier, a significant number of people who undergo a potentially traumatic event are not, in fact, traumatized by the event; they may experience few if any lasting posttraumatic symptoms and thus probably should not be treated.

• For victims of more severe traumas, when physical injury is involved, medical attention takes priority over mental health evaluation and intervention.

• Beyond medical treatment, adequate shelter, clothing, and food are usually the first priority for survivors of floods, earthquakes, fires, and other disasters (National Institute for Mental Health, 2002). For many victims of rape or domestic violence, a major concern may be finding a place to stay that is safe from the perpetrator. In such situations, when physical needs and safety are paramount, psychological treatment is often not an immediate focus (Briere & Jordan, 2004). To the extent that it is provided before (or instead of) these more immediate interventions, in fact, early psychotherapy may even be detrimental.

In the context of acute trauma, very early treatment may seem out of place, intrusive, and even anti-survival to the extent that it distracts from more immediate concerns. After the terrorist attacks of September 11, 2001, for example, anecdotal reports suggested that the services most immediately appreciated by victims and their families were assistance in locating other family members or victims, concrete advice, referral to social services, emotional encouragement, and, in some cases, the human contact and warmth associated with donuts, coffee, blankets, and support at the disaster site. In contrast, however, there were a few complaints that clinicians insisted survivors discuss and process traumatic material, despite protestations of not needing or wanting clinical intervention. This latter group tended to characterize the effects of such treatment more negatively. As care providers, it is important that we not be too rigidly attached to providing "clinical" services to acutely traumatized individuals—there are times when the most important thing we can offer is basic human contact, emotional support, and connection with others.

In some cases, requests for mental health treatment do not come from the victim, but, instead, from family members, clergy, or relief workers. Such referral for clinical intervention can be critically important when the victim is unable or unwilling to seek out needed medical or psychological attention on his or her own. For example, intervention is clearly indicated when the victim is psychotic, suicidal, or otherwise at risk for immediate harm. In less extreme instances, however, trauma-exposed individuals may experience uninvited referrals and interventions as intrusive and irrelevant to their immediate concerns.

Despite these cautions, there is little question that some people are profoundly and immediately affected by traumatic events and that early psychological intervention can be helpful. In general, we suggest that formal psychological treatment for acute stress be considered if the following criteria are met:

- Assessment has indicated significant psychological impairment.
- Significant food, shelter, and medical issues are not present or are under control.
- The client indicates a desire to receive treatment.
- Clinically significant symptoms have persisted for at least 1 or 2 weeks.

Unfortunately, this list runs the risk of making things appear more cut-and-dried than they often are. Perhaps most significantly, in some cases where early intervention could be helpful, given the victim's level of impairment, the victim either denies significant symptoms or actively avoids treatment. As noted at various points in this book, a frequent aspect of posttraumatic response is some form of emotional or behavioral avoidance. The shock and numbing often associated with an overwhelming event may reduce the victim's access to (and therefore description of) his or her internal state. In some cases, the survivor may feel so overwhelmed by negative feelings that he or she understandably avoids conversations (for example, symptom disclosure) and activities (for example, treatment) that might activate the symptoms of ASD described in Chapter 2. Survivors may feel embarrassed or frightened by their symptoms, or by the trauma itself, and thus may be reluctant to disclose their experiences; others may consider emotional expression or help-seeking a sign of weakness. Still others may accept social messages that they should "put their past behind them" or "just get over it," in the hopes that, if suppressed or unacknowledged, trauma symptoms will remit on their own.

Together, these various responses can result in a conundrum for the clinician: The individual appears traumatized, but denies symptoms and rejects offers of treatment. Ultimately, the decision to disclose or to participate in therapy must be the victim's alone. It is rarely wise to insist that even obviously symptomatic individuals enter psychological treatment if they do not want to be treated. On the other hand, when faced with such situations (for example, with a highly symptomatic rape victim who demands to be left alone, or an emotionally distressed police officer who fears stigmatization if he or she discloses PTSD symptoms or enters therapy), it is entirely appropriate for the clinician to gently discuss with the victim his or her current symptomatic state, the possible benefits of current or future therapy, and possible solutions to any barriers preventing him or her from seeking treatment. If it is clear that the victim is unwilling to engage in treatment, it is usually best not to push further. Instead, the clinician may consider one or more of the following:

- Offer information—either verbally or in written form—that describes possible longer-term effects of trauma exposure and outlines ways to receive help in the future.
- Make a follow-up appointment for the victim a month after the current contact, noted on a written appointment slip.
- With the victim's permission, arrange for at least one follow-up phone call from the clinician "just to see how things are going."
- With the victim's permission and signed release form, meet with one or more significant others (for example, a partner or family members) to discuss the victim's situation and the future availability of clinical services. Ideally, this is done with the victim present—in which case release forms may or may not be necessary.
- Refer the victim to a psychiatrist or other medical practitioner for evaluation for possible medication treatment. Some individuals, while concerned about possible stigma associated with psychotherapy, may be willing to consider medication to help with distressing symptoms and may see such intervention as less pathologizing. Medication management, while not affording clients the opportunity to fully process trauma, may provide empathic support as well as a safe environment in which to express concerns. It may also "open the door" to the possibility of future psychological treatment.

In some cases, victims respond to these additional prompts or supports by eventually requesting psychological assistance, albeit well after the fact. For example, the individual may keep a flyer or appointment slip—"just in case"—and then refer to it when symptoms increase or fail to remit. In other instances, unfortunately, it may be years before the trauma survivor seeks mental health services, if at all. Even in these cases, however, the clinician's demeanor, helpfulness, and initial information at the time of the trauma may be remembered and may influence later decisions to seek help.

Once it has been determined that treatment is both indicated and desired by the client, therapy generally proceeds as described in previous chapters. However, because acutely traumatized individuals are sometimes easily overwhelmed, and may rely to a greater extent on avoidance defenses, treatment must be provided with considerable attention to the principles of the self-trauma model, especially vis-à-vis the therapeutic window. Following are a series of special considerations to take into account when working with acute trauma.

Balanced Emotional Support and Compassion

As noted earlier, individuals acutely overwhelmed by traumatic events often have significant, immediate needs for human contact, support, and compassion. This need is often so strong that the less responsive clinician may be seen as uncaring or unapproachable, thereby potentially reducing his or her effectiveness. We suggest that the first moments of interaction with an acute trauma survivor be directed toward making empathic contact and communicating caring. This does not mean that the therapist should be so sympathetic that his or her attentions suggest pity, nor should expressions of concern be intrusive. The goal should be to respond in a manner that communicates appreciation of the client's traumatic situation, provides emotional acceptance and warmth, and yet remains professional and noninvasive. Survivors often remember such caring, professional helper responses, whether in the emergency room or at a disaster site, well into the future.

Active Relatedness

In classic psychotherapy, the clinician often works to communicate therapeutic neutrality and may respond to client disclosures in a relatively reflective, nondirective manner. In contrast, therapy for trauma victims, perhaps especially those acutely exposed to traumatic events, is often more active and directly interactive with the client. To paraphrase Judith Herman (1992b), there is rarely a place for therapeutic neutrality in work with victims of violence or, we suggest, others exposed to major trauma. Further, the potentially overwhelming quality of some acute posttraumatic presentations often requires that the therapist provide concrete advice, make direct referrals, and act as a strong relational figure—someone the client can temporarily rely upon. Importantly, this directive stance is rarely indicated for longer-term therapy, where the client's self-determination and self-directedness are more directly called upon and bolstered (see Chapter 9). Instead, active relatedness is typically a shorter-term response to the disorganizing and destabilizing effects of acute trauma exposure. As the client's immediate needs for structure, access to resources, and therapeutic guidance wanes, so too should the therapist's directiveness.

Greater Than Usual Accessibility

In more traditional, less emergent mental health contexts, contact boundaries are often negotiated between the client and therapist, typically limiting when the client may call or otherwise access the therapist. Such understandings discourage excessive dependency and allow the therapist to have uninterrupted periods of time when he or she is not "on duty." In acute trauma situations, however, the client may experience crises and/or intermittent episodes of overwhelming distress or grief that require more frequent contact. For this reason, professional assistance should be available to the acute trauma victim whenever necessary in the days, weeks, and early months following the trauma. In addition to providing the client with phone numbers for emergency rooms, crisis centers, or on-call or back-up clinicians, the emergency/trauma clinician should consider allowing more phone calls or impromptu sessions (ideally during normal work hours) than would be the case in regular psychotherapy. Because the client may have formed an especially strong attachment to the therapist early in the trauma recovery process, ongoing access to the clinician is often more appreciated (and often more helpful) than interventions provided by more impersonal settings, such as a crisis phone line or back-up clinician. Of course, it is almost never appropriate for even acute trauma clinicians to be available on a 24-hour basis. If the acute trauma survivor appears to require many mental health contacts within a short period of time, more intensive intervention (for example, psychiatric hospitalization) should be considered.

Case Work

Most psychotherapists and other mental health clinicians understandably prefer to focus their attention on evaluating and treating psychological disturbance rather than on other, more extratherapeutic tasks. However, as described earlier in this chapter, many acute trauma survivors require medical, social, legal, and other nonpsychological services above and beyond psychological treatment. The logistics inherent in accessing these additional services and resources are often daunting for the recently traumatized person. For example, in the context of loss, posttraumatic stress, and acute dysphoria, the client may have difficulty arranging for clinic appointments, locating appropriate social services (for example, disaster relief or crime victim support), housing or economic assistance, insurance personnel, or help with legal issues when law enforcement is (or should be) involved. Although assisting the client in such areas may seem to be beyond the therapist's job description, it is often difficult to separate case work issues from psychotherapeutic ones when the client's immediate world has been disrupted (for example, Young et al., 1998). In such situations, the clinician may need to call or write to governmental, legal, or other agencies to advocate for the client, resolve issues, or cut through red tape that the client could not resolve on his or her own.

Social Connection

The psychological effects of trauma include isolation and social disconnection—the survivor may feel that he or she has undergone experiences that cannot be fully understood or appreciated by others. In disasters and other mass trauma phenomena, there also may be *actual* disconnection—during the chaos and confusion of acute traumatic events, victims may be separated from other victims, families, and friends, and helpers may not be able to reach all victims quickly or may themselves be affected by the event (Hobfoll, Dunahoo, & Monnier, 1995; Orner, Kent, Pfefferbaum, Raphael, & Watson, 2006). For these reasons, intervention in acute trauma often

includes reconnecting survivors with relational resources (for example, helping victims locate and establish contact with family members) and broad
sources of social support (for example, involving clergy, when appropriate,
or facilitating access to community resources and groups). In many cases, in
fact, increasing social support and mobilizing community resources may be
more immediately beneficial to the acute trauma survivor than classic psychological interventions (Orner et al., 2006).

Psychoeducation

Most clinicians and researchers view psychoeducation as a critical component of treatment for acute trauma survivors. The acutely traumatized
client should be provided with information regarding self-care. When appropriate, this includes counseling against excessive behavioral avoidance of
trauma cues, such as entirely secluding oneself to avoid triggered memories
of recent interpersonal violence, or attempting to avoid all conversations,
thoughts, or reminders of a traumatic event. Similarly, the excessive use of
alcohol or recreational drugs should be discouraged in the first weeks or
months after a major trauma, since substance abuse may interfere with
trauma processing and reduce inhibitions that otherwise would impede self-
destructive behaviors, suicidality, or danger to others. The general message,
in this regard, is that excessive avoidance of trauma triggers and memories,
although entirely understandable, potentially interferes with psychological
recovery by undercutting the normal process of exposure, activation, and
processing.

In some cases, such advice supports a form of *in vivo* desensitization. For
example, a recent victim of a motor vehicle accident who drives only when
absolutely necessary might be encouraged to drive more often, or to try
driving progressively closer to the area where the accident occurred. Similarly, a self-secluding female rape survivor might be asked to consider walking to the local store with a woman friend or, if possible, attending an
activity (with a friend) where men are present but interaction with them is
limited. In such instances, the clinician ideally does more than advise—he
or she explains the underlying reasons for such advice. In our experience,
clients who are advised that they should, in a sense, avoid avoidance are
considerably more likely to try to do so if they understand the underlying
rationale for such advice.

As described in Chapter 5, the client is typically informed of the range of
symptoms and problems that may follow acute exposure to traumatic
events. This often includes the major symptoms of ASD and PTSD, as well
as other cognitive or behavioral responses that seem relevant to the client's
specific situation. Although, by definition, individuals appropriate for
trauma therapy are to some extent symptomatic, few will experience the
entire range of posttraumatic disturbance. Nevertheless, gentle, nonalarming
education about possible posttraumatic outcomes can serve to validate and

normalize what the client is already experiencing, so that he or she is less likely to feel stigmatized or mentally disordered.

Finally, the acutely traumatized client may benefit from information on how to identify potentially triggering situations and stimuli so that he or she can avoid excessive activation when it is problematic. As noted in Chapter 6, the benefit of this information is that the easily overwhelmed client will feel a greater sense of control to the extent that he or she is able to predict and, to some extent, reduce intrusive flashbacks and trauma-related emotional flooding.

Careful Attention to the Therapeutic Window

Although the relative balance between the effects of trauma memory activation and the client's level of self-capacity must be attended to in all trauma work, this issue is especially relevant to treating acute trauma survivors. Because such individuals are often in the midst of major, intrusive posttraumatic symptoms and equally powerful dysphoric states, it may be relatively easy to overshoot the therapeutic window by intervening too quickly or too evocatively. This is probably the most common error made by clinicians working with the acutely traumatized—beginning formal treatment too early and/or providing too much memory exposure and activation with a client who is acutely dysregulated and who has not yet had a chance to consolidate his or her psychological resources. Because the therapeutic window may initially be quite "small" in such cases, the clinician must approach trauma processing very carefully, and only attempt significant exposure activities when it is clear that the client has sufficient internal stability. In many cases, in fact, the various interventions outlined earlier in this chapter and elsewhere (for example, emotional support, case work, psychoeducation, and, in some instances, strengthening self-capacities) may be required before memory processing is considered. This is not to say that therapeutic exposure is contraindicated in work with acute trauma victims—recent research clearly indicates that it can be quite helpful. Instead the relevant issues are *how soon* and *how intense*. Although prolonged exposure soon after a trauma might be most efficient for those acute survivors who can tolerate it, more often the best approach is to assess for emotional stability and then to provide titrated exposure– only when indicated, only when the client is ready, and with careful attention to the therapeutic window.

Duration of Treatment

A final issue that may discriminate treatment of acute traumatic stress from treatment of more chronic posttraumatic states is that of therapy duration. In some cases, survivors of multiple traumatic events that have occurred over a number of years may require extended therapy before they show major and sustained clinical improvement. In contrast, some acute stress survivors respond to a considerably shorter treatment period. For example, Bryant and Harvey (2000) and Ehlers et al. (2003) describe empirically validated cognitive-behavioral treatments for ASD that range from 5 to 12 sessions. Although such brief therapy may not always be appropriate, for example, when treating acute survivors who have undergone especially invasive or horrific experiences (for example, torture, severe burns, or war atrocities), have substantial comorbidity, or have a history of unresolved prior traumas, the success of these researchers underscores an important point: Many acutely traumatized individuals do not require extended treatment. The reasons for this are several. First, many acute traumas will resolve, to some extent, on their own—the role of therapy in such cases may be to provide more rapid and/or complete recovery. In contrast, PTSD and other posttraumatic conditions can be more chronic, and thus represent more severe and treatment-resistant phenomena. Second, although chronic posttraumatic stress is associated with multiple risk factors (for example, inadequate affect regulation, excessive avoidance), this may not be the case for some instances of acute trauma. Finally, it is possible, although not yet entirely proven, that early, successful intervention "catches" posttraumatic symptoms before they have a chance to generalize and elaborate over time, and thus less comprehensive intervention is required.

It should be reemphasized that not all acute trauma survivors respond to shorter-term treatment. A minority, for example, some victims of mass casualty events, gang rapes, torture, or human rights abuses, are likely to require considerably more extensive clinical attention. Nevertheless, as is true for all trauma therapy, the extent of treatment required to resolve a given instance of acute stress should not be determined by the clinician's preexisting assumptions or by what kind of therapy he or she habitually provides. In many cases, a positive outcome may result from less treatment than otherwise might be anticipated.

Special Issue: Trauma Work in Acute Medical Contexts

Emergency Rooms

The first stop for many individuals, posttrauma, is the emergency room (ER). Though the primary focus of the ER visit is stabilization of critical illness or injury, the ER also is where many survivors will begin to experience psychological effects. In this regard, approximately 12 to 16 percent of survivors of traumatic injury develop ASD, while 30 to 36 percent meet diagnostic criteria for PTSD 12 months postinjury (Thombs, Fauerbach, & McCann, 2005). Despite this, ERs are, on the whole, ill equipped to identify and provide early intervention for individuals suffering from the initial symptoms of an acute stress response. This is not necessarily due to poor organization—in fact, the ER's focus on prioritizing and triaging for appropriate treatment is ideal for such a task. The challenge appears to be more related to lack of time and difficulty identifying early symptoms of traumatic stress. One survey of ER staff indicates that insufficient time to conduct assessments for PTSD is a major barrier to referring traumatized individuals for more thorough assessment and treatment (S. Lee et al., 2004). A possible approach to this issue is for ERs to be staffed with onsite mental health professionals, who can take on the role of identifying patients who may benefit from early intervention for symptoms of acute stress.

Numerous studies of the psychobiological trauma response have been conducted in ERs and provide valuable information as to strategies to detect early risk factors of ASD and/or PTSD. For example, Ehring, Ehlers, Cleare, and Glucksman (2008), in a sample of 53 accident survivors, found that lower levels of salivary cortisol, lower diastolic blood pressure, past emotional problems, and greater dissociation predict PTSD symptoms 6 months after the ER visit. Elevated heart rate in the ER has also been found to predict ASD and PTSD symptoms 6 months posttrauma (Kuhn, Blanchard, Fuse, Hickling, & Broderick, 2006).

Should an ER patient be transferred to the intensive care unit (ICU), his or her chance of developing PTSD appears to increase. The literature describes widely varying prevalence rates of PTSD (from 5 percent to 63 percent) in ICU patients, though it is likely that the higher rates are overestimates (Jackson et al., 2007). The ICU admission itself, independent of demographic factors, premorbid mental health status, and injury characteristics, may contribute significantly to the development of ASD or PTSD (O'Donnell, Creamer, Holmes, et al., 2010)—lighting, noises, high ratio of medical staff, and high potential for invasive procedures may be directly traumatic. As suggested by those studies reviewed previously in this chapter, early psychological interventions in the ICU may decrease the likelihood of later stress disorders. Peris et al., 2011), for example, found that ICU patients receiving early clinical psychologist support demonstrated significantly lower risk for PTSD as compared to a control group (21 percent vs. 57 percent).

Treatment

In general, interventions for trauma survivors in the ER should resemble what has been discussed in this chapter for acute stress, albeit adjusted for the medical emergency context. Often, this will involve the following:

- A gentle, supportive, and empathic clinical approach, wherein the patient is treated with dignity and compassion
- A clinical demeanor that does not appear frightened, repulsed, or condescending in the face of what may be very severe physical injuries, burns, blood, significant disfigurement, or possibly impending death

- Reassurance and optimism, without falsely promising unrealistic recovery
- Psychoeducation, including—if possible and appropriate—a description and likely timeline of future medical procedures as well as any appropriate information about the patient's specific injuries, illness, and/or disabilities
- Cognitive interventions (as adapted from Chapter 7), when indicated, to address guilt, shame, self-blame, or an overly catastrophized view of the immediate future
- Nonoverwhelming and appropriately timed opportunities for trauma processing, as needed and accepted by the patient, such as titrated descriptions of the traumatic event and the circumstances surrounding it
- Intervention with family members and significant others, in order to increase their capacities for support of the trauma victim—including psychoeducation, discussions of any inappropriate blaming of the patient, and opportunities to process the trauma themselves so that they will not respond to the patient in alarming or unhelpful ways
- Appropriate referrals for the patient following discharge from the hospital, potentially including outpatient individual and family/couples psychotherapy, support groups, and linkage to social services

Burn Units

According to the American Burn Association (2011), approximately 450,000 people per year receive some form of medical intervention for a burn injury, and 10 percent of these people require hospitalization. The majority of those who are hospitalized are White males, and most burn injuries take place in the home, by exposure to fire or flame. Currently, the survival rate for burn injuries is 95 percent, with many burn patients requiring several weeks or more of hospitalization and several months or more of rehabilitation.

The medical and psychosocial needs of burn patients can be extensive. As noted in Chapter 1, survivors of burn injuries face a multitude of challenges, beginning with pain management and wound treatment (often surgical in nature, for example, debridement, skin grafts, and, in some cases, amputations), and continuing through a lengthy recovery and rehabilitation process, which may include physical and occupational therapies, therapeutic exercise, psychological interventions with the patient and family members, medical devices such as pressure garments, and vocational counseling.

The most common psychiatric symptoms exhibited by burn-injured patients are posttraumatic stress and depression. In general, PTSD is thought to affect approximately one-third of both the civilian and military burn patient populations (McGhee et al., 2009), although prevalence rates vary from study to study. Several studies of burn patients suggest a clear connection between ASD and later diagnosis of PTSD (Difede et al., 2002; McKibben, Bresnick, Wiechman Askay, & Fauerbach, 2008), reinforcing the need for early intervention with those who exhibit acute symptoms of posttraumatic stress.

Clinical research has demonstrated a variety of risk factors with regard to the development and maintenance of trauma-related symptoms in burn patients. These may involve the early manifestation of certain symptoms, as described more generally in this chapter, including severe intrusive and avoidant symptoms (Difede et al., 2002; N. Gould et al., 2011), peritraumatic dissociation, and acute stress symptoms (Davydow et al., 2009), as well as the presence of a prior psychiatric and/or substance abuse history, premorbid personality factors (especially high neuroticism), burn injury characteristics (such as visibility of burn injury, disfigurement, or percentage of total body surface area burned), peritraumatic and post-admission heart rate, anxiety related to pain, avoidant coping, and blaming others for the injury (Davydow et al., 2009; Dyster-Aas, Willebrand, Wikehult, Gerdin, & Ekselius, 2008; N. Gould et al., 2011; R. T. Jones & Olendick, 2005; J. F. Lambert, Difede, & Contrada, 2004; Madianos, Papaghelis, Ioannovich, & Dafni, 2001; Suominen, Vuola, & Isometsa, 2011).

Treatment

Although medical and mental health care providers cannot change the circumstances of the burn injury, they may be able to address aspects of the treatment experience that can contribute to trauma-related symptoms (Davydow et al., 2009). Inadequate pain management is a major contributor to trauma-related symptoms in burn patients, leading them to feel vulnerable and without adequate emotional resources to manage other aspects of their recovery (Tengvall, Wickman, & Wengstrom, 2010). The degree of recalled negative care experiences during burn-related hospitalization (for example, feelings of uncertainty or powerlessness, fear, and neglect of needs) is associated with more symptoms of PTSD (Wikehult, Hedlund, Marsenic, Nyman, & Willebrand, 2008). It follows, then, that interventions geared toward information sharing and education regarding patients' injuries and prognosis, improving patients' sense of safety and control, and helping patients consider the issues of acceptance and (in some cases, eventually) forgiveness may reduce trauma-related symptoms.

As with ASD in other contexts, active processing of the burn-related event before the patient is able to stabilize and self-soothe may produce poor or even harmful results (Fauerbach et al., 2009). However, in many cases, carefully titrated exposure to burn-related memories, per the therapeutic window described in Chapter 8, may be helpful. Mental health providers who work with burn patients should be aware of the complex issues burn patients confront during the recovery and rehabilitation process, any or all of which may be addressed in psychological treatment—including grief, loss, pain, role changes, disfigurement, reduced functioning, social stigma, financial concerns, legal issues, difficulty returning to work, and overall diminished quality of life (Davydow et al., 2009; Difede, Cukor, Lee, & Yurt, 2009).

The issue of disfigurement is especially prominent for many acutely burned patients. Individuals who have serious facial burns, or severe burns to other visible areas of the body, as well as those whose burns resulted in amputation of a limb, may suffer considerable distress associated with stigma and the negative reactions of others, real or presumed. Those with severe facial scarring, reconstructed eyelids or lips, or missing or misshapen ears may have the experience of witnessing repulsion, or at least gaze aversion, by others, which can engender shame, embarrassment, or even, occasionally, self-hatred in the burn survivor.

In many cases, intervention in this area will involve helping the client to accept himself or herself as he or she is, despite a radically changed appearance—especially in terms of developing a model of self-esteem more focused on resilience, internal qualities (for example, intelligence, humor, caring, or wisdom), and/or relationships with people who are (or eventually become) less affected by superficial appearance, such as invested family members, friends, or other loved ones.

It is our experience that some clinicians, despite themselves, may reflexively reject the idea that horribly burned and disfigured people can make a reasonable adjustment to life, and even may have a chance of lasting happiness. Yet we have seen this outcome on multiple occasions. Although typically not quantified by the scientific literature, the ongoing psychological survival of severely burned people appears to be a testament to the capacity of humans to successfully integrate extremely traumatic events when conditions are right. For this reason, it is very important that the clinician not "give up" on individuals whose physical appearance or medical circumstances seem insurmountable; acceptance, accommodation, and even growth are entirely possible for many physically disfigured or very injured clients, whose recovery might otherwise be limited by therapist or institutional countertransference.

Beyond acute psychological interventions, posthospitalization follow-up or referral is especially important for the burn survivor. Burn patients who do not receive treatment for ASD and/or PTSD symptoms are more likely to struggle with physical and psychosocial functioning following discharge from the hospital (Corry, Klick, & Fauerbach, 2010). Many burn patients benefit from ongoing psychological interventions after hospital discharge, such as peer support groups and regular follow-up visits, since their return to society is likely to be marked by new challenges. Importantly, the families of burn patients may also gain from intervention, both in the early stages of their loved one's injury as well as postdischarge. This is particularly salient with regard to parents of pediatric burn patients, who may be struggling with ASD/PTSD symptoms themselves (Hall et al., 2006).

Suggested Reading

Blanchard, E. B., & Hickling, E. J. (1997). *After the crash: Assessment and treatment of motor vehicle accident survivors.* Washington, DC: American Psychological Association.

Bryant, R. A., & Harvey, A. G. (2000). *Acute stress disorder: A handbook of theory, assessment, and treatment.* Washington, DC: American Psychological Association.

National Child Traumatic Stress Network and National Center for PTSD. (2005). *Psychological First Aid: Field operations guide.* Retrieved from http://www .nctsnet.org/content/psychological-first-aid

Ritchie, E. C., Watson, P. J., & Friedman, M. J. (Eds.). (2007). *Interventions following mass violence and disasters: Strategies for mental health practice.* New York, NY: Guilford.

Shalev, A. Y. (2002). Acute stress reactions in adults. *Biological Psychiatry, 51,* 532–544.

Vasterling, J. J., Bryant, R. A., & Keane, T. M. (Eds.). (2012). *PTSD and mild traumatic brain injury.* New York, NY: Guilford.

12 Psychobiology and Psychopharmacology of Trauma

Catherine Scott, Janelle Jones, and John Briere

This chapter is intended to be useful for psychiatrists and other medical practitioners as well as for nonphysician clinicians. Of necessity, some of the material presented here is relatively technical in nature. Because this information is more medically specialized, it may seem less relevant to the needs of some non prescribing clinicians. It should be noted, however, that many trauma survivors who are in regular psychotherapy take psychiatric medications of one type or another. In this context, the nonprescribing therapist is often the professional most aware of the client's week-to-week psychological state and general physical functioning; in contrast, medical practitioners may only have a fraction of an hour—perhaps once a month or even less often—to evaluate medication effects. This ready access to the client's state may allow the pharmacologically informed therapist to detect drug side effects or emergent need for medication changes, which can then be communicated to the prescribing clinician. In other cases, severely traumatized survivors may not recieve psychiatric medication, but probably would benefit from them. Knowledge of trauma psychopharmacology can assist the nonmedical clinician in making appropriate psychiatric referrals and recommendations for such clients. Issues addressed in this chapter for the nonmedical psychotherapist include (1) the rationale for specific trauma-focused medications, (2) their primary actions on the human nervous system, (3) their major side effects, and (4) their limitations.

For medical practitioners who are interested in increasing their understanding of the practical psychopharmacology of posttraumatic stress and related psychiatric conditions, we include a detailed overview of the major trauma-relevant medications, their appropriate dosages, and their general indications and contraindications for posttraumatic symptom patterns. In this regard, the major clinical trials involving medications for posttraumatic distress are reviewed. This chapter also discusses strategies for medication management in the context of Axis I comorbidity and as an adjunct to trauma-focused psychotherapy. An in-depth discussion of the research in this area is beyond the scope of this book, however; the clinician is referred to the Suggested Reading at the end of the chapter for a more detailed review of the literature on trauma pharmacotherapy. We have also limited this chapter to the treatment of adult survivors. Trauma psychopharmacology for children and adolescents is a highly specialized area; although adolescents often respond to psychoactive medication in ways similar to adults, there are significant differences between adolescent and adult biology. The reader is referred to Donnelly, Amaya-Jackson, and March (1999), Seedat and Stein (2001), and Strawn, Keeshin, DelBello, Geracioti, and Putnam (2010) for more information on the use of medication for traumatized children and adolescents.

Before discussing psychopharmacology, we briefly review the psychobiology of posttraumatic stress, since nervous system dysregulation is the specific target of psychiatric medication. However, because research in this area is still in its infancy, we present an overview of currently proposed biological models, rather than attempting to make a definitive statement about the exact physiological substrates of posttraumatic disturbance.

The Psychobiology of Trauma

The last two decades have witnessed substantial interest in the biology of posttraumatic stress. This growing research base indicates that multiple systems and neurotransmitters are involved in posttraumatic disturbance, although some of the evidence is contradictory and sometimes difficult to interpret. There are several implications of this complexity:

1. There are multiple biological pathways to posttraumatic stress, and it is likely that no one model will suffice to describe the entire pathophysiology involved.

2. Posttraumatic stress disorder (PTSD), as it is currently described, may not represent a single disorder, but rather a collection of outcomes that vary depending on individual differences in genetics, underlying neurophysiology, stress response, and exposure to traumatic events.

3. It is unlikely that there will be one ideal medication for PTSD or other posttraumatic outcomes; rather, there will be a range of pharmacological agents that may be of assistance in treating different symptom clusters.

The Hypothalamic-Pituitary-Adrenal (HPA) Axis and the Adrenergic System

When stressed, the normal response of the body is to activate both the adrenergic and the glucocorticoid systems, releasing (among other compounds) norepinephrine and cortisol (Sherin & Nemeroff, 2011). Under healthy conditions these two systems regulate one another—cortisol appears to act as a "brake" on the adrenergic system, preventing sustained sympathetic activity. In PTSD, this balance is not maintained, and the responses of both systems become dysregulated (Raison & Miller, 2003).

The adrenergic system, also known as the sympathetic nervous system (SNS), is responsible for what is classically known as the fight-or-flight response. It is associated with maintaining arousal and attention and with the consolidation of certain types of memories. Typically, under conditions of stress or threat, the brain increases the synthesis and release of norepinephrine—primarily in the locus ceruleus and reticular activating system—to allow an appropriate response to the situation (for example, running away or fighting). When the stressor is removed, the adrenergic system returns to its usual baseline state. This return to normal levels of arousal appears to be disrupted in PTSD. Adrenergic hyperactivity—involving the release of multiple neurotransmitters and neurohormones such as acetylcholine, epinephrine, and norepinephrine, as well as increased levels of their metabolites—has been demonstrated in individuals with PTSD. Such excess and sustained activation has been associated with multiple posttraumatic symptoms, including hyperarousal, reexperiencing, dissociation, aggression, and both generalized anxiety and panic attacks. In addition, increased adrenergic activity appears to assist in the encoding of emotionally laden memories (Southwick, Bremner, et al., 1999).

The adrenal glands—the end organs of the HPA axis—release both cortisol and adrenergic compounds. The cascade that results in cortisol production begins at the hypothalamus, which secretes corticotropin releasing factor (CRF). CRF stimulates the pituitary to secrete adrenocorticotropin hormone (ACTH), which, in turn, controls the release of cortisol by the adrenals. Cortisol is a hormone with multiple functions, including regulation of immune and stress responses. It has been proposed that cortisol, along with other compounds such as neuropeptide Y (NPY), may serve to modulate the activity of the adrenergic system (Sherin & Nemeroff, 2011; Southwick, Bremner, et al., 1999). NPY is an endogenous anxiolytic that appears to act in concert with cortisol (Kask et al., 2002). At moderate or "tolerable" levels of stress, this means that blood levels of cortisol and NPY are typically high. At such levels, NPY appears to be a protective neurosteroid that confers additional resiliency, acting as a "buffer" in the brain to protect against the development of PTSD when exposed to trauma (Sah et al., 2009). However, when an individual is overwhelmed by a traumatic event, this system may be overwhelmed as well, leading to a drop in levels of cortisol and NPY. The result is a limitation on the brain's capacity to down-regulate adrenergic arousal and a vulnerability to PTSD.

In support of the above argument, decreased cortisol and NPY levels have been demonstrated in individuals living under chronically stressful conditions. Several lines of research have also demonstrated lower cortisol and NPY in individuals with PTSD (Yehuda, 2002). It may be that exposure to trauma itself helps to sensitize the HPA, resulting in some alteration of cortisol levels, whether or not an individual goes on to develop the full spectrum of PTSD symptoms (de Kloet et al., 2007). In addition, low levels of these neurochemicals after a trauma appear to be predictive of later PTSD (C. A. Morgan et al., 2001). For example, in women with a history of sexual abuse who were raped, low cortisol predicted PTSD (Resnick, Yehuda, Pitman, & Foy, 1995). However, not all studies in this area agree. For example, DeBellis et al. (1999) found elevated (as opposed to lower) cortisol in PTSD, and a few studies suggest that the relationship between cortisol and posttraumatic stress may be, at minimum, more complex than otherwise assumed (see Yehuda, 2002; Lindley, Carlson, & Benoit, 2004). Research in this area is ongoing, and current findings—although strongly suggestive—should not be considered definitive.

The HPA axis self-regulates by means of a negative feedback loop. Under "normal" circumstances, a low cortisol level would provide feedback to the hypothalamus and pituitary, resulting in higher levels of CRF and ACTH— ultimately stimulating the adrenals to secrete more cortisol and balance the system. However, in PTSD there appears to be enhanced negative feedback of the HPA axis—ultimately resulting in higher CRF without a resultant increase in cortisol (Raison & Miller, 2003). In addition, individuals with PTSD appear to hypersuppress cortisol upon dexamethasone challenge (Pfeffer, Altemus, Heo, & Jiang, 2009; Yehuda et al., 2004). These data suggest that glucocorticoid receptors may become hypersensitive in some traumatized individuals, leading to lower baseline levels of cortisol and, therefore, increased sympathetic nervous system activity. Excessive glucocorticoid sensitivity also may effect peripheral inflammatory processes and have effects on cognitive functions (Rohleder, Wolf, & Wolf, 2010).

Given this information, it has been proposed that the deficit in PTSD is one of impaired glucocorticoid signaling rather than simply a problem of too little cortisol (Raison & Miller, 2003). And because dexamethasone challenges (and adequate levels of CRF) fail to result in expected ACTH elevations in those experiencing PTSD, the trouble in the HPA system is thought to lie in the pituitary (Ströhle, Scheel, Modell, & Holsboer, 2008). Interestingly, recent research suggests that it may be helpful to give a treatment such as hydrocortisone to restore the HPA axis's ability to dampen subjective distress (M. W. Miller et al., 2011), perhaps including during exposure therapy (Suris, North, Adinoff, Powell, & Greene, 2010).

Taken together, these findings suggest that there is a neurobiological window for optimal stress response, within which various brain compounds (such as NPY and cortisol) operate to "inhibit the continued release of [norepinephrine] so that the SNS does not overshoot" (Southwick et al., 2003, p. 1). In posttraumatic stress, there appears to be a co-occurrence of increased adrenergic activity with decreased glucocorticoid (cortisol) and NPY modulation. This imbalance may lead to the rapid and powerful consolidation of emotionally laden traumatic memories, which, under conditions of ongoing adrenergic stimulation, become intrusive and overwhelming, and lead to symptoms of hyperarousal, agitation, anxiety, and dissociation. HPA-related disruption of the normal immune response, especially under conditions of chronic stress (for example, prolonged torture, childhood physical or sexual abuse), may also contribute to chronic physical complaints and susceptibility to physical illness, as reported by some trauma survivors (Ehlert, Gaab, & Heinrichs, 2001; Pace & Heim, 2011).

Other Biological Correlates of PTSD

As the above discussions indicate, the biology of trauma is highly complex, with multiple systems and circuits, which overlap and interact with each other in a variety of ways. In the coming years, we will undoubtedly learn more about this fascinating area of research.

In addition to the role of the adrenergic and glucocorticoid systems described above, there is a significant body of literature investigating other biological mechanisms in the development of PTSD, as well as neuroanatomical sequelae of HPA axis dysregulation.

PTSD has been associated with changes in serotonin levels, serotonin transporters, opioid dysregulation, and high-normal thyroid hormone levels (Friedman, 2000b), as well as altered immune functioning (Gill, Vythilingam, & Page, 2008) that may contribute to some of the pathophysiology of the illness (Pace & Heim, 2011). Low levels of gamma-Aminobutyric acid (GABA, the primary inhibitory neurotransmitter in the brain, responsible for regulating neuronal excitability) have been implicated in PTSD (Rasmussen et al., 2006; Vaiva et al., 2006). Kindling, in which repeated stress is thought to sensitize limbic neurons so that reactions are set off by stimuli that were once sub-threshold, has also been proposed as a model for the development of PTSD, especially in conditions of chronic stress such as child abuse (Weiss & Post, 1998).

An emerging body of research in neurobiology, which may explain the hippocampal changes seen in neuroimaging (described below) involves "neurogenesis"—the production of new cells within the nervous system. It appears that PTSD, as well as other anxiety and affective disorders, may be related to impaired neurogenesis in the dentate gyrus of the hippocampus. Until recently, it was thought that adult brains could not create new cells; however, in the 1990s, neurogenesis was first demonstrated in the brains of adult rodents (see, for example, Takemura & Kato, 2007). Further research has indicated that neurogenesis occurs in only two places in the mammalian brain, one of which is the hippocampus (Samuels & Hen, 2011). Neurogenesis appears to be impacted by levels of stress and is associated with learning and memory processes (Takemura & Kato, 2007). In fact, it appears that under stressful situations cortisol modulates neurogenesis, with higher levels leading to cell atrophy and lowers levels correlating with cell growth (Samuels & Hen, 2011). While most of the research in this area has been in rodent and primate models of stress and depression, recent human data are also encouraging. Boldrini et al (2009) examined on autopsy the hippocampal tissue of individuals with untreated depression, depression treated with selective serotonin reuptake inhibitors (SSRIs) or tricyclic antidepressants (TCAs), and a set of controls. They found greater numbers of dividing cells in the treated group, compared to both untreated and control subjects.

However, the effects of SSRIs may be more varied than merely increasing available serotonin or enhancing hippocampal growth, indicating an even greater complexity of the underlying biology. Serotonergic agents also have effects on the locus ceruleus, where the adrenergic cell bodies reside—a possible mechanism for SSRIs to affect the HPA. In addition, it has been suggested that one of the actions of the serotonergic agents in PTSD is to increase levels of the neurosteroid allopregnanolone, an endogenous anxiolytic. Allopregnanolone, in turn, impacts anxiety by activating GABA and thus down-regulating neural excitability (Pinna, 2010).

Findings From Neuroimaging Studies

Recent advances in neuroimaging technology allow us to view the brain as it functions *in vivo*, opening a window into how trauma affects both neuroanatomy and neurophysiology. While much of the data is limited by small sample sizes, there do appear to be some consistent findings. In general, PTSD has been associated with amygdaloid hyperactivity, smaller brain white and gray matter, smaller hippocampal volumes, and smaller anterior cingulates (Shin, Rauch, & Pitman, 2006; Villarreal & King, 2004). Accelerated brain atrophy appears to occur in patients with worsening rather than improving symptoms (Cardenas et al., 2011). Small hippocampal volume has also been found in survivors of child abuse (irrespective of PTSD diagnostic status), and the volume loss correlates with the severity of that abuse, with the severity of PTSD symptoms (Fennema-Notestine, Stein, Kennedy, Archibald, & Jernigan, 2002), and, in some cases, with memory disturbance (Tischler et al., 2006). In one study, even new onset PTSD was associated with decreased hippocampal and parahippocampal density and volume (J. Zhang et al., 2011).

A question that remains to be answered is whether smaller hippocampal volume might predate the trauma and therefore predispose an individual to develop PTSD (Gilbertson et al., 2002), or whether the volume decrease occurs as a result of the neurobiological response to a traumatic event (for example, Woon, Sood, & Hedges, 2010). To further complicate the picture, it is possible that both of these processes might occur in an overlapping fashion in some individuals (for example, Apfel et al., 2011).

Imaging also has demonstrated decreased activation of the hippocampus during verbal memory tasks in individuals with PTSD (Bremner et al., 2003), a finding that makes sense given that the hippocampus plays an important role in the consolidation of memory. Interestingly, treatment with the selective serotonin reuptake inhibitors (such as Prozac) has been shown to improve verbal memory as well as increase hippocampal volume (Villarreal & King, 2004). Similarly, researchers have found decreased recruitment of the anterior cingulate during trauma recall, an area of the brain thought to be associated with emotional responsiveness and affect regulation (Shin et al., 2001).

Interestingly, recent research indicates that, in the wake of a trauma, the dorsolateral prefrontal cortex (DLPFC) appears to increase in size, possibly compensating with increased activity to help reduce symptoms stemming from other areas of the brain. The increased thickness of the DLPFC report-edly correlates with greater symptom reduction during recovery and may return to baseline over time (Lyoo et al., 2011).

Integrating Biological Models With the Self-Trauma Model

The psychobiological models presented here are focused on nervous sys-tem pathology, as opposed to the more adaptation-oriented psychological conceptualizations described in earlier chapters. Biological theories tend to suggest that the symptoms of posttraumatic stress arise from excessive acti-vation of the sympathetic nervous system, probably in combination with dysregulation of the HPA axis and related neurohormones, such that trau-matic memories become overconsolidated, easily activated, and overwhelm-ing in their capacity to produce negative emotions. Further, the continuous activation of the sympathetic system is thought to result in sustained auto-nomic arousal and, in the presence of repeated stressors, hyper-reactivity to subsequent stimuli.

In contrast, the psychological model described in earlier chapters suggests that posttraumatic reexperiencing (for example, flashbacks and intrusive trauma-related thoughts) represents a normal psychobiological process—the mind's attempts to desensitize traumatic memory by repeatedly evoking it in the context of safety (that is, the concepts of exposure, disparity, and extinc-tion discussed in Chapter 8).

Although the integration of these two perspectives must remain specula-tive, we suggest that it is possible. We hypothesize that, as described in Chapter 8, the normal exposure/disparity/extinction process "works" only to the extent that reexperiencing phenomena (for example, intrusive thoughts and memories) do not exceed the individual's capacities to regulate and tolerate the associated painful affect. These affect regulation capacities, in turn, are likely to be partially a function of psychobiological phenomena such as the ability of the HPA axis to modulate sympathetic arousal.

Thus, it is possible that chronic PTSD and other posttraumatic responses arise when the natural exposure/extinction system is derailed—that is, when the emotional impacts of a stressor exceed the individual's existing affect regulation "window." This is perhaps especially true in those who already have a sensitive or dysregulated nervous system. In cases where reexperienc-ing appears to be effective—that is, when traumatic memories are successfully exposed and extinguished—we might expect to find less overwhelming stressors, a less "excitable" nervous system (and, therefore, more effective modulation via cortisol), higher levels of NPY, and less overall limbic sensitization.

It is interesting that both biological and psychological researchers have independently hypothesized the notion of a "window" within which optimal stress response occurs. Southwick and colleagues (2003) have suggested that "psychologically resilient individuals maintain SNS activation within a window of adaptive elevation, high enough to respond to danger but not so high as to produce incapacity, anxiety, and fear" (p. 1). As was described in detail in Chapter 8, the self-trauma model (Briere, 2002b) posits a psychological window within which individuals can experience and tolerate emotion and distress without becoming overwhelmed.

Given the preceding discussion, successful treatments for PTSD and other stress disorders would probably involve some combination or subset of the following:

1. Carefully titrated exposure to traumatic memory, so that even compromised biological and psychological systems are not overwhelmed

2. Attempts to increase emotional/stress regulation through the psychological interventions described in Chapter 6, but also, in some instances, through medications thought to stabilize the limbic system and HPA axis

3. A reduction in the overall anxiety/arousal "load" (that is, overactivity and hypersensitivity of the sympathetic nervous system) through relaxation training, meditation, or memory desensitization, as well as dampening of sympathetic activation, when indicated, through medications that treat anxiety

4. Use of medications to reduce comorbid anxiety, depression, or psychosis that otherwise add to overall distress or interfere with affect regulation

Although, as noted in this chapter, currently available medications are rarely sufficient to permanently resolve posttraumatic stress, some trauma survivors suffer from such high levels of anxiety, hyperarousal, and comorbid symptoms that psychotherapy alone is unlikely to be fully effective. As a result, successful treatment of posttraumatic states—especially in the case of severe or chronic symptoms—may sometimes involve both psychological and pharmacological interventions.

Trauma Psychopharmacology

As discussed throughout this volume, posttraumatic outcomes can be extremely complex. Similarly, tailoring treatment—whether it be psychotherapy, psychopharmacology, or a combination of the two—to a given individual's particular circumstances may be far from simple. Although the medications indicated for the treatment of PTSD and related disorders are relatively few in number, the practice of using them and encouraging compliance requires considerable knowledge and attention. It is rarely sufficient to write a prescription and tell the client to return in a month for follow-up. Specific concerns associated with using medications with trauma survivors include the following:

- *Compliance.* Trauma survivors often have a difficult time remembering to take their medications—the result of distractibility, high levels of emotional activation, and, sometimes, dissociation. This may be even more of a concern if a medication regimen requires pills at multiple time points during the day.

- *Anxiety.* Many of the antidepressant medications used to treat PTSD can increase the levels of anxiety that some individuals experience in the initial days of treatment, and in some instances can precipitate panic attacks. Trauma survivors who are highly dissociated, somatically preoccupied, and anxious, or who present with panic attacks, are likely to respond to these medications with more anxious symptoms than are other, less traumatized individuals.

- *Sedation.* Certain psychotropic medications can cause feelings of "dullness," sedation, or of "not being myself" in some individuals. Trauma survivors, in particular, may feel that these side effects impair their ability to sense and respond to danger. Paradoxically, although hypervigilance can be an extremely debilitating component of posttraumatic stress, many individuals do not want to lose the sense of control and safety that "being on edge" provides them.

- *Sleep.* Similarly, although trauma survivors frequently report disturbed and erratic sleep, they may resist taking sleep medications for fear that they will sleep through potential danger.

- *Memory processing.* Some medications, particularly the benzodiazepines (and some "street" and recreational drugs as well) may interfere with the psychological processing of traumatic memories, as described in more detail later in this chapter. As a result, the costs and benefits of using such drugs should be carefully considered when the client is undergoing psychotherapy or otherwise addressing traumatic material.

- *Substance abuse.* The use of illicit and other addictive substances is highly comorbid with posttraumatic stress and may be problematic in combination with certain medications.

- *Distrust of authority.* Many trauma survivors, especially victims of interpersonal violence or political torture, may be distrustful of authority figures, including—in some cases—therapists or physicians, and may therefore be reluctant to take prescribed medications. For example, they may fear that the clinician is trying to control them through drugs or even, in rare instances, poison them.

• *Overmedication.* The chronic and extreme distress that some trauma survivors experience may induce helplessness and frustration in the clinician, leading him or her to medicate clients more aggressively than is appropriate or to overprescribe addictive anti-anxiety medications.

Given these concerns, we make the following initial recommendations:

- Close follow-up of traumatized clients, preferably within a week of starting a new medication
- Patience regarding the client's occasional unwillingness to take medications—it may take more than one visit for him or her to develop the trust necessary to start a psychotropic regimen
- Slow dose increases to avoid side effects that may decrease compliance
- Adequate education about potential side effects, so that, if they occur, they do not surprise or alarm the client or cause him or her to prematurely discontinue medication that ultimately would be tolerable
- Gentle encouragement and support around fears of being overmedicated and therefore less responsive to danger
- Careful consideration of any potential for abuse or overdose when prescribing medications for relief of anxiety
- As always, documentation of informed consent is recommended when prescribing psychiatric medications

Psychotherapy and Psychopharmacology

Throughout this volume, we focus on the importance of processing traumatic material in the context of a supportive therapeutic relationship. In some instances, however, posttraumatic symptoms may be so overwhelming that the individual is unable to participate in therapy altogether, or becomes so anxious and distressed with even low levels of activation that therapy proceeds at a very slow pace. In other situations, comorbid psychological conditions (most commonly depression) interfere with the client's ability to participate fully in psychotherapy. In the worst case, the client may drop out of treatment after a very few sessions, often without explanation, and without returning therapist phone calls.

Psychotropic medications can be a useful adjunct to trauma-focused psychotherapy under such conditions, especially in the early phase of treatment. Appropriate pharmacological intervention can provide some initial relief of intense distress—partly via medication effects on posttraumatic symptomatology and partly via the placebo effect. Medication that improves sleep may be particularly helpful, since sleep disturbance is often one of the most debilitating symptoms of posttraumatic stress.

When some initial symptom reduction can be gained through the use of medication, clients may be more able and willing to engage in the often difficult work of trauma-focused psychotherapy. For clients who are suspicious of treatment, the experience of an initial benefit may help to improve the therapeutic alliance; for those whose negative experiences have caused them to believe there is no possibility of recovery, the demonstration of early symptom relief may provide a glimmer of hope for the future. Seen in this light, pharmacotherapy can be a "stepping stone" in the process of helping clients to recover—a way to help them both enter into and stay engaged with psychotherapy.

Overall, however, medications are rarely curative by themselves and, although helpful, may have less of an impact than psychological therapy. In the practice guidelines of the International Society for Traumatic Stress Studies (Foa, Keane, Friedman, & Cohen, 2009), where the gold standard outcome studies for both psychotherapy (Cahill, Rothbaum, Resick, & Follette, 2009) and pharmacotherapy (Friedman, Davidson, & Stein, 2009) are reviewed, the amount of symptom reduction associated with psychotherapeutic interventions was considerably larger than that found for pharmacological interventions. While there are methodological problems associated with such direct comparisons (including possible differences in symptom severity between the participants in drug and psychotherapy studies), certainly there is no evidence to support the idea that pharmacotherapy for posttraumatic stress is intrinsically more effective than psychotherapy. Nevertheless, in our experience, some individuals may "miss out" on the potential benefits of psychotherapy because their level of symptomatology means that they cannot tolerate—and therefore must avoid—even low levels of activation and distress. For these individuals, medication can be a powerful method of engaging them in psychological treatment, and thus may increase the possibility of recovery.

In the past few years, a handful of studies looking at the combination of psychotherapy and pharmacology in PTSD have shed some light on this rather complex topic. Simon et al. (2008), in a trial of paroxetine augmentation in individuals refractory to prolonged exposure therapy, found that medication was not superior to placebo in reducing residual symptoms. The authors suggest that perhaps novel treatments will be required for those patients who fail both psychotherapy and pharmacotherapy. Rothbaum et al. (2006) compared sertraline continuation treatment to prolonged exposure in a group of patients already on sertraline for 10 weeks. Interestingly, those patients who had responded well to the medication initially experienced no further benefit from either treatment. However, those who were partial medication responders had a further reduction in PTSD symptoms with the addition of psychotherapy. Van der Kolk et al. (2007) compared eye movement desensitization and reprocessing (EMDR) to fluoxetine and placebo over a period of 8 weeks. At 6-month follow up, EMDR was associated with greater reduction in symptoms in survivors of adult traumas. For child onset traumas, both treatments were only partially effective. And lastly, Shalev et al. (2012) compared prolonged exposure, cognitive therapy, medication with citalopram, and placebo in survivors of acute trauma. Results were consistent with the data reported in earlier studies: At 5-month follow up, 20 percent of the individuals who had received psychotherapeutic interventions had PTSD, compared to 60 percent of those on medication, and 58 percent of those receiving placebo. These four studies, all carried out by different investigators, with different groups of patients, confirm a remarkably consistent trend: Psychotherapy in all cases produced greater symptom reduction than did psychiatric medications.

Treatment Outcome Studies and the Limitations of Medications in Posttraumatic Stress

This chapter reviews the medications used to treat posttraumatic states, their indications and side effects, and the major clinical trials (if any) investigating their use in traumatized individuals. There are, however, several limitations of this research that warrant discussion. Many studies of treatment outcome in PTSD, whether involving medication or psychotherapy, have looked at relatively "pure" PTSD, often associated with adult traumas of little complexity. Individuals with comorbid diagnoses of major depression, personality disorders, obsessive-compulsive disorder, and other anxiety disorders are often excluded from such trials (Spinazzola et al., 2005). In addition, many studies exclude those who abuse substances, are suicidal, or have significant dissociative symptoms. Remarkably, even despite these exclusions, dropout rates approach 30 percent in many studies (Spinazzola et al., 2005).

Unfortunately, in the general population (that is, in nonscreened, nonresearch settings), PTSD is highly comorbid with other Axis I diagnoses. In fact, estimates place the comorbidity of PTSD with other Axis I disorders, summing across sex, at up to 80 percent (Kessler et al., 1995). As most clinicians working with trauma survivors in clinics and in private offices will attest, "pure" PTSD is relatively rare. Thus, it is not always easy to generalize the results of treatment outcome studies to the actual environment in which most clinicians practice—a world in which clients often present with a complex array of symptoms and may respond less robustly to treatment or take longer to respond than the studies suggest.

Overall, there is considerable evidence that psychoactive medication is sometimes necessary, but it is rarely sufficient in the treatment of PTSD and other trauma-related states. However, these limitations should not preclude the appropriate use of such medications in clinical practice. For example, a majority of trauma clients seen at LAC + USC Medical Center are taking at least one psychoactive medication—although, admittedly, these individuals may fall on the more severe end of the trauma severity-complexity continuum (Ehrlich & Briere, 2002).

Pregnancy and Lactation

Pregnancy is a time of increased vulnerability, both mentally and physically, as well as potentially a time of role change and financial stress. In this context, psychological stability, physical safety, and social support become especially important during pregnancy and the immediate postpartum period. As noted in Chapter 1, women are overrepresented among trauma survivors, and women are at a higher risk for victimization when they are pregnant (Campbell & Lewandowski, 1997). Trauma history, especially childhood sexual abuse, as well as a diagnosis of PTSD, have been correlated with negative outcomes in pregnancy. As well, childbirth itself can be a trauma that leads to subsequent posttraumatic symptoms and distress, especially when delivery occurs by emergency cesarean section or with the assistance of instrumentation (for example, forceps, episiotomy; L. E. Ross & McLean, 2006).

Being in a violent relationship while pregnant carries a risk of heightened victimization and both fetal and maternal death, most often subsequent to abdominal injury. In fact, the risk of maternal death in pregnancy from all causes is three times higher in abused women than in nonabused women (Boy & Salihu, 2004). Current violence is also a risk factor for kidney infections in pregnancy, prematurity, and low birth weight (Seng, 2002).

A history of sexual trauma, especially in childhood, is also associated with a variety of pregnancy complications and negative pregnancy outcomes. These include, among others, unintended pregnancies, miscarriage, hyperemesis gravidarum (persistent and extreme nausea and vomiting during pregnancy), preterm labor, and low birth weight. Sexual trauma is also associated with negative postnatal outcomes, including difficulties with breastfeeding, attachment, and mothering (Curry, Perrin, & Wall, 1998; Jacob, 1992; Seng, 2002). In addition, reactivation of traumatic memories may occur in the course of medical care and exams, leading to avoidance of necessary prenatal care.

A small but growing body of research has focused on the connection between PSTD and negative outcomes in pregnancy. Woman with PTSD are at higher baseline risk for social and medical sequelae such as poor health perception, revictimization, HIV, eating disorders, depression, and increased use of drugs and alcohol, all of which are independent risk factors for negative pregnancy outcomes. In addition, there is a connection between the diagnosis of PTSD itself and pregnancy complications. These include ectopic pregnancy, pre-eclampsia, miscarriage, hyperemesis gravidarum, excessive fetal growth, and preterm labor. Perinatal PTSD has also been associated with avoidance of the baby, impaired maternal/infant bonding, avoidance of sexual activity, and avoidance of other infants and their mothers—resulting in social isolation (Ross & McLean, 2006; Seng et al., 2001). Interestingly, and not surprisingly, PTSD secondary to child abuse was most strongly predictive of negative outcomes. It is notable that these risks remain even when prenatal care is controlled for (Seng et al., 2011).

Estimates of PTSD prevalence in pregnant populations range from 0 percent to 8 percent, depending on the study and the demographics of the individuals participating (Ross & McLean, 2006). In an attempt to elucidate PTSD status based on the type of trauma history, a recent survey of pregnant women found PTSD in 4.1 percent of never abused women, 11.4 percent of women abused as adults, 16 percent of women abused in childhood, and 39.2 percent abused in both childhood and adulthood (Seng, Sperlich, & Low, 2008).

Given the above, it is important to consider both pregnancy and the potential for pregnancy in women of childbearing age when working with traumatized women. Unfortunately, there have been no studies to date evaluating either (1) the treatment of PTSD in pregnancy or (2) the course of PTSD in the perinatal period. Thus, clinicians must extrapolate from the available studies of medications during pregnancy in women with depression, anxiety, and schizophrenia. There is a paucity of data in this area, and most psychiatric medications have not been studied enough in pregnant women to provide clear guidance on their safety. This is complicated by the fact that it is considered unethical to carry out randomized medication trials on pregnant women.

Prescribing practices during pregnancy vary widely, and a review of the literature reveals a variety of opinions, ranging from encouraging clinicians to aggressively treat psychiatric symptoms in pregnancy, to the view that medications clearly have the potential for harm and should be used only as a last resort (see, for example, Campagne, 2007; L. S. Cohen, Nonacs, Viguera, & Reminick, 2004). Most medications used to treat PTSD are classified by the Food and Drug Administration (FDA) as pregnancy Category C, indicating possible adverse effects on the unborn child. Certain medications, described below, are more clearly contraindicated in pregnancy. Therefore, the decision to treat a pregnant woman with psychotropic medication involves a careful risk-benefit analysis. For example, are the symptoms severe enough that a woman is at risk for harming herself or her baby? Is the risk for harm due to intentional injury or self-neglect greater than the risk posed by use of a medication?

The antidepressants, especially the selective serotonin reuptake inhibitors (SSRIs), generally have been prescribed quite widely during pregnancy. However, in December 2005, the FDA changed the SSRI paroxetine (Paxil) from pregnancy Category C to D, indicating positive evidence of risk. This change occurred as a result of preliminary data suggesting that exposure to this drug during the first trimester may increase the chance of congenital malformations, especially cardiac anomalies (FDA, 2005). It is unclear whether this finding might be a more general SSRI-related effect as opposed to one simply connected with paroxetine. Nonetheless, this change, which was announced rather suddenly, illustrates that there is much we still do not know about this class of medications. In addition, there have been several studies indicating that SSRIs taken in the third trimester of pregnancy can lead to premature birth as well as complications immediately after delivery, including difficulties with breathing and feeding, jitteriness, and need for extended care, collectively described as a "neonatal behavioral syndrome" (Moses-Kalko et al., 2005). Thus, all SSRIs carry a warning regarding third-trimester exposure.

Mood-stabilizing medications, sometimes used in patients with PTSD, are overwhelmingly not recommended in pregnancy due to teratogenicity (causing malformations in the fetus) and are rated pregnancy Category D. For example, lithium taken in the first trimester can cause cardiac malformations, while valproic acid has been associated with spina bifida and neural tube defects, as well as craniofacial malformations.

The use of antipsychotic medications in pregnancy presents challenges. Generally, antipsychotics are rated pregnancy Category C, however available research is limited. Haloperidol (Haldol, one of the first and most extensively used antipsychotics) is the most commonly used in pregnancy, primarily because it has been around the longest. However, there have been multiple reports of malformations with the use of antipsychotics, as well as increased risk for gestational diabetes in the mother, perinatal complications, and movement disorders in the infant (Gentile, 2010).

To the extent possible, it is recommended that the use of psychotropics be avoided during the first trimester, since this is when the most crucial neurological development occurs in the fetus. If medication must be used, it should follow an honest discussion with the patient about the potential risks and side effects of whatever pharmacologic agent is being considered. If a patient becomes pregnant while on medication, then a careful consideration must follow of the need to change medication, and the possibility that the fetus will be exposed to more than one agent if a change is made. If a patient remains on medication through the third trimester, attention is necessary close to labor and delivery, as the infant may need a higher level of care in order for neonatal complications to be addressed.

Most psychotropic medications are secreted in breast milk. The data on the effects of medications taken in by newborns through breast milk is minimal, and there have been no controlled trials of psychotropic medications in lactating women and their infants (V. K. Burt et al., 2001). Therefore, in circumstances where new mothers have symptoms severe enough to require pharmacological intervention, the most prudent choice is to avoid breastfeeding. That being said, prescribing practices for lactating women vary widely, and some have suggested that if a patient took medication during pregnancy, the baby will receive far less of the drug through milk than in utero, and therefore may continue taking it while breastfeeding. As always, a thoughtful risk-benefit analysis is required. While antidepressants may in some cases be acceptable during lactation, antipsychotics and mood stabilizers have the potential for more serious side effects in the baby, and if a mother needs to be on such medication, formula rather than breastfeeding is recommended.

In a review of antidepressant medications in pregnancy, Payne and Meltzer-Brody (2009) suggest the following "clinical pearls" when working with pregnant and lactating women:

- Assume all women of reproductive age will get pregnant and plan ahead.
- All medication changes should be carried out before pregnancy, if possible.
- Ideally, the patient should be stable psychiatrically for at least 3 months before attempting pregnancy.
- Limit the number of exposures for the baby; consider active psychiatric symptoms in the mother an exposure.
- Use medications that we know more about: Older generally means better.
- Consider breastfeeding when planning for pregnancy.
- If a baby was exposed to a medication during pregnancy, it may not make sense to discontinue the medication (or alternatively not breast-feed) for breastfeeding.
- Every case is unique—there are no rules.
- Use a team approach.

Given that there are significant gaps in our knowledge of how medications affect both the course of pregnancy and fetal development, we recommend a careful, cautious approach. To the extent possible, women with PTSD and other sequelae of trauma should be offered psychotherapy as a first treatment option. If a careful risk-benefit analysis suggests that medication is warranted, patient education, fully informed consent, and close monitoring throughout the perinatal period are essential.

In the medication tables throughout this chapter, we have listed the FDA pregnancy ratings, when known, for each drug. In addition, we have listed whether or not each medication is secreted in breast milk, and if breastfeeding while taking the medication poses risks (if this information is known). For reference, the FDA pregnancy ratings are as follows (FDA, 1980):

Category A: Controlled studies in humans show no risk	Adequate and well-controlled human studies have failed to demonstrate a risk to the fetus in the first trimester of pregnancy (and there is no evidence of risk in later trimesters).
Category B: No clear evidence of risk in humans	Animal reproduction studies have failed to demonstrate a risk to the fetus and there are no adequate and well-controlled studies in pregnant women OR Animal studies have shown an adverse effect, but adequate and well-controlled studies in pregnant women have failed to demonstrate a risk to the fetus in any trimester.
Category C: Risk cannot be ruled out	Animal reproduction studies have shown an adverse effect on the fetus and there are no adequate and well-controlled studies in humans, but potential benefits may warrant use of the drug in pregnant women despite potential risks.

Category D: Positive evidence of risk in humans	There is positive evidence of human fetal risk based on adverse reaction data from investigational or marketing experience or studies in humans, but potential benefits may warrant use of the drug in pregnant women despite potential risks.
Category X: Contraindicated in pregnancy	Studies in animals or humans have demonstrated fetal abnormalities and/or there is positive evidence of human fetal risk based on adverse reaction data from investigational or marketing experience, and the risks involved in use of the drug in pregnant women clearly outweigh potential benefits.

Complementary and Alternative Medicine and Psychotropic Medications

Complementary and alternative medicine (CAM) is comprised of a rather loosely defined group of therapeutic modalities that are not often taught in medical schools or available in hospitals. Alternative therapy is generally distinguished from "conventional medicine" and includes such disparate therapies as herbal remedies, homeopathy, massage, chiropractic, acupuncture, vitamins, and "energy healing," among others. We explore the use of alternative therapies in this chapter because there is considerable anecdotal evidence that trauma survivors avail themselves of nontraditional remedies instead of (or in addition to) prescribed psychiatric medication.

Often, such remedies are used in concert with changes in lifestyle such as yoga, meditation, or other mindfulness or spiritual practices. As described in greater detail in Chapter 10, mindfulness can be a powerful tool in work with traumatized individuals. In addition, a growing body of research on spirituality, religion, and coping indicates that a variety of spiritual beliefs and positive religious coping mechanisms (such as prayer, engaging in good deeds, receiving help from clergy, among others) can be associated with more positive psychological outcomes (for example, Ahrens, Abeling, Ahmad, & Hinman, 2010; Boehnlein, 2006; Connor, Davidson, & Lee 2003). Over the past two decades, the use of alternative therapies has become increasingly widespread in the United States; in 1997, 45 percent of respondents to a national phone survey had used at least one form of alternative therapy (Knaudt, Connor, Weisler, Churchill, & Davidson, 1999). While some forms of alternative therapies are provided by licensed practitioners, others are entirely unregulated. For example, herbal supplements, nutritionals, and vitamins, many of which can have significant side effects, and may interact with other drugs, are sold over the counter and are not regulated by the FDA.

In addition, some faith-based approaches to healing have crossover with CAM. For example, at USC Medical Center, we see a number of individuals who have consulted with traditional Mexican spiritual healers, known as *curanderos*. These healers often are greatly respected within their communities, and their opinions can carry significant weight. Sometimes, curanderos will give herbs or other pills to take as part of a healing ritual or will advise patients to stop all other mainstream treatments in order for their rituals to be effective.

Demographic studies have repeatedly indicated that individuals who seek out alternative forms of health care have higher rates of anxiety and depression (for example, J. R. T. Davidson et al., 1998; Knaut et al., 1999). Possible reasons for this include diffuse, ill-defined physical complaints not well addressed by conventional medicine, attempts to find "natural" remedies for both physical and psychiatric complaints, and frustration with the health care system, among others. Whatever the reason, it is important for mental health providers to be aware that their clients may be using alternative remedies and that they are often reluctant to share this information with their doctors and/or therapists. It is a common misconception that herbal or other supplements, because they are "natural," do not have any adverse effects; unfortunately, this is not the case.

An exhaustive discussion of the literature on alternative treatments is beyond the scope of this chapter. However, a general review indicates potential benefit in several areas. There have been few systematic studies of alternative pharmacologic treatments (that is, herbal or other "natural" remedies) for PTSD, in specific. However, there is a growing literature on the use of alternative remedies more generally for symptoms of depression and anxiety. These include acupuncture, St. John's Wort (or Hypericin), Kava Kava, SAMe (s-adenosyl-methionine), omega fatty acids, passionflower, valerian root, aromatherapy, and homeopathy. In addition, there is an abundance of scientifically unsubstantiated information available on the World Wide Web regarding the use of vitamins, tryptophan, and other supplements to treat psychiatric symptoms.

Although not all of these remedies and interventions are necessarily safe, let alone helpful, there are studies indicating that some alternative treatments can have positive results. In a randomized trial, acupuncture was as effective as group CBT in reducing symptoms of PTSD (Hollifield, Sinclair-Lian, Warner, & Hammerschlag, 2007). In a small pilot study, omega-3 fatty acids were helpful for PTSD after a natural disaster (Matsuoka et al., 2011). Multiple trials have shown that St. John's Wort is an effective treatment for mild to moderate depression in adults, and that omega fatty acids and SAMe may be beneficial as an adjunct to antidepressant treatment. Among alternative remedies, Kava Kava has shown the most potential as an anxiolytic (Larzelere, Campbell, & Robertson, 2010). In a double-blind randomized trial, inositol was found to improve depressive symptoms in individuals with PTSD, but had no effect on the PTSD itself (Kaplan, Amir, Swartz, & Levine, 1996). Similarly, a recent review found that there was no support for the use of homeopathy in anxiety/stress disorders, but potentially some efficacy for sleep (J. R. Davidson, Crawford, Ives, & Jonas, 2011).

A few critical points regarding safety are worth mentioning:

1. St. John's Wort (Hypericin) is an herbal supplement available over the counter for treatment of depression and often recommended by alternative providers. It has some SSRI activity, which is presumed to be its mechanism of action. Therefore, it is critical that clients not take St. John's Wort concurrently with an SSRI, since this would increase the risk of serotonin syndrome (see the section on SSRIs, following, for a description of the SSRIs and serotonin syndrome). There are similar potential risks with the use of supplements containing tryptophan, a serotonin precursor. Tryptophan is widely recommended on websites as a "mood enhancer" and is available online and over the counter in various forms.

2. Some natural remedies act as stimulants and activate the sympathetic nervous system (for example, ephedra/ephedrine used for weight control, and yohimbine used for energy and male impotence). As described previously, trauma survivors frequently experience increased sympathetic nervous system activity and therefore are at risk of increased posttraumatic symptoms if they use stimulants. In one series of case reports (Southwick, Morgan, Charney, & High, 1999), dramatic symptom increases were noted in individuals with PTSD who took over-the-counter yohimbine. We therefore recommend that traumatized individuals avoid herbal or other nonprescribed stimulants.

3. Some clients may take supplements that do not come in labeled packaging or that come from other countries. Such supplements may be prescribed by Chinese herbalists, for example, or by curanderos, as described above. If psychotropic medications are indicated, it is imperative to have a frank discussion with the client about additional remedies they are taking. We recommend asking clients to bring all pills and supplements, along with the packaging in which they came, to their appointments, so that the clinician can be as informed as possible about potential problems/interactions.

The potential risks when combining mainstream medications with alternative remedies are real and must be conveyed to the client as well as documented in the medical record. However, maintaining a supportive, nonjudgmental attitude is essential during any such discussion. Often, clients believe that they will be penalized for seeing alternative providers and are afraid to report what they are taking. In such situations, open communication among the nonprescribing therapist, the psychiatrist or other medical practitioner, and the client can be extremely useful.

In the current atmosphere of increasing interest in alternatives to mainstream medicine, we will undoubtedly learn more about these and other alternative approaches to mental health treatment. And as patients become more highly informed consumers of health care, and have more and more access to information via the Internet, clinicians will need to stay informed in order to deliver the safest and most effective care. We recommend an open-minded approach on the part of clinicians. In the best of cases, CAM is just that—a complement to mainstream approaches, that may provide a sense of spirituality, wholeness, and perspective (and in some cases, new efficacy) that otherwise can be lacking in modern medicine.

A Note on the Uses and Limitations of This Chapter

Much of what we present in the following sections is well-known, easily available information regarding the mechanism of action, side effects, contraindications, and dosing of various psychotropic medications. However, in the interest of brevity—and ease for the reader—we have not presented exhaustive general information about each medication. We have, however, focused on the application of such medication in posttraumatic stress, so that interested readers can further their knowledge in this ever-expanding area. Prescribing clinicians should view this book primarily as a guide to the literature on the use of psychopharmacology in trauma; they are referred to more complete and authoritative texts, as well as their own clinical knowledge, for specifics regarding the use of psychiatric medications in actual practice. *In no case should the clinician prescribe or determine medication dosages based solely on information provided in this chapter.* Instead, the prescribing clinician should consult the *Physicians' Desk Reference* (2012) or an other drug reference for the exact and proper dosage and regimen appropriate for any given client.

Medications for PTSD

Antidepressants

Selective Serotonin Reuptake Inhibitors

Most of the research on medications for PTSD has focused on the use of SSRIs. This is logical: SSRIs have demonstrated efficacy for the treatment of depression, generalized anxiety, and panic. Therefore, their use for PTSD, which includes symptoms that overlap with these disorders, is a natural extension. The results of research on SSRIs and PTSD have generally been encouraging, leading to the widespread use of these medications to treat posttraumatic stress. For example, SSRIs are listed as the first-line medication for PTSD in the "Treatment Recommendations for PTSD" made by the International Society for Traumatic Stress Studies (Friedman et al., 2009). And the only medications the FDA has approved for treatment of PTSD are SSRIs—sertraline (Zoloft) and paroxetine (Paxil).

There have been several randomized, double-blind, placebo-controlled studies of SSRIs in PTSD, using paroxetine (Paxil; for example, Marshall et al., 2007; D. J. Stein, Davidson, Seedat, & Beebe, 2003), sertraline (Zoloft;

for example, Brady et al., 2000; J. R. T. Davidson, Rothbaum, van der Kolk, Sikes, & Farfel, 2001; D. J. Stein, van der Kolk, Austin, Fayyad, & Clary, 2006), and fluoxetine (Prozac; for example, Connor, Sutherland, Tupler, Malik, & Davidson, 1999; Martenyi & Soldatenkova, 2006). Results of this research indicate that SSRIs reduce symptoms in all three of the core symptom clusters of PTSD (that is, reexperiencing, hyperarousal, and avoidance).

Two newer SSRIs, citalopram and escitalopram, have not been studied in randomized controlled trials. Both have shown efficacy for treating PTSD in small open-label trials, but larger randomized studies are needed in order to validate and replicate these findings (English, Jewell, Jewell, Ambrose, & Davis, 2006; S. Robert et al., 2009).

Most studies have followed patients over a relatively short 12-week treatment period. One trial of sertraline followed patients for 28 weeks following the acute phase of the study to assess efficacy in preventing relapse (J. R. T. Davidson et al., 2001). The results suggested that sertraline is effective in preventing relapse of PTSD. There have been two placebo-controlled trials of relapse prevention of PTSD with fluoxetine. The first was a 24-week extension of a 12-week study in which fluoxetine was superior to placebo in preventing relapse (Martenyi, Brown, Zhang, Koke, & Prakash, 2002). The second confirmed these findings over a longer period: In a 6-month open trial of fluoxetine followed by 6 months of randomization to placebo control, 22 percent of those individuals taking fluoxetine relapsed, compared to 50 percent of those receiving placebo (J. R. Davidson et al., 2005). In addition, time to relapse was longer with fluoxetine than placebo. These studies suggest that, in order for SSRI treatment to be effective over the long term, it must be maintained for a longer period of time than the usual 12-week duration of most clinical trials. In fact, for PTSD that lasts more than 3 months, it appears that treatment with an SSRI for 9 months to a year after symptom remission may be more appropriate (J. R. T. Davidson, 2004).

It is important to note that SSRIs, while helpful in PTSD, are not necessarily curative. In most studies, although 50–60 percent of participants responded, only 20–30 percent of them no longer met criteria for PTSD by the end of the study (Spinazzola et al., 2005). Put another way, this means that 70–80 percent of individuals in the study still had PTSD after treatment, albeit perhaps in an attenuated form. In addition, despite the studies cited above indicating the efficacy of SSRIs in treating PTSD, some research has suggested a less than robust response to these medications, or cited the presence of comorbidities, overall lower doses of medication, or surprisingly high placebo response as confounders (for example, Martenyi, Brown, & Caldwell, 2007). What this means for clinical practice is that medications for trauma cannot be prescribed in a cookie-cutter fashion: It is essential for clinicians to take into account the entire presentation of the patient and to be especially aware of comorbidities and complexities that may attenuate a given individual's response to any given treatment.

In some studies of SSRIs in PTSD, treatment appears to be less successful in war veterans and in men than in civilians and women (for example, Hertzberg, Feldman, Beckham, Kudler, & Davidson, 2000). There has been much discussion about why this might be the case. The negative studies involved male Vietnam-era participants with persistent PTSD over many years—a cohort with, almost by definition, a particularly treatment-resistant form of the disorder. In addition, many Vietnam-era veterans suffer from longstanding, severe substance dependence, which may complicate the picture. However, more recent studies in civilians have demonstrated no sex difference in response to these medications. In addition, studies with veterans from other combat areas have shown that SSRIs can be effective in PTSD related to war trauma. For example, Zohar et al. (2002) found that sertraline was superior to placebo in Israeli combat veterans with PTSD, albeit with a smaller effect size than in civilians. In addition, a placebo-controlled, randomized study of fluoxetine in male veterans traumatized in the Yugoslavian civil war (1992–1996) demonstrated significant improvement across all three PTSD symptom clusters (Martenyi & Soldatenkova, 2006). More research is required to clearly elucidate the relationships between type of trauma, chronicity, and substance use.

There are some interesting data suggesting that SSRIs may actually have direct effects on the anatomy and neurophysiology that underlie posttraumatic stress, which are described above in the neurobiology section. In a small group of patients with borderline personality disorder, fluvoxamine (Luvox) was found to decrease the hyper-responsiveness of the HPA axis (as measured by dexamethasone challenge) in individuals with a history of childhood abuse (Rinne et al., 2003). Another recent study showed a 5 percent increase in hippocampal volume in individuals with PTSD who were treated for a year with paroxetine (Bremner & Vermetten, 2004). This information, while still preliminary, supports the notion that treatment with SSRIs may be most effective when used over a more extended period of time.

At the time of publication of this book, there are six SSRIs available on the market, listed in Table 12.1. They have been found to be equally effective in reducing symptoms and improving quality of life across most clinical trials for various *Diagnostic and Statistical Manual of Mental Disorders* (*DSM-IV-TR;* American Psychiatric Association, 2000) diagnoses (for example, Mace & Taylor, 2000). As discussed later in this chapter, they differ primarily in terms of side effects. This is an important consideration in choosing a medication for trauma survivors, because noncompliance is especially high in this population. At this time, only sertraline and paroxetine have received FDA approval for the treatment of PTSD. However, as the SSRIs are generally equally effective across disorders, decisions regarding choice of one medication over another are primarily based upon the judgment of the clinician.

Table 12.1   SSRIs

Generic Name	Trade Name	Recommended Dosage	Half Life	Pregnancy Category*	Present in Breast Milk
Citalopram	Celexa	10–40mg	35 hrs.	C, caution in third trimester	Yes, safety unknown
Escitalopram	Lexapro	10–20mg	27–32 hrs.	C, caution in third trimester	Yes, safety unknown
Fluoxetine	Prozac	10–80mg	4–6 days	C, caution in third trimester	Yes, safety unknown
Fluvoxamine	Luvox	100–300mg	15 hrs.	C, caution in third trimester	Yes, probably safe
Paroxetine	Paxil	10–50mg	10–21 hrs.	D	Yes, safe
Sertraline	Zoloft	50–200mg	26 hrs.	C, caution in third trimester	Yes, safe

*See pp. 240–241 for a description of FDA pregnancy ratings.

SSRIs are generally considered to be safer than the older antidepressants (the tricyclics and monoamine oxidase inhibitors, described later in this chapter) and less lethal in overdose. However, they have been associated with a potentially life-threatening condition known as "serotonin syndrome" that results from excess central nervous system serotonin. Symptoms can range from tremor and diarrhea to delirium, neuromuscular rigidity, and hyperthermia. Serotonin syndrome can occur in cases of overdose, drug-drug interactions, or, in rare instances, during therapeutic drug use.

Generally, SSRIs are well tolerated and have the benefit of being relatively nonlethal in overdose (as compared to, for example, the tricyclic antidepressants, which can be fatal when taken in quantities equaling a 15-day supply). However, they all share some potential side effects. These include anxiety, nervousness, sweating, headache, gastrointestinal upset (nausea, diarrhea, dyspepsia), dry mouth, somnolence, insomnia, and disruption of all phases of sexuality (erections in men, and libido and orgasms in both men and women). Although SSRIs treat symptoms of anxiety and are indicated for the treatment of Axis I anxiety disorders, they frequently increase anxiety in the initial days of treatment and can sometimes precipitate panic attacks.

There are certain side effects that are associated more with some SSRIs than others. Fluoxetine tends to be activating and is generally prescribed to be taken in the morning. Paroxetine (as well as fluvoxamine) tends to be more sedating and is typically taken in the evening. Paroxetine can also cause weight gain. Sertraline, escitalopram, and citalopram are more side-effect neutral, with fewer effects on sleep and weight. However, recent data showing an association of high dose citalopram with prolongation of the QTc interval on EKG led to a decrease in the maximum recommended dose from 60mg daily to 40mg, and a caution regarding those with risk for QT abnormalities. In addition, all SSRIs carry a "black box" warning regarding risk for increased suicidality in children, adolescents, and young adults (age < 24 years).

Some clinicians make decisions about which SSRI to give an individual client based upon the most advantageous use of these side effects, a strategy that we have found anecdotally to increase compliance; for example:

- Paroxetine in a nonpregnant client who is highly anxious and unable to sleep and is not bothered by potential weight gain
- Fluoxetine in a client who is tired and apathetic and has a hard time "getting going" in the morning
- Sertraline, citalopram, or escitalopram in a client who is particularly concerned about side effects

Given the potential side effects discussed, client education is essential. It is important to warn very anxious and hyperaroused clients that their anxiety may increase initially and that this is a normal response to the medication. It is also crucial to inform clients about possible sexual side effects and to assure men that erectile difficulties will resolve if the medication is stopped. In addition, it is essential to inform clients that antidepressants do not take effect immediately. Often, it takes up to 2 weeks for an initial response to occur; a full response may not take place until an individual has been taking a therapeutic dose for 4 to 6 weeks.

SSRIs also have the potential to cause significant symptoms if they are stopped abruptly, known as "discontinuation syndrome." Vomiting, diarrhea, nausea, anorexia, dizziness, headache, insomnia, irritability, disturbances of vision, fatigue, and tremor, as well as "electric shock" sensations in the back and arms have all been reported (for example, Coupland, Bell, & Potokar, 1996). Paroxetine, with its short half-life, has been noted to cause discontinuation symptoms more frequently than the other SSRIs (Barr, Goodman, & Price, 1994). Fluoxetine, with a long half-life, rarely causes such difficulties, and in fact is sometimes used short-term to assist in tapering clients off of other SSRIs. Again, educating clients about the potential symptoms associated with stopping SSRIs is important—they should be encouraged to discontinue such medications only when tapered under the supervision of a prescribing clinician. The half-lives of the SSRIs are noted in Table 12.1 for reference purposes regarding this issue.

Other Serotonergic Agents

There has been a dramatic increase in the number of antidepressant medications available to clinicians over the past 15 years. In addition to the

SSRIs, several newer medications have come onto the market that have effects on other neurotransmitters as well as serotonin. These have been demonstrated to be effective antidepressant medications in their own right; however, we know less about their efficacy in treating posttraumatic stress. In the coming years, our knowledge about these medications and their use in trauma will undoubtedly increase considerably. These agents are listed in Table 12.2.

Venlafaxine (Effexor)

Venlafaxine is a potent serotonin-norepinephrine reuptake inhibitor (SNRI) that has been found to be effective in the treatment of depression and anxiety. Its side effect profile is similar to that of the SSRIs. It tends to be activating rather than sedating and has a relatively high likelihood of causing sexual side effects and discontinuation syndrome (both of these are due to its serotonergic activity and are similar to the side effects described above for the SSRIs). The regular form of venlafaxine was associated with elevations in blood pressure in some individuals; this is seen less with the extended-release form of the medication, venlafaxine XR. It

Table 12.2 Other Serotonergic Agents

Generic Name	Trade Name	Recommended Dosage	Pregnancy Category*	Present in Breast Milk
Venlafaxine XR	Effexor XR	75–225mg daily	C, caution in third trimester	Yes, safety unknown
Duloxetine	Cymbalta	60–120mg daily, in divided doses	C, caution in third trimester	Yes, safety unknown
Atomoxetine	Strattera	40–100mg daily	C	Yes, safety unknown
Bupropion	Wellbutrin	150–300mg daily (divided twice daily for the regular and SR forms, once daily for the XL)	C	Yes, possibly unsafe
Mirtazapine	Remeron	15–45mg at bedtime	C	Yes, safety unknown
Trazodone	Desyrel	150–600mg divided twice daily	C	Yes, probably safe
Nefazodone	Serzone	200–600mg divided twice daily	C	Yes, possibly unsafe

*See pp. 240–241 for a description of FDA pregnancy ratings.

Note that the above serotonergic agents, with the exception of nefazodone, carry the same "black box" warning regarding suidicality in children, adolescents, and young adults (age < 24 years) that the SSRIs do.

is nevertheless appropriate to monitor blood pressure in individuals taking venlafaxine. Given its similarity to the SSRIs, one would expect that venlafaxine would be a useful treatment for PTSD; however, there is only a small body of research in this area.

In a 24-week placebo-controlled study of venlafaxine in PTSD, venlafaxine was superior to placebo in alleviating reexperiencing and avoidance/numbing, but not hyperarousal (J. R. Davidson, Baldwin et al., 2006). This is not surprising given venlafaxine has noradrenergic effects and tends to be activating. In a second placebo-controlled study, venlafaxine was compared to both sertraline and placebo (J. R. T. Davidson et al., 2001). In this trial, venlafaxine and sertraline were equivalent in reducing PTSD symptoms, however the placebo response was also relatively high, and the effect sizes for both venlafaxine and sertraline were small. One open trial in refugees showed efficacy in five subjects (Smajkic et al., 2001); other than this trial, there have only been case reports of good response to venlafaxine in PTSD (for example, Hamner & Frueh, 1998). Overall, it appears that venlafaxine is probably a useful medication for PTSD, similar to the SSRIs, but perhaps not an ideal medication for those with high levels of hyperarousal.

Duloxetine (Cymbalta)

Duloxetine is another SNRI, often used to treat depression and chronic pain. There are two reports of duloxetine and PTSD in the literature. The first is an open trial of duloxetine in combat veterans with PTSD. Duloxetine appeared to reduce both posttraumatic and depressive symptoms and improve sleep (Walderhaug et al., 2010). A case report of a man with PTSD who also had refractory depression was treated with duloxetine with significant resultant exacerbation of PTSD symptoms.

Bupropion (Wellbutrin)

Bupropion is unrelated to any other antidepressants. Its precise mechanism of action is unknown—it weakly inhibits the reuptake of serotonin and epinephrine, and more potently inhibits the reuptake of dopamine. It appears to have stimulant-like effects, and therefore it is usually recommended that bupropion be taken before 5 p.m. to prevent insomnia. In line with this activation, a substantial portion of individuals treated with bupropion experience agitation or restlessness, a side effect that must always be kept in mind when treating trauma survivors, who may already complain of autonomic arousal. The most concerning side effect with bupropion is a 0.4 percent risk of causing seizures, which is four times that of other antidepressants. This risk is increased in patients with bulimia, and the medication is therefore contraindicated in those with a prior history of seizure disorder or a history of bulimia. Because some survivors of childhood abuse may engage in tension reduction behaviors, including bingeing/purging (as described in Chapter 2), it is important to ask about a history of eating disorders. Despite these concerns, bupropion is an effective antidepressant and has the significant (and unique) added benefit of causing no sexual side effects. In fact, it is sometimes added to counteract the sexual side effects caused by other medications.

There are only two reports in the literature on the use of bupropion in PTSD. This may be due to concerns that bupropion could be too activating in those with significant posttraumatic distress and anxiety. Interestingly, in an open trial of 17 combat veterans with PTSD, bupropion was found to decrease hyperarousal but have no effect on intrusions or avoidance, or, in fact, on measures of overall PTSD severity (Canive, Clark, Calais, Qualls, & Tuason, 1998). However, in a placebo-controlled trial with a rather small sample size of 43, bupropion was not found to be helpful for either symptoms of depression or PTSD (M. E. Becker et al., 2007). More research is needed before any definitive recommendations can be made regarding the use of this medication in PTSD, but initial reports are not particularly encouraging. Bupropion is available in three formulations—regular, sustained release (SR), and, most recently, an extended release (XL) that is dosed only once a day. It may be that this XL formulation will have fewer acute side effects, such as anxiety and agitation, but this remains to be seen as the medication is used in clinical practice.

Mirtazapine (Remeron)

Mirtazapine is another unique medication that has activity on both serotonin and norepinephrine, as well as some presynaptic alpha-adrenergic blockade. It has antagonism at some serotonin receptor sites, which is hypothesized to be the reason that it has fewer serotonergic side effects than do the SSRIs, including less sexual side effects. It is sedating and is usually given at night to help with sleep. Unfortunately, it also can cause significant weight gain. There have been several open trials and one small randomized controlled trial that have indicated good response to mirtazapine in PTSD (Alderman, Condon, & Gilbert, 2009; J. R. T. Davidson et al., 2003). One randomized open trial in Korean War veterans found mirtazapine to be superior to Zoloft in reducing symptoms of PTSD (Chung et al., 2004). There have also been case reports of the efficacy of mirtazapine for PTSD-related nightmares and sleep disturbance (Lewis, 2002). It has been suggested that this may be due to alpha blockade, a topic that is discussed later in this chapter.

Trazodone (Desyrel)

Trazodone is another serotonergic antidepressant that has alpha-adrenergic blocking activity. It is highly sedating and is used most frequently in psychiatry as a sleep agent. There have been a few case reports and one open trial with six subjects investigating the use of trazodone in PTSD. These reports suggest mild to moderate efficacy across the PTSD symptom clusters (Hertzberg, Feldman, Beckham, & Davidson, 1996). Significant side effects, aside from sedation, include dry mouth, blurred vision, gastrointestinal upset, and in males, risk of priapism (painful sustained erection that may require emergent medical intervention).

Nefazodone (Serzone)

Nefazodone is a potent blocker of postsynaptic serotonin as well as a weak inhibitor of both serotonin and norepinephrine reuptake. It has been shown to have similar efficacy to the SSRIs in treating depression, and it has the benefit of causing minimal sexual side effects. Nefazodone was widely used in those individuals for whom SSRI-related sexual dysfunction was problematic. Unfortunately, it has been associated with several cases of fatal liver failure and has been taken off the market in the United States, Europe, and Canada. There have been no randomized controlled trials with nefazodone; however, several open trials have shown efficacy not only for the three symptom clusters of PTSD, but for improved sleep as well (for example, Davis, Nugent, Murray, Kramer, & Petty, 2000).

Monoamine Oxidase Inhibitors

Monoamine oxidase inhibitors (MAOIs; listed in Table 12.3) are effective antidepressants that have largely been replaced by SSRIs because of their considerable side effects and the dietary restrictions that must be followed when taking them. They are generally used for treatment of depression (especially the melancholic type) when other medications have failed. MAOIs inhibit the action of the enzyme monoamine oxidase, which breaks down epinephrine, norepinephrine, serotonin, and dopamine, thereby increasing the available levels of these neurotransmitters. MAOIs have significant side effects, including dizziness, headache, somnolence, weight gain, constipation, dry mouth, and sexual disturbances. MAOIs can also cause hypertensive crisis, especially in those individuals taking other sympathomimetic agents (such as cold preparations, decongestants, and weight reduction medications) or who eat tyramine-containing foods. The dietary

Table 12.3 Monoamine Oxidase Inhibitors

Generic Name	Trade Name	Recommended Dosage (daily)	Pregnancy Category*	Present in Breast Milk
Phenelzine	Nardil	45–90 mg	C	Not known
Tranylcypromine	Parnate	30–60mg	C	Not known

*See pp. 240–241 for a description of FDA pregnancy ratings.

restrictions are critical, as monoamine oxidase also breaks down tyramine. When tyramine is not metabolized, it displaces epinephrine and norepinephrine in the nervous system and adrenal glands, which can lead to severe headache, sweating, neck rigidity, palpitations, and dramatic blood pressure elevations. On rare occasions, MAOI-induced hypertensive crisis can lead to cardiac arrhythmias and cerebral hemorrhage. Therefore, individuals taking MAOIs must avoid foods containing tyramine (including, but not limited to, aged cheese, yeast extract, red wine, beer, pickled fish, preserved meats, fava beans, overripe bananas and avocados, caffeine, and chocolate). Clearly, MAOIs are not simple to take, and compliance can be very difficult.

There have been three randomized controlled trials of phenelzine in PTSD. One showed efficacy in reducing reexperiencing symptoms and in global improvement, superior to both imipramine and placebo (Kosten, Frank, Dan McDougle, & Giller 1991). Two others were not superior to placebo at all (Frank, Kosten, Giller, & Dan, 1988; Shezatsky, Greenberg & Lerer 1988). Open trials of phenelzine have had similarly equivocal results (for example, Lerer et al., 1987).

Tricyclic Antidepressants

The tricyclic antidepressants (TCAs; listed in Table 12.4) were introduced in the 1950s as a treatment for depression and were the mainstay of pharmacotherapy for depression until the introduction of the SSRIs in the 1980s. TCAs have been used less frequently over the past two decades due to their side effects, which can be quite debilitating, and because of their potential lethality when taken in overdose. Common side effects of TCAs include sedation, dry mouth, gastrointestinal discomfort, constipation, blurry vision, sexual dysfunction, and weight gain. TCAs can also cause prolongation of the QTc interval on EKG and can, in some instances, lead to cardiac arrhythmias.

Table 12.4   Tricyclic Antidepressants

Generic Name	Trade Name	Recommended Dosage (daily)	Pregnancy Category*	Present in Breast Milk
Amitriptyline	Elavil	50–300mg	C	Yes, probably safe
Clomipramine	Anafranil	100–250mg	C	Yes, probably safe
Desipramine	Norpramin	50–300mg	C	Yes, safety unknown
Imipramine	Tofranil	75–300mg	D	Yes, probably safe
Nortriptyline	Pamelor	74–150mg	D	Yes, probably safe

*See pp. 240–241 for a description of FDA pregnancy ratings.

There have been four randomized clinical trials of TCAs in PTSD and multiple open trials. Both imipramine and amitriptyline have shown effectiveness in reducing the reexperiencing and avoidant symptoms of PTSD, but not hyperarousal (Kosten et. al, 1991). One study with desipramine showed no efficacy (Reist et al., 1989). Overall, TCAs appear to be less effective for PTSD than are the SSRIs or the MAOIs (Friedman, Davidson, & Stein 2009). However, all of the randomized controlled studies have involved veterans, not civilians, which may have affected the results.

Some clinicians take advantage of the sedating properties of the tricyclics and use them in low doses as adjunctive sleep medications in PTSD. There is, however, no research data to support this practice.

Like the SSRIs, TCAs can cause a discontinuation syndrome. This is thought to be due to cholinergic excess after the blockade of acetylcholine is removed. Discontinuation symptoms can include abdominal pain, nausea, vomiting, anorexia, chills, diaphoresis, diarrhea, fatigue, headache, malaise, myalgia, and weakness (Lejoyeux, Adès, Mourad, Solomon, & Dilsaver, 1996).

Benzodiazepines

Benzodiazepines are highly addictive medications that are used in psychiatry and general medicine for the treatment of anxiety. The most commonly used benzodiazepines are listed in Table 12.5. They act on GABA and have many similarities to alcohol—in fact, they are used as the primary treatment in alcohol detoxification to prevent withdrawal. Their use is fraught with controversy due to the potential for abuse and dependence. Benzodiazepines are often used in combination with illegal recreational substances, as well as with alcohol, and can be purchased "on the street" as drugs of abuse. Concerns about abuse are especially relevant in the treatment of trauma survivors, who often present complaining of intense, overwhelming anxiety that appears to require immediate relief. For such individuals, benzodiazepines may initially seem a godsend—the only thing that seems to dramatically reduce their level of arousal and/or address their panic. However, in the longer term, many people develop tolerance to the drugs' effects, requiring higher and higher doses to achieve the same result. Some individuals develop physiological and psychological dependence and find that these medications are extremely difficult to discontinue. As mentioned earlier, benzodiazepines have similar actions to alcohol—including a withdrawal syndrome that can be potentially fatal if not managed properly. Although benzodiazepines are excellent antianxiety medications, they are only a short-term solution—they treat anxiety when it happens and for as long as the drug remains active in the bloodstream. Unlike SSRIs and other antidepressants that treat anxiety only after a therapeutic blood level has built up over several weeks, benzodiazepines only work "in the moment."

Table 12.5   Benzodiazepines

Generic Name	Trade Name	Recommended Dosage (used as needed two to three times daily, or taken at bedtime)	Pregnancy Category*	Present in Breast Milk
Alprazolam	Xanax	0.25–0.5mg	D	Yes, possibly unsafe
Clonazepam	Klonopin	0.5–2mg	D	Yes, safety unknown
Diazepam	Valium	2–10mg	D	Yes, possibly unsafe
Lorazepam	Ativan	1–2mg	D	Yes, possibly unsafe
Temazepam	Restoril	7.5–30mg at bedtime	X	Yes, possibly unsafe
Triazolam	Halcion	0.125–0.25mg at bedtime	X	Yes, possibly unsafe
Oxazepam	Serax	10–30mg	D	Yes, possibly unsafe

*See pp. 240–241 for a description of FDA pregnancy ratings.

Another concern with the use of benzodiazepines in trauma survivors, aside from the problems related to abuse and dependence, is the alteration in consciousness that they produce. Benzodiazepines not only treat anxiety and panic, but they may cause euphoria, disinhibition, sedation, diminished response to threat, impaired coordination, and feelings of being "zoned out" or "disconnected." It might appear, at first glance, that this reduction in arousal would be useful in the context of trauma-related psychotherapy. One might imagine, for example, that decreased arousal could reduce the likelihood that the client would be overwhelmed when discussing emotionally laden, traumatic material. However, this is not borne out in clinical practice. Instead, regular use of benzodiazepines may interfere with the processing of traumatic material in therapy and has been hypothesized to produce state-dependent treatment effects that do not persist once medication has been discontinued (Briere, 2002b).

Although this clinical observation has yet to be empirically validated in the specific context of psychotherapeutic interventions, research has clearly demonstrated that benzodiazepines affect both learning and memory performance. Triazolam has been shown to affect memory for emotional content, in a manner consistent with difficulties seen in those who have damage to the amygdala (Buchanan, Karafin, & Adolphs, 2003). Other studies have shown that lorazepam can cause impairment in the ability to learn behavioral strategies, a finding that may be due to impaired consolidation of long-term memory while under the influence of the medication (Matthews, Kirkby, & Martin, 2002). Similar impairments in learning and memory have been found with oxazepam and alcohol (Barbee, 1993; Mattila, Vanakoski, Kalska, & Seppala, 1998). These findings are not surprising, given that benzodiazepines are known amnestics and are used as such in anesthesia.

There are similar data regarding the effects of alcohol on memory and performance that may be generalizable to benzodiazepines, given its similar effects on GABA. Studies with alcohol have shown that information learned while under the effects of alcohol is best retrieved under the same conditions. Some research suggests that alcohol disrupts hippocampal-dependent information processing (that is, explicit or declarative memory) preferentially. This finding might explain why it is difficult to remember specific experiences that occurred while under the influence of alcohol (Melia, Ryabinin, Corodimas, Wilson, & LeDoux, 1996).

It is important to educate clients early on about these concerns if they are taking benzodiazepines. When clients are informed about the potential for addiction and possible longer-term impacts on trauma processing, those not yet addicted are often more careful in how they use medications. In addition, those trauma survivors who are concerned about having less ability to sense danger often appreciate being informed about the potential for benzodiazepines to sedate and impair responsiveness. It may also be helpful to explain to patients that benzodiazepines work only in the short term—much as drinking a glass of wine will help to alleviate acute anxiety but will not treat it longer term.

Unfortunately, when trauma survivors present to medical emergency rooms with complaints of intense anxiety and panic, they are often prescribed benzodiazepines as sole agents, without being provided adequate information about potential problems. All too frequently, the medication prescribed is alprazolam (Xanax), which is the most highly addictive of this class of medication. Alprazolam also produces a type of euphoria that heightens the potential for psychological addiction. Alprazolam can produce a particularly bad withdrawal syndrome with rebound panic, and sometimes the need for medications to manage seizures. The frequent use of alprazolam in emergency room settings means that trauma therapists and mental health professionals often find that they need to intervene and educate clients who have already developed a problem with this medication. In one survey of primary care patients, trauma exposure was associated with increased lifetime use of benzodiazepines (Sansone, Hruschka, Vasudevan, & Miller, 2003).

There are few studies examining the use of benzodiazepines in trauma victims. In the only randomized controlled investigation of benzodiazepines in trauma, alprazolam was noted to help with symptoms of anxiety during the course of the trial, but there was no decrease in posttraumatic symptoms or in risk of later development of PTSD (Braun, Greenberg, Dasberg, & Lerer, 1990). In an open study of clonazepam and alprazolam, administered within the first week posttrauma, benzodiazepine-treated patients showed a decrease in heart rate over time, but no other benefit was found at 6 months. In fact, more of the patients who received medication met diagnostic criteria for PTSD at 6 months than those who did not receive a benzodiazepine (Gelpin, Bonne, Peri, Brandes, & Shalev, 1996). Temazepam, given at bedtime for a week in victims of acute trauma, improved sleep and appeared to decrease symptoms of PTSD 1 week after discontinuation; however, there was no long-term follow-up (Mellman,

Byers, & Augenstein, 1998). Clonazepam, given at bedtime in a small single-blind, placebo-controlled study, was not superior to placebo across multiple sleep measures in combat-related PTSD (Cates, Bishop, Davis, Lowe, & Wooley, 2004).

Girard and colleagues (2007) followed patients who had been mechanically ventilated in an intensive care unit. Six months out, those who received lorazepam during their ICU stay were more likely to have PTSD, and the total dose of lorazepam received correlated with the severity of symptoms. Researchers have attempted to elucidate this correlation in animal models, with interesting initial results: In stressed animals, administration of alprazolam was associated with freezing behaviors, a less favorable response to subsequent traumas, and suppression of corticosteroid levels (Matar, Zohar, Kaplan, & Cohen, 2009).

While more research is needed to elucidate the utility of benzodiazepines in trauma survivors, it is unlikely that they will prove to be therapeutic, either acutely or prescribed long-term. At the present time, we advise that benzodiazepines be used with such individuals only for the management of intense anxiety and panic attacks for which there is no other appropriate intervention. If used, these medications should be prescribed short term, and the initial treatment plan should include a discussion of risks and side effects as well as a plan for discontinuation. In addition, the clinician should have a discussion with the client regarding treatment with a less addictive, more long-term medication for intense, ongoing symptoms, such as an SSRI. Ideally, treatment with an SSRI would begin concomitantly with the benzodiazepine, with the benzodiazepine being tapered over the first 10 to 14 days of treatment. Close follow-up by the prescribing clinician is essential. In emergency settings, dispensing only enough medications to last 4 or 5 days is recommended as well—this ensures that the patient will not develop dependence before follow-up can occur.

Mood Stabilizers

As mentioned earlier, kindling has been hypothesized as one of the mechanisms by which PTSD develops under conditions of chronic stress. Because kindling theory was developed as a way to explain seizure disorders, this sparked interest in the use of mood stabilizing and anti-epileptic medications in PTSD. These medications have also been used to treat aggression and irritability in PTSD and other psychiatric conditions. Only two medications have been FDA approved as mood stabilizers: lithium and valproic acid. Despite the fact that lithium is generally considered to be the "gold standard" for the treatment of classical bipolar disorder, there have been no clinical trials investigating its use in PTSD. Recently, there has been increased interest in using the atypical antipsychotic medications as mood stabilizers, and in fact there are now indications for their use in certain phases of bipolar disorder. These medications and their indications are discussed in the section on antipsychotics. The mood stabilizers are listed in Table 12.6.

Table 12.6 Mood Stabilizers

Generic Name	Trade Name	Recommended Dosage	Pregnancy Category*	Present in Breast Milk
Lithium	Lithobid	300–1800mg (divided two or three times daily, dosed to reach a blood level of 0.6–1.2mEq/L)	D	Yes, possibly unsafe
Lamotrigine	Lamictal	50–200mg daily, dosed once	C	Yes, unsafe
Valproic acid	Depakote	500–1500mg (divided two or three times daily, dosed to reach a blood level of 50–100micrograms/mL)	D	Yes, probably safe
Carbamazepine	Tegretol	200–1200mg (divided twice daily, dosed to reach a blood level of 8–12micrograms/mL)	D	Yes, probably safe
Topiramate	Topamax	100–400mg, divided twice daily	D	Yes, safety unknown
Gabapentin	Neurontin	300–3600mg divided three or four times daily	C	Yes, probably safe
Levetiracetam	Keppra	500–3000mg, divided twice daily	C	Yes, safety unknown
Tiagabine	Gabitril	32–56mg, divided two to four times daily	C	Yes, probably safe

*See pp. 240–241 for a description of FDA pregnancy ratings.

Lithium

There are some studies suggesting that lithium may be helpful for the treatment of PTSD-related aggression (for example, Kitchner & Greenstein, 1985); however, there are no data investigating the use of this medication for PTSD. Lithium can cause weight gain, tremor, rash, kidney failure, and thyroid problems; it is also potentially fatal in overdose.

Lamotrigine (Lamictal)

Lamotrigine is a newer medication that affects N-methyl-D-aspartate (NDMA). In a small cohort of patients, lamotrigine was associated with improvements over placebo in the reexperiencing and avoidance/numbing symptoms of PTSD (Hertzberg et al., 1999). Given the small sample size of this study, little can be extrapolated from these findings until more research has been done. Lamotrigine is well documented as an effective mood stabilizer, as well as having antidepressant effects. Its most concerning potential side effect is Stevens-Johnson syndrome, a rare but life-threatening form of erythema multiforme that presents as a rash over the body, particularly the palms, soles, and backs of hands and feet. It can also involve lesions of the mucous membranes, and in severe cases, the kidneys, lungs, and digestive tract. For this reason, it must be slowly titrated with close observation.

Valproic Acid (Depakote)

Of all the mood stabilizers, valproic acid is probably most commonly used for the control of aggression and irritability. In three small open trials, in addition to multiple case reports, results of valproic acid in PTSD have been positive, but somewhat equivocal—one of the open trials reported benefit in all three symptom clusters of PTSD, the others in reexperiencing/hyperarousal and hyperarousal/avoidance, respectively (for example, R. D. Clark, Canive, Calais, Qualls, & Tuason, 1999; Petty et al., 2002). However, in a recent randomized placebo-controlled study, valproic acid was not found to be superior to placebo, although this may have been due in part to small sample size and the fact that participants were veterans with refractory PTSD (Hamner et al., 2009). Valproic acid can cause weight gain, mental dullness, and liver damage. It can also be fatal in overdose.

Carbamazepine (Tegretol)

Carbamazepine is another anticonvulsant frequently used as a mood stabilizer, although it is not FDA approved as such. It decreases excitability in the brain by stabilizing sodium channels; it also potentiates GABA receptors. In several small open trials, carbamazepine was effective in reducing all three symptom clusters of PTSD (for example, Keck, McElroy, & Friedman, 1992; Looff, Grimley, Kuller, Martin, & Shonfield, 1995). Carbamazepine is generally well tolerated, although it can cause bone marrow suppression that may have serious consequences. It can also cause a significant drop in serum sodium levels. Blood counts and electrolytes, as well as liver and kidney functions, therefore need to be monitored periodically. Common side effects include gastrointestinal upset, weight gain, and sedation. Carbamazepine can be lethal in overdose.

Topiramate (Topamax)

Topiramate is a newer anticonvulsant that is used as an add-on mood stabilizer. It has the added benefit of assisting with weight loss, a notable effect as most of the more commonly used mood stabilizers can cause significant weight gain. The exact mechanism of action is unknown, although topiramate, like other anticonvulsants, appears to have some activity on GABAergic neurons. In case reports and in two small open trials (Berlant, 2004;

Berlant & van Kammen, 2002), topiramate appeared to be effective across the three symptom clusters of PTSD. Topiramate has also been reported to be particularly effective in reducing PTSD-related nightmares and flashbacks, and as an add-on has been found to improve sleep and anxiety (Alderman, McCarthy, et al., 2009). Its most notable side effect is cognitive dulling, which some individuals find intolerable.

Gabapentin (Neurontin)

Gabapentin is another anticonvulsant that is used frequently in psychiatry as an add-on mood stabilizer, and as an adjunct in the management of anxiety and aggression. While gabapentin was designed to have effects on GABA, its exact mechanism of action is unknown. It has the benefit of having relatively few side effects and being less risky in overdose. To date there have been only case reports and retrospective chart reviews of its use as an adjunct to other medications for PTSD. Initial reports suggest that gabapentin may be useful for sleep disturbance and nightmares in PTSD (Hamner, Brodrick, & Labbate, 2001).

Levetiracetam (Keppra)

Levetiracetam is another novel antiepileptic that has unique binding in the nervous system. It is thought to reduce neural transmission through its effects on calcium channels. In a small retrospective study of SSRI nonresponders, levetiracetam was effective in reducing symptoms of PTSD (Kinrys, Wygant, Pardo, & Melo, 2006). It remains to be seen whether these results are reproduced in larger controlled studies. Levetiracetam is generally well tolerated, with minimal adverse effects. The most common side effects are irritability, somnolence, and dizziness; in high doses it can cause some psychotic symptoms.

Tiagabine (Gabitril)

Tiagabine is an antiepileptic that enhances the activity of GABA in the brain. There have been two small trials of tiagabine in PTSD. The first was a double-blind extension of an open trial—responders in the initial phase were randomized to either drug or placebo. Relapse rates were not significantly different between the groups, but tiagabine treatment was associated with greater likelihood of eventual remission, and the authors concluded there was a possible role for tiagabine in the PTSD armamentarium (Connor et al., 2006). However, in a later randomized placebo controlled study, tiagabine was found to be no more effective than placebo (J. R. Davidson et al., 2007). The most common side effects of tiagabine are dizziness, headache, and nausea. Rarely, it has been associated with seizures in those without a history of epilepsy; it also has been reported to cause depression and other psychiatric symptoms. The dose of tiagabine in psychiatry is much lower than that used for seizures—this is because most seizure patients are on other medications that induce the metabolism of tiagabine, requiring higher doses in order to achieve adequate blood levels.

Given this discussion, and the lack of adequate data regarding the use of mood stabilizers, they cannot be recommended as a first-line treatment for PTSD. They are probably most appropriate for use in those who do not respond adequately to treatment with SSRIs or other antidepressants, and in those who have significant behavioral disturbances due to aggression or agitated hyperarousal.

Adrenergic Agents

As described earlier in this chapter, dysregulation of the adrenergic system is clearly part of the biological underpinning of PTSD and other posttraumatic outcomes. Despite research that has demonstrated adrenergic hyperactivity in these states, there has been surprisingly little investigation of the use of anti-adrenergic compounds in the treatment of posttraumatic stress. The most commonly used adrenergic agents are listed in Table 12.7.

Beta-Adrenergic Blockade

Propranolol (Inderal). Propranolol is a nonselective beta-adrenergic blocking agent that has effects on both the central and peripheral nervous systems. While primarily used in general medicine as an antihypertensive and antiarrhythmic medication, propranolol is also used in psychiatry to treat aggression, social phobia, performance anxiety, and akathisia.

There have been three randomized trials of beta-blockers in treating post-traumatic stress. A pilot study investigated the use of a course of propranolol in acute trauma survivors with heart rates of at least 90 beats per minute (Pitman et al., 2002). At 1-month follow-up, fewer victims treated with the beta-blocker met PTSD criteria. However, this difference disappeared by 3 months. Surprisingly, those in the treatment group did not have a significantly greater heart rate decrease after receiving propranolol (at a dose of 40 milligrams) than did those who received a placebo. The authors suggest that this may indicate a need for higher doses in order to effectively counteract trauma-related adrenergic conditioning. A second trial, comparing propranolol and gabapentin to placebo for 13 days after an acute trauma, found no effect (M. B. Stein, Kerridge, Dimsdale, & Hoyt, 2007). A third trial in children with PTSD found no significant effect for propranolol compared to placebo (Nugent et al., 2010).

Smaller open studies, two in acute trauma survivors (Jimenez, Dieguez, & Lopez-Ibor, 2007; Vaiva et al., 2003), one in children with PTSD (Famularo,

Kinscherff, & Fenton, 1988), and a two-client case report (Dias & Jones, 2004) suggest that propranolol may be useful in reducing both current symptoms of posttraumatic stress and later risk for PTSD. However, a case series in acutely traumatized children (Sharp, Thomas, Rosenberg, Rosenberg, & Meyer, 2010) and one in burned servicemen (McGhee et al., 2009) found no incremental benefit for beta-blockers.

Beta-blockers have been shown to interfere with the consolidation of memories (see, for example, Maheu, Joober, & Lupien, 2005). Because of this effect, there has been much speculation, both in academia and in the media, about the ethics of preventing PTSD by giving a beta-blocker and thereby preventing the formation of a traumatic memory (see, for example, E. A. Hurley, 2007). However, as the literature is in fact far from clear that beta blockade prevents or treats PTSD, this ethical debate may be premature.

Frequent side effects of beta-blockers include gastrointestinal upsets (nausea, vomiting, diarrhea, abdominal pain), cold extremities and exacerbation of Raynaud's phenomenon, sleep disturbance, dizziness, and fatigue. Beta-blockers can also cause congestive heart failure and bronchospasm; they are therefore contraindicated in individuals who have preexisting congestive heart failure, bronchospasm, and bronchial asthma, as well as those who have sinus bradycardia or first-degree heart block. In overdose, propranolol can lead to significant cardiac damage.

Table 12.7   Adrenergic Agents

Generic Name	Trade Name	Recommended Dosage	Pregnancy Category*	Present in Breast Milk
Propranolol	Inderal	Initial dose 40mg twice daily. Titration as tolerated to a maximum of 320mg. Usual doses in psychiatry total 120–160mg daily. (Inderal exists in a long-acting form, but there are no studies of its use in psychiatry.)	C	Yes, probably safe
Clonidine	Catapres	Initial dose 0.1mg twice daily. The dose may be increased by 0.1mg per day as indicated clinically—usual doses range from 0.2–0.6mg daily.	C	Yes, safety unknown
Prazosin	Minipress	Initial dose 1mg daily. Slowly increase as tolerated. The doses used in PTSD have ranged from 1–10mg daily. The dose limit for prazosin in medical settings is up to 15mg.	C	Yes, safety unknown

*See pp. 240–241 for a description of FDA pregnancy ratings.

Alpha-Adrenergic Blockade

Clonidine (Catapres). Clonidine, a presynaptic alpha 2-adrenergic agonist, suppresses the release of norepinephrine both centrally and peripherally. It is used as an antihypertensive agent and as an adjunct in the treatment for the autonomic symptoms associated with opiate withdrawal. In open trials, clonidine has been reported as helpful for symptoms of hyperarousal, hypervigilance, sleep disruption, exaggerated startle response, nightmares, behavioral irritability, and aggression in studies of combat veterans (Kolb, Burris, & Griffiths, 1984), Cambodian refugees (Kinzie & Leung, 1989), and children with PTSD (Harmon & Riggs, 1996).

The most common side effects of clonidine include dry mouth, drowsiness, sedation, dizziness, and constipation. Clonidine acts relatively rapidly and can cause severe hypotension acutely, within 30 to 60 minutes after administration. It must therefore be carefully dosed and monitored. Clonidine should not be given to those with severe cardiovascular disease, and care should be taken on discontinuation to avoid rebound hypertension.

A significant problem with the use of clonidine is the development of physiological tolerance, leading to a gradual return of symptoms that sometimes do not respond to higher doses. There have been a few case reports describing the use of guanfacine instead of clonidine, but these are too small in number to recommend its use (for example, Horrigan & Barnhill, 1996).

Prazosin (Minipress). Prazosin is more commonly used in clinical practice than clonidine due to its more favorable side effect profile and the fact that, unlike clonidine, it does not lead to tolerance. Prazosin is an antihypertensive agent that blocks alpha1-adrenergic receptors centrally and peripherally. A small placebo-controlled trial in noncombat PTSD found that prazosin was effective at increasing time asleep as well as decreasing nightmares and awakenings (F. B. Taylor et al., 2008). Similarly, in two small controlled trials in veterans, prazosin was superior to placebo in improving sleep, changing dream content away from trauma-related material, and improving overall PTSD symptoms (Raskind et al., 2007; Raskind et al., 2003). Several open trials of prazosin in both combat- and noncombat-related PTSD have indicated similar efficacy (for example, Boynton, Bentley, Strachan, Barbato, & Raskind, 2009; F. Taylor & Raskind, 2002).

The most common side effects of prazosin are nausea, dizziness, headache, drowsiness, weakness, lack of energy, and palpitations. Prazosin has been noted to cause syncope (sudden loss of consciousness), which is believed in most cases to be due to hypotension. There are no absolute contraindications; however, care must be taken in patients who have preexisting heart disease, and blood pressure must be closely monitored. In overdose, alpha-blockers can cause significant cardiac problems, as well as fatality in very high doses.

A Final Note on Adrenergic Agents

Although there are clear research data that alpha- and beta-adrenergic blockers can be useful adjuncts in the treatment of posttraumatic stress, the investigations to date have been limited to case reports, open trials, and a handful of controlled trials with very few subjects. The data suggest that beta-blockers may be helpful in treating those individuals who suffer from intense symptoms of hyperarousal, while alpha-blockers may be most helpful in those with intractable sleep disturbance and nightmares. Practical precautions to take with patients when prescribing these medications include (1) explaining the nature of and rationale for treatment with these agents, including the fact that their use in psychiatry is "off label," (2) communicating with and obtaining clearance from patients' internists regarding using blood pressure–lowering agents, (3) close monitoring of vital signs, especially in the first few weeks of treatment, and (4) caution regarding risk for falls in elderly or otherwise medically compromised individuals.

Antipsychotics

The antipsychotics are medications that block dopamine in the central nervous system. They differ from each other primarily in the extent of dopamine blockade, the specific receptors that they affect, and their side effects. The "typical" antipsychotics, (for example, haloperidol [Haldol], fluphenazine [Prolixin], chlorpromazine [Thorazine]) were seen as a miracle cure for schizophrenia when they were first introduced in the 1950s. However, because they affect dopamine, they have potentially serious and debilitating motor side effects. These "extrapyramidal symptoms" (EPS—so called because they are thought to originate from the basal ganglia, rather than from the motor "pyramids" of the brainstem) occur often in the first few days or weeks of treatment, and manifest in three ways: (1) Parkinsonism—tremor, rigidity, shuffling gait; (2) akathisia—the subjective experience of feeling restless and unable to sit still; and (3) dystonia—stiffening of the limbs, jaw, or neck, often occurring quite acutely and requiring immediate medical intervention. Tardive dyskinesia (TD) usually occurs after long-term treatment with antipsychotics, although it has also been reported both early in treatment and after treatment is terminated. TD is characterized by rhythmic involuntary movements of the mouth, jaw, tongue, and lips (such as chewing, smacking, and pursing) as well as the extremities. TD is generally irreversible and can be quite disfiguring and debilitating.

The typical antipsychotics have also been associated with a condition known as neuroleptic malignant syndrome (NMS), a potentially life-threatening reaction that is characterized by altered mental status, autonomic dysfunction, fever, and muscle rigidity. In overdose, they can cause arrythmias and can be fatal.

Table 12.8 Atypical Antipsychotics

Generic Name	Trade Name	Recommended Dosage	Major Side Effects	Pregnancy Category*	Present in Breast Milk
Risperidone	Risperdal	0.5–16mg daily, however, doses greater than 4mg daily are rarely more effective	Akathisia, EPS in higher doses, hyperprolactinemia	C	Yes, possibly unsafe
Olanzapine	Zyprexa	5–20mg daily	Sedation, weight gain, increased risk for diabetes	C	Yes, possibly unsafe
Quetiapine	Seroquel	50–800mg daily, in divided doses	Sedation, weight gain, rare risk of cataracts	C	Yes, safety unknown
Ziprasidone	Geodon	40–160mg daily, in divided doses	Rare risk of prolonged QTc on EKG— screening EKG recommended before starting therapy	C	Yes, safety unknown
Aripiprazole	Abilify	10–30mg daily	Agitation, constipation, headache, lightheadedness	C	Yes, safety unknown
Clozapine	Clozaril	100–900mg daily, in divided doses	Sedation, drooling, weight gain, increased risk for diabetes, agranulocytosis	B	Yes, possibly unsafe
Asenapine	Saphris	10–20mg daily, in divided doses	Dizziness, somnolence, tachycardia, weight gain, rare agranulocytosis	C	Yes, safety unknown
Lurasidone	Latuda	40–80mg daily	Somnolence, akathisia, nausea, weight gain	B	Yes, safety unknown
Iloperidone	Fanapt	12–24 mg daily, in divided doses	Dizziness, somnolence, weight gain, fatigue	C	Yes, safety unknown

*See pp. 240–241 for a description of FDA pregnancy ratings.

In the 1980s, a new class of antipsychotics was developed, referred to as "atypical" to distinguish them from the older medications. These newer medications, as a class, have significantly less risk of motor side effects. They also are relatively benign in overdose. Because of this lower risk, they are being used for an increasingly wide spectrum of nonpsychotic psychiatric disturbances, including mania, depression, severe anxiety, personality disorders, aggression, insomnia, and trauma. In fact, the FDA has recently approved the use of several atypical antipsychotics for the treatment of various phases of bipolar disorder. The atypical antipsychotics are listed in Table 12.8.

The use of these medications in nonpsychotic individuals, nonetheless, remains controversial. While the incidence of movement disorders and NMS is greatly reduced with atypical antipsychotics, the risk is not eliminated. The annual incidence of TD with typical antipsychotics has been estimated to be 5 percent in adults; for the atypicals, the annual incidence is around 0.8 percent (Correll, Leucht, & Kane, 2004). However, several lines of research have suggested that individuals with mood disorders have a higher likelihood of developing TD from antipsychotics than do those who have primary psychotic disorders. In one study, depressed individuals treated with typical antipsychotics developed TD at an annual rate of 13.5 percent (Kane, 1999). Such data have yet to be replicated using the newer generation of medications. However, given the high comorbidity of PTSD and depression, it might be reasonable to extrapolate from these data that traumatized individuals could also be at higher risk for these debilitating side effects. Given this potential risk, caution is warranted when using antipsychotics for this broader array of symptoms.

Another emerging concern with the use of the atypicals is metabolic syndrome—a clustering of obesity, impaired glucose tolerance, hypertension, and increased lipids. Metabolic syndrome has been noted to be higher in those with severe mental illnesses than in the general population (for a variety of reasons, including lifestyle and poor self-care, among others) but has also been associated with psychotropic medications, particularly olanzapine, clozapine, and quetiapine. Recent studies have shown high discontinuation rates with all antipsychotics, and researchers and clinicians are beginning to reevaluate the risk-benefit profiles associated with their use (for example, Lieberman et al., 2005).

Antipsychotics for PTSD

Five of the atypical antipsychotics have been evaluated for efficacy in trauma. These are risperidone (Risperdal), olanzapine (Zyprexa), quetiapine (Seroquel), ziprasidone (Geodon) and aripiprazole (Abilify). Lurasidone (Latuda), asenapine (Saphris), and iloperidone (Fanapt) are newer to the market, and it is likely that, in the coming years, their use in trauma will be investigated as well. There is one case report in the literature discussing the efficacy of clozapine (Clozaril) in PTSD with psychosis (Hamner, 1996). Given the dearth of literature, and the significant side effects associated with the use of this medication, however, it would be prudent to continue to restrict its use to those individuals who are psychotic and highly treatment resistant, as is the usual practice.

Risperidone (Risperdal). There have been five randomized controlled trials of risperidone in PTSD. In largest and most recent of these, a 6-month multicenter trial with over 300 subjects, adjunctive risperidone was evaluated in combat veterans with chronic PTSD. Surprisingly, risperidone was not associated with a reduction in symptoms of anxiety, depression or PTSD in this population (Krystal et al., 2011). However, it was associated with a small improvement in hyperarousal and reexperiencing symptoms as compared to avoidance/numbing, consistent with its activity as an alpha-adrenergic blocker. The authors suggest that the lack of efficacy for risperidone in this population may have been in part due to the fact that most participants were taking other medications, such as trazodone or quetiapine, which have similar actions and might have reduced the observed effect. They also question the widespread practice of using risperidone as a treatment for chronic PTSD and suggest care when it is prescribed in such situations.

The four other randomized trials of risperidone were limited by small sample size, the presence of significant comorbidity, and the use of other psychotropic medications. Two of these found that low-dose risperidone was helpful in the treatment of irritability and intrusive reexperiencing (Monnelly, Ciraulo, Knapp, & Keane, 2003; Reich, Winternitz, Hennen, Watts, & Stanculescu, 2004); another found efficacy on the hyperarousal subscale of the CAPS (Bartzokis, Lu, Turner, Mintz, & Saunders, 2005). The last investigated the use of risperidone in veterans with PTSD who also had psychotic symptoms. These individuals had a modest improvement in their psychotic symptoms, but no statistically significant reduction in PTSD symptoms (Hamner, Deitsch, Brodrick, Ulmer, & Lorberbaum, 2003).

In addition, there have been several open studies indicating that risperidone may be helpful for nightmares, intrusive reexperiencing, hyperarousal, suspiciousness, and aggression in PTSD (for example, David, De Faria, & Mellman, 2006; Krashin & Oates, 1999; Monnelly & Ciraulo, 1999). Rothbaum et al. (2008) studied the risperidone augmentation of sertraline in a small sample of civilians with PTSD who had not responded to sertraline alone. While there was no difference between the risperidone and placebo in terms of overall response, there did appear to be some incremental improvement in sleep and suspiciousness/paranoia with risperidone.

Of the atypicals, risperidone has the highest risk of extrapyramidal symptoms, in that sense it is the most "typical" of the atypicals. Risperidone also carries some risk of weight gain, sedation, and increase in prolactin levels, which can be a problem especially in women of childbearing age.

Olanzapine (Zyprexa). There have been two small randomized controlled trials using olanzapine as an adjunctive treatment in nonpsychotic combat veterans with PTSD. The first indicated moderate response in symptoms of PTSD compared to placebo, but no significant difference in clinical global improvement (M. B. Stein, Kline, & Matloff, 2002). The second found a high placebo-response rate and no statistical benefit to olanzapine over placebo (Butterfield et al., 2001). There have been several open trials and case reports suggesting the effectiveness of olanzapine in treating PTSD-associated insomnia, nightmares, intrusive reexperiencing, and depressive symptoms (for example, Jakovljevic, Sagud, & Mihaljevic-Peles, 2003; Pivac, Kozaric-Kovacic, & Muck-Seler, 2004). Olanzapine has a significant risk of weight gain (which patients often find intolerable) and has been associated with the development of diabetes and metabolic syndrome. It is also quite sedating, and it may cause hypotension in some individuals.

Quetiapine (Seroquel). There have been no randomized controlled trials of quetiapine in PTSD, although multiple open-label trials and case reports have described some efficacy. In an open trial of treatment-resistant combat veterans with PTSD and psychosis, quetiapine monotherapy improved both PTSD and psychotic symptoms. Psychosis was improved more than PTSD, and most patients still met criteria for moderate to mild PTSD at the end of the trial (Kozaric-Kovacic & Pivac, 2007). Similarly, in an open-label study in combat veterans a variety of PTSD-related sleep disturbances were improved with quetiapine treatment, although the effect was "modest" (S. Robert et al., 2005).

Several other open trials and case reports of quetiapine as adjunctive therapy have indicated effectiveness across all PTSD symptom clusters, particularly the reexperiencing symptoms, and in positive symptoms of psychosis (for example, Hamner et al., 2003; Sokolski, Denson, Lee, & Reist, 2003).

Quetiapine can cause significant weight gain and sedation, and has been identified as a risk factor for the development of metabolic syndrome. Seroquel has attained a "street value" among substance-addicted individuals and for this reason has been taken off formulary in some clinical settings such as prisons.

Aripiprazole (Abilify). There have been no randomized trials of aripiprazole in PTSD. Several open trials and case reports indicate some effectiveness; however, across all studies there were high rates of dropout due to adverse effects. In a recent open-label trial of aripiprazole augmentation, overall PTSD symptoms improved, most interestingly the avoidance/numbing symptoms—in contrast to risperidone and olanzapine, which appear to be most useful in targeting reexperiencing and hyperarousal (S. Robert et al., 2009). Similarly, a retrospective chart review of patients with PTSD and depression found that both PTSD and depressive symptoms improved with aripiprazole augmentation, with depressive symptoms improving slightly more (Richardson, Fikretoglu, Liu, & McIntosh, 2011).

Aripiprazole as monotherapy appeared to be quite effective in two open trials, with up to two-thirds of the participants showing significant symptom improvement. However, in these trials one-fourth and one-third of the subjects, respectively, dropped out due to adverse side effects (Villareal et al., 2007).

Aripiprazole is a unique medication, billed as a "dopamine equalizer"—it blocks dopamine in some areas of the brain, while increasingly its activity in others. This can lead to paradoxical activation in some individuals, along with sedation and gastrointestinal upset. Interestingly, in studies of PTSD and aripiprazole there appear to be more dropouts due to adverse effects than with other antipsychotics. It may be that the activation is intolerable to some already-hyperaroused trauma survivors. However, the associated benefits are that aripiprazole appears to be more efficacious for avoidance/numbing and depression than the other medications in its class, for those who can tolerate it. Aripiprazole does not appear to cause significant weight gain, and it carries less risk of metabolic syndrome.

Ziprasidone (Geodon). The one randomized placebo-controlled study of ziprasidone was discontinued due to participant dropout—the cases were unblinded and it turned out that all of the dropouts receiving ziprasidone suffered adverse events (Kellner, Muhtz, & Wiedemann, 2010). In two case reports of individuals with refractory nonpsychotic combat PTSD, posttraumatic symptoms responded well to ziprasidone (Siddiqui, Marcil, Bhatia, Ramaswamy, & Petty, 2005). Ziprasidone has a good metabolic profile, with little weight gain. It must be taken with food, as this increases its absorption into the blood by a factor of 2.

The above data regarding antipsychotics suggest that, for treatment-refractory PTSD, particularly when there are psychotic symptoms present, atypical antipsychotics can be a useful addition to pharmacotherapy. In fact, in clinical practice, antipsychotics appear to be prescribed for symptoms of hyperarousal, insomnia, and aggression in significant quantities. However, given the high risk of side effects, the limited number of randomized, controlled trials to guide their use, and the limited amount of data regarding their true efficacy for nonpsychotic posttraumatic stress, caution is recommended. A recent study comparing quetiapine to prazosin is illustrative: In this chart review, both medications were equally effective for sleep disturbance, but prazosin was ultimately more effective in the long term as patients were more likely to continue taking it due to fewer negative sides effects (Byers, Allison, Wendel, & Lee, 2010). In line with these results, it behooves the clinician to look for the intervention with the least adverse effects.

It may be particularly difficult to convince highly anxious, distrustful individuals, especially those who do not want to be sedated, that antipsychotics are a reasonable alternative. At the present time, there is no indication that the antipsychotics are as effective as the SSRIs for PTSD, nor is there any evidence to suggest that antipsychotics represent a first-line choice for PTSD (Friedman et al., 2009).

For those instances in which an antipsychotic is clinically warranted, the literature indicates some trends that may prove useful:

- Atypicals are likely to be most helpful in patients with symptoms that have not responded or have partially responded to other pharmacologic interventions.
- Olanzapine and risperidone appear to be most effective for symptoms of reexperiencing, intrusion, and hyperarousal.

- Quetiapine appears to be particularly effective in improving sleep and reducing nightmares.
- Aripiprazole may be most useful for patients with significant numbing/ avoidance and/or comorbid depression.

Medications for Trauma-Related Psychosis

As noted earlier in this volume, posttraumatic stress is occasionally accompanied by psychosis. Severe trauma can lead to brief psychotic disorder with marked stressors (BPDMS), and it can exacerbate symptoms in those with an underlying psychotic disorder such as schizophrenia. PTSD has been found to occur four times more frequently in people with psychotic depression than in those with nonpsychotic depression (Zimmerman & Mattia, 1999). Some individuals may have intense reexperiencing symptoms that can be very difficult to distinguish from psychotic symptoms; others may have trauma-associated fear and avoidance responses that generalize to a wide range of stimuli and are hard to discriminate from paranoid delusions. Although there is no *DSM-IV* category for "PTSD with psychotic features," there do appear to be some individuals with PTSD who have psychotic symptoms, who do not appear to have another underlying psychotic disorder, and who do not meet criteria for psychotic depression. (See Chapter 2 for a more complete discussion of this issue and the diagnostic dilemma involved.)

In instances when trauma leads acutely to psychosis, the recommended treatment is antipsychotic medication. Often, as in BPDMS, the psychotic symptoms resolve over a relatively brief time period. In such situations, the antipsychotic may be tapered off over a course of several weeks, with close monitoring for recurrence as well as for the development of other posttraumatic symptomatology. The literature on BPDMS (and on its predecessor in *DSM-III* [American Psychiatric Association, 1987], "Acute Reactive Psychosis") is extremely sparse, and there are no clinical trials investigating the use of medications specifically for this condition.

Major depression with psychotic features, a not uncommon disorder in trauma survivors (see Chapter 2), is a particularly difficult condition both to diagnose and treat. When PTSD occurs comorbidly with psychotic depression, treatment with both an antidepressant (generally an SSRI) and an antipsychotic is indicated (see Schatzberg, 2003, for a review). Tricyclic antidepressants as monotherapy have generally been found to be ineffective for psychotic depression, as have SSRIs and antipsychotic medications (for example, Schatzberg, 2003; G. M. Simpson, El Sheshai, Rady, Kingsbury, & Fayek, 2003). Overall, response rates with the combination of an SSRI and an atypical antipsychotic have ranged in the area of 50–60 percent. Over the course of treatment, the symptoms of PTSD, depression, and psychosis should be followed closely. The decision to continue antipsychotic medication once psychotic symptoms have resolved must be made on an individual basis. This involves an assessment of risk of recurrence, prior history of psychosis, severity of depression, current levels of stress, and presence or absence of debilitating medication side effects. Recent research indicates that treatment with an antipsychotic for at least 4 months is associated with a decreased risk of relapse (Rothschild & Duval, 2003).

There is an emerging literature on the use of medications that inhibit the HPA axis, such as mifepristone, for psychotic depression. This practice is based on the finding that psychotic depression appears to be associated with abnormal HPA axis activity and elevated cortisol levels (Schatzberg, 2003). Note that the reconciliation of this finding with the generally low HPA axis activity and low cortisol associated with PTSD, as described earlier, is as yet unclear. Some recent research has suggested that nonpsychotic depression in trauma survivors is biologically (in terms of HPA axis activity) more similar to PTSD than it is to "regular" depression that is not associated with trauma (Yehuda et al., 2004). Perhaps, as research continues, we will find a similar biological difference between psychotic depression that is associated with trauma and PTSD and psychotic depression that occurs in the absence of trauma. This conundrum, again, illustrates the complexity associated with studying and treating trauma. As of yet, there is no data examining the use of HPA inhibition in psychotic depression that is comorbid with PTSD.

For those situations where PTSD is accompanied by psychotic symptoms in the absence of depression or another Axis I disorder, the literature provides little in the way of direction. Clinical and anecdotal experience suggest that, as for PTSD with comorbid psychotic depression, treatment with an antidepressant and an antipsychotic is indicated, with similar close follow-up and assessment of the need for ongoing medication. In our experience, antipsychotics are rarely helpful when the reexperiencing symptoms of PTSD mimic psychosis (see Table 12.8).

Medications for Acute Traumatic Stress

As described in Chapter 6, there is a dearth of literature on acute stress disorder (ASD). This is especially apparent in the area of pharmacological treatment. There have been very few randomized controlled trials of medications for acute stress; in fact, when treating acute trauma victims, clinicians must often extrapolate from the literature on PTSD in order to provide treatment that is validated and up to date with current research. Most of the literature on treating victims in the emergency setting, or in a less emergent but nonetheless acute setting, focuses on psychosocial rather than pharmacological interventions (see Chapter 11).

Benzodiazepines

Acute survivors of trauma often experience a great amount of distress, with significant anxiety, panic attacks, agitation, and sleep disturbance.

Victims (and often their families and loved ones) may request that medical practitioners provide sedating medications to relieve the intense distress associated with the trauma. In addition, clinicians may have their own emotional reactions to traumatic material and to the distress of their clients, which may prompt them to provide powerful medications for immediate symptomatic relief. Unfortunately, the literature is equivocal on the benefits to be derived from acutely treating the anxiety that acute trauma victims experience.

As described earlier, the benzodiazepines, although technically effective for the amelioration of acute anxiety, are not useful treatments for acute trauma and, in fact, may be associated with an increased risk for the development of PTSD (Gelpin et al., 1996). Some have suggested that benzodiazepines might be useful in the acute setting to prevent the memory consolidation that leads to PTSD; again, this hypothesis has not been borne out in clinical practice. Nevertheless, there are situations in which distress (for example, following a gang rape or witnessing the murder of a family member), especially in the emergency room setting, can only be adequately addressed by using a benzodiazepine. Under these circumstances, cautious use is acceptable, preferably in conjunction with beginning an SSRI or other antidepressant. However, because of the especially high risk for abuse and dependence associated with alprazolam, its use is not recommended (see Table 12.5).

Antidepressants

There is only sparse data on the use of antidepressants in the acutely traumatized. In a single, small open trial of imipramine in pediatric burn victims who met ASD criteria, moderate improvement across all three symptom clusters was seen after 7 days (R. Robert, Blakeney, Villarreal, Rosenberg, & Meyer, 1999). Surprisingly, there has been no research on the use of SSRIs in acute traumatic stress, despite the fact that SSRIs are the first-line medication treatment for PTSD and appear to have efficacy for all three of its symptom clusters.

Notwithstanding the absence of empirical data, in actual clinical practice clinicians often prescribe SSRIs for those individuals who have been diagnosed with ASD, or who are otherwise experiencing acute posttraumatic symptoms, particularly panic attacks. In addition, SSRIs are often prescribed in the hope that they will prevent the development of lasting posttraumatic disturbance. The use of SSRIs in ASD seems reasonable, given (1) the fact that the *DSM-IV* criteria for ASD are similar to those for PTSD and (2) the data mentioned earlier suggesting that SSRIs may "reregulate" the HPA dysfunction thought to be involved in posttraumatic stress.

For these reasons, the SSRIs are a reasonable choice for those individuals suffering from ASD who require intervention with medications. In light of the problems associated with the use of benzodiazepines, an SSRI is probably the best candidate for intervening in the acute anxiety of ASD, since these medications are efficacious in the treatment of both generalized anxiety and panic attacks, in addition to PTSD. Clearly, however, research is needed to clarify this issue (see Tables 12.1–12.4).

Adrenergic Agents

As described earlier, the use of adrenergic medications in trauma is theoretically promising, but the few studies done to date have yielded equivocal results. Propranolol given to acute trauma survivors appears to reduce risk for PTSD initially, but this difference disappeared by 3 months (Pitman et al., 2002). However, script-driven imagery at 3 months revealed decreased physiological reactivity in those who had received the treatment as compared to controls. There has been some speculation that adrenergic blockade, if given within hours of a trauma, might work to prevent sensitization of the adrenergic system; this has yet to be adequately studied, however. At this time, no definitive recommendation regarding these agents in acute trauma can be made (see Table 12.7).

Other Agents

As with the SSRIs, there is very little literature on the use of other psychotropic agents in ASD. Research is necessary to evaluate the potential benefit of mood stabilizers to interfere at an early stage with the kindling that might lead to PTSD.

Medications for Sleep

Disturbances of sleep can be one of the most distressing and debilitating aspects of posttraumatic stress. Trauma survivors often complain of initial insomnia, frequent nighttime wakenings, nightmares, early morning wakenings, and subjective feelings of being not rested even when they have slept. Sleep studies have been inconclusive in terms of the underlying physiological mechanisms of disordered sleep in traumatized individuals. Although some research has indicated that trauma leads to disordered rapid eye movement (REM) sleep and that nightmare sufferers have more frequent nighttime wakenings (Harvey, Jones, & Schmidt, 2003; Mellman, Bustamante, Fins, Pigeon, & Nolan, 2002), other studies have found no correlation between subjective complaints of sleep disturbance and abnormalities on polysomnographic sleep studies in the laboratory (for example, Hurwitz, Mahowald, Kuskowski, & Engdahl, 1998). Regardless, sleep problems remain a frequent complaint in trauma survivors. Finding medication that improves the quality and quantity of sleep without causing daytime drowsiness or oversedation can be challenging.

The literature on treating PTSD-related sleep disturbance is limited. However, many of the medications that improve posttraumatic symptomatology can help with sleep—including the mood stabilizers, the antipsychotics, the tricyclics, and some antidepressants. Many of these medications are also sedating, and clinicians can take advantage of this side effect by prescribing them to be taken at night. Although the SSRIs as a class do improve symptoms across all three clusters of PTSD symptomatology, they can sometimes cause an increase in levels of anxiety and activation, especially in the first few weeks of treatment, and often require the addition of a sleep agent. The major nonbenzodiazepine sleep agents are listed in Table 12.9.

Trazodone (Desyrel)

Trazodone, as discussed earlier, is a highly sedating antidepressant. In fact, it is used more commonly as a sleep agent (in low doses) than as a treatment for depression. Trazodone is an effective hypnotic, and it does not cause dependence or withdrawal. However, it can cause a feeling of being "hungover," and daytime drowsiness, that some patients cannot tolerate. There are no reports of its use as a sleep agent in PTSD survivors, but a few case reports suggest that trazodone improves sleep as well as other symptoms of PTSD (Hertzberg et al., 1996). As a sleep agent, there is an optimal "window" of effectiveness—it is generally recommended to go to bed within 1 to 1.5 hours after taking trazodone in order for it to effectively bring on sleep. Trazodone is generally considered a safe adjunct to other psychotropics. See pages 251–252 for more information on this medication.

Antihistamines

There is no specific literature on the use of antihistamines in PTSD. However, diphenhydramine (Benadryl, which is available over the counter), and

Table 12.9 Nonbenzodiazepine Sleeping Medications

Generic Name	Trade Name	Recommended Doses (for sleep)	Pregnancy Category*	Present in Breast Milk
Trazodone	Desyrel	50–200 mg	C	Yes, probably safe
Diphenhydramine	Benadryl	25–50mg	B	Yes, probably safe
Hydroxyzine	Atarax, Vistaril	50–100mg	C	Yes, probably safe
Zolpidem	Ambien	5–10mg	C	Yes, possibly unsafe
Zaleplon	Sonata	5–10mg	C	Yes, probably safe
Eszopiclone	Lunesta	1–3mg	C	Yes, safety unknown

*See pp. 240–241 for a description of FDA pregnancy ratings.

hydroxyzine (Atarax, Vistaril) are used commonly as sleep agents because of their sedating properties (Ringdahl, Pereira, & Delzell, 2004). They have relatively few side effects, little risk associated with overdose, and no potential for abuse or dependence. The major problems with their use as sleep agents are dry mouth and the potential for morning drowsiness.

Zolpidem (Ambien)

Zolpidem is a commonly prescribed nonbenzodiazepine sleep agent. It has a rapid onset of action and causes minimal daytime sedation, due to a short half-life of about 2.5 hours. Compared to benzodiazepines, it has significantly fewer effects on cognition and memory (Terzano, Rossi, Palomba, Smerieri, & Parrino, 2003) and appears to have less risk of abuse. In a series of case reports of the use of zolpidem in veterans with PTSD, it was found to be an effective sleep agent with no development of tolerance over treatment periods of up to 20 months (Dieperink & Drogemuller, 1999). However, caution is warranted as the manufacturer notes the potential for tolerance and rebound insomnia in some individuals, as well as psychological dependence, and recommends limiting the use of this medication to no more than 3 weeks. The main side effects associated with zolpidem are headache, drowsiness, fatigue, and dizziness. Zolpidem has also been noted to cause perceptual disturbances shortly after administration; this is thought to be due to the rapid induction of a hypnotic or dreamlike state associated with peak plasma levels. It is also available in a controlled-release formulation (Zolpidem CR), which has a longer length of action.

Zaleplon (Sonata)

Zaleplon is another nonbenzodiazepine hypnotic. It is ultra-short-acting, with a half-life of about 1 hour. There have been no studies investigating its use in PTSD. However, because of its short length of action, zaleplon may be a good choice for those traumatized individuals who are particularly concerned about sedation and decreased responsiveness to threats. Conversely, for individuals who suffer from early wakening, or who wake frequently throughout the night due to trauma-related nightmares, the effects of zaleplon may not be long-lasting enough. The main side effects associated with zaleplon are headache, nausea, and dizziness. Zaleplon can also cause a hypnagogic state similar to that caused by zolpidem (Terzano et al., 2003).

Eszopiclone (Lunesta)

Eszopiclone is the newest nonbenzodiazepine sleep agent, and it is related to zolpidem and zaleplon. It appears to be generally well tolerated. Its use in PTSD has not been investigated. The main side effects are a bad taste in the mouth on waking, which some report as intolerable, and headache, as well as the possibility of a hypnagogic state, as described earlier.

Benzodiazepines

As discussed earlier in this chapter, there are significant risks associated with the use of benzodiazepines. If at all possible, clinicians should try other agents before using benzodiazepines as sleep agents. The risk for physiological and psychological dependence is high, as is the potential for abuse. This being said, there are times when no other treatment for the severe insomnia associated with posttraumatic stress is adequate. In such cases, benzodiazepines should be prescribed for short periods of time only, and with careful monitoring of patterns of use and reported need for dose increases (see Table 12.5).

Strategy for Medicating Sleep Disturbances in Posttraumatic Stress

The recommendations for medicating posttraumatic sleep disturbance can be summarized as follows:

- Maximize use of current psychotropic regimen for sleep efficacy (for example, paroxetine, TCAs, trazodone, mirtazapine, antipsychotics, mood stabilizers). Often this can be accomplished by switching from twice daily to once daily at bedtime dosing.
- If necessary, add a nonaddictive sleep agent such as trazodone or an antihistamine.
- In those individuals with nightmares as well as sleep disturbance, consider prazosin.
- Switch to one of the nonbenzodiazepine hypnotics such as zolpidem or zaleplon.
- If these are ineffective, judicious use of a benzodiazepine may be supportable.

Medications for Dissociation

The literature on pharmacological approaches to the treatment of dissociative symptomatology is extremely sparse, and many clinicians make the presumption that medications will not be helpful for dissociation. To some extent, this is correct; currently available medications do not do much for such symptoms as amnesia, cognitive disengagement, depersonalization, rapid switching from one state to another, or losing track of time. However, because dissociative symptoms do appear to intensify under stress, much of the literature encourages treatment of the conditions that may occur comorbidly with dissociative disorders, including depression, anxiety, and PTSD.

A few open trials (for example, Bohus et al., 1999) have suggested that naltrexone may help to reduce dissociative symptoms and posttraumatic flashbacks in borderline patients, while others have described its effectiveness in reducing self-injurious behavior in dissociative identity disorder (Loewenstein, 2005).

The differentiation of posttraumatic reexperiencing from psychotic hallucinations (as described in detail in Chapter 3) can be particularly difficult in highly dissociated individuals. Unfortunately, some clients are treated unnecessarily, sometimes for long periods of time, with antipsychotics that have little effect and have significant side effects, because they were incorrectly judged to be psychotic. Some clinicians find that low doses of antipsychotics are helpful in treating the anxiety and intrusive symptoms of PTSD that can accompany dissociation (Loewenstein, 2005). However, in our anecdotal experience there are times when such medications can in fact increase dissociative responses by decreasing awareness of the environment, much in the way benzodiazepines do.

C. A. Morgan, Krystal, and Southwick (2003), in a review, suggest several approaches that might be beneficial for dissociation, given what we know about the biology of dissociative states: (1) treatment of hyperarousal with adrenergic blockers, as traumatized individuals often dissociate when stressed or overwhelmed; (2) treatment with medications that affect GAB Aergic neurons, such as SSRIs; and (3) use of medications that affect N-methyl-D-aspartate (NMDA), such as lamotrigine. However, these recommendations are based on presumptions about biology rather than clinical outcome data.

Our general approach to the treatment of dissociation involves psychotherapy as the primary intervention; in the best-case scenario, as clients process trauma and learn skills that assist with affect regulation and interpersonal relatedness, dissociation recedes as part of the clinical picture. However, when dissociating clients have significant posttraumatic, depressive, or other anxiety symptoms, treatment with pharmacotherapy is appropriate.

Medication for Traumatic Brain Injury (TBI)

The FDA has yet to approve any medications for specific post-TBI mental health indications. Given that lesions in different areas of the brain present with often markedly different clinical pictures, pharmacologic interventions generally aim to address the specific symptom cluster in a given patient. For example, impulsivity, poor concentration, psychosis, mood disturbance, and anxiety stemming from TBI might each require different treatment approaches. Although the numbers vary significantly depending on patient population and type of injury, best estimates are that post-TBI, 11–48 percent of individuals develop major depression, 5–23 percent develop mania, and up to 20 percent develop posttraumatic psychosis, any of which may first emerge many years after the initial injury (Kim et al., 2007). Recommendations for medication management of these symptom clusters are consistent with symptom management in non-TBI patients, with a few caveats, as described below.

Cognitive impairment after TBI is widely described and can be an extremely frustrating and debilitating collection of symptoms. Writer et al. (2009), in a review of available studies, found that while the greatest body of evidence was for the efficacy of stimulants in treating the cognitive sequelae of TBI, different types of cognitive deficits appeared to respond best to different medications. Attentional deficits responded best to stimulants, memory deficits to stimulants and cholinergic medications, and executive impairments to stimulants and nonstimulant dopamine enhancing agents. This heterogeneity likely reflects the diverse nature of TBI presentations as well as confounding factors such as depression and PTSD.

While this section focuses on the pharmacologic management of post-TBI symptomatology, it should be noted that both ASD and PTSD symptoms have been shown to respond to cognitive-behavioral therapy and psychoeducation in the presence of brain injury (for example, Bryant 2003, 2011). Particularly in light of the recent findings that early intervention with prolonged exposure or cognitive behavioral therapy is more effective than treatment with an SSRI (Shalev et al., 2012), it is important to remember that counseling and non-pharmacologic interventions remain at the core of trauma treatment.

Stimulants (Dopamine Enhancers)

Stimulant refers to a general class of medications that are psychoactive and increase wakefulness, attention, and psychomotor activity, as well as heart rate and blood pressure—and includes such substances as caffeine, nicotine, cocaine, and amphetamines. The primary stimulant used in the treatment of TBI is methylphenidate (MPH or Ritalin, which increases the release of both dopamine and norepinephrine in the brain), a common medication used in the treatment of attention deficit hyperactivity disorder (ADHD). Multiple studies, including seven randomized placebo controlled trials, have shown efficacy for methylphenidate in the treatment of cognitive and distractibility symptoms (Plenger et al., 1996; Whyte et al., 2004). Methylphenidate may also help with impulsivity in TBI patients (Jin & Schachar, 2004). Methylphenidate has also been shown to help correct the sleep-wake cycle disturbances that often trouble individuals with TBI, as well as improving focus and reaction times (H. Lee et al., 2005). Lee (2005) found that in a comparison of methylphenidate and sertraline, methylphenidate helped with depressive symptoms, sleep-wake troubles, as well as cognitive tasks, whereas sertraline improved only depressive symptoms. Interestingly, the stimulant also was better tolerated.

Willmott and Ponsford (2009) found that methylphenidate improves cognitive processing speed after TBI and that the more severe the injury, the better the response. In a study of early intervention with methylphenidate after TBI, concentration, mental control, symbol search, and digit span all improved (Kaelin, Cifu, & Matthies, 1996). Of note, this early improvement was sustained even after the drug was removed. There are data as well to suggest that stimulants can be used during ICU stays, possibly shortening length of hospitalization after a TBI (Moein, Khalili, & Keramatian, 2006).

Typical doses of methylphenidate range from 5 to 60mg daily, in divided doses. Common side effects include jitteriness, drowsiness, insomnia, gastrointestinal disturbances, headache, loss of appetite, and cardiac arrhythmias. It is a pregnancy category C drug and is probably safe in breastmilk; however, caution when breastfeeding is advised.

Cholinergics

Cholinergic drugs, also known as parasympathomimetics, mimic or increase the action of the neurotransmitter acetylcholine in the brain. That cholinergic drugs would help in TBI makes inherent sense, since TBI has been identified in many cases as being a hypocholinergic state. The most common cholinergic drug used both for dementia and TBI is donepezil (Aricept), an acetylcholinesterase inhibitor. New research indicates that donepezil may aid patients with TBI to improve attention, cognition, processing speed, and learning (for example, Ballesteros, Guemes, Ibarra, & Quemada, 2008; S. L. Griffin, van Reekum, & Masanic, 2003). In a group of 10 TBI patients, 8 reported cognitive improvement on donepezil, and testing showed increased speed of processing, learning, and attention (Khateb, Ammann, Annoni, & Diserens, 2005). Similarly, in a double-blind crossover study with 18 TBI patients, donepezil improved short-term memory and sustained attention compared to placebo (Zhang, Plotkin, Wang, Sandel, & Lee, 2004). The typical dose of donepezil is 5 to 10mg daily; common side effects include slowed heart rate, nausea, diarrhea, anorexia, abdominal pain, and vivid dreams. It is a pregnancy Category C drug, with unknown safety in breast milk.

Nonstimulant Dopamine Enhancers

There are several disparate medications in this class, which all serve to increase dopamine or dopaminergic activity in the brain, without being stimulants. These include amantadine, bromocriptine, and pramipexole (among others), all used to treat Parkinson's disease and restless leg syndrome. Two randomized controlled studies (McDowell, Whyte, & D'Esposito, 1998; Meythaler, Brunner, & Johnson, 2002), as well as several open trials, have demonstrated efficacy for this class of medication in TBI-related cognitive disturbance, especially executive functioning and global cognitive functioning.

- Amantadine (Symmetrel) is typically dosed 100 to 400mg daily in divided doses. Common side effects include nervousness, insomnia, anxiety, difficulty concentrating, and exacerbation of both seizures and other underlying psychiatric illness. Pregnancy Category C; unknown safety in breast milk.

- Bromocriptine (Parlodel, Cycloset) is typically dosed 10 to 30mg three times daily. Common side effects include nausea, headache, fatigue and dizziness, and elevated liver enzymes. It can also precipitate seizures. Pregnancy Category C; unsafe in breast milk.
- Pramipexole (Mirapex) is typically dosed 0.5 to 1.5mg twice daily. Common side effects are similar to bromocriptine. Pregnancy Category C; unknown safety in breast milk.
- Atomoxetine (Strattera) is another unique agent used for the treatment of adult ADHD. It increases both norepinephrine and dopamine in the brain and might be a candidate for treating cognitive deficits. To date, there is no research into this possibility.

Antidepressants

Many patients who suffer from TBI have concomitant symptoms of PTSD or depression. In these cases, alleviation of as many of such symptoms as possible helps to improve outcome significantly. There is also some research evidence for the use of antidepressants for the cognitive sequelae of TBI, and it may be that cognition and affective symptoms respond to serotonergic treatment.

Given their known efficacy both for anxiety and depressive disorder, and their relatively benign safety profile, the SSRIs are typically the first choice for treating mood symptoms after TBI. Fann, Hart, and Schomer (2009) reviewed 27 studies and found that treatment of depression after a traumatic brain injury with both serotonergic agents and cognitive behavioral interventions was the most beneficial approach. In an earlier study (Fann, Uomoto, & Katon, 2001), it was noted that symptoms of depression as well as cognition improved when post-injury depression was treated with sertraline for 8 weeks. Verbal recall, visual memory, psychomotor speed, and general cognitive efficiency improved as well as other depressive symptoms. The authors suggest that sertraline may be particularly effective after TBI since it has the greatest dopaminergic effects of the SSRIs. In an open-label study of fluoxetine, after 8 months of treatment patients had improved cognitive symptoms across multiple domains. In addition, symptoms of depression had been alleviated (Horsfield et al., 2002).

The multireceptor effects of the TCAs, including increases in norepinephrine, make them promising candidates in treating cognitive difficulties as well as depression in TBI. However, TCAs are also significantly anticholinergic, which has the potential to be problematic in the context of already low levels of acetylcholine in TBI. For this reason, of the TCAs, desipramine, which has the least anticholinergic activity of its class, is preferable. Wroblewski et al. (1996) found that a group of 10 patients with severe TBI and particularly longstanding depression had an improvement in perceived affect and mood when treated with desipramine, although two patients dropped out due to seizures and development of manic symptoms. Desipramine and amitriptyline in three anecdotal cases improved cognition, arousal, and verbal expression (Reinhard, Whyte, & Sandel, 1996).

Mood Stabilizers

Impulse control problems and mood lability problems are often part of the post-TBI constellation of symptoms. Since most mood stabilizers are also anticonvulsant medications, they have the added benefit of helping prevent seizures, which can also occur after brain injury. Valproic acid may be best tolerated without impairing cognition further; both valproic acid and carbamazepine have been shown to aid in management of TBI-related aggression (Chew & Zafonte, 2009). Anticonvulstant medications such as gabapentin may provide additional relief by addressing chronic pain, which can also be an important symptom of head trauma.

Antipsychotics

Neuroleptics are often used to manage agitated behavior as well as psychotic symptoms. Individuals with TBI may be particularly prone to adverse side effects with the use of antipsychotic medications and should be monitored with extra vigilance (Harmsen, Geurts, Fasotti, & Bevarrt, 2004). That said, several atypical antipsychotics have been used effectively to reduce aggression in TBI patients, particularly quetiapine and ziprasidone (Kim & Bijlani, 2006; Noe, Ferri, Trenor, & Chirivella, 2007).

Medications for Other Comorbid Disorders

As described in Chapter 2, PTSD is highly comorbid with other Axis I disorders, including depression, other anxiety disorders, and psychotic disorders. The trauma-focused clinician should not presume that psychotherapy for traumatic stress will necessarily address this broader range of symptoms. In cases where clients present with one or more comorbid disorders, appropriate pharmacological treatment for these conditions is recommended. Fortunately, when depression or other anxiety symptoms are involved, SSRIs are the treatment of choice, and symptoms of posttraumatic stress can be treated simultaneously. As described earlier, clear psychotic symptoms require the addition of an antipsychotic medication. The general principles of medication management in trauma survivors, described earlier in this chapter, especially regarding side effects and concerns about overmedication, are relevant when treating comorbidities as well as when treating posttraumatic stress.

A Consideration of Larger-Picture Treatment Strategies

In *Effective Treatments for PTSD: Practice Guidelines From the International Society for Traumatic Stress Studies*, Friedman et al. (2009) confirm the general understanding that serotonergic antidepressants are the first-line treatment for PTSD. They summarize their findings regarding pharmaco-therapy in five key points: (1) many individuals are receiving some form of medication for PTSD and related conditions, (2) some patients benefit greatly from short-term therapy but may in due time require more prolonged treatment, (3) SSRIs and SNRIs[1] are the best established medications for the treatment of PTSD, (4) the use of atypical antipsychotics in treatment refractory individuals is warranted, and (5) much more research in this area is necessary.

The treatment guidelines of the American Psychiatric Association (APA) work group on ASD and PTSD (APA, 2004) make similar recommenda-tions: (1) SSRIs are recommended as first-line treatment; (2) benzodiaze-pines may be helpful for anxiety and sleep, but caution is warranted regard-ing dependence and potential for increased PTSD symptoms; (3) atypical antipsychotics may be useful adjunctive therapy in those refractory to SSRIs; and (4) anticonvulsant medications may be useful in individual cases, but data for recommending them are lacking.

The Department of Veterans Affairs and the Department of Defense (2010) guidelines caution more strongly against the use of atypical antipsy-chotics and benzodiazepines. They recommend initial monotherapy with an SSRI or SNRI, which have the strongest support in the literature for efficacy in treating PTSD. They note that while there is insufficient evidence for most antipsychotics as pharmacotherapy for PTSD, the recent findings regarding lack of efficacy of risperidone as adjunctive therapy (Krystal et al., 2011) indicate that the metabolic risks of this medication outweigh any potential small benefit. In addition, they caution, "Benzodiazepine administration should be discouraged both in acute stress disorder (ASD) and post-traumatic stress disorder (PTSD), due to lack of evidence for effectiveness and risks that outweigh potential benefits" (p. 153).

A recent review from the Harvard Psychopharmacology Algorithm Project suggests a slightly different approach (Bajor, Ticlea, & Osser, 2011). The authors propose that antidepressants may not in fact be the best first-line treatment in all cases. Instead, the most effective initial use of psychopharmacology might be to target sleep, nightmares, and reexpe-riencing through the use of prazosin or trazodone. Next, a trial of SSRI for ongoing symptoms of PTSD would be warranted. The authors suggest that antipsychotics be reserved for PTSD-related psychosis, or as augmentation for residual symptoms.

Our approach to trauma clients incorporates elements of the recommen-dations above, knowledge of the literature reviewed in this chapter, and our

---

[1]Note that here, and below, as well as elsewhere in the literature, the SNRIs are referred to collectively. It is worth mentioning that the only SNRI with demonstrated efficacy in PTSD is venlafaxine. There is not enough research to recommend others in this class.

practical experience with patients. Generally, the psychopharmacological treatment algorithm we recommend is as follows:

First-line treatments:

1. For patients with significant posttraumatic symptoms, an SSRI or SNRI is the first-line treatment.

2. If sleep disturbance or nightmares are prominent, trazodone or prazosin may be started concurrently with an SSRI. Alternatively, a sedating agent such as mirtazapine may be used to help with sleep difficulties.

3. In patients with overwhelming hyperarousal, treatment with an alpha- or beta-blocker may be considered.

4. When clear psychosis is present, an atypical antipsychotic should be started concurrently with an SSRI.

Second-line treatments for refractory symptoms or partial responders:

1. In patients who do not respond to an SSRI, or who have a partial response, a trial of a second antidepressant is warranted.

2. If prominent symptoms still remain, adjunctive low-dose antipsychotic medication may be initiated.

3. When significant aggression is present that is refractory to SSRI treatment, or when antipsychotic medication is contraindicated or unacceptable to the patient, treatment with a mood stabilizer should be considered.

4. As described above, benzodiazepines should be reserved for cases of overwhelming anxiety and/or acute distress that requires immediate down-regulation.

Once a treatment response is obtained, ideally medication should be continued for 1 year to maintain benefits.

Conclusion

This chapter has reviewed the wide range of medications that appear to be helpful in the treatment of posttraumatic stress. Two points should be reemphasized, however.

First, there is little reason to believe, based on the extant clinical literature, that psychiatric medication can, by itself, resolve most cases of PTSD or other forms of posttraumatic disturbance. Such medication is often helpful, but it tends to be palliative rather than curative. In many cases medication will effect some level of symptom reduction but will not completely remove all symptomatology, and may only be effective for certain posttraumatic symptom clusters. In addition, among those clients who experience significant symptom remission, a significant proportion will relapse when medication is discontinued. Finally, some clients are unable or unwilling to tolerate the side effects of psychotropic medication, regardless of whether or not the drug might technically be effective.

Second, although psychiatric medication will rarely permanently resolve all posttraumatic symptoms in a given client, it is often helpful. In our experience, the effective use of medication can provide initial symptom relief (medically and via the placebo effect)—sometimes before initial psychotherapy effects. This initial response may increase compliance, discourage clinical dropout, and reduce the sleep deprivation and/or autonomic hyperarousal that contributes significantly to many clients' distress. In this way, psychiatric medication may provide benefits that allow the client to participate in psychotherapy long enough for the more substantial and enduring effects of psychological intervention to emerge.

Suggested Reading

Davidson, J. R. T. (2004). Long-term treatment and prevention of posttraumatic stress disorder. *Journal of Clinical Psychiatry, 65*, 44–48.

Davidson, J. R. T. (2006). Pharmacologic treatment of acute and chronic stress following trauma: 2006. *Journal of Clinical Psychiatry, 68*(Suppl. 2), 34–39.

Friedman, M. J. (2000). What might the psychobiology of posttraumatic stress disorder teach us about future approaches to pharmacotherapy? *Journal of Clinical Psychiatry, 61*(Suppl. 7), 44–51.

Friedman, M. J., Davidson, J. R. T., & Stein, D. J. (2009). Psychopharmacotherapy for adults. In E. B. Foa, T. M. Keane, M. J. Friedman, & J. A. Cohen (Eds.), *Effective treatments for PTSD: Practice guidelines from the International Society for Traumatic Stress Studies* (pp. 245–268). New York, NY: Guilford.

Morgan, C. A., Krystal, J. H., & Southwick, S. M. (2003). Toward early pharmacological posttraumatic stress intervention. *Biological Psychiatry, 53*, 834–843.

13

Conclusions

This book has provided an overview of the assessment and treatment of various forms of posttraumatic distress and disorder. In it, we have offered a general philosophy of intervention that stresses a nonpathologizing, growth-oriented, and, ultimately, hopeful view of recovery from trauma. We have suggested that human relationships provide not only the context for a huge amount of violence in our world, but also the essential environment in which the effects of violence can be addressed. Healing relationships need not always involve psychotherapy; many people recover from trauma exposure without seeking professional assistance, instead processing and resolving their injuries in the context of family, friendship, and other relationships.

Unfortunately, some posttraumatic outcomes are of sufficient severity and chronicity that a more specialized relationship is often necessary, one generally referred to as psychotherapy. Probably regardless of culture, some trauma effects appear to require a supportive other who is trained to listen and respond in an empathic and relatively objective manner and who is able to call on a variety of techniques and approaches that directly address psychological injury. We have outlined the range of interventions that are relevant to this process. At the same time, clinical techniques—although often providing great specificity and efficiency in treating posttraumatic stress—generally require an additional element: a compassionate, safe, and supportive therapeutic relationship in which the past can be explored and processed.

This focus on the therapeutic relationship is sometimes dismissed by proponents of shorter-term therapy, who may consider the relational effects of therapy to be nonspecific or placebo phenomena. We suggest, in contrast, that the therapeutic relationship activates important psychological and physiological processes that—far from being placebo effects—serve to evoke, countercondition, and otherwise process traumatic (especially relational) memories. Therapeutic intervention in these attachment-relational processes requires considerable training and skill, in part because relational dynamics also affect the therapist. At the same time, the largely cognitive-behavioral activities of exposure, activation, disparity, counterconditioning, and extinction/resolution can be found—in one form or another—in most effective trauma therapies. In fact, it is hard to imagine how successful psychological treatment for posttraumatic stress could fail to include at least some of these components.

The need for both relational and cognitive-behavioral interventions in the treatment of chronic and/or complex posttraumatic disturbance is not particularly surprising, especially when real-world clinical practice is examined. Probably all good trauma therapy is cognitive-behavioral, to the extent that it involves exploration of traumatic material (exposure) in a safe relationship (disparity), wherein the client is encouraged to feel and think about what happened to him or her (emotional and cognitive activation and processing). On the other hand, most effective therapy for complex trauma effects also is relational and "psychodynamic," involving the effects of activated attachment relationships and interpersonal processes.

Ultimately, the complex interrelationships between exposure to adverse events, biology, psychology, culture, social support, and symptomatology mean that no two trauma survivors are clinically similar. A corollary of this fact is that the therapy required to intervene in posttraumatic outcomes will necessarily differ from case to case, as a function of a wide variety of variables. As we hope has been apparent in this book, this means that trauma treatment must be flexible, inclusive of various perspectives, relevant to the client's specific issues and concerns, and responsive to his or her specific relational context. In combination with the remarkable survival capacity of traumatized people, such therapy can be a powerful agent for psychological recovery and, in many cases, growth.

Appendix 1 _____

Initial Trauma Review-3 (ITR-3)

Childhood Questions:

1. [Physical abuse questions] *"<u>Before you were age 18,</u> did a parent or another adult ever hurt or punish you in a way that left a bruise, cut, scratches, or made you bleed?"*

Yes__   No__   [Yes = physical abuse]

If yes:

"When this happened, did you ever feel very afraid, horrified, or helpless?"

Yes__   No__

"Did you ever think you might be injured or killed?"

Yes__   No__

2. [Sexual abuse questions] *"<u>Before you were age 18,</u> did anyone who was <u>5 or more years older</u> than you ever do something sexual with you or to you?"*

Yes__   No__   [Yes = sexual abuse]

If yes:

"Did the person ever put their penis, a finger, or an object into your vagina or anus, or a penis in your mouth?"

Yes__   No__   [Yes = sexual abuse with penetration]

"Was this ever done against your will or when you couldn't defend yourself (for example, when you were asleep or intoxicated)?"

Yes__   No__   [Yes = sexual abuse]

"When this happened, did you ever feel very afraid, horrified, or helpless?"

[NOTE: For sexual abuse only; this part is not necessary for PTSD Criterion A]

Yes___   No___

"Did you ever think you might be injured or killed?"
[NOTE: For sexual abuse only; this part is not necessary for PTSD Criterion A]

Yes___   No___

3. [Peer sexual assault questions] *"Before you were age 18, did anyone who was less than 5 years older than you ever do something sexual to you that was against your will or that happened when you couldn't defend yourself (for example, when you were asleep or intoxicated)?"*

Yes___   No___   [Yes = peer child sexual assault]

If yes:

"Did the person ever put their penis, a finger, or an object into your vagina, anus, or mouth?"

Yes___   No___   [Yes = peer child rape if any insertion in vagina or anus, or penile insertion in mouth]

"When this happened, did you ever feel very afraid, horrified, or helpless?"

Yes___   No___

"Did you ever think you might be injured or killed?"

Yes___   No___

4. [Disaster questions] *"Before you were age 18, were you ever involved in a serious fire, earthquake, flood, or other disaster?"*

Yes___   No___   [Yes = childhood exposure to disaster]

If yes:

"When this happened, did you ever feel very afraid, horrified, or helpless?"

Yes___   No___

"Did you ever think you might be injured or killed?"

Yes___   No___

5. [Motor vehicle accident questions] *"Before you were age 18, were you ever involved in a serious automobile accident?"*

Yes___   No___   [Yes = childhood exposure to MVA]

If yes:

"When this happened, did you ever feel very afraid, horrified, or helpless?"

Yes___   No___

"Did you ever think you might be injured or killed?"

Yes___   No___

6. **[Witnessing trauma questions]** *"Before you were age 18, did you ever see someone get killed or badly hurt?"*

Yes___   No___   [Yes = childhood witnessing trauma]

If yes:

"When this happened, did you ever feel very afraid, horrified, or helpless?"

Yes___   No___

"Did you ever think you might be injured or killed?" *[Not required for PTSD Criterion A]*

Yes___   No___

Adulthood Questions:

1. **[Adult sexual assault questions]** *"Since you were 18 or older, has anyone done something sexual to you against your will or when you couldn't defend yourself (for example, when you were asleep or intoxicated)?"*

Yes___   No___   [Yes = Adult sexual assault]

If yes:

"Did the person ever put their penis, a finger, or an object into your vagina or anus, or a penis in your mouth?"

Yes___   No___   [Yes = adult rape]

"When this happened, did you ever feel very afraid, horrified, or helpless?"

Yes___   No___

"Did you ever think you might be injured or killed?"

Yes___   No___

"Did this ever happen on a date, or with a sexual/romantic partner or spouse?

Yes___   No___   [Yes = date/partner/marital sexual assault or rape]

2. **[Spouse/partner abuse questions]** *"Since you were 18 or older, have you ever been slapped, hit, or beaten in a sexual or marital relationship?"*

Yes__   No__   [Yes = partner battering]

"Since you were 18 or older, have you ever been shot, shot at, stabbed, or nearly strangled in a sexual or marital relationship?"

Yes__   No__   [Yes = partner battering and possible attempted murder]

If yes to either:

"When this happened, did you ever feel very afraid, horrified, or helpless?"

Yes__   No__

"Did you ever think you might be injured or killed?"

Yes__   No__

3. **[Nonintimate assault questions]** *"Since you were 18 or older, have you ever been physically attacked, assaulted, stabbed, or shot at by someone who wasn't a sex partner or husband/wife?"*

Yes__   No__   [Yes = nonintimate assault and possible attempted murder]

If yes:

"When this happened, did you ever feel very afraid, horrified, or helpless?"

Yes__   No__

"Did you ever think you might be injured or killed?"

Yes__   No__

4. **[War questions]** *"Since you were 18 or older, have you ever experienced combat, fought in a war, or lived in a place where war was happening?"*

Yes__   No__   [Yes = combat exposure]

If yes:

"When this happened, did you ever feel very afraid, horrified, or helpless?"

Yes__   No__

"Did you ever think you might be injured or killed?"

Yes__   No__

5. **[Motor vehicle accident questions]** *"Since you were 18 or older, were you ever involved in a serious automobile accident?"*

Yes__   No__   [Yes = motor vehicle accident]

If yes:

"When this happened, did you ever feel very afraid, horrified, or helpless?"

Yes__   No__

"Did you ever think you might be injured or killed?"

Yes__   No__

6. **[Disaster questions]** *"Since you were 18 or older, were you ever involved in a serious fire, earthquake, flood, or other disaster?"*

Yes__   No__   [Yes = disaster exposure]

If yes:

"When this happened, did you ever feel very afraid, horrified, or helpless?"

Yes__   No__

"Did you ever think you might be injured or killed?"

Yes__   No__

7. **[Torture questions—If client is an immigrant from another country]** *"In the country where you used to live, were you ever tortured by the government or by people against the government?"*

Yes__   No__   [Yes = torture]

If yes:

"When this happened, did you ever feel very afraid, horrified, or helpless?"

Yes__   No__

"Did you ever think you might be injured or killed?"

Yes__   No__

8. **[Police trauma questions]** *"In this country, have you ever been hit, beaten, assaulted, or shot at by the police or other law enforcement officials, during or after an arrest, or at some other time?"*

Yes__   No__   [Yes = police trauma]

If yes:

"When this happened, did you ever feel very afraid, horrified, or helpless?"

Yes__   No__

"Did you ever think you might be injured or killed?"

Yes__   No__

9. **[Witnessing trauma questions]** *"Since you were 18 or older, did you ever see someone else killed or badly hurt?"*

Yes__   No__   [Yes = adult witnessing trauma]

If yes:

"When this happened, did you ever feel very afraid, horrified, or helpless?"

Yes__   No__

"Did you ever think you might be injured or killed?" [NOTE: For witnessing trauma, this part is not necessary for DSM-IV Criterion A]

Yes__   No__

Appendix 2 _____

Brief Interview for Posttraumatic Disorders (BIPD)

A semi-structured interview for the diagnosis of *DSM-IV* acute stress disorder, posttraumatic stress disorder, and brief psychotic disorder with marked stressor

Date: _____/_____/_____
Patient Name: _____
Sex: _____
Age: _____
Evaluator Name: _____

Instructions for Completing the Brief
_____ Interview for Posttraumatic Disorders

First: Determine whether the traumatic event occurred within the last month or longer in the past, and whether psychotic symptoms are part of the clinical presentation.

If the trauma has occurred within the last month, and there are no significant psychotic symptoms, use the <u>Acute Stress Disorder</u> screen.

If the trauma occurred in the last month, but significant psychotic symptoms are present, use the <u>Brief Psychotic Disorder</u> <u>with Marked Stressor</u> screen.

If the trauma occurred a month or more ago, use the <u>Posttraumatic Stress Disorder</u> screen.

Second: For each numbered diagnostic criterion, place a ✓ mark in the ( ) space for each symptom that is present for the patient you are evaluating.

For example, if a nonpsychotic patient reported recent recurrent, intrusive, and distressing dreams and thoughts about a traumatic event that happened 3 months ago, and intense psychological distress upon exposure to environmental reminders of the event, you would mark the following in the "B" PTSD section of the BIPD:

B. Has the traumatic event been persistently reexperienced in <u>at least one</u> of the following symptom categories <u>within the last month?</u>

    (1) recurrent and intrusive distressing recollections of the event, including images ( ), thoughts (✓), or perceptions ( ).

    (2) recurrent distressing dreams of the event (✓)

    (3) acting or feeling as if the event were recurring, including a sense of reliving the experience ( ), nonpsychotic hallucinations of the event ( ), and flashbacks ( ), including those which occur upon awakening or when intoxicated.

    (4) intense psychological distress (e.g., fear, anger) upon exposure to internal or external/environmental cues that symbolize or resemble the traumatic event (✓)

    (5) physiological reactivity (e.g., sweating, flushing, dizziness, increased heart rate, shortness of breath) upon exposure to internal or external cues that symbolize or resemble the traumatic event ( )

Third: Review all check marks to see if they indicate sufficient symptoms to satisfy the lettered criterion. If so, check the "Yes" box. For example, for this patient, your response to the following question would be "yes" and you would check the box:

Yes, criterion B is met (at least one numbered category checked) _✓_

Fourth: Review all checked boxes to determine if sufficient criteria have been met to meet the diagnosis. For example, if criteria A, C, D, E, and F were also met in this example, you would check "yes" to the following:

G. Yes, PTSD diagnostic criteria are all met ("Yes" responses to criteria A through F) _✓_

Based on this example, you would assign a diagnosis of posttraumatic stress disorder.

Fifth: If you determine that a disorder is present, complete the "associated features" section to document additional difficulties associated (or comorbid) with posttraumatic stress.

_____ **Acute Stress Disorder (ASD) Screen**

Diagnosis potentially relevant to this patient (trauma occurred within the last month and there are no significant psychotic symptoms) _____

Diagnosis not relevant to this patient (skip to PTSD section) _____

A. Has the patient been exposed to a traumatic event in which <u>both</u> of the following were present <u>within the last month:</u>

(1) the patient experienced/witnessed/was confronted with an event that

- involved the death of another person(s) ( ) or
- potential death of the patient ( ) or
- serious potential or actual injury to the patient ( ) or
- a threat to the physical integrity of the patient or others ( ) or
- had developmentally inappropriate sexual experiences in childhood
- (e.g., sexual abuse), in which case there need not be threatened or actual violence or injury ( )

<u>AND</u>

(2) the patient's response to this event involved intense fear ( ), helplessness ( ), or horror ( ) <u>OR,</u> in children, disorganized or agitated behavior ( )

Yes, both criteria A1 and A2 are met (at least one check in each category) _____

No, criteria A1 and A2 are not both met _____

<u>If no,</u> stop ASD screen. (Check here _____ if screen stopped)
<u>If yes,</u> **briefly describe the trauma, including when it occurred:**

B. <u>During the event</u> or <u>within the last month,</u> has the patient had at least three of the following dissociative symptom categories?

(1) Numbing (not being able to feel emotions as well or at all), emotional detachment (feeling emotionally distant or uninvolved), or an absence of emotional responsiveness ( )

(2) Reduced awareness of his or her surroundings ( )

(3) Derealization: an altered perception/experience of the external world so that it seems strange or unreal ( )

(4) Depersonalization: an altered perception or experience of self so that the person feels detached from—or an outside observer on—his/her mental processes or body (e.g., out-of-body experiences, distorted sense of one's body or body parts) ( )

(5) An inability to recall an important aspect of the trauma ( )

Yes, criterion B is met (at least three numbered categories checked) ____

No, criterion B is not met ____

C. Has the traumatic event been persistently reexperienced in at least one of the following ways within the last month: recurring images ( ), thoughts ( ), dreams ( ), flashbacks ( ), or reliving the experience as if it were happening again ( ); or distress upon exposure to reminders of the event ( )?

Yes, criterion C is met (at least one symptom checked) ____

No, criterion C is not met ____

D. Has there been marked avoidance of stimuli that might cause recollections of the trauma [e.g., avoidance of thoughts ( ), feelings ( ), conversations ( ), activities ( ), places ( ), people ( )] within the last month?

Yes, criterion D is met (at least one symptom checked) ____

No, criterion D is not met ____

E. Have there been marked symptoms of anxiety ( ) or increased arousal [e.g., difficulty sleeping ( ), irritability ( ), poor concentration ( ), hypervigilance ( ), exaggerated startle response ( ), motor restlessness ( )] that were not present before the trauma and that occurred <u>within the last month</u>?

Yes, criterion E is met (at least one symptom checked) ____

No, criterion E is not met ____

F. Have these symptoms caused clinically significant distress or impairment in social ( ), occupational ( ), or other important areas of functioning ( ), or impaired the patient's ability to pursue some necessary task ( ) within the last month?

Yes, criterion F is met (at least one form of impairment checked)

No, criterion F is not met ____

G. Have these symptoms both ____

    (1) lasted for a minimum of 2 days and a maximum of 4 weeks ( ) and

    (2) occurred within 4 weeks of the trauma ( )?

Yes, both G1 and G2 are met ____

No, both G1 and G2 are not met ____

Assign an ASD diagnosis?

Yes, ASD criteria are all met ("yes" responses to criteria A through G) ____

No, ASD criteria are not all met ____

Posttraumatic Stress Disorder (PTSD) Screen

Diagnosis potentially relevant to this patient (trauma occurred a month or more ago) _____

Diagnosis not relevant to this patient (skip to BPDMS section) _____

A. <u>Prior to the last month,</u> was the patient exposed to a traumatic event in which <u>both</u> of the following were present:

(1) the patient experienced/witnessed/was confronted with an event that
- involved the death of another person(s) ( ) or
- potential death of the patient ( ) or
- serious potential or actual injury to the patient ( ) or
- a threat to the physical integrity of the patient or others ( ) or
- had developmentally inappropriate sexual experiences in childhood (e.g., sexual abuse), in which case there need not be threatened or actual violence or injury ( )

<u>AND</u>

(2) the patient's response to this event involved intense fear ( ), help-lessness ( ), or horror ( ) <u>OR,</u> in children, disorganized or agitated behavior ( )

Yes, both criteria A1 and A2 are met (at least one check in each category) _____

No, criteria A1 and A2 are not both met _____

If no, stop PTSD screen. (Check here _____ if screen stopped)

If yes, briefly describe trauma, including when it occurred:

B. Has the traumatic event been persistently reexperienced in at <u>least one</u> of the following symptom categories <u>within the last month</u>?

(1) recurrent and intrusive distressing recollections of the event, including images ( ), thoughts ( ), or perceptions ( )

(2) recurrent distressing dreams of the event ( )

(3) acting or feeling as if the event were recurring [including a sense of reliving the experience ( ), nonpsychotic hallucinations of the event ( ), and flashbacks ( )], including those which occur upon awakening or when intoxicated.

(4) intense distress upon exposure to internal or external cues that symbolize/resemble the traumatic event ( )

(5) physiological reactivity (e.g., sweating, flushing, dizziness, increased heart rate, shortness of breath) upon exposure to internal or external cues that symbolize or resemble the traumatic event ( )

Yes, criterion B is met (at least one numbered category checked) ____

No, criterion B is not met ____

C. Has there been persistent avoidance of stimuli associated with the trauma and numbing of general responsiveness that was not present before the trauma, as indicated by at least three of the following symptom categories, within the last month?

(1) efforts to avoid thoughts ( ), feelings ( ), or conversations ( ) associated with the trauma

(2) efforts to avoid activities ( ), places ( ), or people ( ) that might stimulate or trigger recollections of the trauma

(3) inability to recall an important aspect of the trauma ( )

(4) markedly diminished interest or participation in significant activities ( )

(5) feelings of detachment/estrangement from others ( ), or restricted range of affect (e.g., unable to have loving feelings) ( )

(6) sense of foreshortened future (e.g., patient does not expect to have a career, marriage, children, or a normal life span) ( )

Yes, criterion C is met (at least three numbered categories checked) ____

No, criterion C is not met ____

D. Have there been persistent symptoms of increased arousal that were not present before the trauma, as indicated by at least two of the following symptom categories:

(1) difficulty falling or staying asleep ( )

(2) irritability or outbursts of anger ( )

(3) difficulty concentrating ( )

(4) hypervigilance ( )

(5) exaggerated startle response ( )

Yes, criterion D is met (at least two numbered categories checked) ____

No, criterion D is not met ____

E. Have these symptoms lasted for more than one month?

Yes, criterion E is met ____

No, criterion E is not met ____

F. Have these symptoms caused clinically significant distress or impairment in social ( ), occupational ( ), or other important areas of functioning ( )?

Yes, criterion F is met (at least one form of impairment checked) ____

No, criterion F is not met ____

Assign a PTSD diagnosis?

Yes, PTSD criteria are all met ("yes" responses to criteria A through F) _____

No, PTSD criteria are not all met _____

If yes, specify: **Acute** (the duration of symptoms has been less than 3 months to date) _____
Chronic (the duration of symptoms has been 3 months or longer) _____
With Delayed Onset (the onset of symptoms was at least 6 months after the stressor) _____

Brief Psychotic Disorder With Marked Stressors (BPDMS) Screen

Diagnosis potentially relevant to this patient (trauma occurred in the last month and psychotic symptoms are present) _____

Diagnosis not relevant to this patient _____

A. Has the patient been exposed to one or more traumatic events within the last month that, alone or in combination, would be markedly stressful to almost anyone in similar circumstances in his or her culture ( )?

Yes _____ No _____

If no, stop BPDMS screen. (Check here ✓ if screen stopped)

If yes, briefly describe trauma:

B. Has the patient's response to this trauma(s) involved the development of at least one of the following symptoms:

(1) **Delusions** ( )

If yes, describe briefly:

(2) **Psychotic hallucinations** ( )

If yes, describe briefly:

(3) **Psychotically disorganized speech** ( )

If yes, describe briefly:

(4) **Grossly disorganized or catatonic behavior** ( )

If yes, describe briefly:

Yes, criterion B is met (at least one numbered category is checked) _____

No, criterion B is not met _____

Assign a BPDMS diagnosis?

Yes, BPDMS criteria are both met ("yes" responses to criteria A and B) ____

No, BPDMS criteria are not met ____

Associated Features

(for any diagnosis documented on BIPD)

Mark "Yes" for currently present, "No" for not currently present, and/or "Premorbid" if the problem or symptom was present when the trauma occurred (regardless of whether or not it is present now). NOTE: "Premorbid" can be marked along with either "Yes" or "No" for the same problem.

(1) Suicidal ideation: Yes ____ No ____ Premorbid ____

(2) Suicidal behavior: Yes ____ No ____ Premorbid ____

If "yes" or "premorbid" for either, describe (including estimate of probable <u>current</u> lethality):

(3) Current or recent aggressive behavior: Yes ____ No ____ Premorbid ____

If "yes" or "premorbid," describe (including estimate of potential current danger to others):

(4) Significant alcohol abuse: Yes ____ No ____ Premorbid ____

(5) Significant substance abuse: Yes ____ No ____ Premorbid ____

If "yes" or "premorbid" for either, describe (including if addiction present):

(6) Other associated features (evaluate for each):

   A. Significant despair or hopelessness Yes ____ No ____ Premorbid ____

   B. Significant depression Yes ____ No ____ Premorbid ____

   C. Significant fears or phobias about people, animals, places, or things Yes ____ No ____ Premorbid ____

   D. Significant guilt or shame Yes ____ No ____ Premorbid ____

   E. Lack of concern about personal health or safety Yes ____ No ____ Premorbid ____

   F. Impulsive behavior Yes ____ No ____ Premorbid ____

   G. Unnecessary risk taking Yes ____ No ____ Premorbid ____

H. Unstable affect or mood swings Yes ____ No ____ Premorbid ____

I. Significant dissociative symptoms Yes ____ No ____ Premorbid ____

J. Somatic symptoms or bodily preoccupation Yes ____ No ____ Premorbid ____

K. Significant social withdrawal Yes ____ No ____ Premorbid ____

L. Chronic perception of danger in environment or relationships Yes ____ No ____ Premorbid ____

M. Sexual dysfunction or distress Yes ____ No ____ Premorbid ____

N. Significant personality change Yes ____ No ____ Premorbid ____

O. Other significant feature (describe): Yes ____ No ____ Premorbid ____

Appendix 3 _____

Breath Training Protocol

_____ Introductory Information

• Explain that learning to pay attention to breathing, and learning to breathe deeply, can both help with relaxation and reduce anxiety. Note that when we get anxious or have a panic attack, one of the first things that happens is that our breathing becomes shallow and rapid.

• Explain that, initially, some people become dizzy when they start breathing deeply—this is a normal reaction. For this reason, they should not try breathing exercises standing up until they have become experienced and comfortable with them.

• Explain that the exercises may feel strange at first because the client will be asked to breathe into his or her belly. Most of us are used to holding our stomachs in, because of tight clothes or because we are self-conscious of weight or how we look.

_____ Practicing Breathing in the Session

• Have the client sit in a comfortable position.

• Go through the sequence below with the client—the whole process should take about 10 to 15 minutes. After each step, "check in" to see how the client is feeling and if there are any problems or questions.

1. If the client is comfortable with closing his or her eyes, ask him or her to do so. Some trauma survivors will feel more anxious with their eyes closed and will want to keep them open. This is entirely acceptable.

2. Ask the client to try to stay "in the moment" while doing breathing exercises. If his or her mind wanders (e.g., thinking about what to make for

dinner, ruminating over an argument with someone), he or she should gently try to bring it back to the immediate experience of breathing.

3. Ask the client to begin breathing through his or her nose, paying attention to the breath coming in and going out. Ask him or her to pay attention to how long each inhalation and exhalation lasts. Do this for 5 or 6 breaths.

4. It is usually helpful for the clinician to breathe along with the client at the beginning of this exercise. You can guide him or her for each inhalation and exhalation, saying "in" and "out" to help him or her along.

Instruct the client to start breathing more deeply into his or her abdomen. This means that the belly should visibly rise and fall with each breath. This sort of breathing should feel different from normal breathing, and the client should notice that each breath is deeper than normal. Do this for another 5 or 6 breaths.

5. Ask the client to imagine that each time he or she breathes in, air is flowing in to fill up the abdomen and lungs. It goes into the belly first, and then rises up to fill in the top of the chest cavity. In the same way, when breathing out, the breath first leaves the chest, and then the abdomen. Some people find it helpful to imagine the breath coming in and out like a wave. Do this for another 5 or 6 breaths.

6. Explain that once the client is breathing deeply and fully into the belly and chest, the next step is to slow the breath down. Ask the client to slowly count to three with each inhalation and exhalation—in for three counts, out for three counts. With practice, the client may begin to slow his or her breath even further. Tell him or her that there is no specific amount of time necessary for each inhalation and exhalation, only that he or she try to slow his or her breathing. Do this for 5 or 6 breaths.

- Ask the client to practice this sequence at home for 5 to 10 minutes a day. He or she should choose a specific time of day (e.g., in the morning, before work or school), and make this exercise a regular part of his or her daily routine. The client should sit or lie down at home in a comfortable position, with no distractions, for this practice.

- Eventually, the client can extend this exercise to other times in the day as well, especially when relaxation would be a good idea (e.g., before important meetings, in stressful social situations, whenever he or she feels especially anxious). Remind the client to count during each inhalation and exhalation, since counting, itself, will come to stimulate the relaxation response.

References _____

Abbas, C. C., Schmid, J.-P., Guler, E., Wiedemar, L., Begré, S., Saner, H., . . . von Känel, R. (2009). Trajectory of posttraumatic stress disorder caused by myocardial infarction: A two-year follow-up study. *International Journal of Psychiatry in Medicine, 39*, 359–379.

Abouzeid, M., Kelsall, H. L., Forbes, A. B., Sim, M. R., & Creamer, M. C. (2011). Posttraumatic stress disorder and hypertension in Australian veterans of the 1991 Gulf War. *Journal of Psychosomatic Research, 72*(1), 33–38.

Abueg, F. R., & Fairbank, J. A. (1992). Behavioral treatment of posttraumatic stress disorder and co-occurring substance abuse. In P. A. Saigh (Ed.), *Posttraumatic stress disorder: A behavioral approach to assessment and treatment* (pp. 111–146). Needham Heights, MA: Allyn & Bacon.

Acierno, R., Resnick, H. S., Kilpatrick, D. G., Saunders, B. E., & Best, C. L. (1999). Risk factors for rape, physical assault, and posttraumatic stress disorder in women: Examination of differential multivariate relationships. *Journal of Anxiety Disorders, 13*, 541–563.

Adler, A. B., Litz, B. T., Castro, C. A., Suvak, M., Thomas, J. L., Burrell, L., . . . Bliese, P. D. (2008). A group randomized trial of critical incident stress debriefing provided to U.S. peacekeepers. *Journal of Traumatic Stress, 21*, 253–263.

Afifi, T. O., Mather, A., Boman, J., Fleisher, W., Enns, M. W., MacMillan, H., & Sareen, J. (2011). Childhood adversity and personality disorders: Results from a nationally representative population-based study. *Journal of Psychiatric Research, 45*, 814–822.

Agar, K., & Read, J. (2002). What happens when people disclose sexual or physical abuse to staff at a community mental health centre? *International Journal of Mental Health Nursing, 11*, 70–79.

Ahrens, C. E., Abeling, S., Ahmad, S., & Hinman, J. (2010). Spirituality and well-being: The relationship between religious coping and recovery from sexual assault. *Journal of Interpersonal Violence, 25*, 1242–1263.

Akagi, H., & House, A. (2002) The clinical epidemiology of hysteria: Vanishingly rare, or just vanishing? *Psychological Medicine, 32*, 191–194.

Alaggiaa, R. (2005). Disclosing the trauma of child sexual abuse: A gender analysis. *Journal of Loss and Trauma: International Perspectives on Stress & Coping, 10*, 453–470.

Alderman, C. P., Condon, J. T., & Gilbert, A. L. (2009). An open-label study of mirtazapine as treatment for combat-related PTSD. *Annals of Pharmacotherapy, 43*, 1220–1226.

Alderman, C. P., McCarthy, L. C., Condon, J. T., Marwood, A. C., & Fuller, J. R. (2009). Topiramate in combat-related posttraumatic stress disorder. *Annals of Pharmacotherapy, 43*, 635–641.

Alemany, S., Arias, B., Aguilera, M., Villa, H., Moya, J., Ibáñez, M. I., . . . Fañanás, L. (2011). Childhood abuse, the BDNF-Val66Met polymorphism and adult psychotic-like experiences. *British Journal of Psychiatry, 199*, 38–42.

Alexander, F. et al. (1946). *Psychoanalytic therapy: Principles and activations.* New York, NY: Ronald Press.

Alexander, P. C. (1992). Effect of incest on self and social functioning: A developmental psychopathology perspective. *Journal of Consulting and Clinical Psychology, 60*, 185–195.

Allden, K., Poole, C., Chantavanich, S., & Ohmar, K. (1996). Burmese political dissidents in Thailand: Trauma and survival among young adults in exile. *American Journal of Public Health, 86*, 1561–1569.

Allen, J. G. (2001). *Traumatic relationships and serious mental disorders.* Chichester, UK: Wiley.

Allen, J. G. (2005). *Coping with trauma: Hope through understanding* (2nd ed.). Washington, DC: American Psychiatric Press.

Álvarez, M.-J., Roura, P., Osés, A., Foguet, Q., Solà, J., & Arrufat, F.-X. (2011). Prevalence and clinical impact of childhood trauma in patients with severe mental disorders. *Journal of Nervous and Mental Disease, 199*, 156–161.

American Burn Association. (2011). *Burn incidence and treatment in the United States: 2011 fact sheet.* Retrieved from http://www.ameriburn.org/resources_factsheet.php

American Congress of Rehabilitation Medicine. (1993). Definition of mild traumatic brain injury. *Journal of Head Trauma Rehabilitation, 8*(3), 86–87.

American Educational Research Association, American Psychological Association, & National Council of Measurement in Education. (1999). *Standards for educational and psychological testing.* Washington, DC: American Educational Research Association.

American Psychiatric Association. (1987). *Diagnostic and statistical manual of mental disorders* (3rd ed., Rev.). Washington, DC: Author.

American Psychiatric Association. (2000). *Diagnostic and statistical manual of mental disorders* (4th ed., Text Rev.). Washington, DC: Author.

American Psychiatric Association. (2001). *Practice guideline for the treatment of patients with borderline personality disorder.* Washington, DC: Author.

American Psychiatric Association. (2004). Practice guideline for the treatment of patients with acute stress disorder and posttraumatic stress disorder. *Psychiatry Online.* Retrieved from http://psychiatryonline.org/content.aspx?bookid=28&sectionid=1670530.

American Psychiatric Association. (2012a). *G 02 acute stress disorder.* Retrieved from http://www.dsm5.org/ProposedRevisions/Pages/proposedrevision.aspx?rid=166

American Psychiatric Association (2012b). *G 03 posttraumatic stress disorder.* Retrieved from http://www.dsm5.org/proposedrevision/pages/proposedrevision.aspx?rid=165

American Psychiatric Association. (2012c). *Persistent complex bereavement-related disorder.* Retrieved from http://www.dsm5.org/ProposedRevision/Pages/proposedrevision.aspx?rid=577

Amir, N., Stafford, J., Freshman, M. S., & Foa, E. B. (1998). Relationship between trauma narratives and trauma pathology. *Journal of Traumatic Stress, 11*, 385–393.

Amnesty International. (2008). *State of the world's human rights*. Retrieved from http://archive.amnesty.org/report2008/eng/

Amnesty International. (2010). *Invisible victims: Migrants on the move in Mexico*. Retrieved from http://amnesty.org/en/library/info/AMR41/014/2010/en

Amnesty International. (2012). *Torture and accountability*. Retrieved from http://www.amnesty.org/en/campaigns/counter-terror-with-justice/issues/torture-and-accountability

Amstadter, A. B., Elwood, L. S., Begle, A. M., Gudmundsdottir, B., Smith, D. W., Resnick, H. S., . . . Kilpatrick, D. G. (2011). Predictors of physical assault victimization: Findings from the National Survey of Adolescents. *Addictive Behaviors, 36*, 814–820.

Anastasi, A., & Urbina, S. (1997). *Psychological Testing* (7th ed.). Upper Saddle River, NJ: Prentice Hall.

Anders, S. L., Frazier, P. A., & Frankfurt, S. B. (2011). Variations in criterion A and PTSD rates in a community sample of women. *Journal of Anxiety Disorders, 25*, 176–184.

Anderson, C. A., & Huesmann, L. R. (2003). Human aggression: A social-cognitive view. In M. A. Hogg & J. Cooper (Eds.), *The handbook of social psychology* (Rev. ed., pp. 296–323). London, UK: Sage.

Anderson, J. R., & Bower, G. H. (1972). Recognition and retrieval processes in free recall. *Psychological Review, 79*, 97–123.

Andrews, B., Brewin, C. R., Rose, S., & Kirk, M. (2000). Predicting PTSD symptoms in victims of violent crime: The role of shame, anger, and childhood abuse. *Journal of Abnormal Psychology, 109*, 69–73.

Apfel, B. A., Ross, J., Hlavin, J., Meyerhoff, D. J., Metzler, T. J., Marmar, C. R., . . . Neylan, T. C. (2011). Hippocampal volume differences in Gulf War veterans with current versus lifetime posttraumatic stress disorder symptoms. *Biological Psychiatry, 69*, 541–548.

Armstrong, J. G., & Kaser-Boyd, N. (2003). Projective assessment of psychological trauma. In D. Segal & M. Hilsenroth (Eds.), *The comprehensive handbook of psychological assessment, Volume 2: Personality assessment* (pp. 500–512). New York, NY: Wiley.

Asmundson, G. J. G., & Taylor, S. (2006). PTSD and chronic pain: Cognitive-behavioral perspectives and practical implications. In G. Young, A. W. Kane, K. Nicholson, G. Young, A. W. Kane, & K. Nicholson (Eds.), *Psychological knowledge in court: PTSD, pain, and TBI* (pp. 225–241). New York, NY: Springer Science + Business Media.

Atkeson, B., Calhoun, K., Resick, P., & Ellis, E. (1982). Victims of rape: Repeated assessment of depressive symptoms. *Journal of Consulting and Clinical Psychology, 50*, 96–102.

Baer, R. A. (2003). Mindfulness training as a clinical intervention: A conceptual and empirical review. *Clinical Psychology: Science and Practice, 10*, 125–143.

Bailey, J. N., Goenjian, A. K., Noble, E. P., Walling, D. P., Ritchie, T. L., & Goenjian, H. A. (2010). PTSD and dopaminergic genes, DRD2 and DAT, in multigenerational families exposed to the Spitak earthquake. *Psychiatry Research, 178*, 507–510.

Bajor, L. A., Ticlea, A. N., & Osser, D. N. (2011). The Psychopharmacology Algorithm Project at the Harvard South Shore Program: An update on posttraumatic stress disorder. *Harvard Review of Psychiatry, 19*, 240–258.

Baker, R. (1992). Psychosocial consequences for tortured refugees seeking asylum and refugee status in Europe. In M. Basoglu (Ed.), *Torture and its consequences: Current treatment approaches* (pp. 83–106). Cambridge, UK: Cambridge University Press.

Baldwin, M. W., Fehr, B., Keedian, E., Seidel, M., & Thompson, D. W. (1993). An exploration of the relational schemata underlying attachment styles: Self-report and lexical decision approaches. *Personality and Social Psychology Bulletin, 19*, 746–754.

Ballesteros, J., Guemes, I., Ibarra, N., & Quemada, J. I. (2008). The effectiveness of donepezil for cognitive rehabilitation after traumatic brain injury: A systematic review. *Journal of Head Trauma Rehabilitation, 23*, 171–180.

Barbee, J. G. (1993). Memory, benzodiazepines, and anxiety: Integration of theoretical and clinical perspectives. *Journal of Clinical Psychiatry, 54*(Suppl.), 86–97.

Barnett, O. W. (2001). Why battered women do not leave, part 2: External inhibiting factors—social support and internal inhibiting factors. *Trauma Violence & Abuse, 2*, 30–35.

Barr, L. C., Goodman, W. K., & Price, L. H. (1994). Physical symptoms associated with paroxetine discontinuation. *American Journal of Psychiatry, 151*, 289.

Bartzokis, G., Lu, P. H., Turner, J., Mintz, J., & Saunders, C. S. (2005). Adjunctive risperidone in the treatment of chronic combat-related posttraumatic stress disorder. *Biological Psychiatry, 57*, 474–479.

Basoglu, M. (1992). *Torture and its consequences: Current treatment approaches.* Cambridge, UK: Cambridge University Press.

Bassuk, E. L., Dawson, R., Perloff, J. N., & Weinreb, L. F. (2001). Post-traumatic stress disorder in extremely poor women: Implications for health care clinicians. *Journal of the American Medical Women's Association, 56*, 79–85.

Batchelor, S. (1997). *Buddhism without belief: A contemporary guide to awakening.* New York, NY: Riverhead Books.

Batchelor, S. (2010). *Confessions of a Buddhist atheist.* New York, NY: Spiegel & Grau.

Batten, S. V., Follette, V. M., Rasmussen Hall, M. L., & Palm, K. M. (2002). Physical and psychological effects of written disclosure among sexual abuse survivors. *Behavior Therapy, 33*, 107–122.

Baugher, S. N., Elhai, J. D., Monroe, J. R., & Gray, M. J. (2010). Rape myth acceptance, sexual trauma history and posttraumatic stress disorder. *Journal of Interpersonal Violence, 25*, 2036–2053.

Beck, J. S. (1995). *Cognitive therapy: Basics and beyond.* New York, NY: Guilford.

Becker, E., Rankin, E., & Rickel, A. U. (1998). *High-risk sexual behavior: Intervention with vulnerable populations.* New York, NY: Plenum.

Becker, M. E., Hertzberg, M. A., Moore, S. D., Dennis, M. F., Bukenya, D. S., & Beckham, J. C. (2007). A placebo-controlled trial of bupropion SR in the treatment of chronic posttraumatic stress disorder. *Journal of Clinical Psychopharmacology, 27*, 193–197.

Beckham, J. C., Moore, S. D., Feldman, M. E., Hertzberg, M. A., Kirby, A. C., & Fairbank, J. A. (1998). Health status, somatization, and severity of posttraumatic stress disorder in Vietnam combat veterans with posttraumatic stress disorder. *American Journal of Psychiatry, 155*, 1565–1569.

Bell, M.D. (1995). *Bell Object Relations and Reality Testing Inventory.* Los Angeles, CA: Western Psychological Services.

Bem, S. L. (1976). Sex typing and the avoidance of cross-sex behavior. *Journal of Personality and Social Psychology, 33*, 48–54.

Benedek, D. M., Fullerton, C., & Ursano, R. J. (2007). First responders: Mental health consequences of natural and human-made disasters for public health and public safety workers. *Annual Review of Public Health, 28*, 55–68.

Benedict, A. L., Mancini, L., & Grodin, M. A. (2009). Struggling to meditate: Contextualising integrated treatment of traumatised Tibetan refugee monks. *Mental Health, Religion & Culture, 12*, 485–499.

Benish, S. G., Imel, Z. E., & Wampold, B. E. (2008). The relative efficacy of bona fide psychotherapies for treating posttraumatic stress disorder: A meta-analysis of direct comparisons. *Clinical Psychology Review, 28,* 746–758.

Benson, H., & Klipper, M.Z. (2000). *The relaxation response: Updated and expanded.* New York, NY: HarperTorch.

Berg, S. H. (2006). Everyday sexism and posttraumatic stress disorder in women: A correlational study. *Violence Against Women, 12,* 970–988.

Bergner, R. M., Delgado, L. K., & Graybill, D. (1994). Finkelhor's risk factor checklist: A cross-validation study. *Child Abuse & Neglect, 18,* 331–340.

Berlant, J. L. (2004). Prospective open-label study of add-on and monotherapy topiramate in civilians with chronic nonhallucinatory posttraumatic stress disorder. *BMC Psychiatry, 4,* 24.

Berlant, J. L., & van Kammen, D. P. (2002). Open-label topiramate as primary, or adjunctive therapy in chronic civilian posttraumatic stress disorder: A preliminary report. *Journal of Clinical Psychiatry, 63,* 15–20.

Berlin, H. A., Rolls, E. T., & Iversen, S. D. (2005). Borderline personality disorder, impulsivity, and the orbitofrontal cortex. *American Journal of Psychiatry, 162,* 2360–2373.

Berliner, L., & Briere, J. (1998). Trauma, memory, and clinical practice. In L. Williams (Ed), *Trauma and memory* (pp. 3–18). Thousand Oaks, CA: Sage.

Berman, H., Girón, E., & Marroquín, A. (2006). A narrative study of refugee women who have experienced violence in the context of war. *Canadian Journal of Nursing Research, 38,* 32–53.

Bernstein, E. M., & Putnam, F. W. (1986). Development, reliability, and validity of a dissociation scale. *Journal of Nervous and Mental Diseases, 174,* 727–734.

Bernstein, I. H., Ellason, J. W., Ross, C. A., & Vanderlinden, J. (2001). On the dimensionalities of the Dissociative Experiences Scale (DES) and the Dissociation Questionnaire (DIS-Q). *Journal of Trauma and Dissociation, 2,* 103–123.

Berthold, S. M. (2000). War traumas and community violence: Psychological, behavioral, and academic outcomes among Khmer refugee adolescents. *Journal of Multicultural Social Work, 8,* 15–46.

Best, C. L., & Ribbe, D. P. (1995). Accidental injury: Approaches to assessment and treatment. In J. R. Freedy & S. E. Hobfoll (Eds.), *Traumatic stress: From theory to practice* (pp. 315–337). New York, NY: Plenum.

Bhikkhu Bodhi. (2005). *In the Buddha's words: An anthology of discourses from the Pali Canon.* Somerville, MA: Wisdom.

Bienvenu, O. J., & Neufeld, K. J. (2011). Post-traumatic stress disorder in medical settings: Focus on the critically ill. *Current Psychiatry Reports, 13,* 3–9.

Bills, C. B., Dodson, N., Stellman, J. M., Southwick, S., Sharma, V., Herbert, R., . . . Katz, C. L. (2009). Stories behind the symptoms: A qualitative analysis of the narratives of 9/11 rescue and recovery workers. *Psychiatric Quarterly, 80,* 173–189.

Bishop, S. R., Lau, M., Shapiro, S., Carlson, L., Anderson, N. D., Carmody, J., . . . Devins, G. (2004). Mindfulness: A proposed operational definition. *Clinical Psychology: Science and Practice, 11,* 230–241.

Bisson, J. I. (2003). Single-session early psychological interventions following traumatic events. *Clinical Psychology Review, 23,* 481–499.

Bisson, J. I., McFarlane, A. C., & Rose, S. (2000). Psychological debriefing. In E. B. Foa, T. M. Keane, & M. J. Friedman (Eds.), *Effective treatments for PTSD* (pp. 39–59). New York, NY: Guilford.

Black, M. C., Basile, K. C., Breiding, M. J., Smith, S. G., Walters, M. L., Merrick, M. T., & Stevens, M. R. (2011). *The National Intimate Partner and Sexual*

Violence Survey (NISVS): 2010 summary report. Atlanta, GA: National Center for Injury Prevention and Control, Centers for Disease Control and Prevention.

Blake, D. D., Weathers, F. W., Nagy, L. M., Kaloupek, D. G., Gusman, F. D., Charney, D. S., & Keane, T. M. (1995). The development of a clinician-administered PTSD scale. *Journal of Traumatic Stress, 8,* 75–90.

Blanchard, E. B., & Hickling, E. J. (1997). *After the crash: Assessment and treatment of motor vehicle accident survivors.* Washington, DC: American Psychological Association.

Bobrow, J. (2007). Tending, attending, and healing. *Psychologist-Psychoanalyst, 27,* 16–18.

Bobrow, J. (2010). *Zen and psychotherapy: Partners in liberation.* New York, NY: W. W. Norton.

Bobrow, J. (2011). Isolation kills and community heals. *Huffington Post.* Retrieved from http://www.huffingtonpost.com/

Boehnlein, J, K. (2006). Religion and spirituality in psychiatric care: Looking back, looking ahead. *Transcultural Psychiatry, 43,* 634–651.

Bohus, M. J., Landwehrmeyer, G. B., Stiglmayr, C. E., Limberger, M. F., Bohme, R., & Schmahl, C. G. (1999). Naltrexone in the treatment of dissociative symptoms in patients with borderline personality disorder: An open-label trial. *Journal of Clinical Psychiatry, 60,* 598–603.

Boldrini, M., Underwood, M. D., Hen, R., Rosoklija, G. B., Dwork, A. J., John Mann, J., & Arango, V. (2009). Antidepressants increase neural progenitor cells in the human hippocampus. *Neuropsychopharmacology, 34,* 2376–2389.

Boorstein, S. (2002). *Pay attention, for goodness' sake: Practicing the perfections of the heart—the Buddhist path of kindness.* New York, NY: Ballantine Books.

Bormann, J. E., Liu, L., Thorp, S. R., & Lang, A. J. (2011). Spiritual wellbeing mediates PTSD change in veterans with military-related PTSD [Electronic version]. *International Journal of Behavioral Medicine,* August 28, 2011.

Boscarino, J. A., Adams, R. E., & Figley, C. R. (2005). A prospective cohort study of the effectiveness of employer-sponsored crisis interventions after a major disaster. *International Journal of Emergency Mental Health, 7*(1), 9–22.

Bowen, S., Chawla, N., & Marlatt, G. A. (2011). *Mindfulnessbased relapse prevention for addictive behaviors: A clinician's guide.* New York, NY: Guilford.

Bowlby, J. (1982). *Attachment and loss. Vol. 1: Attachment* (2nd ed.). New York, NY: Basic Books.

Bowlby, J. (1988). *A secure base: Parent-child attachment and healthy human development.* New York, NY: Basic Books.

Boy, A., & Salihu, H. M. (2004). Intimate partner violence and birth outcomes: A systematic review. *International Journal of Fertility & Women's Medicine, 49,* 159–164.

Boynton, L., Bentley, J., Strachan, E., Barbato, A., & Raskind, M. (2009). Preliminary findings concerning the use of prazosin for the treatment of posttraumatic nightmares in a refugee population. *Journal of Psychiatric Practice, 15,* 454–459.

Brach, T. (2003). *Radical acceptance: Embracing your life with the heart of a Buddha.* New York, NY: Bantam.

Brach, T. (in press). *True refuge: Three gateways to a fearless heart.* New York, NY: Bantam.

Bracken, P., Giller, J., & Summerfield, D. (1995). Psychological responses to war and atrocity: The limitations of the current concepts. *Social Science & Medicine, 40,* 1073–1082.

Bradley, R. G., Greene, J., Russ, E., Dutra, L., & Westen, D. (2005). A multidimensional meta-analysis of psychotherapy for PTSD. *American Journal of Psychiatry, 162,* 214–227.

Brady, K., Pearlstein, T., Asnis, G. M., Baker, D., Rothbaum, B., Sikes, C. R., & Farfel, G. M. (2000). Efficacy and safety of sertraline treatment of posttraumatic stress disorder: A randomized controlled trial. *Journal of the American Medical Association, 283,* 1837–1844.

Braun, P., Greenberg, D., Dasberg, H., & Lerer, B. (1990). Core symptoms of posttraumatic stress disorder unimproved by alprazolam treatment. *Journal of Clinical Psychiatry, 51,* 236–238.

Bremner, J. D., Southwick, S., Brett, E., Fontana, A., Rosenheck, R., & Charney, D. S. (1992). Dissociation and posttraumatic stress disorder in Vietnam combat veterans. *American Journal of Psychiatry, 149,* 328–332.

Bremner, J. D., & Vermetten, E. (2004). Neuroanatomical changes associated with pharmacotherapy in posttraumatic stress disorder. *Annals of the New York Academy of Sciences, 1032,* 154–157.

Bremner, J. D., Vythilingham, M., Vermetten, E., Southwick, S. M., McGlashan, T., Nazeer, A., . . . Charney, D. S. (2003). MRI and PET study of deficits in hippocampal structure and function in women with childhood sexual abuse and posttraumatic stress disorder. *American Journal of Psychiatry, 160,* 924–932.

Brennan, K. A., & Shaver, P. R. (1995). Dimensions of adult attachment, affect regulation, and romantic relationship functioning. *Personality and Social Psychology Bulletin, 21,* 267–283.

Brent, D., Melhem, N., Donohoe, M. B., & Walker, M. (2009). The incidence and course of depression in bereaved youth 21 months after the loss of a parent to suicide, accident, or sudden natural death. *American Journal of Psychiatry, 166,* 786–794.

Breslau, N., Chilcoat, H. D., Kessler, R. C., & Davis, G. C. (1999). Previous exposure to trauma and PTSD effects of subsequent trauma: Results from the Detroit Area Survey of Trauma. *American Journal of Psychiatry, 156,* 902–907.

Breslau, N., Davis, G. C., Andreski, P., & Peterson, E. L. (1991). Traumatic events and posttraumatic stress disorder in an urban population of young adults. *Archives of General Psychiatry, 48,* 216–222.

Breslau, N., Kessler, R. C., Chilcoat, H. D., Schultz, L. R., Davis, G. C., & Andreski, P. (1998). Trauma and posttraumatic stress disorder in the community: The 1996 Detroit Area Survey of Trauma. *Archives of General Psychiatry, 55,* 626–632.

Breslau, N., Peterson, E. L., & Schultz, L. R. (2008). A second look at prior trauma and the posttraumatic stress disorder effects of subsequent trauma: A prospective epidemiological study. *Archives of General Psychiatry, 65,* 431–437.

Breslau, N., Wilcox, H. C., Storr, C. L., Lucia, V., & Anthony, J. C. (2004). Trauma exposure and PTSD: A non-concurrent prospective study of youth in urban America. *Journal of Urban Health, 81,* 530–544.

Briere, J. (1992). *Child abuse trauma: Theory and treatment of the lasting effects.* Newbury Park, CA: Sage.

Briere, J. (1995). *Trauma Symptom Inventory professional manual.* Odessa, FL: Psychological Assessment Resources.

Briere, J. (1996). *Therapy for adults molested as children* (2nd ed.). New York, NY: Springer.

Briere, J. (1998). *Brief Interview for Posttraumatic Disorders (BIPD).* Unpublished psychological test, University of Southern California.

Briere, J. (2000a). *Cognitive Distortions Scale (CDS)*. Odessa, FL: Psychological Assessment Resources.

Briere, J. (2000b). *Inventory of Altered Self Capacities (IASC)*. Odessa, FL: Psychological Assessment Resources.

Briere, J. (2001). *Detailed Assessment of Posttraumatic Stress (DAPS)*. Odessa, FL: Psychological Assessment Resources.

Briere, J. (2002a). *Multiscale Dissociation Inventory*. Odessa, FL: Psychological Assessment Resources.

Briere, J. (2002b). Treating adult survivors of severe childhood abuse and neglect: Further development of an integrative model. In J. E. B. Myers, L. Berliner, J. Briere, C. T. Hendrix, T. Reid, & C. Jenny (Eds.), *The APSAC handbook on child maltreatment* (2nd ed., pp. 175–202). Newbury Park, CA: Sage.

Briere, J. (2003). Integrating HIV/AIDS prevention activities into psychotherapy for child sexual abuse survivors. In L. Koenig, A. O'Leary, L. Doll, & W. Pequenat (Eds.), *From child sexual abuse to adult sexual risk: Trauma, revictimization, and intervention* (pp. 219–232). Washington DC: American Psychological Association.

Briere, J. (2004). *Psychological assessment of adult posttraumatic states: Phenomenology, diagnosis, and measurement* (2nd ed.). Washington, DC: American Psychological Association.

Briere, J. (2006). Dissociative symptoms and trauma exposure: Specificity, affect dysregulation, and posttraumatic stress. *Journal of Nervous and Mental Disease, 194*, 78–82.

Briere, J. (2011). *Trauma Symptom Inventory-2 (TSI-2)*. Odessa, FL: Psychological Assessment Resources.

Briere, J. (2012a). Working with trauma: Mindfulness and compassion. In C. K. Germer & R. D. Siegel (Eds.), *Wisdom and compassion in psychotherapy* (pp. 265–279). New York, NY: Guilford.

Briere, J. (2012b). When people do bad things: Evil, suffering, and dependent origination. In A. Bohart, E. Mendelowitz, B. Held, & K. Schneider (Eds.), *Humanity's dark side: Explorations in psychotherapy and beyond* (pp. 141-156). Washington, DC: American Psychological Association.

Briere, J. (2012c). Mindfulness, insight, and trauma therapy. In C. K. Germer, R. D. Siegel, & P. R. Fulton (Eds.), *Mindfulness and Psychotherapy*, 2nd edition. NY: Guilford.

Briere, J., & Armstrong, J. (2007). Psychological assessment of posttraumatic dissociation. In E. Vermetten, M. Dorahy, & D. Spiegel (Eds.), *Traumatic dissociation: Neurobiology and treatment* (pp. 259–274). Arlington, VA: American Psychiatric.

Briere, J., & Elliott, D. M. (2000). Prevalence, characteristics, and long-term sequelae of natural disaster exposure in the general population. *Journal of Traumatic Stress, 13*, 661–679.

Briere, J., & Elliott, D. M. (2003). Prevalence and symptomatic sequelae of self-reported childhood physical and sexual abuse in a general population sample of men and women. *Child Abuse and Neglect, 27*, 1205–1222.

Briere, J., Henschel, D., & Smiljanich, K. (1992). Attitudes toward sexual abuse: Sex differences and construct validity. *Journal of Research in Personality, 26*, 398–406.

Briere, J., & Hodges, M. (2010). Assessing the effects of early and later childhood trauma in adults. In R. Lanius, E. Vermetten, & C. Pain (Eds.), *The impact of early life trauma on health and disease* (pp. 207–216). Cambridge, UK: Cambridge University Press.

Briere, J., Hodges, M., & Godbout, N. (2010). Traumatic stress, affect dysregulation, and dysfunctional avoidance: A structural equation model. *Journal of Traumatic Stress, 23*, 767–774.

Briere, J., Kaltman, S., & Green, B. L. (2008). Accumulated childhood trauma and symptom complexity. *Journal of Traumatic Stress, 21*, 223–226.

Briere, J., & Lanktree, C. (2011). *Treating complex trauma in adolescents and young adults.* Thousand Oaks, CA: Sage.

Briere, J., & Rickards, S. (2007). Self-awareness, affect regulation, and relatedness: Differential sequels of childhood versus adult victimization experiences. *Journal of Nervous and Mental Disease, 195*, 497–503.

Briere, J., & Runtz, M. G. (1989). The trauma symptom checklist (TSC-33): Early data on a new scale. *Journal of Interpersonal Violence, 4*, 151–163.

Briere, J., Scott, C., & Weathers, F. (2005). Peritraumatic and persistent dissociation in the presumed etiology of PTSD. *American Journal of Psychiatry, 162*, 2295–2301.

Briere, J., & Spinazzola, J. (2005). Phenomenology and psychological assessment of complex posttraumatic states. *Journal of Traumatic Stress, 18*, 401–412.

Briere, J., & Spinazzola, J. (2009). Assessment of the sequelae of complex trauma: Evidence-based measures. In C. A. Courtois & J. D. Ford (Eds.), *Treating complex traumatic stress disorders: An evidence-based guide* (pp. 104–123). New York, NY: Guilford.

Briere, J., Weathers, F. W., & Runtz, M. (2005). Is dissociation a multidimensional construct? Data from the Multiscale Dissociation Inventory. *Journal of Traumatic Stress, 18*, 221–231.

Briere, J., & Zaidi, L. Y. (1989). Sexual abuse histories and sequelae in female psychiatric emergency room patients. *American Journal of Psychiatry, 146*, 1602–1606.

Brown, A. (2009). Trauma and holocaust video testimony: The intersection of history, memory, and judgment in the interview process. *Traumatology, 15*, 44–54.

Brown, L. S. (2008). *Cultural competence in trauma therapy: Beyond the flashback.* Washington, DC: American Psychological Association.

Brown, P. J., Read, J. P., & Kahler, C. W. (2003). Comorbid posttraumatic stress disorder and substance use disorders: Treatment outcomes and the role of coping. In P. Ouimette & P. J. Brown (Eds.), *Trauma and substance abuse: Causes, consequences, and treatment of comorbid disorders* (pp. 171–188). Washington, DC: American Psychological Association.

Brown, P. J., & Wolfe, J. (1994). Substance abuse and post-traumatic stress disorder comorbidity. *Drug and Alcohol Dependence, 35*, 51–59.

Brown, R. P., & Gerbarg, P. L. (2009). Yoga breathing, meditation, and longevity. *Annals of the New York Academy of Sciences, 1172*, 54–62.

Browne, A. L., Andrews, R., Schug, S. A., & Wood, F. (2011). Persistent pain outcomes and patient satisfaction with pain management after burn injury. *Clinical Journal of Pain, 27*, 136–145.

Bruce, N., Shapiro, S. L., Constantino, M. J., & Manber, R. (2010). Psychotherapist mindfulness and the psychotherapy process. *Psychotherapy: Theory, Research, Practice, Training, 47*, 83–97.

Bryant, R. A. (2003). Treating acute stress disorder following mild traumatic brain injury. *American Journal of Psychiatry, 160*, 585–587.

Bryant, R. A. (2011a). Acute stress disorder as a predictor of posttraumatic stress disorder: A systematic review. *Journal of Clinical Psychiatry, 72*, 233–239.

Bryant, R. A. (2011b). Post-traumatic stress disorder vs traumatic brain injury. *Dialogues in Clinical Neuroscience, 13*, 251–262.

Bryant, R. A., Creamer M., O'Donnell M., Silove, D. Clark, C. R., & McFarlane, A. C. (2009). Post-traumatic amnesia and the nature of post-traumatic stress disorder after mild traumatic brain injury. *Journal of the International Neuropsychological Society, 15*, 862–867.

Bryant, R. A., Friedman, M. J., Spiegel, D., Ursano, R. J., & Strain, J. J. (2011). A review of acute stress disorder in DSM-5. *Depression and Anxiety, 28*, 802–817.

Bryant, R. A., & Harvey, A. G. (2000). *Acute stress disorder: A handbook of theory, assessment, and treatment.* Washington, DC: American Psychological Association.

Bryant, R. A., & Harvey, A. G. (2002). Delayed-onset posttraumatic stress disorder: A prospective evaluation. *Australian and New Zealand Journal of Psychiatry, 36*, 205–209.

Bryant, R. A., Harvey, A. G., Dang, S. T., & Sackville, T. (1998). Assessing acute stress disorder: Psychometric properties of a structured clinical interview. *Psychological Assessment, 10*, 215–220.

Bryant, R. A., Moulds, L. M., & Nixon, R. V. D. (2003). Cognitive behaviour therapy of acute stress disorder: A four-year follow-up. *Behaviour Research and Therapy, 41*, 489–494.

Bryant, R. A., Sackville, T., Dang, S., Moulds, M., & Guthrie, R. (1999). Treating acute stress disorder: An evaluation of cognitive behavior therapy and counseling techniques. *American Journal of Psychiatry, 156*, 1780–1786.

Buchanan, T. W., Karafin, M. S., & Adolphs, R. (2003). Selective effects of triazolam on memory for emotional, relative to neutral, stimuli: Differential effects on gist versus detail. *Behavioral Neuroscience, 117*, 517–525.

Bureau, J.-F., Martin, J., & Lyons-Ruth, K. (2010). Inadequate early caregiving and psychopathology. In R. Lanius & E. Vermetten (Eds), *The hidden epidemic: The impact of early life trauma on health and disease* (pp. 48–56). Cambridge, UK: Cambridge University Press.

Burns, J. K., Jhazbhay, K., Esterhuizen, T., & Emsley, R. (2011). Exposure to trauma and the clinical presentation of first-episode psychosis in South Africa. *Journal of Psychiatric Research, 45*, 179–184.

Burt, M. R. (1980). Cultural myths and support for rape. *Journal of Personality and Social Psychology, 38*, 217–230.

Burt, V. K., Suri, R., Altshuler, L., Stowe, Z., Hendrick, V. C., & Muntean, E. (2001). The use of psychotropic medications during breast-feeding. *American Journal of Psychiatry, 158*, 1001–1009.

Butcher, J. N., Dahlstrom, W. G., Graham, J. R., Tellegen, A., & Kaemmer, B. (1989). *Minnesota Multiphasic Personality Inventory (MMPI-2): Manual for administration and scoring.* Minneapolis: University of Minnesota Press.

Butcher, J. N., Williams, C. L., Graham, J. R., Archer, R. P., Tellegen, A., Ben-Porath, Y. S., & Kaemmer, B. (1992). *MMPI-A (Minnesota Multiphasic Personality Inventory–Adolescent): Manual for administration, scoring, and interpretation.* Minneapolis: University of Minnesota Press.

Butterfield, M. I., Becker, M. E., Connor, K. M., Sutherland, S., Churchill, L. E., & Davidson, J. R. (2001). Olanzapine in the treatment of post-traumatic stress disorder: A pilot study. *International Clinical Psychopharmacology, 16*, 197–203.

Byers, M. G., Allison, K. M., Wendel, C. S., & Lee, J. K. (2010). Prazosin versus quetiapine for nighttime posttraumatic stress disorder symptoms in veterans: An assessment of long-term comparative effectiveness and safety. *Journal of Clinical Psychopharmacology, 30,* 225–229.

Cahill, S. P., Rothbaum, B. O., Resick, P. A., & Follette, V. M. (2009). Cognitive behavioral therapy for adults. In E. B. Foa, T. M. Keane, M. J. Friedman, & J. A. Cohen (Eds.), *Effective treatments for PTSD: Practice guidelines from the International Society for Traumatic Stress Studies* (pp. 139–222). New York, NY: Guilford.

Campagne, D. M. (2007). Fact: Antidepressants and anxiolytics are not safe during pregnancy. *European Journal of Obstetrics & Gynecology and Reproductive Biology, 135,* 145–148.

Campbell, J. C. (2002). Health consequences of intimate partner violence. *Lancet, 359,* 1331–1336.

Campbell, J. C., & Lewandowski, L. A. (1997). Mental and physical health effects of intimate partner violence on women and children. *Psychiatric Clinics of North America, 20,* 353–374.

Campbell, J. C., & Soeken, K. L. (1999). Forced sex and intimate partner violence: Effects on women's risk and women's health. *Violence Against Women, 5,* 1017–1035.

Canive, J. M., Clark, R. D., Calais, L. A., Qualls, C., & Tuason, V. B. (1998). Bupropion treatment in veterans with posttraumatic stress disorder: An open study. *Journal of Clinical Psychopharmacology, 18,* 379–383.

Cardenas, V. A., Samuelson, K., Lenoci, M., Studholme, C., Neylan, T. C., Marmar, C. R., . . . Weiner, M. W. (2011). Changes in brain anatomy during the course of posttraumatic stress disorder. *Psychiatry Research, 192,* 93–100.

Carleton, R. N., Peluso, D. L., Collimore, K. C., & Asmundson, G. J. G. (2011). Social anxiety and posttraumatic stress symptoms: The impact of distressing social events. *Journal of Anxiety Disorders, 25,* 49–57.

Carlson, E. A. (1998). A prospective longitudinal study of attachment disorganization/disorientation. *Child Development, 69,* 1107–1128.

Carlson, E. B. (1997). *Trauma assessments: A clinician's guide.* New York, NY: Guilford.

Carlson, E. B., & Dalenberg, C. J. (2000). A conceptual framework for the impact of traumatic experiences. *Trauma, Violence, and Abuse: A Review Journal, 1,* 4–28.

Carlson, E. B., Putnam, F. W., Ross, C. A., Torem, M., Coons, P., Dill, D. L., . . . Braun, B. G. (1993). Validity of the Dissociative Experiences Scale in screening for multiple personality disorder: A multicenter study. *American Journal of Psychiatry, 150,* 1030–1036.

Carrión, V. G., & Steiner, H. (2000). Trauma and dissociation in delinquent adolescents. *Journal of the American Academy of Child & Adolescent Psychiatry, 39,* 353–359.

Carter, R. T. (2007). Racism and psychological and emotional injury: Recognizing and assessing race-based traumatic stress. *Counseling Psychologist, 35,* 13–105.

Carter, R. T., & Forsyth, J. (2010). Reactions to racial discrimination: Emotional stress and help-seeking behaviors. *Psychological Trauma: Theory, Research, Practice, and Policy, 2,* 183–191.

Cassidy, J., & Mohr, J. J. (2001). Unsolvable fear, trauma, and psychopathology. *Clinical Psychology: Science and Practice, 8,* 275–298.

Cassidy, J., & Shaver, P. R. (Eds). (1999). *Handbook of attachment: Theory, research, and clinical applications.* New York, NY: Guilford.

Cassidy, J., & Shaver, P. R. (2010). (Eds.). *Handbook of attachment: Theory, research, and clinical applications* (2nd ed.). New York, NY: Guilford.

Cates, M. E., Bishop, M. H., Davis, L. L., Lowe, J. S., & Woolley, T. W. (2004). Clonazepam for treatment of sleep disturbances associated with combat-related posttraumatic stress disorder. *Annals of Pharmacotherapy, 38,* 1395–1399.

Chang, J. C., Cluss, P. A., Burke, J. G., Hawker, L., Dado, D., Goldstrohm, S., & Scholle, S. H. (2011). Partner violence screening in mental health. *General Hospital Psychiatry, 33,* 58–65.

Chard, K. M., Weaver, T. L., & Resick, P. A. (1997). Adapting cognitive processing therapy for child sexual abuse survivors. *Cognitive and Behavioral Practice, 4,* 31–52.

Chew, E., & Zafonte, R. D. (2009). Pharmacological management of neurobehavioral disorders following traumatic brain injury: A state-of-the-art review. *Journal of Rehabilitation Research and Development,46,* 851–879.

Chilcoat, H. D., & Breslau, N. (1998). Investigations of causal pathways between PTSD and drug use disorders. *Addictive Behaviors, 23,* 827–840.

Chödrön, P. (2000). *When things fall apart: Heart advice for difficult times.* Boston, MA: Shambhala Classics.

Chu, J. A. (1988). Ten traps for therapists in the treatment of trauma survivors. *Dissociation: Progress in the Dissociative Disorders, 1,* 24–32.

Chu, J. A. (2011). *Rebuilding shattered lives: Treating complex PTSD and dissociative disorders* (2nd ed.). Hoboken, NJ: Wiley.

Chung, M. Y., Min, K. H., Jun, Y. J., Kin, S. S., Kin, W. C., & Jun, E. M. (2004). Efficacy and tolerability of mirtazapine and sertraline in Korean veterans with posttraumatic stress disorder: A randomized open label trial. *Human Psychopharmacology, 19,* 489–494.

Cioffi, D., & Holloway, J. (1993). Delayed costs of suppressed pain. *Journal of Personality and Social Psychology, 64,* 274–282.

Cisler, J. M., Amstadter, A. B., Begle, A. M., Resnick, H. S., Danielson, C. K., Saunders, B. E., & Kilpatrick, D. G. (2011). A prospective examination of the relationships between PTSD, exposure to assaultive violence, and cigarette smoking among a national sample of adolescents. *Addictive Behaviors, 36,* 994–1000.

Clark, D. M., Ball, S., & Pape, D. (1991). An experimental investigation of thought suppression. *Behaviour Research and Therapy, 29,* 253–257.

Clark, R. D., Canive, J. M., Calais, L. A., Qualls, C. R., & Tuason, V. B. (1999). Divalproex in posttraumatic stress disorder: An open-label clinical trial. *Journal of Traumatic Stress, 12,* 395–401.

Classen, C. C., Nevo, R., Koopman, C., Nevill-Manning, K., Gore-Felton, C., Rose, D. S., & Spiegel, D. (2002). Recent stressful life events, sexual revictimization, and their relationship with traumatic stress symptoms among women sexually abused in childhood. *Journal of Interpersonal Violence, 17,* 1274–1290.

Classen, C. C., Palesh, O. G., & Aggarwal, R. (2005). Sexual revictimization: A review of the empirical literature. *Trauma, Violence, and Abuse: A Review Journal, 6,* 103–129.

Cloitre, M., Courtois, C. A., Charuvastra, A., Carapezza, R., Stolbach, B. C., & Green, B. J. (2011). Treatment of complex PTSD: Results of the ISTSS Expert Clinician Survey on Best Practices. *Journal of Traumatic Stress, 24,* 615–627.

Cloitre, M., Koenen, K. C., Cohen, L. R., & Han, H. (2002). Skills training in affective and interpersonal regulation followed by exposure: A phase-based treatment for PTSD related to childhood abuse. *Journal of Consulting and Clinical Psychology, 70*, 1067–1074.

Cloitre, M., Stovall-McClough, K. C., Miranda, R., & Chemtob, C. M. (2004). Therapeutic alliance, negative mood regulation, and treatment outcome in child abuse-related posttraumatic stress disorder. *Journal of Consulting and Clinical Psychology, 72*, 411–416.

Cloitre, M., Stovall-McClough, K. C., Nooner, K., Zorbas, P., Cherry, S., Jackson, C. L., & Petkova, E. (2010). Treatment for PTSD related to childhood abuse: A randomized controlled trial. *American Journal of Psychiatry, 167*, 915–924.

Cochran, S. V. (2005). Evidence-based assessment with men. *Journal of Clinical Psychology, 61*, 649–660.

Coe, M. T., Dalenberg, C. J., Aransky, K. M., & Reto, C. S. (1995). Adult attachment style, reported childhood violence history and types of dissociative experiences. *Dissociation: Progress in the Dissociative Disorders, 8*, 142–154.

Coelho, H. F., Canter, P. H., & Ernst, E. (2007). Mindfulness-based cognitive therapy: Evaluating current evidence and informing future research. *Journal of Consulting and Clinical Psychology, 75*, 1000–1005.

Coffey, S. F., Dansky, B. S., & Brady, K. T. (2003). Exposure-based, trauma-focused therapy for comorbid posttraumatic stress disorder-substance use disorder. In P. Ouimette & P. J. Brown (Eds.), *Trauma and substance abuse: Causes, consequences, and treatment of comorbid disorders* (pp. 127–146). Washington, DC: American Psychological Association.

Cohen L. R., & Hien D. A. (2006). Treatment outcomes for women with substance abuse and PTSD who have experienced complex trauma. *Psychiatric Services, 57*, 100–106.

Cohen, L. S., Nonacs, R., Viguera, A. C., & Reminick, A. (2004). Diagnosis and treatment of depression during pregnancy. *CNS Spectrums, 9*, 209–216.

Coker, A. L., Smith, P. H., Thompson, M. P., McKeown, R. E., Bethea, L., & Davis, K. E. (2002). Social support protects against the negative effects of partner violence on mental health. *Journal of Women's Health and Gender-Based Medicine, 11*, 465–476.

Cole, P. M., & Putnam, F. W. (1992). Effect of incest on self and social functioning: A developmental psychopathology perspective. *Journal of Consulting and Clinical Psychology, 60*, 174–184.

Connor, K. M., Davidson, J. R. T., & Lee, L. C. (2003). Spirituality, resilience, and anger in survivors of violent trauma: A community survey. *Journal of Traumatic Stress, 16*, 487–494.

Connor, K. M., Davidson, J. R., Weisler, R. H., Zhang, W., & Abraham, K. (2006). Tiagabine for posttraumatic stress disorder: Effects of open-label and double-blind discontinuation treatment. *Psychopharmacology, 184*, 21–25.

Connor, K. M., Sutherland, S. M., Tupler, L. A., Malik, M. L., & Davidson, J. R. (1999). Fluoxetine in post-traumatic stress disorder: Randomised, double-blind study. *British Journal of Psychiatry, 175*, 17–22.

Cook, A., Spinazzola, J., Ford, J., Lanktree, C., Blaustein, M., Cloitre, M., . . . van der Kolk, B. (2005). Complex trauma in children and adolescents. *Psychiatric Annals, 35*, 390–398.

Cooper, B. S., Kennedy, M. A., & Yuille, J. C. (2001). Dissociation and sexual trauma in prostitutes: Variability of responses. *Journal of Trauma and Dissociation, 2*, 27–36.

Correll, C. U., Leucht, S., & Kane, J. M. (2004). Lower risk for tardive dyskinesia associated with second-generation antipsychotics: A systematic review of 1-year studies. *American Journal of Psychiatry, 161,* 414–425.

Corry, N., Klick, B., & Fauerbach, J. (2010). Posttraumatic stress disorder and pain impact functioning and disability after major burn injury. *Journal of Burn Care & Research, 31*(1), 13–25.

Cottler, L. B., Compton, W. M., Mager, D., Spitznagel, E. L., & Janka, A. (1992). Posttraumatic stress disorder among substance users from the general population. *American Journal of Psychiatry, 149,* 664–670.

Cougle, J. R., Feldner, M. T., Keough, M. E., Hawkins, K. A., & Fitch, K. E. (2010). Comorbid panic attacks among individuals with posttraumatic stress disorder: Associations with traumatic event exposure history, symptoms, and impairment. *Journal of Anxiety Disorders, 24,* 183–188.

Cougle, J. R., Timpano, K. R., Sachs-Ericsson, N., Keough, M. E., & Riccardi, C. J. (2010). Examining the unique relationships between anxiety disorders and childhood physical and sexual abuse in the National Comorbidity Survey-Replication. *Psychiatry Research, 177,* 150–155.

Coupland, N. J., Bell, C. J., & Potokar, J. P. (1996). Serotonin reuptake inhibitor withdrawal. *Journal of Clinical Psychopharmacology, 16,* 356–362.

Courtois, C. A. (2004). Complex trauma, complex reactions: Assessment and treatment. *Psychotherapy: Theory, Research, Practice, and Training, 41,* 412–425.

Courtois, C. A. (2010). *Healing the incest wound: Adult survivors in therapy* (2nd ed.). New York, NY: W. W. Norton.

Courtois, C. A., & Ford, J. D. (Eds.). (2009). *Treating complex traumatic stress disorders: An evidence-based guide.* New York, NY: Guilford.

Courtois, C. A., & Ford, J. D. (in press). *Relational integrated treatment of complex trauma: A practical guide for therapists.* New York, NY: Guilford.

Courtois, C. A., Ford, J. D., & Cloitre, M. (2009). Best practices in psychotherapy for adults. In C. A. Courtois & J. D. Ford (Eds.), *Treating complex traumatic stress disorders: An evidence based guide* (pp. 82–103). New York, NY: Guilford.

Currier, G., & Briere, J. (2000). Trauma orientation and detection of violence histories in the psychiatric emergency service. *Journal of Nervous and Mental Disease, 188,* 622–624.

Curry, M. A., Perrin, N., & Wall, E. (1998). Effects of abuse on maternal complications and birth weight in adult and adolescent women. *Obstetrics & Gynecology, 92,* 530–534.

Dalai Lama, & Goleman, D. (2003). *Destructive emotions: How can we overcome them? A scientific dialogue with the Dalai Lama.* New York, NY: Bantam Books.

Dalenberg, C. J. (2000). *Countertransference and the treatment of trauma.* Washington, DC: American Psychological Association.

Dalgleish, T., Meiser-Stedman, R., Kassam-Adams, N., Ehlers, A., Winston, F., Smith, P., . . . Yule, W. (2008). Predictive validity of acute stress disorder in children and adolescents. *British Journal of Psychiatry, 192,* 392–393.

David, D., De Faria, L., & Mellman, T. A. (2006). Adjunctive risperidone treatment and sleep symptoms in combat veterans with chronic PTSD. *Depression and Anxiety, 23,* 489–491.

David, D., Kutcher, G. S., Jackson, E. I., & Mellman, T. A. (1999). Psychotic symptoms in combat-related posttraumatic stress disorder. *Journal of Clinical Psychiatry, 60,* 29–32.

Davidson, J. R., Brady, K., Mellman, T. A., Stein, M. B., & Pollack, M. H. (2007). The efficacy and tolerability of tiagabine in adult patients with post-traumatic stress disorder. *Journal of Clinical Psychopharmacology, 27,* 85–88.

Davidson, J. R., Connor, K. M., Hertzberg, M. A., Weisler, R. H., Wilson, W. H., & Payne, V. M. (2005). Maintenance therapy with fluoxetine in posttraumatic stress disorder: A placebo-controlled discontinuation study. *Journal of Clinical Psychopharmacology, 25,* 166–169.

Davidson, J. R., Crawford, C., Ives, J. A., & Jonas, W. B. (2011). Homeopathic treatments in psychiatry: A systematic review of randomized placebo-controlled studies. *Journal of Clinical Psychiatry, 72,* 795–805.

Davidson, J. R. T. (1994). Issues in the diagnosis of posttraumatic stress disorder. In R. S. Pynoos (Ed.), *Posttraumatic stress disorder: A clinical review* (pp. 1–15). Lutherville, MD: Sidran.

Davidson, J. R. T. (2004). Long-term treatment and prevention of posttraumatic stress disorder. *Journal of Clinical Psychiatry, 65,* 44–48.

Davidson, J. R. T., Book, S. W., Colket, J. T., Tupler, L. A., Roth, S. H., David, D., . . . Feldman, M. E. (1997). Assessment of a new self-rating scale for posttraumatic stress disorder. *Psychological Medicine, 27,* 153–160.

Davidson, J. R. T., Rampes, H., Eisen, M., Fisher, P., Smith, R. D., & Malik, M. (1998). Psychiatric disorders in primary care patients receiving complementary medical treatments. *Comprehensive Psychiatry, 39,* 16–20.

Davidson, J. R. T., Rothbaum, B. O., van der Kolk, B. A., Sikes, C. R., & Farfel, G. M. (2001). Multi-center, double-blind comparison of sertraline and placebo in the treatment of posttraumatic stress disorder. *Archives of General Psychiatry, 58,* 485–492.

Davidson, J. R. T., Weisler, R. H., Butterfield, M. I., Casat, D. C., Connor, K. M., Barnett, S., & Van Meter, S. (2003). Mirtazapine vs. placebo in posttraumatic stress disorder: A pilot trial. *Biological Psychiatry, 53,* 188–191.

Davidson, P. R., & Parker, K. C. H. (2001). Eye movement desensitization and reprocessing (EMDR): A meta-analysis. *Journal of Consulting and Clinical Psychology, 69,* 305–316.

Davis, L. L., Nugent, A. L., Murray, J., Kramer, G. L., & Petty, F. (2000). Nefazodone treatment for chronic posttraumatic stress disorder: An open trial. *Journal of Clinical Psychopharmacology, 20,* 159–164.

Davydow, D., Katon, W., & Zatzick, D. (2009). Psychiatric morbidity and functional impairments in survivors of burns, traumatic injuries, and ICU stays for other critical illnesses: A review of the literature. *International Review of Psychiatry, 21,* 531–538.

De Bellis, M. D., Baum, A. S., Birmaher, B., Keshavan, M. S., Eccard, C. H., Boring, A. M., . . . & Ryan, N. D. (1999). Developmental traumatology, Part I: Biological stress systems. *Biological Psychiatry, 45,* 1259–1270.

Deckersbach, T., Hölzel, B. K., Eisner, L. R., Stange, J. P., Peckham, A. D., Dougherty, D. D., & Nierenberg, A. A. (2011). Mindfulness-based cognitive therapy for nonremitted patients with bipolar disorder. *CNS Neuroscience & Therapeutics, 18,* 133–141.

de Kloet, C. S., Vermetten, E., Heijnen, C. J., Geuze, E., Lentjes, E. G., & Westenberg H. G. (2007). Enhanced cortisol suppression in response to dexamethasone administration in traumatized veterans with and without posttraumatic stress disorder. *Psychoneuroendocrinology, 32,* 215–226.

Del Gaizo, A. L., Elhai, J. D., & Weaver, T. L. (2011). Posttraumatic stress disorder, poor physical health and substance use behaviors in a national trauma-exposed sample. *Psychiatry Research, 188,* 390–395.

Dell, P. F. (2006). The Multidimensional Inventory of Dissociation (MID): A comprehensive measure of pathological dissociation. *Journal of Trauma and Dissociation, 7,* 77–106.

Department of Veterans Affairs & Department of Defense. (2010). *VA/DoD clinical practice guideline for management of post-traumatic stress.* Retrieved from http://www.healthquality.va.gov/ptsd/PTSD-FULL-2010a.pdf

DePrince, A. P., Combs, M. D., & Shanahan, M. (2009). Automatic relationship–harm associations and interpersonal trauma involving close others. *Psychology of Women Quarterly, 33,* 163–171.

Derogatis, L. R. (1983). *SCL-90-R administration, scoring, and procedures manual II for the revised version* (2nd ed.). Towson, MD: Clinical Psychometrics Research.

Descilo, T., Vedamurtachar, A., Gerbarg, P. L., Nagaraja, D., Gangadhar, B. N., Damodaran, B., . . . Brown, R. P. (2009). Effects of a yoga breath intervention alone and in combination with an exposure therapy for post-traumatic stress disorder and depression in survivors of the 2004 South-East Asia tsunami. *Acta Psychiatrica Scandinavica, 121,* 289–300.

Dias, C. P., & Jones, J. (2004, April). *Propranolol in the treatment of hyperarousal symptoms in posttraumatic stress disorder.* Paper presented at the West Coast Colleges of Biological Psychiatry, Pasadena, CA.

Dieperink, M. E., & Drogemuller, L. (1999). Zolpidem for insomnia related to PTSD. *Psychiatric Services, 50,* 421.

Dietrich, A. M. (2007). Childhood maltreatment and revictimization: The role of affect dysregulation, interpersonal relatedness difficulties and posttraumatic stress disorder. *Journal of Trauma and Dissociation, 8,* 25–51.

Difede, J., Cukor, J., Lee, F., & Yurt, R. (2009). Treatments for common psychiatric conditions among adults during acute, rehabilitation, and reintegration phases. *International Review of Psychiatry, 21,* 559–569.

Difede, J., Ptacek, J. T., Roberts, J., Barocas, D., Rives, W., Apfeldorf, W., & Yurt, R. (2002). Acute stress disorder after burn injury: A predictor of posttraumatic stress disorder? *Psychosomatic Medicine, 64,* 826–834.

DiGrande, L., Neria, Y., Brackbill, R. M., Pulliam, P., & Galea, S. (2010). Long-term posttraumatic stress symptoms among 3,271 civilian survivors of the September 11, 2001, terrorist attacks on the World Trade Center. *American Journal of Epidemiology, 173,* 271–281.

Dobie, D. J., Kivlahan, D. R., Maynard, C., Bush, K. R., Davis, T. M., & Bradley, K. A. (2004). Posttraumatic stress disorder in female veterans: Association with self-reported health problems and functional impairment. *Archives of Internal Medicine, 164,* 394–400.

Donnelly, C. L., Amaya-Jackson, L., & March, J. S. (1999). Psychopharmacology of pediatric posttraumatic stress disorder. *Journal of Child and Adolescent Psychopharmacology, 9,* 203–220.

Drescher, K. D., Foy, D. W., Kelly, C., Leshner, A., Schutz, K., & Litz, B. (2011). An exploration of the viability and usefulness of the construct of moral injury in war veterans. *Traumatology, 17,* 8–13.

Duckworth, M. P., & Follette, V. M. (2011). *Retraumatization: Assessment, treatment, and prevention*. New York, NY: Routledge.

Du Mont, J., Macdonald, S., Rotbard, N., Asllani, E., Bainbridge, D., & Cohen, M. M. (2009). Factors associated with suspected drug-facilitated sexual assault. *Canadian Medical Association Journal, 180,* 513–519.

Duran, E., & Duran, B. (1995). *Native American postcolonial psychology.* Albany: State University of New York Press.

Dutra, L., Callahan, K., Forman, E., Mendelsohn, M., & Herman, J. (2008). Core schemas and suicidality in a chronically traumatized population. *Journal of Nervous and Mental Disease, 196,* 71–74.

Dyster-Aas, J., Willebrand, M., Wikehult, B., Gerdin, B., & Ekselius, L. (2008). Major depression and posttraumatic stress disorder symptoms following severe burn injury in relation to lifetime psychiatric morbidity. *Journal of Trauma Injury, Infection & Critical Care, 64,* 1349–1356.

Echeburúa, E., De Corral, P., Sarasua, B., & Zubizarreta, I. (1996). Treatment of acute posttraumatic stress disorder in rape victims: An experimental study. *Journal of Anxiety Disorders, 10,* 185–199.

Ehlers, A., Bisson, J., Clark, D. M., Creamer, M., Pilling, S., Richards, D., . . . Yule, W. (2010). Do all psychological treatments really work the same in posttraumatic stress disorder? *Clinical Psychology Review, 30,* 269–276.

Ehlers, A., Clark, D. M., Hackman, A., McManus, F., Fennell, M., Herbert, C., & Mayou, R. A. (2003). A randomized controlled trial of cognitive therapy, self-help, and repeated assessment as early interventions for PTSD. *Archives of General Psychiatry, 60,* 1024–1032.

Ehlert, U., Gaab, J., & Heinrichs, M. (2001). Psychoneuroendocrinological contributions to the etiology of depression, posttraumatic stress disorder, and stress-related bodily disorders: The role of the hypothalamus-pituitary-adrenal axis. *Biological Psychology, 57,* 141–152.

Ehring, T., Ehlers, A., Cleare, A. J., & Glucksman, E. (2008). Do acute psychological and psychobiological responses to trauma predict subsequent symptom severities of PTSD and depression? *Psychiatry Research, 161*(1), 67–75.

Ehrlich, C., & Briere, J. (2002). The Psychological Trauma Clinic at Los Angeles County-USC Medical Center. *Los Angeles Psychologist, 16,* 12–13.

Elhai, J. D., & Palmieri, P. A. (2011). The factor structure of posttraumatic stress disorder: A literature update, critique of methodology, and agenda for future research. *Journal of Anxiety Disorders, 25,* 849–854.

Elklit, A., Armour, C., & Shevlin, M. (2010). Testing alternative factor models of PTSD and the robustness of the dysphoria factor. *Journal of Anxiety Disorders, 24,* 147–154.

Elklit, A., & Brink, O. (2004). Acute stress disorder as a predictor of post-traumatic stress disorder in physical assault victims. *Journal of Interpersonal Violence, 19,* 709–726.

Elliott, D. M. (1994). Impaired object relationships in professional women molested as children. *Psychotherapy, 31,* 79–86.

Elliott, D. M. (1997). Traumatic events: Prevalence and delayed recall in the general population. *Journal of Consulting and Clinical Psychology, 65,* 811–820.

Elliott, D. M., & Briere, J. (1992). Sexual abuse trauma among professional women: Validating the Trauma Symptom Checklist-40 (TSC-40). *Child Abuse & Neglect: The International Journal, 16,* 391–398.

Elliott, D. M., & Briere, J. (1995). Posttraumatic stress associated with delayed recall of sexual abuse: A general population study. *Journal of Traumatic Stress, 8,* 629–647.

Elliott, D. M., & Briere, J. (2003). *Prevalence and symptomatic sequelae of physical and sexual domestic violence in a general population sample of women.* Unpublished manuscript, University of Southern California, Los Angeles, CA.

Elliott, D. M., Mok, D., & Briere, J. (2004). Adult sexual assault: Prevalence, symptomatology, and sex differences. *Journal of Traumatic Stress, 17,* 203–211.

Elwood, L. A., Smith, D. W., Resnick, H. S., Gudmundsdottir, B., Amstadter, A. B., Hanson, R. F., . . . Kilpatrick, D. G. (2011). Predictors of rape: Findings from the National Survey of Adolescents. *Journal of Traumatic Stress, 24,* 166–173.

EMDR Institute. (2011a). *EMDR evaluated clinical applications.* Retrieved from http://www.emdr.com/general-information/clinical-applications.html

EMDR Institute. (2011b). What is EMDR? Retrieved from http://www.emdr.com/general-information/what-is-emdr.html

Emerson, D., & Hopper, E. (2011). *Overcoming trauma through yoga: Reclaiming your body.* Berkeley, CA: North Atlantic Books.

English, B. A., Jewell, M., Jewell, G., Ambrose, S., & Davis, L. L. (2006). Treatment of chronic posttraumatic stress disorder in combat veterans with citalopram: An open trial. *Journal of Clinical Psychopharmacology, 26,* 84–88.

Epstein, M. (2008). *Psychotherapy without the self: A Buddhist perspective.* New Haven, CT: Yale University Press.

Epstein, R. S., Fullerton, C. S., & Ursano, R. J. (1998). Posttraumatic stress disorder following an air disaster: A prospective study. *American Journal of Psychiatry, 155,* 934–938.

Erickson, M. F., & Egeland, B. (2011). Child neglect: The invisible assault. In J. E. B. Myers (Ed.), *The handbook of child maltreatment* (3rd ed.,) (pp. 103–124). Thousand Oaks, CA: Sage.

Evans, S., Ferrando, S., Findler, M., Stowell, C., Smart, C., & Haglin, D. (2008). Mindfulness based cognitive therapy for generalized anxiety disorder. *Journal of Anxiety Disorders, 22,* 716–721.

Expert Consensus Guideline Series. (1999). Treatment for posttraumatic stress disorder: The Expert Consensus Panels for PTSD. *Journal of Clinical Psychiatry, 60*(Suppl. 16), 3–76.

Eytan, A., Guthmiller, A., Durieux-Paillard, S., Loutan, L., & Gex-Fabry, M. (2011). Mental and physical health of Kosovar Albanians in their place of origin: A post-war 6-year follow-up study. *Social Psychiatry and Psychiatric Epidemiology, 46,* 953–963.

Falsetti, S. A., & Resnick, H. S. (1997). Frequency and severity of panic attack symptoms in a treatment seeking sample of trauma victims. *Journal of Traumatic Stress, 10,* 683–689.

Famularo, R., Kinscherff, R., & Fenton, T. (1988). Propranolol treatment for childhood PTSD acute type. *American Disorders of Childhood 142,* 1244–1247.

Fann, J. R., Hart, T., & Schomer, K. G. (2009). Treatment for depression after traumatic brain injury: A systematic review. *Journal of Neurotrauma, 26,* 2383–2402.

Fann J. R., Uomoto, J. M., & Katon, W. J. (2001). Cognitive improvement with treatment of depression following mild traumatic brain injury. *Psychosomatics. 42,* 48.

Farber, B. A., & Hall, D. (2002). Disclosure to therapists: What is and is not discussed in psychotherapy. *Journal of Clinical Psychology, 58,* 359–370.

Farley, M. (Ed.). (2003). *Prostitution, trafficking, and traumatic stress.* Binghamton, NY: Hayworth.

Farley, M. (2004). "Bad for the body, bad for the heart": Prostitution harms women even if legalized or decriminalized. *Violence Against Women, 10,* 1087–1125.

Fauerbach, J., Lawrence, J., Fogel, J., Richter, L., Magyar-Russell, G., McKibben, J., & McCann, U. (2009). Approach-avoidance coping conflict in a sample of burn patients at risk for posttraumatic stress disorder. *Depression and Anxiety, 26,* 838–850.

Fauerbach, J. A., McKibben, J. B. A., Bienvenu, O. J., Magyar-Russell, G., Smith, M. T., Holavanahalli, R., . . . Lezotte, D. (2007). Psychological distress after major burn injury. *Psychosomatic Medicine, 69,* 473–482.

Fauerbach, J. A., Richter, L., & Lawrence, J. W. (2002). Regulating acute posttrauma distress. *Journal of Burn Care and Rehabilitation, 23,* 249–257.

Federal Bureau of Investigation. (2010). *Crime in the United States by volume and rate per 100,000 inhabitants, 1991–2010.* Retrieved from http://www.fbi.gov/about-us/cjis/ucr/crime-in-the-u.s/2010/crime-in-the-u.s.-2010/tables/10tbl01.xls

Fennema-Notestine, C., Stein, M. B., Kennedy, C. M., Archibald, S. L., & Jernigan, T. L. (2002). Brain morphometry in female victims of intimate partner violence with and without posttraumatic stress disorder. *Biological Psychiatry, 51,* 1089–1101.

Feuer, C., Jefferson, D. L., & Resick, P. A. (2002). Post-traumatic stress disorder. In J. Worell (Ed.), *Encyclopedia of gender* (pp. 827–836). San Diego, CA: Academic Press.

Finkelhor, D., Hotaling, G., Lewis, I. A., & Smith, C. (1990). Sexual abuse in a national survey of adult men and women: Prevalence, characteristics, and risk factors. *Child Abuse and Neglect, 14,* 19–28.

Finkelhor, D., Ormrod, R. K., Turner, H. A., & Hamby, S. L. (2005). Measuring poly-victimization using the JVQ. *Child Abuse & Neglect, 29,* 1297–1312.

Finkelhor, D., & Yllo, K. (1985). *License to rape: Sexual abuse of wives.* New York, NY: Holt, Rinehart & Winston.

Fitzgerald, S. G., & Gonzalez, E. (1994). Dissociative states induced by relaxation training in a PTSD combat veteran: Failure to identify trigger mechanisms. *Journal of Traumatic Stress, 7,* 111–115.

Foa, E. B. (1995). *Posttraumatic Stress Diagnostic Scale.* Minneapolis, MN: National Computer Systems.

Foa, E. B., Ehlers, A., Clark, D., Tolin, D. F., & Orsillo, S. M. (1999). The Posttraumatic Cognitions Inventory (PTCI): Development and validation. *Psychological Assessment, 11,* 303–314.

Foa, E. B., Hearst-Ikeda, D., & Perry, K. J. (1995). Evaluation of a brief cognitive-behavioral program for the prevention of chronic PTSD in recent assault victims. *Journal of Consulting and Clinical Psychology, 63,* 948–955.

Foa, E. B., Hembree, E. A., & Rothbaum, B. O. (2007). *Prolonged exposure therapy for PTSD: Emotional processing of traumatic experiences: Therapist guide.* New York, NY: Oxford University Press.

Foa, E. B., Huppert, J. D., & Cahill, S. P. (2006). Emotional processing theory: An update. In B. O. Rothbaum (Ed.), *Pathological anxiety: Emotional processing in etiology and treatment* (pp. 3–24). New York, NY: Guilford.

Foa, E. B., Keane, T. M., & Friedman, M. J. (Ed.). (2000). *Effective treatments for PTSD: Practice guidelines from the International Society of Traumatic Stress Studies.* New York, NY: Guilford.

Foa, E. B., Keane, T. M., Friedman, M. J., & Cohen, J. A. (2009). *Effective treatments for PTSD: Practice guidelines of the International Society for Traumatic Stress Studies* (2nd ed). New York, NY: Guilford.

Foa, E. B., & Kozak, M. J. (1986). Emotional processing of fear: Exposure to corrective information. *Psychological Bulletin, 99,* 20–35.

Foa, E. B., Molnar, C., & Cashman, L. (1995). Changes in rape narrative during exposure therapy for posttraumatic stress disorder. *Journal of Traumatic Stress, 8,* 675–690.

Foa, E. B., & Rothbaum, B. O. (1998). *Treating the trauma of rape: Cognitive-behavioral therapy for PTSD.* New York, NY: Guilford.

Foa, E. B., Zinbarg, R., & Rothbaum, B. O. (1992). Uncontrollability and unpredictability in post-traumatic stress disorder: Experimental evidence. *Psychological Bulletin, 112,* 218–238.

Follette, V. M., Palm, K. M., & Hall, M. L. R. (2004). Acceptance, mindfulness, and trauma. In S. C. Hayes, V. M. Follette, & M. M. Linehan (Eds.), *Mindfulness and acceptance: Expanding the cognitive-behavioral tradition* (pp. 192–208). New York, NY: Guilford.

Follette, V. M., & Pistorello, J. (2007). *Finding life beyond trauma: Using Acceptance and Committment Therapy to heal from posttraumatic stress and trauma related problems.* Oakland, CA: New Harbinger.

Follette, V. M., Polusny, M. A., Bechtle, A., & Naugle, A. (1996). Cumulative trauma: Impact of child sexual abuse, sexual assault, and spouse abuse. *Journal of Traumatic Stress, 9,* 25–35.

Follette, V. M., & Vijay, A. (2009). Mindfulness for trauma and posttraumatic stress disorder. In F. Didonna (Ed.), *Clinical handbook of mindfulness* (pp. 299–317). New York, NY: Springer.

Food and Drug Administration. (1980). *Federal Register, 44,* 37434–37467.

Food and Drug Administration. (2005). *Public health advisory: Paroxetine.* Retrieved from http://www.fda.gov/Drugs/DrugSafety/PostmarketDrugSafety InformationforPatientsandProvidersDrugSafetyInformationforHeathcare Professionals/PublicHealthAdvisories/ucm051731.htm

Ford, J. D., Connor, D. F., & Hawke, J. M. (2009). Complex trauma among psychiatrically impaired children: A cross-sectional, chart-review study. *Journal of Clinical Psychiatry, 79,* 1155–1163.

Ford, J. D., Courtois, C. A., Steele, K., van der Hart, O., & Nijenhuis, E. R. S. (2005). Treatment of complex posttraumatic self-regulation. *Journal of Traumatic Stress, 18,* 437–447.

Foy, D. W., Resnick, H. S., Sipprelle, R. C., & Carroll, E. M. (1987). Premilitary, military, and postmilitary factors in the development of combat-related post-traumatic stress disorder. *Behavior Therapist, 10,* 3–9.

Frank, A. F., & Gunderson, J. G. (1990). The role of the therapeutic alliance in the treatment of schizophrenia. *Archives of General Psychiatry, 47,* 228–236.

Frank, J. B., Kosten, T. R., Giller, E. L., Jr., & Dan, E. (1988). A randomized clinical trial of phenelzine and imipramine for posttraumatic stress disorder. *American Journal of Psychiatry, 145,* 1289–2291.

Frayne, S. M., Seaver, M. R., Loveland, S., Christiansen, C. L., Spiro, A., Parker, V. A., & Skinner, K. M. (2004). Burden of medical illness in women with depression and posttraumatic stress disorder. *Archives of Internal Medicine, 164,* 1306–1312.

Freed, W. (2003). From duty to despair: Brothel prostitution in Cambodia. *Journal of Trauma Practice, 2,* 133–146.

Freedman, S. A., Gluck, N., Tuval-Mashiach, R., Brandes, D., Peri, T., & Shalev, A. Y. (2002). Gender differences in responses to traumatic events: A prospective study. *Journal of Traumatic Stress, 15,* 407–413.

Freedman, S. A., & Shalev, A. Y. (2000). Prospective studies of the recently traumatized. In A. Y. Shalev, R. Yehuda, & A. C. McFarlane (Eds.), *International handbook of human response to trauma* (pp. 249–261). New York, NY: Kluwer.

Friedman, M. J. (2000a). *Posttraumatic stress disorder.* Kansas City, MO: Compact Clinicals.

Friedman, M. J. (2000b). What might the psychobiology of posttraumatic stress disorder teach us about future approaches to pharmacotherapy? *Journal of Clinical Psychiatry, 61*(Suppl. 7), 44–51.

Friedman, M. J., Davidson, J. R., & Stein, D. J. (2009). Psychopharmacotherapy for adults. In E. B. Foa, T. M. Keane, M. J. Friedman, & J. A. Cohen (Eds.), *Effective treatments for PTSD: Practice guidelines from the International Society for Traumatic Stress Studies* (pp. 245–268). New York, NY: Guilford.

Friedman, M. J., & Jaranson, J. M. (1994). The applicability of the PTSD concept to refugees. In A. J. Marsella, T. H. Borneman, S. Ekblad, & J. Orley (Eds.), *Amid peril and pain: The mental health and well-being of the world's refugees* (pp. 207–228). Washington, DC: American Psychological Association.

Friedman M. J., Resick P. A., Bryant R. A., Brewin C. R. (2011). Considering PTSD for *DSM-5. Depression and Anxiety, 28,* 750–769.

Fullerton, C. S., Ursano, R. J., & Wang, L. (2004). Acute stress disorder, posttraumatic stress disorder, and depression in disaster or rescue workers. *American Journal of Psychiatry, 161,* 1370–1376.

Gal, G., Levav, I., & Gross, R. (2011). Psychopathology among adults abused during childhood or adolescence: Results from the Israel-based world mental health survey. *Journal of Nervous and Mental Disease, 199,* 222–229.

Galea, S., Ahern, J., Resnick, H. S., Kilpatrick, D. G., Bucuvalas, M. J., Gold, J., & Vlahov, D. (2002). Psychological sequelae of the September 11 terrorist attacks in New York City. *New England Journal of Medicine, 346,* 982–987.

Gelpin, E., Bonne, O., Peri, T., Brandes, D., & Shalev, A. Y. (1996). Treatment of recent trauma survivors with benzodiazepines: A prospective study. *Journal of Clinical Psychiatry, 57,* 390–394.

Gentile, S. (2010). Antipsychotic therapy during early and late pregnancy: A systematic review. *Schizophrenia Bulletin, 36,* 518–544.

Germer, C. K. (2005). Teaching mindfulness in therapy. In C. K. Germer, R. D. Siegel, & P. R. Fulton (Eds.), *Mindfulness and psychotherapy* (pp. 113–129). New York, NY: Guilford.

Germer, C. K. (2009). *The mindful path to self-compassion: Freeing yourself from destructive thoughts and emotions.* New York, NY: Guilford.

Germer, C. K., & Siegel, R. D. (Eds.). (2012) *Wisdom and compassion in psychotherapy.* New York, NY: Guilford.

Giaconia, R. M., Reinherz, H. Z., Silverman, A. B., & Pakiz, B. (1995). Traumas and posttraumatic stress disorder in a community population of older adolescents. *Journal of the American Academy of Child & Adolescent Psychiatry, 34,* 1369–1380.

Gilbert, J. (2009). Power and ethics in psychosocial counselling: Reflections on the experience of an international NGO providing services for Iraqi refugees in Jordan. *Intervention, 7,* 50–60.

Gilbert, P. (2009). Introducing compassion-focused therapy. *Advances in Psychiatric Treatment, 15,* 199–208.

Gilbertson, M. W., Shenton, M. E., Ciszewski, A., Kasai, K., Lasko, N. B., Orr, S. P., & Pitman, R. K. (2002). Smaller hippocampal volume predicts pathologic vulnerability to psychological trauma. *Nature Neuroscience, 5,* 1242–1247.

Gilboa, D., Friedman, M., Tsur, H., & Fauerbach, J. A. (1994). The burn as a continuous traumatic stress: Implications for emotional treatment during hospitalization. *Journal of Burn Care and Rehabilitation, 15,* 86–94.

Gill, J., Vythilingam, M., & Page, G. C. (2008). Low cortisol, high DHEA, and high levels of stimulated TNF-alpha and IL-6 in women with PTSD. *Journal of Traumatic Stress, 21,* 530–539.

Ginzburg, K., & Solomon, Z. (2011). Trajectories of stress reactions and somatization symptoms among war veterans: A 20-year longitudinal study. *Psychological Medicine: A Journal of Research in Psychiatry and the Allied Sciences, 41,* 353–362.

Girard, T. D., Shintani, A. K., Jackson, J. C., Gordon, S. M., Pun, B. T., Henderson, M. S., . . . Ely, E. W. (2007). Risk factors for post-traumatic stress disorder symptoms following critical illness requiring mechanical ventilation: A prospective cohort study. *Critical Care, 11,* R28.

Glaesmer, H., Braehler, E., Riedel-Heller, S. G., Freyberger, H. J., & Kuwert, P. (2011). The association of traumatic experiences and posttraumatic stress disorder with health care utilization in the elderly—A German population based study. *General Hospital Psychiatry, 33,* 177–184.

Goin, M. K. (1997). A psychoanalyst's look at common and uncommon factors in psychodynamic and cognitive-behavioral psychotherapies. *Journal of Practical Psychiatry and Behavioral Health, 3,* 308–309.

Goin, M. K. (2002). When it really hurts to listen: Psychotherapy in the aftermath of September 11. *Psychiatric Services, 53,* 561–562.

Gold, D. B., & Wegner, D. M. (1995). Origins of ruminative thought: Trauma, incompleteness, nondisclosure, and suppression. *Journal of Applied Social Psychology, 25,* 1245–1261.

Goldberg, J., True, W. R., Eisen, S. A., & Henderson, W. G. (1990). A twin study of the effects of the Vietnam War on posttraumatic stress disorder. *Journal of the American Medical Association, 263,* 1227–1232.

Goldstein, E. (2009). *Radical acceptance: An interview with Tara Brach.* Retrieved from http://blogs.psychcentral.com/mindfulness/2009/09/radical-acceptance-an-interview-with-tara-brach/

Goodman, L. A., Corcoran, C. B., Turner, K., Yuan, N., & Green, B. L. (1998). Assessing traumatic event exposure: General issues and preliminary findings for the Stressful Life Events Screening Questionnaire. *Journal of Traumatic Stress, 11,* 521–542.

Gould, K. R., Ponsford, J. L., Johnston, L., & Schonberger, M. (2011). Relationship between psychiatric disorders and 1-year psychosocial outcome following traumatic brain injury. *Journal of Head Trauma and Rehabilitation, 26*(1), 79–89.

Gould, N., McKibben, J., Hall, R., Corry, N., Amoyal, N., Mason, S., . . . & Fauerbach, J. (2011). Peritraumatic heart rate and posttraumatic stress disorder in patients with severe burns. *Journal of Clinical Psychiatry, 72,* 539–547.

Gradus, J. L., Qin, P., Lincoln, A. K., Miller, M., Lawler, E., Sørensen, H. T., & Lash, T. L. (2010). Acute stress reaction and completed suicide. *International Journal of Epidemiology, 39,* 1478–1484.

Green, B. L., Grace, M. C., Lindy, J. D., & Gleser, G. C. (1990). War stressor and symptom persistence in posttraumatic stress disorder. *Journal of Anxiety Disorder, 4,* 31–39.

Green, B. L., Krupnick, J. L., Stockton, P., Goodman, L., Corcoran, C., & Petty, R. (2005). Effects of adolescent trauma exposure on risky behavior in college women. *Psychiatry: Interpersonal and Biological Processes, 68,* 363–378.

Green, B. L., Lindy, J. D., Grace, M. C., Gleser, G. C., Leonard, A. C., Korol, M., & Winget, C. (1990). Buffalo Creek survivors in the second decade: Stability of stress symptoms. *American Journal of Orthopsychiatry, 60,* 43–54.

Green, B. L., & Solomon, S. D. (1995). The mental health impact of natural and technological disasters. In J. R. Freedy & S. E. Hobfoll (Eds.), *Traumatic stress: From theory to practice* (pp. 163–180). New York, NY: Plenum.

Grella, C. E., & Joshi, V. (2003). Treatment processes and outcomes among adolescents with a history of abuse who are in drug treatment. *Child Maltreatment, 8,* 7–18.

Griffin, M. G., Resick, P. A.. Waldrop, A. E., & Mechanic, M. B. (2003). Participation in trauma research: Is there evidence of harm? *Journal of Traumatic Stress, 16,* 221–227.

Griffin, S. L., van Reekum, R., & Masanic, C. (2003). A review of cholinergic agents in the treatment of neurobehavioral deficits following traumatic brain injury. *Journal of Neuropsychiatry and Clinical Neuroscience 15,* 17–26.

Grilo, C. M., Martino, S., Walker, M. L., Becker, D. F., Edell, W. S., & McGlashan, T. H. (1997). Controlled study of psychiatric comorbidity in psychiatrically hospitalized young adults with substance use disorders. *American Journal of Psychiatry, 154,* 1305–1307.

Gros, D. F., Simms, L. J., & Acierno, R. (2010). Specificity of posttraumatic stress disorder symptoms: An investigation of comorbidity between posttraumatic stress disorder symptoms and depression in treatment-seeking veterans. *Journal of Nervous and Mental Disease, 198,* 885–890.

Grossman, P., Niemann, L., Schmidt, S., & Walach, H. (2004). Mindfulness-based stress reduction and health benefits: A meta-analysis. *Journal of Psychosomatic Research, 57,* 35–43.

Haden, S. C., Scarpa, A., Jones, R. T., & Ollendick, T. H. (2007). Posttraumatic stress disorder symptoms and injury: The moderating role of perceived social support and coping for young adults. *Personality and Individual Differences, 42,* 1187–1198.

Hahn, T. H. (1987). *The miracle of mindfulness.* Boston, MA: Beacon Press.

Hall, E., Saxe, G., Stoddard, F., Kaplow, J., Koenen, K., Chawla, N., . . . King, D. (2006). Posttraumatic stress symptoms in parents of children with acute burns. *Journal of Pediatric Psychology, 31,* 403–412.

Halpern, J., Maunder, R. G., Schwartz, B., & Gurevich, M. (2011). Identifying risk of emotional sequelae after critical incidents. *Emergency Medicine Journal, 28*(1), 51–56.

Hamner, M. B. (1996). Clozapine treatment for a veteran with comorbid psychosis and PTSD. *American Journal of Psychiatry, 153,* 841.

Hamner, M. B., Brodrick, P. S., & Labbate, L. A. (2001). Gabapentin in PTSD: A retrospective, clinical series of adjunctive therapy. *Annals of Clinical Psychiatry, 13,* 141–146.

Hamner, M. B., Deitsch, S. E., Brodrick, P. S., Ulmer, H. G., & Lorberbaum, J. P. (2003). Quetiapine treatment in patients with posttraumatic stress disorder: An open trial of adjunctive therapy. *Journal of Clinical Psychopharmacology, 23,* 15–20.

Hamner, M. B., Faldowski, R. A., Robert, S., Ulmer, H. G., Horner, M. D., & Lorberbaum, J. P. (2009). A preliminary controlled trial of divalproex in post-traumatic stress disorder. *Annals of Clinical Psychiatry, 21,* 89–94.

Hamner, M. B., & Frueh, B. C. (1998). Response to venlafaxine in a previously antidepressant treatment-resistant combat veteran with post-traumatic stress disorder. *International Clinical Psychopharmacology, 13,* 233–234.

Harari, D., Bakermans-Kranenburg, M. J., & van Ijzendoorn, M. J. (2007). Attachment, disorganization, and dissociation. In E. Vermetten, M. Dorahy, & D. Spiegel (Eds.), *Traumatic dissociation: Neurobiology and treatment* (pp. 31–54). Arlington, VA: American Psychiatric.

Hardy, A., Fowler, D., Freeman, D., Smith, B., Steel, C., Evans, J., . . . Dunn, G. (2005). Trauma and hallucinatory experience in psychosis. *Journal of Nervous and Mental Disease, 193,* 501–507.

Harmon, R. J., & Riggs, P. D. (1996). Clonidine for posttraumatic stress disorder in preschool children. *Journal of the American Academy of Child and Adolescent Psychiatry, 35,* 1247–1249.

Harmsen, M., Geurts, A. C., Fasotti, L., & Bevarrt, B. J. (2004). Positive behavioural disturbances in the rehabilitation phase after severe traumatic brain injury: An historic cohort study. *Brain Injury, 18,* 787–796.

Hart, S. N., Brassard, M., Davidson, H. A., Rivelis, E., Diaz, V., & Binggeli, N. J. (2011). Psychological maltreatment. In J. E. B. Myers (Ed.), *American Professional Society on the Abuse of Children (APSAC) handbook on child maltreatment* (3rd ed., pp. 125–144). Thousand Oaks, CA: Sage.

Harvard Mental Health Letter. (2009, April). *Yoga for anxiety and depression.* Cambridge, MA: Harvard Health.

Harvey, A. G., & Bryant, R. A. (2002). Acute stress disorder: A synthesis and critique. *Psychological Bulletin, 128,* 886–902.

Harvey, A. G., Jones, C., & Schmidt, D. A. (2003). Sleep and posttraumatic stress disorder: A review. *Clinical Psychology Review, 23,* 377–407.

Haskell, S. G., Mattocks, K., Goulet, J. L., Krebs, E. E., Skanderson, M., Leslie, D., . . . Brandt, C. (2011). The burden of illness in the first year home: Do male and female VA users differ in health conditions and healthcare utilization. *Women's Health Issues, 21,* 92–97.

Hayes, S. C. (2004). Acceptance and commitment therapy, relational frame theory, and the third wave of behavioral and cognitive therapies. *Behavior Therapy, 35,* 639–665.

Hayes, S. C., Follette, V. M., & Linehan, M. M. (Eds.). (2004). *Mindfulness and acceptance: Expanding the cognitive-behavioral tradition.* New York, NY: Guilford.

Hayes, S. C., Luoma, J., Bond, F., Masuda, A., & Lillis, J. (2006). Acceptance and commitment therapy: Model, processes, and outcomes. *Behavior Research & Therapy, 44,* 1–25.

Hayes, S. C., Strosahl, K. D., & Wilson, K. G. (2011). *Acceptance and commitment therapy: The process and practice of mindful change* (2nd ed). New York, NY: Guilford.

Hedtke, K. A., Ruggiero, K. J., Fitzgerald, M. M., Zinzow, H. M., Saunders, B. E., Resnick, H. S., & Kilpatrick, D. G. (2008). A longitudinal investigation of interpersonal violence in relation to mental health and substance use. *Journal of Consulting and Clinical Psychology, 76,* 633–647.

Heidenreich, F., Ruiz-Casares, M., & Rousseau, C. (2009). The psychosocial consequences of organized violence on children. In R. Lanius, E. Vermetten, & C. Pain (Eds.), *The impact of early life trauma on health and disease: The hidden epidemic* (pp. 234–241). Cambridge, UK: Cambridge University Press.

Herman, J. L. (1992a). Complex PTSD: A syndrome in survivors of prolonged and repeated trauma. *Journal of Traumatic Stress, 5,* 377–392.

Herman, J. L. (1992b). *Trauma and recovery: The aftermath of violence—from domestic abuse to political terror.* New York, NY: Basic Books.

Herman, J. L., Perry, C., & van der Kolk, B. A. (1989). Childhood trauma in borderline personality disorder. *American Journal of Psychiatry, 146,* 490–494.

Herpertz, S., Gretzer, A., Steinmeyer, E. M., Muehlbauer, V., Schuerkens, A., & Sass, H. (1997). Affective instability and impulsivity in personality disorder: Results of an experimental study. *Journal of Affective Disorders, 44,* 31–37.

Hertzberg, M. A., Butterfield, M. I., Feldman, M. E., Beckham, J. C., Sutherland, S. M., Connor, K. M., & Davidson, J. R. T. (1999). A preliminary study of lamotrigine for the treatment of posttraumatic stress disorder. *Biological Psychiatry, 45,* 1226–1229.

Hertzberg, M. A., Feldman, M. E., Beckham, J. C., & Davidson, J. R. T. (1996). Trial of trazodone for posttraumatic stress disorder using a multiple baseline group design. *Journal of Clinical Psychopharmacology, 16,* 294–298.

Hertzberg, M. A., Feldman, M. E., Beckham, J. C., Kudler, H. S., & Davidson, J. R. T. (2000). Lack of efficacy for fluoxetine in PTSD: A placebo controlled trial in combat veterans. *Annals of Clinical Psychiatry, 12,* 101–105.

Hesse, E., Main, M., Abrams, K. Y., & Rifkin, A. (2003). Unresolved states regarding loss or abuse can have "second generation" effects: Disorganization, role inversion, and frightening ideation in the offspring of traumatized, non-maltreating parents. In M. F. Solomon & D. Siegel (Eds.), *Healing trauma: Attachment, mind, body, and brain* (pp. 57–106). New York, NY: Norton.

Hickling, E. J., Blanchard, E. B., & Hickling, M. T. (2006). The psychological impact of litigation: Compensation neurosis, malingering, PTSD, secondary traumatization, and other lessons from MVAs. *DePaul Law Review, 55,* 617–633.

Hickling, E. J., Gillen, R., Blanchard, E. B., Buckley, T. C., & Taylor, A. E. (1998). Traumatic brain injury and posttraumatic stress disorder: A preliminary investigation of neuropsychological test results in PTSD secondary to motor vehicle accidents. *Brain Injury, 12,* 265–274.

Hien, D. A., & Ruglass, L. M. (2009). Interpersonal partner violence and women in the United States: An overview of prevalence rates, psychiatric correlates and consequences and barriers to help seeking. *International Journal of Law and Psychiatry, 32,* 48–55.

Hien, D. A., Wells, E. A., Jiang, H., Suarez-Morales, L., Campbell, A. N. C., Cohen, L. R., . . . Nunes, E. V. (2009). Multisite randomized trial of behavioral interventions for women with co-occurring PTSD and substance use disorders. *Journal of Consulting and Clinical Psychology, 77,* 607–619.

Hinton, D. E., Hinton, S., Um, K., Chea, A. S., & Sak, S. (2002). The Khmer "weak heart" syndrome: Fear of death from palpitations. *Transcultural Psychiatry, 39,* 323–344.

Hinton, D. E., & Lewis-Fernández, R. (2011). The cross-cultural validity of posttraumatic stress disorder: Implications for DSM-5. *Depression and Anxiety, 28,* 783–801.

Hinton, D. E., Pich, V., Marques, L., Nickerson, A., & Pollack, M. H. (2010). Khyâl attacks: A key idiom of distress among traumatized Cambodia refugees. *Culture, Medicine and Psychiatry, 34,* 244–278.

Hobfoll, S. E., Dunahoo, C. A., & Monnier, J. (1995). Conservation of resources and traumatic stress. In J. R. Freedy & S. E. Hobfoll (Eds.), *Traumatic stress: From theory to practice* (pp. 29–47). New York, NY: Plenum.

Hoffman, A., Eisenkraft, A., Finkelstein, A., Schein, O., Rotman, E., & Dushnitsky, T. (2007). A decade after the Tokyo sarin attack: A review of neurological follow-up of the victims. *Military Medicine, 172,* 607–610.

Hofmann, S. G., Sawyer, A. T., Witt, A. A., & Oh, D. (2010). The effect of mindfulness-based therapy on anxiety and depression: A meta-analytic review. *Journal of Consulting and Clinical Psychology, 78,* 169–183.

Hofmann, S. G., & Smits, J. A. J. (2008). Cognitive-behavioral therapy for adult anxiety disorders: A meta-analysis of randomized placebo-controlled trials. *Journal of Clinical Psychiatry, 69,* 621–632.

Hoge, C. W., Castro, C. A., Messer, S. C., McGurk, D., Cotting, D. I., & Koffman, R. L. (2004). Combat duty in Iraq and Afghanistan, mental health problems, and barriers to care. *New England Journal of Medicine, 351,* 13–22.

Holbrook, T. L., Hoyt, D. B., Stein, M. B., & Sieber, W. J. (2001). Perceived threat to life predicts posttraumatic stress disorder after major trauma: Risk factors and functional outcome. *Journal of Trauma: Injury, Infection, and Critical Care, 51,* 287–293.

Holgersen, K., Klöckner, C. A., Boe, H., Weisæth, L., & Holen, A. (2011). Disaster survivors in their third decade: Trajectories of initial stress responses and long-term course of mental health. *Journal of Traumatic Stress, 24,* 334–341.

Hollifield, M., Sinclair-Lian, N., Warner, T. D., & Hammerschlag, R. (2007). Acupuncture for posttraumatic stress disorder: A randomized controlled pilot trial. *Journal of Nervous & Mental Disease, 195,* 504–513.

Hooberman, J. B., Rosenfeld, B., Lhewa, D., Rasmussen, A., & Keller, A. (2007). Classifying the torture experiences of refugees living in the United States. *Journal of Interpersonal Violence, 22,* 108–123.

Hooberman, J. B., Rosenfeld, B., Rasmussen, A., & Keller, A. S. (2010). Resilience in trauma-exposed refugees: The moderating effect of coping style on resilience variables. *American Journal of Orthopsychiatry, 80,* 557–563.

Horowitz, M., Wilner, N., & Alvarez, W. (1979). Impact of Event Scale: A measure of subjective stress. *Psychosomatic Medicine, 41,* 209–218.

Horowitz, M. J. (1978). *Stress response syndromes.* New York, NY: Jason Aronson.

Horowitz, M. J., Siegel, B., Holen, A., Bonanno, G. A., Milbrath, C., & Stinson, C. H. (1997). Diagnostic criteria for complicated grief disorder. *American Journal of Psychiatry, 154,* 904–910.

Horrigan, J. P., & Barnhill, L. J. (1996). The suppression of nightmares with guanfacine. *Journal of Clinical Psychiatry, 57,* 371.

Horsfield, S. A., Rosse, R. B., Tomasino V., Schwartz B. L., Mastropaolo, J., & Deutsch, S. I. (2002). Fluoxetine's effects on cognitive performance in patients with traumatic brain injury. *International Journal of Psychiatry in Medicine. 32,* 337–344.

Horvath, A. O. (2007). The alliance in context: Accomplishments, challenges, and future directions. *Psychotherapy: Theory, Research, Practice, Training, 43,* 258–263.

Human Rights Watch. (2009). *World report 2009.* Retrieved from http://www.hrw.org/world-report-2009.

Hung, N., & Rabin, L. A. (2009). Psychological implications of parental bereavement by suicide: A review of the literature and recommendations for future research. *Death Studies, 33,* 781–814.

Hurley, E. A. (2007). The moral costs of prophylactic propranolol. *American Journal of Bioethics, 7,* 35–36.

Hurley, M., Parker, H., & Wells, D. L. (2006). The epidemiology of drug facilitated sexual assault. *Journal of Clinical and Forensic Medicine, 13,* 181–185.

Hurwitz, T. D., Mahowald, M. W., Kuskowski, M., & Engdahl, B. E. (1998). Polysomnographic sleep is not clinically impaired in Vietnam combat veterans with chronic posttraumatic stress disorder. *Biological Psychiatry, 44,* 1066–1073.

Institute of Medicine. (2010). *Gulf War and health: Volume 8. Health effects of serving in the Gulf War.* Retrieved from http://www.iom.edu/Reports/2010/Gulf-War-and-Health-Volume-8-Health-Effects-of-Serving-in-the-Gulf-War.aspx

Jackson, J. C., Hart, R. P., Gordon, S. M. Hopkins, R. O., Girard, T. D., & Ely, E. W. (2007). Post-traumatic stress disorder and post-traumatic stress symptoms following critical illness in intensive care unit patients: Assessing the magnitude of the problem. *Critical Care, 11*(1), R27.

Jacob, J. (1992). Child sexual abuse victimization and later sequelae during pregnancy and childbirth. *Journal of Child Sexual Abuse, 1,* 103–112.

Jacobs, J., Horne-Moyer, H. L., & Jones, R. (2004). The effectiveness of critical incident stress debriefing in primary and secondary trauma victims. *International Journal of Emergency Mental Health, 6*(1), 5–14.

Jacobson, E. (1938). *Progressive relaxation.* Chicago, IL: University of Chicago Press.

Jakovljevic, M., Sagud, M., & Mihaljevic-Peles, A. (2003). Olanzapine in the treatment-resistant, combat-related PTSD—A series of case reports. *Acta Psychiatrica Scandinavica, 107,* 394–396.

Janakiramaiah N., Gangadhar, B. N., Naga Venkatesha Murthy, P. J., Harish, M. G., Subbakrishna D. K., & Vedamurthachar, A. (2000). Antidepressant efficacy of Sudarshan Kriya yoga (SKY) in melancholia: A randomized comparison with electroconvulsive therapy (ECT) and Imipramine. *Journal of Affective Disorders, 57,* 255–259.

Janoff-Bulman, B. (1992). *Shattered assumptions: Towards a new psychology of trauma.* New York, NY: Free Press.

Jaycox, L. H., Foa, E. B., & Morral, A. R. (1998). Influence of emotional engagement and habituation on exposure therapy for PTSD. *Journal of Consulting and Clinical Psychology, 66,* 185–192.

Jin, C., & Schachar, R. (2004). Methylphenidate treatment of attention-deficit/hyperactivity disorder secondary to traumatic brain injury: A critical appraisal of treatment studies. *CNS Spectrums 9,* 217–226.

Johnson, K., Scott, J., Rughita, B., Kisielewski, M., Asher, J., Ong, R., & Lawry, L. (2010). Association of sexual violence and human rights violations with physical and mental health in territories of the eastern Democratic Republic of the Congo. *JAMA: Journal of the American Medical Association, 304,* 553–562.

Jones, E., & Wessely, S. C. (2003). "Forward psychiatry" in the military: Its origins and effectiveness. *Journal of Traumatic Stress, 16,* 411–419.

Jones, R. T., & Ollendick, T. H. (2005). Risk factors for psychological adjustment following residential fire: The role of avoidant coping. In E. Cardena & K. Croyle (Eds.), *Acute reactions to trauma and psychotherapy: A multidisciplinary and international perspective* (pp. 85–99). New York, NY: Haworth.

Jordan, C. E., Nietzel, M. T., Walker, R., & Logan, T. K. (2004). *Intimate partner violence: Clinical and practice issues for mental health professionals.* New York, NY: Springer.

Jordan, R. G., Nunley, T. V., & Cook, R. R. (1992). Symptom exaggeration in a PTSD inpatient population: Response set or claim for compensation. *Journal of Traumatic Stress, 5,* 633–642.

Joseph, S. A., & Linley, P. A. (2008). *Psychological assessment of growth following adversity: A review.* Hoboken, NJ: Wiley.

Kabat-Zinn, J. (1982). An outpatient program in behavioral medicine for chronic pain patients based on the practice of mindfulness meditation: Theoretical considerations and preliminary results. *General Hospital Psychiatry, 4,* 33–47.

Kabat-Zinn, J. (2003). Mindfulness-based stress reduction (MBSR). *Constructivism in the Human Sciences, 8,* 73–107.

Kaelin, D. L., Cifu, D. X., & Matthies, B. (1996). Methylphyenidate effect on attention deficit in the acutely brain-injured adult. *Archives of Physical Medicine & Rehabilitation, 77,* 6–9.

Kaltman, S., & Bonnano, G. A. (2003). Trauma and bereavement: Examining the impact of sudden and violent deaths. *Journal of Anxiety Disorders, 17,* 131–147.

Kane, J. M. (1999). Tardive dyskinesia in affective disorders. *Journal of Clinical Psychiatry, 60*(Suppl. 5), 43–47.

Kang, H. K., Dalager, N. A., Mahan, C. M., & Ishii, E. (2005). The role of sexual assault on the risk of PTSD among Gulf War veterans. *Annals of Epidemiology, 15,* 191–195.

Kaplan, Z., Amir, M., Swartz, M., & Levine, J. (1996). Inositol treatment of posttraumatic stress disorder. *Anxiety, 2,* 51–52.

Kask, A., Harro, J., von Horsten, S., Redrobe, J. P., Dumont, Y., & Quirion, R. (2002). The neurocircuitry and receptor subtypes mediating anxiolytic-like effects of neuropeptide Y. *Neuroscience and Behavioral Reviews, 26,* 259–283.

Keane, T. M. (1995). The role of exposure therapy in the psychological treatment of PTSD. *National Center for PTSD Clinical Quarterly, 5*(1), 3–6.

Kearney, P. (n.d.). *Still crazy after all these years: Why meditation isn't psychotherapy.* Retrieved from http://www.buddhanet.net/crazy.htm

Keck, P., McElroy, S., & Friedman, L. (1992). Valproate and carbamazepine in the treatment of panic and posttraumatic stress disorders, withdrawal states, and behavioral dyscontrol syndromes. *Journal of Clinical Psychopharmacology, 12,* 368–418.

Kellner, M., Muhtz, C., & Wiedemann, K. (2010). Primary add-on of ziprasidone in sertraline treatment of posttraumatic stress disorder: Lessons from a stopped trial? *Journal of Clinical Psychopharmacology, 30,* 471–473.

Kendall-Tackett, K. (2009). Psychological trauma and physical health: A psychoneuroimmunology approach to etiology of negative health effects and possible interventions. *Psychological Trauma: Theory, Research, Practice, and Policy, 1,* 35–48.

Kendler, K. S., Bulik, C. M., Silberg, J., Hettema, J. M., Myers, J., & Prescott, C. A. (2000). Childhood sexual abuse and adult psychiatric and substance use disorders in women: An epidemiological and cotwin control analysis. *Archives of General Psychiatry, 57,* 953–959.

Kendler, K. S., Myers, J., & Prescott, C. A. (2002). The etiology of phobias: An evaluation of the stress-diathesis model. *Archives of General Psychiatry, 59,* 242–248.

Kennedy, J. E., Jaffee, M. S., Leskin, G. A., Stokes, J. W., Leal, F. O., & Fitzpatrick, P. J. (2007). Posttraumatic stress disorder and posttraumatic stress disorder–like symptoms and mild traumatic brain injury. *Journal of Rehabilitation Research & Development, 44,* 895–920.

Kernberg, O. F. (1976). *Borderline conditions and pathological narcissism.* New York, NY: Jason Aronson.

Kersting, A., Kroker, K., Horstmann, J., Ohrmann, P., Baune, B. T., Arolt, V., & Suslow, T. (2009). Complicated grief in patients with unipolar depression. *Journal of Affective Disorders, 118,* 201–204.

Kessler, R. C., Sonnega, A., Bromet, E., Hughes, M., & Nelson, C. B. (1995). Posttraumatic stress disorder in the national comorbidity survey. *Archives of General Psychiatry, 52,* 1048–1060.

Khan, A. Y., & Margoob, M. A. (2006). Paediatric PTSD: Clinical presentation, traumatic events and socio-demographic variables—experience from a chronic conflict situation. *JK-Practitioner, 13*(Supplement 1), S40–S44.

Khantzian, E. J. (1997). The self-medication hypothesis of substance use disorders: A reconsideration and recent applications. *Harvard Review of Psychiatry, 4,* 231–244.

Khateb, A., Ammann, J., Annoni, J. M., & Diserens, K. (2005). Cognition-enhancing effects of donepezil in traumatic brain injury. *European Neurology, 54,* 39–45.

Kianpoor, M., & Rhoades, G. F. (2005). "Djinnati," a possession state in Baloochistan, Iran. *Journal of Trauma Practice, 4,* 147–155.

Kilcommons, A. M., Morrison, A. P., Knight, A., & Lobban, F. (2008). Psychotic experiences in people who have been sexually assaulted. *Social Psychiatry and Psychiatric Epidemiology, 43,* 602–611.

Kilpatrick, D. G., & Resnick, H. S. (1993). Posttraumatic stress disorder associated with exposure to criminal victimization in clinical and community populations. In J. R. T. Davidson & E. B. Foa (Eds.), *Posttraumatic stress disorder: DSM-IV and beyond* (pp. 113–143). Washington, DC: American Psychiatric Press.

Kim, E., & Bijlani, M. (2006). A pilot study of quetiapine treatment of aggression due to traumatic brain injury. *Journal of Neuropsychiatry and Clinical Neuroscience, 18,* 547–549.

Kim, E., Lauterbach, E. D., Reeve, A., Arcineagas, D. B., Coburn, K. L., Mendez, M. F., . . . Coffey, E. C. (2007). Neuropsychiatric complications of traumatic brain injury: A critical review of the literature. *Journal of Neuropsychiatry Clin Neuroscience, 19,* 106–127.

Kimbrough, E., Magyari, T., Langenberg, P., Chesney, M. A., & Berman, B. (2010). Mindfulness intervention for child abuse survivors. *Journal of Clinical Psychology, 66,* 17–33.

Kimerling, R., Ouimette, P., & Wolfe, J. (Eds.). (2002). *Gender and PTSD.* New York, NY: Guilford.

Kimerling, R., Street, A. E., Pavao, J., Smith, M. W., Cronkite, R. C., Holmes, T. H., & Frayne, S. M. (2010). Military-related sexual trauma among Veterans Health Administration patients returning from Afghanistan and Iraq. *American Journal of Public Health, 100,* 1409–1412.

Kinrys, G., Wygant, L. E., Pardo, T. B., & Melo, M. (2006). Levetiracetam for treatment-refractory posttraumatic stress disorder. *Journal of Clinical Psychiatry, 67,* 211–214.

Kinsler, P. J., Courtois, C. A., & Frankel, A. S. (2009). Therapeutic alliance and risk management. In C. A. Courtois, & J. D. Ford (Eds.), *Treating complex traumatic stress disorders: An evidence-based guide* (pp. 183–201). New York, NY: Guilford.

Kinzie, J. D., & Leung, P. (1989). Clonidine in Cambodian patients with posttraumatic stress disorder. *Journal of Nervous and Mental Disease, 177,* 546–550.

Kirmayer, L. J. (1996). Confusion of the senses: Implications of ethnocultural variation in somatoform and dissociative disorders for PTSD. In A. J. Marsella, M. J. Friedman, E. T. Gerrity, & R. M. Scurfield (Eds.), *Ethnocultural aspects of posttraumatic stress disorder: Issues, research, and clinical applications* (pp. 131–163). Washington, DC: American Psychological Association.

Kitchner, I., & Greenstein, R. A. (1985). Low dose lithium carbonate in the treatment of post traumatic stress disorder: Brief communication. *Military Medicine, 150,* 378–381.

Kliem, S., Kröger, C., & Kosfelder, J. (2010). Dialectical behavior therapy for borderline personality disorder: A meta-analysis using mixed-effects modeling. *Journal of Consulting and Clinical Psychology, 78,* 936–951.

Knaudt, P. R., Connor, K. M., Weisler, R. H., Churchill, L. E., & Davidson, J. R. T. (1999). Alternative therapy use by psychiatric outpatients. *Journal of Nervous & Mental Disease, 187,* 692–695.

Koenen, K. C., Harley, R. M., Lyons, M. J., Wolfe, J., Simpson, J. C., Goldberg, J., . . . Tsuang, M. T. (2002). A twin registry study of familial and individual risk factors for trauma exposure and posttraumatic stress disorder. *Journal of Nervous and Mental Disease, 190,* 209–218.

Kohrt, B. A., & Hruschka, D. J. (2010). Nepali concepts of psychological trauma: The role of idioms of distress, ethnopsychology and ethnophysiology in alleviating suffering and preventing stigma. *Culture, Medicine and Psychiatry, 34,* 322–352.

Kolb, L. C., Burris, B. C., & Griffiths, S. (1984). Propranolol and clonidine in the treatment of the chronic post-traumatic stress disorders of war. In B. A. van der Kolk (Ed.), *Post traumatic stress disorder: Psychological and biological sequelae* (pp. 98–108). Washington, DC: American Psychiatric Press.

Koopman, C., Classen, C., & Speigel, D. (1996). Dissociative responses in the immediate aftermath of the Oakland/Berkeley firestorm. *Journal of Traumatic Stress, 9,* 521–540.

Kornfield, J. (2008). *The wise heart: A guide to the universal teachings of Buddhist psychology.* New York, NY: Bantam.

Kornfield, J. (n.d.). *Even the best meditators have old wounds to heal.* Retrieved from http://www.buddhanet.net/psymed1.htm

Kosten, T. R., Frank, J. B., Dan, E., McDougle, C. J., & Giller, E. L. (1991). Pharmacotherapy for posttraumatic stress disorder using phenelzine or imipramine. *Journal of Nervous and Mental Disorders, 179,* 366–370.

Kozaric-Kovacic, D., & Pivac, N. (2007). Quetiapine treatment in an open trial in combat-related post-traumatic stress disorder with psychotic features. *International Journal of Neuropsychopharmacology, 10,* 285–289.

Krashin, D., & Oates, E. W. (1999). Risperidone as an adjunct therapy for post-traumatic stress disorder. *Military Medicine, 164,* 605–606.

Krause, E. D., DeRosa, R. R., & Roth, S. (2002). Gender, trauma themes, and PTSD: Narratives of male and female survivors. In R. Kimerling, P. Ouimette, & J. Wolfe (Eds.), *Gender and PTSD* (pp. 349–381). New York, NY: Guilford.

Krippner, S., & McIntyre, T. (2003). *The psychological impact of war trauma on civilians: An international perspective.* Westport, CT: Praeger.

Krysinska, K., & Lester, D. (2010). Post-traumatic stress disorder and suicide risk: A systematic review. *Archives of Suicide Research, 14,* 1–23.

Krystal, J. H., Rosenheck, R. A., Cramer, J. A., Vessicchio, J. C., Jones, K. M., Vertrees, J. E., . . . Stock, C. (2011). Adjunctive risperidone treatment for antidepressant-resistant symptoms of chronic military service-related PTSD: A randomized trial. *Journal of the American Medical Association, 306,* 493–502.

Kubany, E. S., Ralston, T. C., & Hill, E. E. (2010). Intense fear, helplessness, "and" horror? An empirical investigation of DSM-IV PTSD Criterion A2. *Psychological Trauma: Theory, Research, Practice, and Policy, 2,* 77–82.

Kudler, H. S., & Davidson, J. R. T. (1995). General principles of biological intervention following trauma. In J. R. Freedy & S. E. Hobfoll (Eds.), *Traumatic stress: From theory to practice* (pp. 73–98). New York, NY: Plenum.

Kudler, H. S., Krupnick, J. L., Blank, A. S., Jr., Herman, J. L., & Horowitz, M. J. (2009). Psychodynamic therapy for adults. In E. B. Foa, T. M. Keane, M. J. Friedman, & J. A. Cohen (Eds.), *Effective treatments for PTSD: Practice guidelines from the International Society for Traumatic Stress Studies* (2nd ed., pp. 346–369). New York, NY: Guilford.

Kuhn, E., Blanchard, E. B., Fuse, T., Hickling, E. J., & Broderick, J. (2006). Heart rate of motor vehicle accident survivors in the emergency department, peritraumatic psychological reactions, ASD, and PTSD severity: A 6-month prospective study. *Journal of Traumatic Stress, 19,* 735–740.

Kulka, R. A., Schlenger, W. E., Fairbank, J. A., Hough, R. L., Jordan, B. K., Marmar, C. R., & Weiss, D. S. (1988). *The National Vietnam Veterans Readjustment Study (NVVRS): Description, current status, and initial PTSD prevalence estimates.* Washington, DC: Veterans Administration.

Kyriacou, D. N., Anglin, D., Taliaferro, E., Stone, S., Tubb, T., Linden, J. A., . . . Kraus, J. F. (1999). Risk factors for injury to women from domestic violence. *New England Journal of Medicine, 341,* 1892–1898.

LaFauci Schutt, J. M., & Marotta, S. A. (2011). Personal and environmental predictors of posttraumatic stress in emergency management professionals. *Psychological Trauma: Theory, Research, Practice, and Policy, 3*(1), 8–15.

LaGarde, G., Doyon, J., & Brunet, A. (2010). Memory and executive dysfunctions associated with acute posttraumatic stress disorder. *Psychiatry Research, 177*(1–2), 144–149.

Lambert, J. F., Difede, J., & Contrada, R. J. (2004). The relationship of attribution of responsibility to acute stress disorder among hospitalized burn patients. *Journal of Nervous and Mental Disease, 192,* 304–312.

Lambert, M. J., & Barley, D. E. (2001). Research summary on the therapeutic relationship and psychotherapy outcome. *Psychotherapy, 38,* 357–361.

Lambert, M. J., & Okishi, J. C. (1997). The effects of the individual psychotherapist and implications for future research. *Clinical Psychology: Science and Practice, 4,* 66–75.

Langer, A. I., Cangas, A. J., Salcedo, E., & Fuentes, B. (2011). Applying mindfulness therapy in a group of psychotic individuals: A controlled study. *Behavioral and Cognitive Psychotherapy, 40,* 105–109.

Lanktree, C. B., & Briere, J. (2008). *Integrative treatment of complex trauma for children ages 8 to 12 (ITCT-C).* Long Beach, CA: MCAVIC-USC, National Child Traumatic Stress Network, U.S. Substance Abuse and Mental Health Services Administration.

Lanktree, C. B., Briere, J., Godbout, N., Hodges, M., Chen, K., Trimm, L., . . . Freed, W. (in press). Treating multi-traumatized, socially-marginalized children: Results of a naturalistic treatment outcome study. *Journal of Aggression, Maltreatment & Trauma.*

Larsson, G., Michel, P.-O., & Lundin, T. (2000). Systematic assessment of mental health following various types of posttrauma support. *Military Psychology, 12,* 121–135.

Lawrence, J. W., Fauerbach, J. A., & Munster, A. M. (1996). Early avoidance of traumatic stimuli predicts chronicity of intrusive thoughts following burn injury. *Behaviour Research and Therapy, 34,* 643–646.

LeDoux, J. (1998). *The emotional brain*. New York, NY: Simon & Schuster.

Lee, A., Isaac, M. K., & Janca, A. (2002). Post-traumatic stress disorder and terrorism. *Current Opinion in Psychiatry, 15*, 633–637.

Lee, H., Kim, S. W., Kim, J. M., Shin, I. S., Yang, S. J., & Yoon, J. S. (2005). Comparing effects of methylphenidate, sertraline and placebo on neuropsychiatric sequelae in patients with traumatic brain injury. *Human Psychopharmacology, 20*, 97–104.

Lee, S., Brasel, K., & Lee, B. (2004). Emergency care practitioners' barriers to mental health assessment, treatment, and referral of post-injury patients. *Wisconsin Medical Journal, 103*(6), 78–82.

Leff, J. P. (1988). *Psychiatry around the globe: A transcultural view* (2nd ed.). London, UK: Gaskell.

Leidholdt, D. A. (2003). Prostitution and trafficking in women: An intimate relationship. *Journal of Trauma Practice, 2*, 167–183.

Lejoyeux, M., Adès, J., Mourad, I., Solomon, J., & Dilsaver, S. (1996). Antidepressant withdrawal syndrome: Recognition, prevention and management. *CNS Drugs, 5*, 278–292.

Lensvelt-Mulders, G., van Der Hart, O., van Ochten, J. M., van Son, M. J. M., Steele, K., & Breeman, L. (2008). Relations among peritraumatic dissociation and posttraumatic stress: A meta-analysis. *Clinical Psychology Review, 28*, 1138–1151.

Lerer, B., Bleich, A., Kotler, M., Garb, R., Hertzberg, M., & Levin, B. (1987). Posttraumatic stress disorder in Israeli combat veterans: Effect of phenelzine treatment. *Archives of General Psychiatry, 44*, 976–981.

Leskela, J., Dieperink, M. E., & Thuras, P. (2002). Shame and posttraumatic stress disorder. *Journal of Traumatic Stress, 15*, 223–226.

Leskin, G. A., & Sheikh, J. I. (2002). Lifetime trauma history and panic disorder: Findings from the National Comorbidity Survey. *Journal of Anxiety Disorders, 16*, 599–603.

Leslie, K., Chan, M. T. V., Myles, P. S., Forbes, A., & McCulloch, T. J. (2010). Posttraumatic stress disorder in aware patients from the B-Aware Trial. *Anesthesia & Analgesia, 110*, 823–828.

Levant, R. F., & Pollack, W. S. (Eds.). (1995). *A new psychology of men*. New York, NY: Basic Books.

Lewis, J. D. (2002). Mirtazapine for PTSD nightmares. *American Journal of Psychiatry, 159*, 1948–1949.

Lewis-Fernández, R., Gorritz, M., Raggio, G. A., Peláez, C., Chen, H., & Guarnaccia, P. J. (2010). Association of trauma-related disorders and dissociation with four idioms of distress among Latino psychiatric outpatients. *Culture, Medicine and Psychiatry, 34*, 219–243.

Lieberman, J. A., Stroup, T. S., McEvoy, J. P., Swartz, M. S., Rosenheck, R. A., Perkins, D. O., . . . Hsiao, J. K. (2005). Effectiveness of antipsychotic drugs in patients with chronic schizophrenia. *New England Journal of Medicine, 353*, 1209–1223.

Lindley, S. E., Carlson, E. B., & Benoit, M. (2004). Basal and dexamethasone suppressed salivary cortisol concentrations in a community sample of patients with posttraumatic stress disorder. *Biological Psychiatry, 55*, 940–945.

Linehan, M. M. (1993a). *Cognitive-behavioral treatment of borderline personality disorder*. New York, NY: Guilford.

Linehan, M. M. (1993b). *Skills training manual for treating borderline personality disorder.* New York, NY: Guilford.

Loewenstein, R. J. (2005). Psychopharmacologic treatments for dissociative identity disorder. *Psychiatric Annals.*

Loo, C. M., Fairbank, J. A., Scurfield, R. M., Ruch, L. O., King, D. W., Adams, L. J., & Chemtob, C. M. (2001). Measuring exposure to racism: Development and validation of a Race-Related Stressor Scale (RRSS) for Asian American Vietnam veterans. *Psychological Assessment, 13,* 503–520.

Looff, D., Grimley, P., Kuller, F., Martin, A., & Shonfield, L. (1995). Carbamazepine for PTSD. *Journal of the American Academy of Child and Adolescent Psychiatry, 34,* 703–704.

Lundin, T. (1995). Transportation disasters: A review. *Journal of Traumatic Stress, 8,* 381–389.

Luterek, J. A., Bittinger, J. N., & Simpson, T. L. (2011). Posttraumatic sequelae associated with military sexual trauma in female veterans enrolled in VA outpatient mental health clinics. *Journal of Trauma & Dissociation, 12,* 261–274.

Luterek, J. A., Orsillo, S. M., & Marx, B. P. (2005). An experimental examination of emotional experience, expression, and disclosure in women reporting a history of child sexual abuse. *Journal of Traumatic Stress, 18,* 237–244.

Luxenberg, T., & Levin, P. (2004). The utility of the Rorschach in the assessment and treatment of trauma. In J. Wilson & T. Keane (Eds.), *Assessing psychological trauma and PTSD* (2nd ed., pp. 190–225). New York, NY: Guilford.

Lynch, T. R., Trost, W. T., Salsman, N., & Linehan, M. M. (2007). Dialectical behavior therapy for borderline personality disorder. *Annual Review of Clinical Psychology, 3,* 181–205.

Lyoo, I. K., Kim, J. E., Yoon, S. J., Hwang, J., Bae, S., & Kim D. J. (2011). The neurobiological role of the dorsolateral prefrontal cortex in recovery from trauma. Longitudinal brain imaging study among survivors of the South Korean subway disaster. *Archives of General Psychiatry, 68,* 701–713.

Mace, S., & Taylor, D. (2000). Selective serotonin reuptake inhibitors: A review of efficacy and tolerability in depression. *Expert Opinion in Pharmacotherapy, 1,* 917–933.

Madianos, M., Papaghelis, M., Ioannovich, J., & Dafni, R. (2001). Psychiatric disorders in burn patients: A follow-up study. *Psychotherapy and Psychosomatics, 70*(1), 30–37.

Maeda, M., & Higa, M. (2006). Transportation disasters and posttraumatic responses: A review of studies on major sea, air, and rail accidents. *Japanese Journal of Traumatic Stress, 4,* 49–60.

Maguen, S., Luxton, D. D., Skopp, N. A., Gahm, G. A., Reger, M. A., Metzler, T. J., & Marmar, C. R. (2011). Killing in combat, mental health symptoms, and suicidal ideation in Iraq war veterans. *Journal of Anxiety Disorders, 25,* 563–567.

Maguen, S., Metzler, T. J., Litz, B. T., Seal, K. H., Knight, S. J., & Marmar, C. R. (2009). The impact of killing in war on mental health symptoms and related functioning. *Journal of Traumatic Stress, 22,* 435–443.

Maheu, F. S., Joober, R., & Lupien, S. J. (2005). Declarative memory after stress in humans: Differential involvement of the β-adrenergic and corticosteroid systems. *Journal of Clinical Endocrinology & Metabolism, 90,* 1697–1704.

Maida, C. A., Gordon, N. S., Steinberg, A. M., & Gordon, G. (1989). Psychosocial impact of disasters: Victims of the Baldwin Hills fire. *Journal of Traumatic Stress, 2*, 37–48.

Main, M., & Morgan, H. J. (1996). Disorganization and disorientation in infant strange situation behavior: Phenotypic resemblance to dissociative states. In L. K. Michelson & W. J. Ray (Eds.), *Handbook of dissociation: Theoretical, empirical, and clinical perspectives* (pp. 107–138). New York, NY: Plenum.

Manson, S. M., Beals, J., O'Nell, T. D., Piasecki, J., Bechtold, D. W., Keane, E. M., & Jones, M. C. (1996). Wounded spirits, ailing hearts: PTSD and related disorders among American Indians. In A. J. Marsella, M. J. Friedman, E. T. Gerrity, & R. M. Scurfield (Eds.), *Ethnocultural aspects of posttraumatic stress disorder: Issues, research, and clinical applications* (pp. 255–283). Washington, DC: American Psychological Association.

Mansour, F. (1987). Egyptian psychiatric casualties in the Arab-Israeli wars. In G. Belenky & G. Belenky (Eds.), *Contemporary studies in combat psychiatry* (pp. 157–163). New York, NY: Greenwood Press.

Marlatt, G. A., & Gordon, J. R. (1985). *Relapse prevention: Maintenance strategy in the treatment of addictive behaviors.* New York, NY: Guilford.

Marsella, A. J., Bornemann, T., Ekblad, S., & Orley, J. (Eds.). (1994). *Amidst peril and pain: The mental health and wellbeing of world's refugees.* Washington, DC: American Psychological Association.

Marsella, A. J., Friedman, M. J., Gerrity, E. T., & Scurfield, R. M. (Eds.). (1996). *Ethnocultural aspects of posttraumatic stress disorder: Issues, research, and clinical applications.* Washington, DC: American Psychological Association.

Marshall, R. D., Lewis-Fernandez, R., Blanco, C., Simpson, H. B., Lin, S. H., Vermes, D., . . . Liebowitz, M. R. (2007). A controlled trial of paroxetine for chronic PTSD, dissociation, and interpersonal problems in mostly minority adults. *Depression & Anxiety, 24*, 77–84.

Marshall, R. D., Spitzer, R. L., & Liebowitz, M. R. (1999). Review and critique of the new DSM-IV diagnosis of acute stress disorder. *American Journal of Psychiatry, 156*, 1677–1685.

Marshall, R. D., Turner, J. B., Lewis-Fernandez, R., Koenan, K., Neria, Y., & Dohrenwend, B. P. (2006). Symptom patterns associated with chronic PTSD in male veterans: New findings from the National Vietnam Veterans Readjustment Study. *Journal of Nervous and Mental Disease, 194*, 275–278.

Martenyi, F., Brown, E. B., & Caldwell, C. D. (2007). Failed efficacy of fluoxetine in the treatment of posttraumatic stress disorder: Results of a fixed-dose, placebo-controlled study. *Journal of Clinical Psychopharmacology, 27*, 166–170.

Martenyi, F., Brown, E. B., Zhang, H., Koke, S. C., & Prakash, A. (2002). Fluoxetine v. placebo in prevention of relapse in post-traumatic stress disorder. *British Journal of Psychiatry, 181*, 315–320.

Martenyi, F., & Soldatenkova, V. (2006). Fluoxetine in the acute treatment and relapse prevention of combat-related post-traumatic stress disorder: Analysis of the veteran group of a placebo-controlled, randomized clinical trial. *European Neuropsychopharmacology, 16*, 340–349.

Martin, D. J., Garske, J. P., & Davis, M. K. (2000). Relation of the therapeutic alliance with outcome and other variables: A meta-analytic review. *Journal of Consulting and Clinical Psychology, 68*, 438–450.

Matar, M. A., Zohar, J., Kaplan, Z., & Cohen, H. (2009). Alprazolam treatment immediately after stress exposure interferes with the normal HPA-stress response and increases vulnerability to subsequent stress in an animal model of PTSD. *European Neuropsychopharmacology, 19,* 283–295.

Matsuoka, Y., Nishi, D., Yonemoto, N., Hamazaki, K., Hamazaki, T., & Hashimoto, K. (2011). Potential role of brain-derived neurotrophic factor in omega-3 fatty acid supplementation to prevent posttraumatic distress after accidental injury: An open-label pilot study. *Psychotherapy and Psychosomatics, 80,* 310–312.

Matthews, A., Kirkby, K. C., & Martin, F. (2002). The effects of single-dose lorazepam on memory and behavioural learning. *Journal of Psychopharmacology, 16,* 345–354.

Mattila, M. J., Vanakoski, J., Kalska, H., & Seppala, T. (1998). Effects of alcohol, zolpidem, and some other sedatives and hypnotics on human performance and memory. *Pharmacology, Biochemistry and Behavior, 59,* 917–923.

Mattis, J. S., Bell, C. C., Jagers, R. J., & Jenkins, E. J. (1999). A critical approach to stress-related disorders in African Americans. *Journal of the National Medical Association, 91,* 80–85.

Mayou, R. A., Bryant, B., & Ehlers, A. (2001). Prediction of psychological outcomes one year after a motor vehicle accident. *American Journal of Psychiatry, 158,* 1231–1238.

Mayou, R. A., Ehlers, A., & Hobbs, M. (2000). A three–year follow-up of psychological debriefing for road traffic accident victims. *British Journal of Psychiatry, 176,* 589–593.

McAllister, T. W., & Stein, M. B. (2010). Effects of psychological and biomechanical trauma on brain and behavior. *Annals of the New York Academy of Sciences, 1208,* 46–57.

McCann, B. S., & Roy-Byrne, P. R. (1998). Attention-deficit/hyperactivity disorder, substance abuse, and post-traumatic stress disorder: A case study with implications for harm reduction. *In Session: Psychotherapy in Practice, 4,* 53–67.

McCann, I. L., & Pearlman, L. A. (1990). *Psychological trauma and the adult survivor: Theory, therapy, and transformation.* New York, NY: Brunner/Mazel.

McCutcheon, V. V., Sartor, C. E., Pommer, N. E., Bucholz, K. K., Nelson, E. C., Madden, P. A. F., & Heath, A. C. (2010). Age at trauma exposure and PTSD risk in young adult women. *Journal of Traumatic Stress, 23,* 811–814.

McDowell, S., Whyte, J., & D'Esposito, M. (1998). Differential effect of a dopaminergic agonist on prefrontal function in traumatic brain injury patients. *Brain, 121,* 1155–1164.

McFarlane, A. C. (1988). The phenomenology of post-traumatic stress disorders following a natural disaster. *Journal of Nervous and Mental Disorders, 176,* 22–29.

McFarlane, A. C. (1998). Epidemiological evidence about the relationship between PTSD and alcohol abuse: The nature of the association. *Addictive Behaviors, 23,* 813–825.

McFarlane, A. C., Barton, C. A., Yehuda, R., & Wittert, G. (2011). Cortisol response to acute trauma and risk of posttraumatic stress disorder. *Psychoneuroendocrinology, 36,* 720–727.

McGhee, L., Maani, C., Garza, T., DeSocio, P., Gaylord, K., & Black, I. (2009). The effect of propranolol on posttraumatic stress disorder in burned service members. *Journal of Burn Care and Research, 30*(1), 92–97.

McGregor, K., Thomas, D. R., & Read, J. (2006). Therapy for child sexual abuse: Women talk about helpful and unhelpful therapy experiences. *Journal of Child Sexual Abuse, 15,* 35–59.

McKay, M. M., Lynn, C. J., & Bannon, W. M. (2005). Understanding inner city child mental health need and trauma exposure: Implications for preparing urban service providers. *American Journal of Orthopsychiatry, 75,* 201–210.

McKibben, J., Bresnick, M., Wiechman Askay, S., & Fauerbach, J. (2008). Acute stress disorder and posttraumatic stress disorder: A prospective study of prevalence, course, and predictors in a sample with major burn injuries. *Journal of Burn Care and Research, 29*(1), 22–35.

McLaughlin, K. A., Fairbank, J. A., Gruber, M. J., Jones, R. T., Lakoma, M. D., Pfefferbaum, B., . . . Kessler, R. C. (2009). Serious emotional disturbance among youth exposed to Hurricane Katrina 2 years postdisaster. *Journal of the American Academy of Child & Adolescent Psychiatry, 48,* 1069–1078.

McMillan, T. M. (2001). Errors in diagnosing post-traumatic stress disorder after traumatic brain injury. *Brain Injury, 15*(1), 39–46.

Meichenbaum, D. (1994). *A clinical handbook/practical therapist manual for assessing and treating adults with post-traumatic stress disorder (PTSD).* Waterloo, Ontario, Canada: Institute Press.

Meichenbaum, D., & Fong, G. T. (1993). Toward a theoretical model of the role of reasons in nonadherence to health-related advice. In D. M. Wegner & J. W. Pennebaker (Eds.), *Handbook of mental control* (pp. 473–490). Englewood Cliffs, NJ: Prentice Hall.

Melhem, N. M., Walker, M., Moritz, G., & Brent, D. A. (2008). Antecedents and sequelae of sudden parental death in offspring and surviving caregivers. *Archives of Pediatric and Adolescent Medicine, 162,* 403–410.

Melia, K. R., Ryabinin, A. E., Corodimas, K. P., Wilson, M. C., & LeDoux, J. E. (1996). Hippocampal-dependent learning and experience-dependent activation of the hippocampus are preferentially disrupted by ethanol. *Neuroscience, 74,* 313–322.

Mellman, T. A., Bustamante, V., Fins, A. I., Pigeon, W. R., & Nolan, B. (2002). REM sleep and the early development of posttraumatic stress disorder. *American Journal of Psychiatry, 159,* 1696–1701.

Mellman, T. A., Byers, P. M., Augenstein, J. S. (1998). Pilot evaluation of hypnotic medication during acute traumatic stress response. *Journal of Traumatic Stress, 11,* 563–569.

Mendel, M. P. (1995). *The male survivor: The impact of sexual abuse.* Thousand Oaks, CA: Sage.

Mendelsohn, M., & Sewell, K. W. (2004). Social attitudes toward traumatized men and women: A vignette study. *Journal of Traumatic Stress, 17,* 103–111.

Mercer, K. B., Orcutt, H. K., Quinn, J. F., Fitzgerald, C. A., Conneely, K. N., Barfield, R. T., ... Ressler, K. J. (2011). Acute and posttraumatic stress symptoms in a prospective gene x environment study of a university campus shooting. *Archives of General Psychiatry, 69*(1), 89–97.

Messman-Moore, T. L., & Coates, A. A. (2007). The impact of childhood psychological abuse on adult interpersonal conflict: The role of early maladaptive schemas and patterns of interpersonal behavior. *Journal of Emotional Abuse, 7,* 75–92.

Meythaler, J. M., Brunner, R. C., & Johnson, A. (2002). Amantadine to improve neurorecovery in traumatic brain injury-associated diffuse axonal injury: A pilot double-blind randomized trial. *Journal of Head Trauma Rehabilitation, 17,* 300–313.

Miller, K. E., & Rasco, L. M. (2004). *The mental health of refugees: Ecological approaches to healing and adaptation.* Mahwah, NJ: Lawrence Erlbaum.

Miller, M. W., McKinney, A. E., Kanter, F. S., Korte, K. J., & Lovallo, W. R. (2011). Hydrocortisone suppression of the fear-potentiated startle response and post-traumatic stress disorder. *Psychoneuroendocrinology, 36,* 970–980.

Millon, T., Davis, R., & Millon, C. (1997). *MCMI-III manual* (2nd ed.). Minneapolis, MN: National Computer Systems.

Mitchell, J. T. (1983). When disaster strikes: The critical incident stress debriefing process. *Journal of Emergency Medical Services, 8,* 36–39.

Moein, H., Khalili, H. A., Keramatian, K. (2006). Effect of methylphenidate on ICU and hospital length of stay in patients with severe and moderate traumatic brain injury. *Clinical Neurology and Neurosurgery, 108,* 539–42.

Monnelly, E. P., & Ciraulo, D. A. (1999). Risperidone effects on irritable aggression in posttraumatic stress disorder. *Journal of Clinical Psychopharmacology, 19,* 377–378.

Monnelly, E. P., Ciraulo, D. A., Knapp, C., & Keane, T. (2003). Low-dose risperidone as adjunctive therapy for irritable aggression in posttraumatic stress disorder. *Journal of Clinical Psychopharmacology, 23,* 193–196.

Monson, C. M., Schnurr, P. P., Resick, P. A., Friedman, M. J., Young-Xu, Y., & Stevens, S. P. (2006). Cognitive processing therapy for veterans with military-related posttraumatic stress disorder. *Journal of Consulting and Clinical Psychology, 74,* 898–907.

Moor, A. (2007). When recounting the traumatic memories is not enough: Treating persistent self-devaluation associated with rape and victim-blaming rape myths. *Women and Therapy, 30,* 19–33.

Moracco, K. E., & Cole, T. B. (2009). Preventing intimate partner violence: Screening is not enough. *Journal of the American Medical Association, 302,* 568–570.

Morey, L. C. (1991). *Personality Assessment Inventory: Professional manual.* Odessa, FL: Psychological Assessment Resources.

Morgan, C., & Fisher, H. (2007). Environmental factors in schizophrenia: Childhood trauma—A critical review. *Schizophrenia Bulletin, 33,* 3–10.

Morgan, C. A., Krystal, J. H., & Southwick, S. M. (2003). Toward early pharmacological posttraumatic stress intervention. *Biological Psychiatry, 53,* 834–843.

Morgan, C. A., Wang, S., Rasmusson, A., Hazlett, G., Anderson, G., & Charney, D. S. (2001). Relationship among plasma cortisol, catecholamines, neuropeptide Y, and human performance during exposure to uncontrollable stress. *Psychosomatic Medicine, 63,* 412–422.

Morgan, W. D., & Morgan, S. T. (2005). Cultivating attention and empathy. In C. K. Germer, R. D. Siegel, & P. R. Fulton (Eds.), *Mindfulness and psychotherapy* (pp. 73–90). New York, NY: Guilford.

Morina, N. (2007). The role of experiential avoidance in psychological functioning after war-related stress in Kosovar civilians. *Journal of Nervous and Mental Disease, 195,* 697–700.

Morina, N., & Ford, J. D. (2008). Complex sequelae of psychological trauma among Kosovar civilian war victims. *International Journal of Social Psychiatry, 54,* 425–436.

Moses-Kolko, E. L., Bogen, D., Perel, J., Bregar, A., Uhl, K., & Levin, B. (2005). Neonatal signs after late in utero exposure to serotonin reuptake inhibitors: Literature review and implications for clinical applications. *Journal of the American Medical Association, 293,* 2372–2383.

Mueser, K. T., Rosenberg, S. D., & Rosenberg, H. J. (2009). Psychoeducation about posttraumatic reactions. In K. T. Mueser, S. D. Rosenberg, & H. J. Rosenberg (Eds.), *Treatment of posttraumatic stress disorder in special populations: A cognitive restructuring program* (pp. 81–97). Washington, DC: American Psychological Association.

Murray, J., Ehlers, A., & Mayou, R. A. (2002). Dissociation and post-traumatic stress disorder: Two prospective studies of road traffic accident survivors. *British Journal of Psychiatry, 180,* 363–368.

Myers, J. E. B. (1998). *Legal issues in child abuse and neglect practice.* Thousand Oaks, CA: Sage.

Nader, K. O., Dubrow, N., & Stamm, B. H. (1999). *Honoring differences: Cultural issues in the treatment of trauma and loss.* Philadelphia, PA: Brunner/Mazel.

Naeem, F., Ayub, M., Masood, K., Gul, H., Khalid, M., Farrukh, A., . . . Chaudhry, H. R. (2011). Prevalence and psychosocial risk factors of PTSD: 18 months after Kashmir earthquake in Pakistan. *Journal of Affective Disorders, 130,* 268–274.

Najavits, L. M. (2002). *Seeking safety: A treatment manual for PTSD and substance abuse.* New York, NY: Guilford.

Nanni, V., Uher, R., & Danese, A. (2012). Childhood maltreatment predicts unfavorable course of illness and treatment outcome in depression: A meta-analysis. *American Journal of Psychiatry, 169,* 141–151.

National Institute for Mental Health. (2002). *Mental health and mass violence— Evidence-based early psychological intervention for victims/survivors of mass violence: A workshop to reach consensus.* (NIMH Publication No. 02–5138). Washington, DC: U.S. Government Printing Office.

Neill, J. R. (1993). How psychiatric symptoms varied in World War I and II. *Military Medicine, 158,* 149–151.

Neuner, F., Schauer, M., Klaschik, C., Karunakara, U. K., & Elbert, T. (2004). A comparison of narrative exposure therapy, supportive counseling, and psycho-education for treating posttraumatic stress disorder in an African refugee settle-ment. *Journal of Consulting and Clinical Psychology, 72,* 579–587.

Newman, E., Briere, J., & Kirlic, N. (in press). Clinical assessment as a form of listen-ing and intervention. In B. McMackon, J. Foley, E. Newman, & T. Keane (Eds.), *Trauma therapy in context: The science and craft of evidence-based practice.* Washington, DC: American Psychological Association.

Nickerson, A., Bryant, R. A., Silove, D., & Steel, Z. (2011). A critical review of psychological treatments of posttraumatic stress disorder in refugees. *Clinical Psychology Review, 31,* 399–417.

Noe, D., Ferri, J., Trenor, C., & Chirivella, J. (2007). Efficacy of ziprasidone in control-ling agitation during post-traumatic amnesia. *Behavioral Neurology, 18,* 7–11.

Norris, F. H. (1992). Epidemiology of trauma: Frequency and impact of different potentially traumatic events on different demographic groups. *Journal of Consulting and Clinical Psychology, 60,* 409–418.

Norris, F. H., & Alegria, M. (2005). Mental health care for ethnic minority indi-viduals and communities in the aftermath of disasters and mass violence. *CNS Spectrums, 10,* 132–140.

Norris, F. H., Friedman, M. J., Watson, P. J., Byrne, C. M., Diaz, E., & Kaniasty, K. (2002). 60,000 disaster victims speak, Part 1: An empirical review of the empirical literature, 1981–2001. *Psychiatry, 65,* 207–239.

Norris, F. H., Tracy, M., & Galea, S. (2009). Looking for resilience: Understanding the longitudinal trajectories of responses to stress. *Social Science & Medicine, 68,* 2190–2198.

North, C. S., Nixon, S. J., Shariat, S., Mallonee, S., McMillen, J. C., Spitznagel, E. L., & Smith, E. M. (1999). Psychiatric disorders among survivors of the Oklahoma City bombing. *Journal of the American Medical Association, 282,* 755–762.

North, C. S., Smith, E. M., & Spitznagel, E. L. (1994). Violence and the homeless: An epidemiologic study of victimization and aggression. *Journal of Traumatic Stress, 7,* 95–110.

Nrugham, L., Holen, A., & Sund, A. M. (2010). Associations between attempted suicide, violent life events, depressive symptoms, and resilience in adolescents and young adults: Erratum. *Journal of Nervous and Mental Disease, 198,* 389.

Nugent, N. R., Christopher, N. C., Crow, J. P., Browne, L., Ostrowski, S., & Delahanty, D. L. (2010). The efficacy of early propranolol administration at reducing PTSD symptoms in pediatric injury patients: A pilot study. *Journal of Traumatic Stress, 23,* 282–287.

O'Connor, M. (2010). PTSD in older bereaved people. *Aging & Mental Health, 14,* 310–318.

O'Connor, M., Lasgaard, M., Shevlin, M., Guldin, M. B. (2010). A confirmatory factor analysis of combined models of the Harvard Trauma Questionnaire and the Inventory of Complicated Grief-Revised: Are we measuring complicated grief or posttraumatic stress? *Journal of Anxiety Disorders, 24,* 672–679.

O'Donnell, M. L., Creamer, M., Holmes, A. C. N., Ellen, S., McFarlane, A. C., Judson, R., . . . Bryant, R. A. (2010). Posttraumatic stress disorder after injury: Does admission to intensive care unit increase risk? *Journal of Trauma, 69,* 627–32.

O'Donnell, M. L., Creamer, M., McFarlane, A. C., Silove, D., & Bryant, R. A. (2010). Should A2 be a diagnostic requirement for posttraumatic stress disorder in DSM-V? *Psychiatry Research, 176,* 257–260.

Ogata, K., Ishikawa, T., Michiue, T., Nishi, Y., & Maeda, H. (2011). Posttraumatic symptoms in Japanese bereaved family members with special regard to suicide and homicide cases. *Death Studies, 35,* 525–535.

Ogata, S. N., Silk, K. R., Goodrich, S., Lohr, N. E., Westen, D., & Hill, E. M. (1990). Childhood sexual and physical abuse in adult patients with borderline personality disorder. *American Journal of Psychiatry, 147,* 1008–1013.

Ogawa, J. R., Sroufe, L. A., Weinfield, N. S., Carlson, E. A., & Egeland, B. (1997). Development and the fragmented self: Longitudinal study of dissociative symptomatology in a nonclinical sample. *Development and Psychopathology, 9,* 855–879.

Ogden, P., Minton, K., & Pain, C. (2000). *Trauma and the body.* New York, NY: Norton.

Okuda, M., Olfson, M., Hasin, D. S., Grant, B. F., Lin, K., Blanco, C. (2011). Mental health of victims of intimate partner violence: Results from a national epidemiologic survey. *Psychiatric Services, 62,* 959–962.

O'Leary, D. K. (1999). Psychological abuse: A variable deserving critical attention in domestic violence. *Violence and Victims, 14,* 3–23.

O'Leary, V. E. (1998). Strength in the face of adversity: Individual and social thriving. *Journal of Social Issues, 54,* 425–446.

Olsen, M. A., & Fazio, R. H. (2002). Implicit acquisition and manifestation of classically conditioned attitudes. *Social Cognition, 20,* 89–103.

Orlinski, D. E., Grawe, K., & Parks, B. K. (1994). Process and outcome in psychotherapy. In A. E. Bergin & S. L. Garfield (Eds.), *Handbook of psychotherapy and behavior change* (4th ed., pp. 272–281). New York, NY: Wiley.

Orner, R., Kent, A. T., Pfefferbaum, B., Raphael, B., & Watson, P. (2006). Context for providing immediate intervention post-event. In E. C. Ritchi, P. J. Watson, & M. J. Friedman (Eds.), *Interventions following mass violence and disasters: Strategies for mental health practice* (pp. 121–133). New York, NY: Guilford.

Orsillo, S. M. (2001). Measures for acute stress disorder and posttraumatic stress disorder. In M. M. Antony & S. M. Orsillo (Eds.), *Practitioner's guide to empirically based measures of anxiety* (pp. 255–307). New York, NY: Kluwer Academic/Plenum.

Orsillo, S. M., & Batten, S. V. (2005). Acceptance and commitment therapy in the treatment of posttraumatic stress disorder. *Behavior Modification, 29,* 95–129.

Öst, L. G. (2008). Efficacy of the third wave of behavioral therapies: A systematic review and meta-analysis. *Behavior Research and Therapy, 46,* 296–321.

Ouimette, P., & Brown, P. J. (2003). *Trauma and substance abuse: Causes, consequences, and treatment of comorbid disorders.* Washington, DC: American Psychological Association.

Ouimette, P., Moos, R. H., & Brown, P. J. (2003). Substance use disorder-posttraumatic stress disorder comorbidity: A survey of treatments and proposed practice guidelines. In P. Ouimette & P. J. Brown (Eds.), *Trauma and substance abuse: Causes, consequences, and treatment of comorbid disorders* (pp. 1–110). Washington DC: American Psychological Association.

Ozer, E. J., Best, S. R., Lipsey, T. L., & Weiss, D. S. (2003). Predictors of posttraumatic stress disorder and symptoms in adults: A meta-analysis. *Psychological Bulletin, 129,* 52–73.

Pace, T. W., & Heim, C. M. (2011). A short review on the psychoneuroimmunology of posttraumatic stress disorder: From risk factors to medical comorbidities. *Brain, Behavior, and Immunity, 25,* 6–13.

Palm, K. M., & Follette, V. M. (2011). The roles of cognitive flexibility and experiential avoidance in explaining psychological distress in survivors of interpersonal victimization. *Journal of Psychopathology and Behavioral Assessment, 33,* 79–86.

Paras, M. L., Murad, M. H., Chen, L. P., Goranson, E. N., Sattler, A. L., Colbenson, K. M., ... Zirakzadeh, A. (2009). Sexual abuse and lifetime diagnosis of somatic disorders: A systematic review and meta-analysis. *Journal of the American Medical Association, 302,* 550–561.

Pastrana Jimenez J., Catalina Romero C., Garcia Dieguez N., & Lopez-Ibor Alino J. (2007). Pharmacological treatment of acute stress disorder with propranolol and hypnotics. *Actas Espanolas de Psiquiatria, 35,* 351–358.

Payne, J. L., & Meltzer-Brody, S. (2009). Antidepressant use during pregnancy: Current controversies and treatment strategies. *Clinical Obstetrics and Gynecology, 52,* 469–482.

Pearlman, L. A. (2003). *Trauma and Attachment Belief Scale.* Los Angeles, CA: Western Psychological Services.

Pearlman, L. A., & Courtois, C. A. (2005). Clinical applications of the attachment framework: Relational treatment of complex trauma. *Journal of Traumatic Stress, 18,* 449–459.

Pearlman, L. A., & Saakvitne, K. W. (1995). *Trauma and the therapist: Countertransference and vicarious traumatization in psychotherapy with incest survivors.* New York, NY: Norton.

Pechtel, P., & Pizzagalli, D. A. (2011). Effects of early life stress on cognitive and affective function: An integrated review of human literature. *Psychopharmacology, 214*, 55–70.

Pelcovitz, D., van der Kolk, B. A., Roth, S., Mandel, F., Kaplan, S., & Resick, P. (1997). Development of a criteria set and a structured interview for disorders of extreme stress (SIDES). *Journal of Traumatic Stress, 10*, 3–16.

Pennebaker, J. W. (1993). Putting stress into words: Health, linguistic, and therapeutic implications. *Behaviour Research and Therapy, 31*, 539–548.

Pennebaker, J. W., & Campbell, R. S. (2000). The effects of writing about traumatic experience. *National Center for PTSD Clinical Quarterly, 9*, 17–21.

Perez, M. C., & Fortuna, L. (2005). Psychosocial stressors, psychiatric diagnoses and utilization of mental health services. *Journal of Immigrant and Refugee Services, 3*, 107–124.

Peris, A., Bonizzoli, M., Iozzelli, D., Migliaccio, M. L., Zagli, G., Bacchereti, A., . . . Belloni, L. (2011). Early intra-intensive care unit psychological intervention promotes recovery from past posttraumatic stress disorders, anxiety, and depression symptoms in critically ill patiens. *Critical Care, 15*, Article R41.

Petrak, J. (2002). Rape: History, myths and reality. In J. Petrak & B. Hedge (Eds.), *The trauma of sexual assault: Treatment prevention and practice* (pp. 1–18). London, UK: Wiley.

Petrakis, I. L., Rosenheck, R., & Desai, R. (2011). Substance use comorbidity among veterans with posttraumatic stress disorder and other psychiatric illness. *American Journal on Addictions, 20*, 185–189.

Petty, F., Davis, L. L., Nugent, A. L., Kramer, G. L., Teten, A., Schmitt, A., & Stone, R. C. (2002). Valproate therapy for chronic, combat-induced posttraumatic stress disorder. *Journal of Clinical Psychopharmacology, 22*, 100–101.

Pfeffer, C. R., Altemus, M., Heo, M., & Jiang, H. (2009). Salivary cortisol and psychopathology in adults bereaved by the September 11, 2001 terror attacks. *International Journal of Psychiatry in Medicine, 39*, 215–226.

Pfefferbaum, B. C., Call, J. A., Lensgraf, S. J., Miller, P. D., Flynn, B. W., Doughty, D. E., . . . Dickson, W. L. (2001). Traumatic grief in a convenience sample of victims seeking support services after a terrorist incident. *Annals of Clinical Psychiatry, 13*, 19–24.

Phifer, J. E., Skelton, K., Weiss, T. E., Schwartz, A. C., Wingo, A. P., Gillespie, C. F., . . . Ressler, K. J. (2011). Pain symptomatology and pain medication use in civilian PTSD. *Pain, 152*, 2233–2240.

Phillips, C. J., LeardMann, C. A., Gumbs, G. R., & Smith, B. (2010). Risk factors for posttraumatic stress disorder among deployed US male Marines. *BMC Psychiatry, 10*, 52.

Physicians' desk reference (66th ed.). (2012). Montvale, NJ: Thomson Healthcare.

Piet, J., & Hougaard, E. (2011). The effect of mindfulness-based cognitive therapy for prevention of relapse in recurrent major depressive disorder: A systematic review and meta-analysis. *Clinical Psychology Review, 31*, 1032–1040.

Pietrzak, R. H., Harpaz-Rotem, I., Southwick, S. M. (2011). Cognitive-behavioral coping strategies associated with combat-related PTSD in treatment-seeking OEF-OIF Veterans. *Psychiatry Research, 189*, 251–258.

Pilver, C. E., Levy, B. R., Libby, D. J., & Desai, R. A. (2011). Posttraumatic stress disorder and trauma characteristics are correlates of premenstrual dysphoric disorder. *Archives of Women's Mental Health, 14*, 383–393.

Pinna, G. (2010). In a mouse model relevant for post-traumatic stress disorder, selective brain steroidogenic stimulants (SBSS) improve behavioral deficits by normalizing allopregnanolone biosynthesis. *Behavioural Pharmacology, 21,* 438–450.

Pinto, P. A., & Gregory, R. J. (1995). Posttraumatic stress disorder with psychotic features. *American Journal of Psychiatry, 152,* 471.

Pitman, R. K., Altman, B., Greenwald, E., Longpre, R. E., Macklin, M. L., Poiré, R. E., & Steketee, G. S. (1991). Psychiatric complications during flooding therapy for posttraumatic stress disorder. *Journal of Clinical Psychiatry, 52,* 17–20.

Pitman, R. K., Sanders, K. M., Zusman, R. M., Healy, F. C., Lasko, N. B., Cahill, L., & Orr, S. P. (2002). Pilot study of secondary prevention of posttraumatic stress disorder with propranolol. *Biological Psychiatry, 51,* 189–142.

Pivac, N., Kozaric-Kovacic, D., & Muck-Seler, D. (2004). Olanzapine versus flu-phenazine in an open trial in patients with psychotic combat-related post-traumatic stress disorder. *Psychopharmacology, 175,* 451–456.

Pizarro, J., Silver, R. C., & Prause, J. (2006). Physical and mental health costs of traumatic war experiences among Civil War veterans. *Archives of General Psychiatry, 63,* 193–200.

Plenger, P. M., Dixon, C. E., Castillo, R. M., Frankowski, R. F., Yablon, S. A., & Levin, H. S. (1996). Subacute methylphenidate treatment for moderate to moder-ately severe traumatic brain injury: A preliminary double-blind placebo-controlled study. *Archives of Physical Medicine & Rehabilitaion, 77,* 536–540.

Plumb, J. C., Orsillo, S. M., & Luterek, J. A. (2004). A preliminary test of the role of experiential avoidance in post-event functioning. *Journal of Behavior Therapy and Experimental Psychiatry, 35,* 245–257.

Poole, G. V., Lewis, J. L., Devidas, M., Hauser, C. J., Martin, R. W., & Thomae, K. R. (1997). Psychopathologic risk factors for intentional and nonintentional injury. *Journal of Trauma, 42,* 711–715.

Potter, A. R., Baker, M. T., Sanders, C. S., & Peterson, A. L. (2009). Combat stress reactions during military deployments: Evaluation of the effectiveness of combat stress control treatment. *Journal of Mental Health Counseling, 31,* 137–148.

Powers, M. B., Halpern, J. M., Ferenschak, M. P., Gillihan, S. J., & Foa, E. B. (2010). A meta-analytic review of prolonged exposure for posttraumatic stress disorder. *Clinical Psychology Review, 30,* 635–641.

Pratchett, L. C., & Yehuda, R. (2011). Foundations of posttraumatic stress disorder: Does early life trauma lead to adult posttraumatic stress disorder? *Development and Psychopathology, 23,* 477–491.

Prigerson, H. G., Shear, M. K., Jacobs, S. C., Reynolds, C. F., Maciejewski, P. K., Davidson, J., . . . Zisook, S. (1999). Consensus criteria for traumatic grief: A preliminary empirical test. *British Journal of Psychiatry, 174,* 67–73.

The Protection Project. (2011). *The Protection Project review of the Trafficking in Persons Report.* Washington, DC: Johns Hopkins University.

Punamäki, R.-L., Qouta, S. R., & El Sarraj, E. (2010). Nature of torture, PTSD, and somatic symptoms among political ex-prisoners. *Journal of Traumatic Stress, 23,* 532–536.

Pynoos, R. S., Steinberg, A. M., & Piacentini, J. C. (1999). A developmental psycho-pathology model of childhood traumatic stress and intersection with anxiety disorders. *Biological Psychiatry, 46,* 1542–1554.

Raison, C. L., & Miller, A. H. (2003). When not enough is too much: The role of insufficient glucocorticoid signaling in the pathophysiology of stress-related disorders. *American Journal of Psychiatry, 169,* 1554–1565.

Ramsay, C. E., Flanagan, P., Gantt, S., Broussard, B., & Compton, M. T. (2011). Clinical correlates of maltreatment and traumatic experiences in childhood and adolescence among predominantly African American, socially disadvantaged, hospitalized, first-episode psychosis patients. *Psychiatry Research, 188,* 343–349.

Raskind, M. A., Peskind, E. R., Hoff, D. J., Hart, K. L., Holmes, H. A., Warren, D., . . . McFall, M. E. (2007). A parallel group placebo controlled study of prazosin for trauma nightmares and sleep disturbance in combat veterans with post-traumatic stress disorder. *Biological Psychiatry, 61,* 928–934.

Raskind, M. A., Peskind, E. R., Kanter, E. D., Petrie, E. C., Radant, A., Thompson, C. E., . . . McFall, M. M. (2003). Reduction of nightmares and other PTSD symptoms in combat veterans by prazosin: A placebo-controlled study. *American Journal of Psychiatry, 160,* 371–373.

Rasmusson, A. M., Pinna, G., Paliwal, P., Weisman, D., Gottschalk, C., Charney, D., . . . Guidotti, A. (2006). Decreased cerebrospinal fluid allopregnanolone levels in women with posttraumatic stress disorder. *Biological Psychiatry, 60,* 704–713.

Rau, P. J., & Goldfried, M. R. (1994). The therapeutic alliance in cognitive-behaviour therapy. In A. O. Horvath & L. S. Greenberg (Eds.), *The working alliance: Theory, research and practice* (pp. 31–152). New York, NY: Wiley.

Rayburn, N. R., Wenzel, S. L., Elliott, M. N., Hambarsoomian, K., Marshall, G. N., & Tucker, J. S. (2005). Trauma, depression, coping, and mental health service seeking among impoverished women. *Journal of Consulting and Clinical Psychology, 73,* 667–677.

Read, J., Agar, K., Argyle, N., & Aderhold, V. (2003). Sexual and physical abuse during childhood and adulthood as predictors of hallucinations, delusions and thought disorder. *Psychology and Psychotherapy: Theory, Research and Practice, 76,* 1–22.

Read, J., Perry, B. D., Moskowitz, A., & Connolly, J. (2001). The contribution of early traumatic events to schizophrenia in some patients: A traumagenic neuro-developmental model. *Psychiatry: Interpersonal and Biological Processes, 64,* 319–345.

Read, J., Van Os, J., Morrison, A. P., & Ross, C. A. (2005). Childhood trauma, psychosis and schizophrenia: A literature review with theoretical and clinical implications. *Acta Psychiatrica Scandinavica, 112,* 330–350.

Read, J. P., Ouimette, P., White, J., Colder, C., & Farrow, S. (2011). Rates of DSM–IV–TR trauma exposure and posttraumatic stress disorder among newly matriculated college students. *Psychological Trauma: Theory, Research, Practice, and Policy, 3,* 148–156.

Rees, S., Silove, D., Chey, T., Ivancic, L., Steel, Z., Creamer, M., . . . Forbes, D. (2011). Lifetime prevalence of gender-based violence in women and the relationship with mental disorders and psychosocial function. *Journal of the American Medical Association, 306,* 513–521.

Reich, D. B., Winternitz, S., Hennen, J., Watts, T., & Stanculescu, C. (2004). A preliminary study of risperidone in the treatment of posttraumatic stress disorder related to childhood abuse in women. *Journal of Clinical Psychiatry, 65,* 1601–1606.

Reid, J. A., & Jones, S. (2011). Exploited vulnerability: Legal and psychological perspectives on child sex trafficking victims. *Victims & Offenders, 6,* 207–231.

Reinhard D. L., Whyte J., & Sandel, M. E. (1996). Improved arousal and initiation following tricyclic antidepressant use in severe brain injury. *Archives of Physical Medicine & Rehabilitation, 77,* 80–83.

Reist, C., Kauffmann, C. D., Haier, R. J., Sangdahl, C., DeMet, E. M., Chicz-DeMet, A., & Nelson, J. N. (1989). A controlled trial of desipramine in 18 men with posttraumatic stress disorder. *American Journal of Psychiatry, 146,* 513–516.

Renzetti, C. M., & Curran, D. J. (2002). *Women, men, and society* (5th ed.). Boston, MA: Allyn & Bacon.

Resick, P. A., & Schnicke, M. K. (1992). Cognitive processing therapy for sexual assault victims. *Journal of Consulting and Clinical Psychology, 60,* 748–756.

Resick, P. A., & Schnicke, M. K. (1993). *Cognitive processing therapy for rape victims: A treatment manual.* Newbury Park, CA: Sage.

Resnick, H. S., Yehuda, R., & Acierno, R. (1997). Acute post-rape cortisol, alcohol abuse, and PTSD symptom profile among recent rape victims. In R. Yehuda & A. C. McFarlane (Eds.), *Psychobiology of posttraumatic stress disorder* (Vol. 821, pp. 433–436). New York, NY: New York Academy of Sciences.

Resnick, H. S., Yehuda, R., Pitman, R. K., & Foy, D. W. (1995). Effect of previous trauma on acute plasma cortisol level following rape. *American Journal of Psychiatry, 152,* 1675–1677.

Rholes, W. S., & Simpson, J. A. (2004). Ambivalent attachment and depressive symptoms: The role of romantic and parent-child relationships. *Journal of Cognitive Psychotherapy, 18,* 67–78.

Richardson, J. D., Fikretoglu, D., Liu, A., & McIntosh, D. (2011). Aripiprazole augmentation in the treatment of military-related PTSD with major depression: A retrospective chart review. *BMC Psychiatry, 11,* 86.

Rimm, D. C., & Masters, J. (1979). *Behavior theory* (2nd ed.). New York, NY: Academic Research.

Ringdahl, E. N., Pereira, S. L., & Delzell, J. E., Jr. (2004). Treatment of primary insomnia. *Journal of the American Board of Family Practice, 17,* 212–219.

Rinne, T., de Kloet, E. R., Wouters, L., Goekoop, J. G., de Rijk, R. H., & van den Brink, W. (2003). Fluvoxamine reduces responsiveness of HPA axis in adult female BPD patients with a history of sustained childhood abuse. *Neuropsychopharmacology, 28,* 126–132.

Ritchie, E. C., Watson, P. J., & Friedman, M. J. (2006). *Mental health intervention following disasters and mass violence.* New York, NY: Guilford.

Rivard, J. M., Dietz, P., Martell, D., & Widawski, M. (2002). Acute dissociative responses in law enforcement officers involved in critical shooting incidents: The clinical and forensic implications. *Journal of Forensic Sciences, 47,* 1093–1100.

Robert, R., Blakeney, P. E., Villarreal, C., Rosenberg, L., & Meyer, W. J. (1999). Imipramine treatment in pediatric burn patients with symptoms of acute stress disorder: A pilot study. *Journal of the American Academy of Child and Adolescent Psychiatry, 38,* 873–882.

Robert, S., Hamner, M. B., Durkalski, V. L., Brown, M. W., & Ulmer, H. G. (2009). An open-label assessment of aripiprazole in the treatment of PTSD. *Psychopharmacology Bulletin, 42,* 69–80.

Robert, S., Hamner, M. B., Kose, S., Ulmer, H. G., Deitsch, S. E., & Lorberbaum, J. P. (2005). Quetiapine improves sleep disturbances in combat veterans with PTSD: Sleep data from a prospective, open-label study. *Journal of Clinical Psychopharmacology, 25,* 387–388.

Roberts, N. P., Kitchiner, N. J., Kenardy, J., & Bisson, J. I. (2010). Early psychological interventions to treat acute traumatic stress symptoms. *Cochrane Database of Systematic Reviews, 2010*(3).

Roelofs, K., Keijsers, G. P. J., Hoogduin, K. A. L., Naring, G. W. B., & Moene, F. C. (2002). Childhood abuse in patients with conversion disorder. *American Journal of Psychiatry, 159,* 1908–1913.

Roemer, L., Orsillo, S. M., Borkovec, T. D., & Litz, B. T. (1998). Emotional response at the time of a potentially traumatizing event and PTSD symptomatology: A preliminary retrospective analysis of the DSM-IV criterion A-2. *Journal of Behavior Therapy and Experimental Psychiatry, 29,* 123–130.

Rogers, C. R. (1957). The necessary and sufficient conditions of therapeutic personality change. *Journal of Consulting Psychology, 21,* 95–103.

Rogers, C. R. (1961). *On becoming a person.* Oxford, UK: Houghton Mifflin.

Rohleder, N., Wolf, J. M., & Wolf, O. T. (2010). Glucocorticoid sensitivity of cognitive and inflammatory processes in depression and posttraumatic stress disorder. *Neurosciences & Biobehavioral Reviews, 35,* 104–114.

Root, M. P. P. (1996). Women of color and traumatic stress in "domestic captivity": Gender and race as disempowering statuses. In A. J. Marsella, M. J. Friedman, E. T. Gerrity, & R. M. Scurfield (Eds.), *Ethnocultural aspects of posttraumatic stress disorder: Issues, research, and clinical applications* (pp. 363–387). Washington, DC: American Psychological Association.

Rorschach, H. (1981). *Psychodiagnostics: A diagnostic test based upon perception* (P. Lemkau & B. Kronemberg, Eds. & Trans.; 9th ed.). New York, NY: Grune & Stratton. (Original work published 1921)

Rose, S., Bisson, J., & Wessely, S. (2002). Psychological debriefing for presenting post traumatic stress disorder (PTSD). *Cochrane Library, 2.* Oxford, UK: Update software.

Rosenman, S. (2002). Trauma and posttraumatic stress disorder in Australia: Findings in the population sample of the Australian national survey of mental health and wellbeing. *Australian and New Zealand Journal of Psychiatry, 36,* 515–520.

Rosenthal, J. Z., Grosswald, S., Ross, R. J., & Rosenthal, N. (2011). Effects of transcendental meditation in veterans of operation enduring freedom and Operation Iraqi Freedom with posttraumatic stress disorder: A pilot study. *Military Medicine, 176,* 626–630.

Ross, C. A., Anderson, G., & Clark, P. (1994). Childhood abuse and the positive symptoms of schizophrenia. *Hospital and Community Psychiatry, 45,* 489–491.

Ross, C. A., Joshi, S., & Currie, R. (1991). Dissociative experiences in the general population: A factor analysis. *Hospital and Community Psychiatry, 42,* 297–301.

Ross, L. E., & McLean, L. M., (2006). Anxiety disorders during pregnancy and the postpartum period: A systematic review. *Journal of Clinical Psychiatry, 67,* 1285–1298.

Rothbaum, B. O., Cahill, S. P., Foa, E. B., Davidson, J. R., Compton, J., Connor, K. M., . . . Hahn, C. G. (2006). Augmentation of sertraline with prolonged exposure in the treatment of posttraumatic stress disorder. *Journal of Traumatic Stress, 19,* 625–638.

Rothbaum, B. O., Foa, E. G., Riggs, D. S., Murdock, T. B., & Walsh, W. (1992). A prospective examination of post-traumatic stress disorder in rape victims. *Journal of Traumatic Stress, 5,* 455–475.

Rothbaum, B. O., Killeen, T. K., Davidson, J. R., Brady, K. T., Connor, K. M., & Heekin, M. H. (2008). Placebo-controlled trial of risperidone augmentation for selective serotonin reuptake inhibitor-resistant civilian posttraumatic stress disorder. *Journal of Clinical Psychiatry, 69,* 520–525.

Rothbaum, B. O., Meadows, E. A., Resick, P., & Foy, D. W. (2000). Cognitive-behavioral therapy. In E. B. Foa, T. M. Keane, & M. J. Friedman (Eds), *Effective treatments for PTSD: Practice guidelines from the International Society for Traumatic Stress Studies* (pp. 60–83). New York, NY: Guilford.

Rothschild, A. J., & Duval, S. E. (2003). How long should patients with psychotic depression stay on the antipsychotic medication? *Journal of Clinical Psychiatry, 64,* 390–396.

Ruch, L. O., & Chandler, S. M. (1983). Sexual assault trauma during the acute phase: An exploratory model and multivariate analysis. *Journal of Health and Social Behavior, 24,* 184–185.

Ruiz, J. (2010). A review of acceptance and commitment therapy (ACT) empirical evidence: Correlational, experimental psychopathology, component and outcome studies. *International Journal of Psychology and Psychological Therapy, 10,* 125–162.

Rusiewicz, A., DuHamel, K. N., Burkhalter, J., Ostroff, J., Winkel, G., Scigliano, E., . . . Redd, W. (2008). Psychological distress in long-term survivors of hematopoietic stem cell transplantation. *Psycho-Oncology, 17,* 329–337.

Sah, R., Ekhator, N. N., Strawn, J. R., Sallee, F. R., Baker, D. G., Horn, P. S., & Geracioti, T. D., Jr. (2009). Low cerebrospinal fluid neuropeptide Y concentrations in posttraumatic stress disorder. *Biological Psychiatry, 66,* 705–707.

Saha, S., Varghese, D., Slade, T., Degenhardt, L., Mills, K., McGrath, J., & Scott, J. (2011). The association between trauma and delusional-like experiences. *Psychiatry Research, 189,* 259–264.

Salib, E., & Cortina-Borja, M. (2009). Effect of 7 July 2005 terrorist attacks in London on suicide in England and Wales. *British Journal of Psychiatry, 194,* 80–85.

Salloum, A., Carter, P., Burch, B., Garfinkel, A., & Overstreet, S. (2011). Impact of exposure to community violence, Hurricane Katrina, and Hurricane Gustav on posttraumatic stress and depressive symptoms among school age children. *Anxiety, Stress & Coping, 24,* 27–42.

Salter, A. C. (1995). *Transforming trauma: A guide to understanding and treating adult survivors of child sexual abuse.* Thousand Oaks, CA: Sage.

Salzberg, S. (1995). *Lovingkindness: The revolutionary art of happiness.* Boston, MA: Shambhala.

Samelius, L., Wijma, B., Wingren, G., & Wijma, K. (2007). Somatization in abused women. *Journal of Women's Health, 16,* 909–918.

Samoilov, A., & Goldfried, M. R. (2000). Role of emotion in cognitive-behavior therapy. *Clinical Psychology: Science and Practice, 7,* 373–385.

Sansone, R. A., Hruschka, J., Vasudevan, A., & Miller, S. N. (2003). Benzodiazepine exposure and history of trauma. *Psychosomatics, 44,* 523–524.

Sansone, R. A., Songer, D. A., & Miller, K. A. (2005). Childhood abuse, mental healthcare utilization, self-harm behavior, and multiple psychiatric diagnoses among inpatients with and without a borderline diagnosis. *Comprehensive Psychiatry, 46,* 117–120.

Şar, V., Akyüz, G., & Doğan, O. (2007). Prevalence of dissociative disorders among women in the general population. *Psychiatry Research, 149,* 169–176.

Şar, V., Akyüz, G., Dogan, O., & Öztü, E. (2009). The prevalence of conversion symptoms in women from a general Turkish population. *Psychosomatics: Journal of Consultation Liaison Psychiatry, 50,* 50–58.

Şar, V., Akyüz, G., Kundakci, T., Kiziltan, E., & Dogan, O. (2004). Childhood trauma, dissociation, and psychiatric comorbidity in patients with conversion disorder. *American Journal of Psychiatry, 161,* 2271–2276.

Schäfer, I., & Fisher, H. L. (2011). Childhood trauma and psychosis—What is the evidence? *Dialogues in Clinical Neuroscience, 13,* 360–365.

Schalinski, I., Elbert, T., & Schauer, M. (2011). Female dissociative responding to extreme sexual violence in a chronic crisis setting: The case of Eastern Congo. *Journal of Traumatic Stress, 24,* 235–238.

Schatzberg, A. F. (2003). New approaches to managing psychotic depression. *Journal of Clinical Psychiatry, 64*(Suppl. 1), 19–23.

Schmahl, C., & Bremner, J. D. (2006). Neuroimaging in borderline personality disorder. *Journal of Psychiatric Research, 40,* 419–427.

Schnurr, P. P., & Green, B. L. (Eds.). (2004). *Trauma and health: Physical health consequences of exposure to extreme stress.* Washington, DC: American Psychological Association.

Schnyder, U., Wittman, L., Friedrich-Perez, J., Hepp, U., & Moergeli, H. (2008). Posttraumatic stress disorder following accidental injury: Rule or exception in Switzerland? *Psychotherapy and Psychosomatics, 77*(2), 111–118.

Schonenberg, M., Jusyte, A., Hautzinger, M., & Badke, A. (2011). Early predictors of posttraumatic stress in accident victims. *Psychiatry Research, 190,* 152–155.

Schore, A. N. (1994). *Affect regulation and the origin of the self: The neurobiology of emotional development.* Hillsdale, NJ: Lawrence Erlbaum.

Schore, A. N. (1996). The experience-dependent maturation of a regulatory system in the orbital prefrontal cortex and the origin of developmental psychopathology. *Development and Psychopathology, 8,* 59–87.

Schore, A. N. (2002). Dysregulation of the right brain: A fundamental mechanism of traumatic attachment and the psychopathogenesis of posttraumatic stress disorder. *Australian and New Zealand Journal of Psychiatry, 36,* 9–30.

Schore, A. N. (2003). *Affect dysregulation and disorders of the self.* New York, NY: Norton.

Schulman, E. A., & DePold Hohler, A. (2012). The American Academy of Neurology position statement on abuse and violence. *Neurology, 78,* 433–435.

Schwab-Stone, M. E., Ayers, T. S., Kasprow, W., Voyce, C., Barone, C., Shriver, T., & Weissberg, R. P. (1995). No safe haven: A study of violence exposure in an urban community. *Journal of the American Academy of Child and Adolescent Psychiatry, 34,* 1343–1352.

Sedlak, A. J., & Broadhurst, D. D. (1996). *Third National Incidence Study of Child Abuse and Neglect.* Washington, DC: National Center on Child Abuse and Neglect.

Seedat, S., & Stein, D. J. (2001). Biological treatment of PTSD in children and adolescents. In S. Eth (Ed.), *PTSD in children and adolescents* (pp. 87–116). Washington, DC: American Psychiatric Press.

Segal, Z. V., Williams, J. M. G., & Teasdale, J. D. (2002). *Mindfulness-based cognitive therapy for depression: A new approach to preventing relapse*. New York, NY: Guilford Press.

Segman, R. H., Cooper-Kazaz, R., Macciardi, F., Goltser, T., Halfon, Y., Dobroborski, T., & Shalev, A. Y. (2002). Association between the dopamine transporter gene and posttraumatic stress disorder. *Molecular Psychiatry, 7*, 903–907.

Segura, D. A., & Zavella, P. (2007). *Women and migration in the U.S.-Mexico borderlands: A reader*. Durham, NC: Duke University Press.

Seidler, G. H., & Wagner, F. E. (2006). Comparing the efficacy of EMDR and trauma-focused cognitive-behavioral therapy in the treatment of PTSD: A meta-analytic study. *Psychological Medicine: A Journal of Research in Psychiatry and the Allied Sciences, 36*, 1515–1522.

Selley, C., King, E., Peveler, R., Osola, K., Martin, N., & Thompson, C. (1997). Posttraumatic stress disorder symptoms and the Clapham rail accident. *British Journal of Psychiatry, 171*, 478–482.

Sells, D. J., Rowe, M., Fisk, D., & Davidson, L. (2003). Violent victimization of persons with co-occurring psychiatric and substance use disorders. *Psychiatric Services, 54*, 1253–1257.

Semple, R. J., & Lee, J. (2011). *Mindfulness-based cognitive therapy for anxious children: A manual for treating childhood anxiety*. Oakland, CA: New Harbinger.

Seng, J. S. (2002). A conceptual framework for research on lifetime violence, posttraumatic stress, and childbearing. *Journal of Midwifery & Women's Health, 47*, 337–346.

Seng, J. S., Low, L. K., Sperlich, M., Ronis, D. L., Liberzon, I. (2011). Post-traumatic stress disorder, child abuse history, birthweight and gestational age: A prospective cohort study. *BJOG: An International Journal of Obstetrics & Gynaecology, 118*, 1329–1339.

Seng, J. S., Oakley, D. J., Sampselle, C. M., Killion, C., Graham-Bermann, S., & Liberzon, I. (2001). Posttraumatic stress disorder and pregnancy complications. *Obstetrics & Gynecology, 97*, 17–22.

Seng, J. S., Sperlich, M., & Low, L. K. (2008). Mental health, demographic, and risk behavior profiles of pregnant survivors of childhood and adult abuse. *Journal of Midwifery & Women's Health, 53*, 511–521.

Shalev, A. Y. (2002). Acute stress reactions in adults. *Biological Psychiatry, 51*, 532–544.

Shalev, A. Y., Ankri, Y. L. E., Israeli-Shalev, Y., Peleg, T., Adessky, R. S., & Freedman, S. A. (2012). Prevention of posttraumatic stress disorder by early treatment: Results from the Jerusalem trauma outreach and prevention study. *Archives of General Psychiatry, 69*, 166–176.

Shapiro, D. H. (1992). Adverse effects of meditation: A preliminary investigation of long-term meditators. *International Journal of Psychosomatics, 39*, 62–66.

Shapiro, F. (1995). *Eye movement desensitization and reprocessing: Basic principles, protocols, and procedures*. New York, NY: Guilford.

Shapiro, F. (2002). EMDR 12 years after its introduction: Past and future research. *Journal of Clinical Psychology, 58*, 1–22.

Shapiro, S. L., & Carlson, L. E. (2009). *The art and science of mindfulness: Integrating mindfulness into psychology and the helping professions*. Washington DC: American Psychological Association.

Sharp, S., Thomas, C., Rosenberg, L., Rosenberg, M., & Meyer, W., III. (2010). Propranolol does not reduce risk for acute stress disorder in pediatric burn trauma. *Journal of Trauma: Injury, Infection, & Critical Care, 68*, 193–197.

Shay, J. (1995). *Achilles in Vietnam: Combat trauma and the undoing of character.* New York, NY: Touchstone.

Shear, M. K., McLaughlin, K., Ghesquire, A., Guber, M., Sampson, N., & Kessler R. (2011). Complicated grief associated with Hurricane Katrina. *Depression and Anxiety, 28*, 648–657.

Shear, M. K., Simon, N., Wall, M., Zisook, S., Neimeyer, R., Duan, N., . . . Keshaviah, A. (2011). Complicated grief and related bereavement issues for DSM-5. *Depression and Anxiety, 28*, 103–117.

Shear, M. K., & Smith-Caroff, K. (2002). Traumatic loss and the syndrome of complicated grief. *PTSD Research Quarterly, 13*, 1–7.

Sherin, J. E., & Nemeroff, C. B. (2011). Post-traumatic stress disorder: The neurobiological impact of psychological trauma. *Dialogues in Clinical Neuroscience, 13*, 263–278.

Shestatzky, M., Greenberg, D., & Lerer, B. (1988). A controlled trial of phenelzine in posttraumatic stress disorder. *Psychiatry Research, 24*, 149–155.

Shin, L. M., Rauch, S. L., & Pitman, R. K. (2006). Amygdala, medial prefrontal cortex, and hippocampal function in PTSD. *Annals of the New York Academy of Sciences, 1071*, 67–79.

Shin, L. M., Whalen, P. J., Pitman, R. K., Bush, G., Macklin, M. L., Lasko, N. B., . . . Rauch, S. L. (2001). An fMRI study of anterior cingulate function in posttraumatic stress disorder. *Biological Psychiatry, 50*, 932–942.

Shipherd, J. C., Street, A. E., & Resick, P. A. (2006). Cognitive therapy for posttraumatic stress disorder. In V. M. Follette, J. I. Ruzek, V. M. Follette, & J. I. Ruzek (Eds.), *Cognitive-behavioral therapies for trauma* (2nd ed., pp. 96–116). New York, NY: Guilford.

Siddiqui, Z., Marcil, W. A., Bhatia, S. C., Ramaswamy, S., & Petty, F. (2005). Ziprasidone therapy for post-traumatic stress disorder. *Journal of Psychiatry and Neuroscience, 30*, 430–431.

Siegel, D. J. (1999). *The developing mind: Toward a neurobiology of interpersonal experience.* New York, NY: Guilford.

Siegel, D. J. (2007). *The mindful brain.* New York, NY: W. W. Norton.

Siegel, D. J. (2012). *The developing mind: How relationships and the brain interact to shape who we are* (2nd ed.). New York, NY: Guilford.

Siegel, K., & Schrimshaw, E. W. (2000). Perceiving benefits in adversity: Stress-related growth in women living with HIV/AIDS. *Social Science and Medicine, 51*, 1543–1554.

Silver, J. M., McAllister, T. W., & Arciniegas, D. B. (2009). Depression and cognitive complaints following mild traumatic brain injury. *American Journal of Psychiatry, 166*, 653–661.

Silver, R. C., Holman, E. A., McIntosh, D. N., Poulin, M., & Gil-Rivas, V. (2002). Nationwide longitudinal study of psychological responses to September 11. *Journal of the American Medical Association, 288*, 1235–1244.

Simeon, D., Bartz, J., Hamilton, H., Crystal, S., Braun, A., Ketay, S., & Hollander, E. (2011). Oxytocin administration attenuates stress reactivity in borderline personality disorder: A pilot study. *Psychoneuroendocrinology, 36*, 1418–1421.

Simeon, D., Greenberg, J., Nelson, D., Schmeidler, J., & Hollander, E. (2005). Dissociation and posttraumatic stress 1 year after the World Trade Center disaster: Follow-up of a longitudinal survey. *Journal of Clinical Psychiatry, 66*, 231–237.

Simon, N. M., Connor, K. M., Lang, A. J., Rauch, S, Krulewicz, S., LeBeau, R. T., . . . Pollack, M. H. (2008). Paroxetine CR augmentation for posttraumatic stress disorder refractory to prolonged exposure therapy. *Journal of Clinical Psychiatry, 69,* 400–405.

Simpson, G. M., El Sheshai, A. E., Rady, A., Kingsbury, S. J., & Fayek, M. (2003). Sertraline and monotherapy in the treatment of psychotic and nonpsychotic depression. *Journal of Clinical Psychiatry, 64, 959–965.*

Simpson, J. A., & Rholes, W. S. (1994). Stress and secure base relationships in adulthood. In K. Bartholomew, D. Perlman, K. Bartholomew, & D. Perlman (Eds.), *Attachment processes in adulthood* (pp. 181–204). London, UK: Jessica Kingsley.

Simpson, T. L., Kaysen, D. L., Bowen, S., MacPherson, L. M., Chawla, N., Blume, A., . . . Larimer, M. E. (2007). PTSD symptoms, substance use, and vipassana meditation among incarcerated individuals. *Journal of Traumatic Stress, 20,* 239–249.

Singer, M. I., Anglin, T. M., Song, L. Y., & Lunghofer, L. (1995). Adolescents' exposure to violence and associated symptoms of psychological trauma. *Journal of the American Medical Association, 273,* 477–482.

Smajkic, A., Weine, S., Djuric-Bijedic, Z., Boskailo, E., Lewis, J., & Pavkovic, I. (2001). Sertraline, paroxetine, and venlafaxine in refugee posttraumatic stress disorder with depression symptoms. *Journal of Traumatic Stress, 14,* 445–542.

Smith, J. D. (2009). *Mindfulness-based stress reduction (MBSR) for women with PTSD surviving domestic violence dissertation* (Unpublished doctoral dissertation). Fielding Graduate University, Santa Barbara, CA.

Smyth, J., Hockemeyer, J., & Tulloch, H. (2008). Expressive writing and posttraumatic stress disorder: Effects on trauma symptoms, mood states, and cortisol reactivity. *British Journal of Health Psychology, 13,* 85–93.

Sokolski, K. N., Denson, T. F., Lee, R. T., & Reist, C. (2003). Quetiapine for treatment of refractory symptoms of combat-related post-traumatic stress disorder. *Military Medicine, 168,* 486–489.

Solomon, M. F., & Siegel, D. J. (2003). *Healing trauma: Attachment, mind, body, and brain.* New York, NY: Norton.

Solomon, Z., & Benbenishty, R. (1986). The role of proximity, immediacy, and expectancy in frontline treatment of combat stress reaction among Israelis in the Lebanon war. *American Journal of Psychiatry, 143,* 613–617.

Solomon, Z., Shklar, R., & Mikulincer, M. (2005). Frontline treatment of combat stress reaction: A 20-year longitudinal evaluation study. *American Journal of Psychiatry, 162,* 2309–2314.

Southwick, S. M., Bremner, J. D., Rasmusson, A., Morgan, C. A., Arnsten, A., & Charney, D. S. (1999). Role of norepinephrine in the pathophysiology and treatment of posttraumatic stress disorder. *Biological Psychiatry, 46,* 1192–1204.

Southwick, S. M., Morgan, C. A., Charney, D. S., & High, J. R. (1999). Yohimbine use in a natural setting: Effects on posttraumatic stress disorder. *Biological Psychiatry, 46,* 442–444.

Southwick, S. M., Morgan, C. A., Vythilingam, M., & Charney, D. S. (2003). Emerging neurobiological factors in stress resilience. *PTSD Research Quarterly, 14,* 1–8.

Spates, C., Koch, E., Cusack, K., Pagoto, S., & Waller, S. (2008). Eye movement desensitization and reprocessing. In Foa, E., Keane, T., Friedman, M., &

Cohen, J. (Eds), *Effective treatments for PTSD: Practice guidelines from the International Society for Traumatic Stress Studies* (2nd ed.). New York, NY: Guilford.

Spinazzola, J., Blaustein, M., & van der Kolk, B. A. (2005). Treatment outcome research: The study of unrepresentative samples? *Journal of Traumatic Stress, 18,* 425–436.

Spitzer, C., Barnow, S., Völzke, H., John, U., Freyberger, H. J., & Grabe, H. J. (2009). Trauma, posttraumatic stress disorder, and physical illness: Findings from the general population. *Psychosomatic Medicine, 71,* 1012–1017.

Sroufe, L. A., Carlson, E. A., Levy, A. K., & Egeland, B. (1999). Implications of attachment theory for developmental psychopathology. *Development and Psychopathology, 11,* 1–13.

Steel, Z., Chey, T., Silove, D., Marnane, C., Bryant, R. A., & van Ommeren, M. (2009). Association of torture and other potentially traumatic events with mental health outcomes among populations exposed to mass conflict and displacement: A systematic review and meta-analysis. *Journal of the American Medical Association, 302,* 537–549.

Steil, R., Dyer, A., Priebe, K., Kleindienst, N., & Bohus, M. (2011). Dialectical behavior therapy for posttraumatic stress disorder related to childhood sexual abuse: A pilot study of an intensive residential treatment program. *Journal of Traumatic Stress, 24,* 102–106.

Stein, D. J., Davidson, J., Seedat, S., & Beebe, K. (2003). Paroxetine in the treatment of post-traumatic stress disorder: Pooled analysis of placebo-controlled studies. *Expert Opinion on Pharmacotherapy, 4,* 1829–1838.

Stein, D. J., van der Kolk, B. A., Austin, C., Fayyad, R., & Clary, C. (2006). Efficacy of sertraline in posttraumatic stress disorder secondary to interpersonal trauma or childhood abuse. *Annals of Clinical Psychiatry, 18,* 243–249.

Stein M.B., Kerridge C., Dimsdale J.E., & Hoyt D.B. (2007). Pharmacotherapy to prevent PTSD: Results from a randomized controlled proof-of-concept trial in physically injured patients. *Journal of Traumatic Stress. 20,* 923-32.

Stein, M. B., Kline, N. A., & Matloff, J. L. (2002). Adjunctive olanzapine for SSRI-resistant combat-related PTSD: A double-blind, placebo-controlled study. *American Journal of Psychiatry, 159,* 1777–1779.

Steinberg, M. (1994). *Structured Clinical Interview for DSM-IV Dissociative Disorders-Revised (SCID-D-R).* Washington, DC: American Psychiatric Press.

Steinberg, M. (2004). Systematic assessment of posttraumatic dissociation: The structured clinical interview for DSM-IV dissociative disorders. In. J. P. Wilson & T. M. Keane (Eds.), *Assessing psychological trauma and PTSD* (pp. 122–143). New York, NY: Guilford.

Stern, D. N. (1985). *The interpersonal world of the infant: A view from psychoanalysis and developmental psychology.* New York, NY: Basic Books.

Stiglmayer, A. (1994). *Mass rape: The war against women in Bosnia-Herzegovina.* Lincoln: University of Nebraska Press.

Stramrood, C. A., Wessel, I., Doornbos, B., Aarnoudse, J. G., van den Berg, P. P., Schultz, W. C., & van Pampus, M. G. (2011). Posttraumatic stress disorder following preeclampsia and PPROM: A prospective study with 15 months follow-up. *Reproductive Sciences, 18,* 645–653.

Straus, M. A., & Gelles, R. J. (1990). *Physical violence in American families: Risk factors and adaptation to violence in 8,145 families.* New Brunswick, NJ: Transaction.

Strawn, J. R., Keeshin, B. R., DelBello, M. P., Geracioti, T. D., & Putnam, F. W. (2010). Psychopharmacologic treatment of posttraumatic stress disorder in children and adolescents: A review. *Journal of Clinical Psychiatry, 71,* 932–941.

Ströhle, A., Scheel, M., Modell, S., & Holsboer, F. (2008). Blunted ACTH response to dexamethasone suppression-CRH stimulation in posttraumatic stress disorder. *Journal of Psychiatric Research, 42,* 1185–1188.

Sugar, J. A., & Ford, J. D. (2012). Peritraumatic dissociation and PTSD in psychiatrically impaired youth. *Journal of Traumatic Stress, 25,* 41–49.

Sullivan P. F. (2005). The genetics of schizophrenia. *PLoS Medicine, 2*(7), e212. doi:10.1371/journal.pmed.0020212

Suominen, K., Vuola, J., & Isometsa, E. (2011). Mental disorders after burn injury: A prospective study. *Burns, 37,* 601–609.

Suris, A., North, C., Adinoff, B., Powell, C. M., & Greene, R. (2010). Effects of exogenous glucocorticoid on combat-related PTSD symptoms. *Annals of Clinical Psychiatry, 22,* 274–279.

Talbot, N. L., Houghtalen, R. P., Cyrulik, S., Betz, A., Barkun, M., Duberstein, P. R., & Wynne, L. C. (1998). Women's safety in recovery: Group therapy for patients with a history of childhood sexual abuse. *Psychiatric Services, 49,* 213–217.

Taylor, F., & Raskind, M. A. (2002). The alpha1-adrenergic antagonist prazosin improves sleep and nightmares in civilian trauma posttraumatic stress disorder. *Journal of Clinical Psychopharmacology, 22,* 82–85.

Taylor, F. B., Martin, P., Thompson, C., Williams, J., Mellman, T. A., Gross, C., . . . Raskind, M. A. (2008). Prazosin effects on objective sleep measures and clinical symptoms in civilian trauma posttraumatic stress disorder: A placebo-controlled study. *Biological Psychiatry, 63,* 629–632.

Taylor, S. (2003). Outcome predictors for three PTSD treatments: Exposure therapy, EMDR, and relaxation training. *Journal of Cognitive Psychotherapy, 17,* 149–162.

Teasdale, J. D., Segal, Z., & Williams, J. M. G. (1995). How does cognitive therapy prevent depressive relapse and why should attentional control (mindfulness) training help? *Behaviour Research and Therapy, 33,* 25–39.

Tengvall, O., Wickman, M., & Wengstrom, Y. (2010). Memories of pain after burn injury—The patient's experience. *Journal of Burn Care and Research, 31,* 319–327.

Terzano, M. G., Rossi, M., Palomba, V., Smerieri, A., & Parrino, L. (2003). New drugs for insomnia: Comparative tolerability of zopiclone, zolpidem and zaleplon. *Drug Safety, 26,* 261–282.

Thanissaro Bhikkhu. (Trans.). (1997). *Sallatha sutta: The arrow.* Retrieved from http://www.accesstoinsight.org/tipitaka/sn/sn36/sn36.006.than.html

Thombs, B. D., Fauerbach, J. A., & McCann, U. D. (2005). Stress disorders following traumatic injury: Assessment and treatment considerations. *Primary Psychiatry, 12*(3), 51–55.

Thompson, A., Nelson, B., McNab, C., Simmons, M., Leicester, S., McGorry, P. D., . . . Yung, A. R. (2010). Psychotic symptoms with sexual content in the "ultra high risk" for psychosis population: Frequency and association with sexual trauma. *Psychiatry Research, 177,* 84–91.

Thompson, B. L., & Waltz, J. (2010). Mindfulness and experiential avoidance as predictors of posttraumatic stress disorder avoidance symptom severity. *Journal of Anxiety Disorders, 24,* 409–415.

Thurman, D. J., Alverson, C., Dunn, K. A., Guerrero, J., & Sniezek, J. E. (1999). Traumatic brain injury in the United States: A public health perspective. *Journal of Head Trauma Rehabilitaion, 14,* 602–615.

Tischler, L., Brand, S. R., Stavitsky, K., Labinsky, E., Newmark, R., Grossman, R., . . . Yehuda, R. (2006). The relationship between hippocampal volume and declarative memory in a population of combat veterans with and without PTSD. *Annals of the New York Academy of Science, 1071,* 405–409.

Tjaden, P., & Thoennes, N. (2000). *Full report of the prevalence, incidence, and consequences of violence against women: Findings from the National Violence Against Women Survey* (NCJ Publication No. 183781). Washington, DC: U.S. Department of Justice & Centers for Disease Control and Prevention.

Treanor, M. (2011). The potential impact of mindfulness on exposure and extinction learning in anxiety disorders. *Clinical Psychology Review, 31,* 617–625.

Turner, S., Yüksel, S., & Silove, D. (2003). Survivors of mass violence and torture. In B. L. Green, M. J. Friedman, J. T. V. M. de Jong, S. D. Solomon, T. M. Keane, J. A. Fairbank, B. Donelan, & E. Frey-Wouters (Eds.), *Trauma interventions in war and peace: Prevention, practice, and policy* (pp. 185–211). New York: Kluwer Academic/Plenum

Ullman, S. E., & Filipas, H. H. (2001). Predictors of PTSD symptom severity and social reactions in sexual assault victims. *Journal of Traumatic Stress, 14,* 393–413.

United Nations Treaty Collection. (1984). *Convention against Torture and Other Cruel, Inhuman or Degrading Treatment or Punishment.* Retrieved from http://treaties.un.org/Pages/ViewDetails.aspx?src=TREATY&mtdsg_no=IV-9&chapter=4&lang=en

Updegraff, J. A., & Taylor, S. E. (2000). From vulnerability to growth: Positive and negative effects of stressful life events. In J. H. Harvey & E. D. Miller (Eds.), *Loss and trauma: General and close relationship perspectives* (pp. 3–28). Philadelphia, PA: Brunner-Routledge.

Ursano, R. J., Fullerton, C. S., Epstein, R. S., Crowley, B., Kao, T.-C., Vance, K., . . . Baum, A. S. (1999). Acute and chronic posttraumatic stress disorder in motor vehicle accident victims. *American Journal of Psychiatry, 156,* 589–595.

Ursano, R. J., Fullerton, C. S., Kao, T.-C., & Bhartiya, V. R. (1995). Longitudinal assessment of posttraumatic stress disorder and depression after exposure to traumatic death. *Journal of Nervous and Mental Disease, 183,* 36–42.

Ursano, R. J., Fullerton, C. S., & McCaughey, B. G. (1994). Trauma and disaster. In R. J. Ursano, B. G. McCaughey, & C. S. Fullerton (Eds.), *Individual and community responses to trauma and disaster: The structure of human chaos* (pp. 3–27). Cambridge, UK: Cambridge University Press.

U.S. Department of Health and Human Services, Office of Refugee Resettlement. (2012). *Services for survivors of torture.* Retrieved from http://www.acf.hhs.gov/programs/orr/programs/services_survivors_torture.htm

U.S. Department of Health and Human Services, Office on Women's Health. (2008). *Date rape drugs fact sheet.* Retrieved from http://www.womenshealth.gov/publications/our-publications/fact-sheet/date-rape-drugs.cfm

U.S. Department of State. (2005). *Trafficking in persons report.* Retrieved from http://www.state.gov/j/tip/rls/tiprpt/2005

U.S. Department of Veterans Affairs. (2011). Mindfulness practice in the treatment of traumatic stress. Retrieved from http://www.ptsd.va.gov/public/pages/mindful-ptsd.asp

U.S. Drug Enforcement Administration. (n.d.). *GHB, GBL and 1,4BD as date rape drugs.* Retrieved from http://www.justice.gov/dea/ongoing/daterape.html

U.S. Surgeon General. (2001). *Mental health: Culture, race, and ethnicity: A supplement to mental health: Report of the Surgeon General.* Retrieved from http://www.namiscc.org/newsletters/August01/Surgeon General Report.htm

Vaage, A. B., Thomsen, P. H., Silove, D., Wentzel-Larsen, T., Van Ta, T., & Hauff, E. (2010). Long-term mental health of Vietnamese refugees in the aftermath of trauma: Errata. *British Journal of Psychiatry, 196*, 122–125.

Vaiva, G., Boss, V., Ducrocq, F., Fontaine, M., Devos, P., Brunet, A., . . . Thomas, P. (2006). Relationship between posttrauma GABA plasma levels and PTSD at 1-year follow-up. *American Journal of Psychiatry, 163*, 1446–1448.

Vaiva, G., Ducrocq, F., Jezequel, K., Averland, B., Lestavel, P., Brunet, A., & Marmar, C. R. (2003). Immediate treatment with propranolol decreases posttraumatic stress disorder two months after trauma. *Biological Psychiatry, 52*, 947–949.

van der Kolk, B. A., & D'Andrea, W. (2010). Towards a developmental trauma disorder diagnosis for childhood interpersonal trauma. In R. Lanius, E. Vermetten, & C. Pain (Eds.), *The impact of early life trauma on health and disease: The hidden epidemic.* Cambridge, UK: Cambridge University Press.

van der Kolk, B. A., Roth, S., Pelcovitz, D., Sunday, S., & Spinazzola, F. (2005). Disorders of extreme stress: The empirical foundation of a complex adaptation to trauma. *Journal of Traumatic Stress, 18*, 389–399.

van der Kolk, B. A., Spinazzola, J., Blaustein, M. E., Hopper, J. W., Hopper, E. K., Korn, D. L., & Simpson, W. B. (2007). A randomized clinical trial of eye movement desensitization and reprocessing (EMDR), fluoxetine, and pill placebo in the treatment of posttraumatic stress disorder: Treatment effects and long-term maintenance. *Journal of Clinical Psychiatry, 68*, 37–46.

Van der Veer, G. (1995). Psychotherapeutic work with refugees. In R. J. Kleber, C. R. Figley, & B. P. R. Gersons (Eds.), *Beyond trauma: Cultural and societal dynamics* (pp. 151–170). New York, NY: Plenum Press.

van Dijke, A., Ford, J. D., van der Hart, O., van Son, M., van der Heijden, P., & Buhring, M. (2012). Complex posttraumatic stress disorder in patients with borderline personality disorder and somatoform disorders. *Psychological Trauma: Theory, Research, Practice, and Policy, 4* , 162–168.

van Emmerik, A. A., Kamphuis, J. H., Hulsbosch, A. M., & Emmelkamp, P. M. (2002). Single session debriefing after psychological trauma: A meta-analysis. *Lancet, 360*(9335), 766–771.

Van Etten, M. L., & Taylor, S. (1998). Comparative efficacy of treatments for posttraumatic stress disorder: A meta-analysis. *Clinical Psychology and Psychotherapy, 5*, 126–144.

Van Ommeren, M., de Jong, J. T. V. M., Sharma, B., Komproe, I., Thapa, S. B., & Cardeña, E. (2001). Psychiatric disorders among tortured Bhutanese refugees in Nepal. *Archives of General Psychiatry, 58*, 475–482.

Verba, H., Bering, R., & Fischer, G. (2007). KO-Tropfen und "date rape"— Verabreichung von drogen zur begehung von sexualstraftaten [Spiked drinks and date rape – The use of drugs to proceed date rape]. *Zeitschrift für Psychotraumatologie, Psychotherapiewissenschaft, Psychologische Medizin, 5*, 35–46.

Videlock, E. J., Adeyemo, M., Licudine, A., Hirano, M., Ohning, G., Mayer, M., . . . Chang, L. (2009). Childhood trauma is associated with hypothalamic-pituitary-adrenal (HPA) axis responsiveness in irritable bowel syndrome. *Gastroenterology, 137*, 1954–1962.

Villarreal, G., Calais, L. A., Canive, J. M., Lundy, S. L., Pickard, J., & Toney, G. (2007). Prospective study to evaluate the efficacy of aripiprazole as a monotherapy in patients with severe chronic posttraumatic stress disorder: An open trial. *Psychopharmacology Bulletin, 40*, 6–18.

Villarreal, G., & King, C. Y. (2004). Neuroimaging studies reveal brain changes in posttraumatic stress disorder. *Psychiatric Annals, 34,* 845–856.

Vogel, M., Meier, J., Grönke, S., Waage, M., Schneider, W., Freyberger, H. J., & Klauer, T. (2011). Differential effects of childhood abuse and neglect: Mediation by posttraumatic distress in neurotic disorder and negative symptoms in schizophrenia? *Psychiatry Research, 189,* 121–127.

Vujanovic, A. A., Niles, B. L., Pietrefesa, A., Schmertz, S. K., & Potter, C. M. (2011). Mindfulness in the treatment of posttraumatic stress disorder among military veterans. *Professional Psychology, 42,* 24–31.

Waelde, L. C. (2004). Dissociation and meditation. *Journal of Trauma and Dissociation, 5,* 147–162.

Wagner, A. W., & Linehan, M. M. (2006). Applications of dialectical behavior therapy to posttraumatic stress disorder and related problems. In V. M. Follette & J. I. Ruzek (Eds.), *Cognitive-behavioral therapies for trauma* (2nd ed., pp. 117–145). New York, NY: Guilford.

Walderhaug, E., Kasserman, S., Aikins, D., Vojvoda, D., Nishimura, C., & Neumeister, A. (2010). Effects of duloxetine in treatment-refractory men with posttraumatic stress disorder. *Pharmacopsychiatry, 43,* 45–49.

Walker, E. A., Katon, W. J., Roy-Byrne, P. P., Jemelka, R. P., & Russo, J. (1993). Histories of sexual victimization in patients with irritable bowel syndrome or inflammatory bowel disease. *American Journal of Psychiatry, 150,* 1502–1506.

Walker, E. F. & Diforio, D. (1997). Schizophrenia: a neural diathesis-stress model. *Psychological Review, 104,* 667–685.

Walker, L. E. (1984). *The battered woman syndrome.* New York, NY: Springer.

Wallace, B. A. (2006). *The attention revolution.* Somerville, MA: Wisdom.

Walser, R., & Westrup, D. (2007). *Acceptance and commitment therapy for the treatment of post-traumatic stress disorder and trauma-related problems: A practitioner's guide to using mindfulness and acceptance strategies.* Oakland, CA: New Harbinger.

Walsh, R. (1988). Two Asian psychologies and their implications for Western psychotherapists. *American Journal of Psychotherapy, 42,* 543–560.

Watkins, K. E., Hunter, S. B., Burnam, M. A., Pincus, H. A., & Nicholson, G. (2005). Review of treatment recommendations for persons with a co-occurring affective or anxiety and substance use disorder. *Psychiatric Services, 56,* 913–926.

Weathers, F. W., Litz, B. T., Herman, D. S., Huska, J. A., & Keane, T. M. (1993, October). *The PTSD Checklist (PCL): Reliability, validity, and diagnostic utility.* Paper presented at the annual convention of the International Society for Traumatic Stress Studies, San Antonio, TX.

Weathers, F. W., Litz, B. T., & Keane, T. M. (1995). Military trauma. In J. R. Freedy & S. E. Hobfoll (Eds.), *Traumatic stress: From theory to practice* (pp. 103–128). New York, NY: Plenum.

Weiss, S. R. B., & Post, R. M. (1998). Sensitization and kindling phenomena in mood, anxiety, and obsessive-compulsive disorders: The role of serotonergic mechanisms in illness progression. *Biological Psychiatry, 44,* 193–206.

Wessely, S., Bryant, R. A., Greenberg, N., Earnshaw, M., Sharpley, J., & Hughes, J. H. (2008). Does psychoeducation help prevent posttraumatic psychological distress? *Psychiatry: Interpersonal and Biological Processes, 71,* 287–302.

Westen, D., Novotny, C. M., & Thompson-Brenner, H. (2004). The empirical status of empirically supported psychotherapies: Assumptions, findings, and reporting in controlled clinical trials. *Psychological Bulletin, 130,* 631–663.

White, J. W., Koss, M. P., & Kazdin, A. E. (Eds.). (2011). *Violence against women and children: Volume I: Mapping the terrain.* Washington, DC: American Psychological Association.

Whyte, J., Hart, T., Vaccaro, M., Grieb-Neff, P., Risser, A., Polansky, M., & Coslett, H. B. (2004). Effects of methylphenidate on attention deficits after traumatic brain injury: A multidimensional, randomized, controlled trial. *American Journal of Physical Medicine & Rehabilitation, 83,* 401–420.

Wikehult, B., Hedlund, M., Marsenic, M., Nyman, S., & Willebrand, M. (2008). Evaluation of negative emotional care experiences in burn care. *Journal of Clinical Nursing, 17,* 1923–1929.

Wilcox, H. C., Kuramoto, S. J., Lichtenstein, P., Långström, N., Brent, D. A., & Runeson, B. (2010). Psychiatric morbidity, violent crime and suicide among children and adolescents exposed to parental death. *Journal of the American Academy of Child and Adolescent Psychiatry, 49,* 514–523.

Williams, J. M. G., & Swales, M. (2004). The use of mindfulness-based approaches for suicidal patients. *Archives of Suicide Research, 8,* 315–329.

Willmott, C., & Ponsford, J. (2009). Efficacy of methylphenidate in the rehabilitation of attention following traumatic brain injury: A randomised, crossover, double blind, placebo controlled inpatient trial. *Journal of Neurology, Neurosurgery & Psychiatry, 80,* 552–557.

Wilson, J. P., & Drožðek, B. (2004). *Broken spirits: The treatment of traumatized asylum seekers, refugees, war and torture victims.* New York, NY: Brunner-Routledge.

Wisnivesky, J. P., Teitelbaum, S. L., Todd, A. C., Boffetta, P., Crane, M., Crowley, L., . . . Landrigan, P. J. (2011). Persistence of multiple illnesses in World Trade Center rescue and recovery workers: A cohort study. *The Lancet, 378,* 888–897.

Wolpe, J. (1958). *Psychotherapy by reciprocal inhibition.* Stanford, CA: Stanford University Press.

Woon, F. L., Sood, S., & Hedges, D. W. (2010). Hippocampal volume deficits associated with exposure to psychological trauma and posttraumatic stress disorder in adults: A meta-analysis. *Progress in Neuro-Psychopharmacology and Biological Psychiatry, 34,* 1181–1188.

Writer, B. W., Schillerstrom, J. E. (2009). Psychopharmacological treatment for cognitive impairment in survivors of traumatic brain injury: A critical review. *Journal of Neuropsychiatry & Clinical Neurosciences, 21,* 362–270.

Wroblewski, B. A., Joseph, A. B., Cornblatt, R. R. (1996). Antidepressant pharmacotherapy and the treatment of depression in patients with severe traumatic brain injury: A controlled, prospective study. *Journal of Clinical Psychiatry, 57,* 582–587.

Xie, P., Kranzler, H. R., Poling, J., Stein, M. B., Anton, R. F., Farrer, L. A., & Gelernter, J. (2010). Interaction of FKBP5 with childhood adversity on risk for post-traumatic stress disorder. *Neuropsychopharmacology, 35,* 1684–1692.

Xu, J., & Song, X. (2011). A cross-sectional study among survivors of the 2008 Sichuan earthquake: Prevalence and risk factors of posttraumatic stress disorder. *General Hospital Psychiatry, 33,* 386–392.

Yaşan, A., Güzel, A., Tamam, Y., & Ozkan, M. (2009). Predictive factors for acute stress disorder and posttraumatic stress disorder after motor vehicle accidents. *Psychopathology, 42,* 236–241.

Yehuda, R. (2002). Status of cortisol findings in PTSD. *Psychiatric Clinics of North America, 25*, 341–368.

Yehuda, R. (2004). Posttraumatic stress disorder. *New England Journal of Medicine, 346*, 108–114.

Yehuda, R., & Bierer, L. M. (2009). The relevance of epigenetics to PTSD: Implications for the DSM-V. *Journal of Traumatic Stress, 22*, 427–434.

Yehuda, R., Halligan, S. L., Golier, J. A., Grossman, R., & Bierer, L. M. (2004). Effects of trauma exposure on the cortisol response to dexamethasone administration in PTSD and major depressive disorder. *Psychoneuroendocrinology, 29*, 389–404.

Yeomans, P. D., Herbert, J. D., & Forman, E. M. (2008). Symptom comparison across multiple solicitation methods among Burundians with traumatic event histories. *Journal of Traumatic Stress, 21*, 231–234.

Young, B. H., Ford, J. D., Ruzek, J. I., Friedman, M. J., & Gusman, F. D. (1998). *Disaster mental health services: A guidebook for clinicians and administrators.* St. Louis, MO: National Center for PTSD, Department of Veterans Affairs Employee Education System.

Yuan, C., Wang, Z., Inslicht, S. S., McCaslin, S. E., Metzler, T. J., Henn-Haase, C., . . . Marmar, C. R. (2011). Protective factors for posttraumatic stress disorder symptoms in a prospective study of police officers. *Psychiatry Research, 188*, 45–50.

Zatzick, D. F., Rivara, F. P, Jurkovich, G. J., Hoge, C. W., Wang, J., Fan, M. Y., . . . Mackenzie, E. J. (2010). Multisite investigation of traumatic brain injuries, posttraumatic stress disorder, and self reported health and cognitive impairments. *Archives of General Psychiatry, 67*, 1291–1300.

Zayfert, C., Becker, C. B., Unger, D. L., & Shearer, D. K. (2002). Comorbid anxiety disorders in civilians seeking treatment for posttraumatic stress disorder. *Journal of Traumatic Stress, 15,* 31–38.

Zayfert, C., De Viva, J. C., Becker, C. B., Pike, J. L., Gillock, K. L., & Haynes, S. A. (2005). Exposure utilization and completion of cognitive behavioral therapy for PTSD in "real world" clinical practice. *Journal of Traumatic Stress, 18*, 637–645.

Zayfert, C., Dums, A. R., Ferguson, R. J., & Hegel, M. T. (2003). Health functioning impairments associated with posttraumatic stress disorder, anxiety disorders, and depression. *Journal of Nervous and Mental Disease, 190*, 233–240.

Zhang, J., Tan, Q., Yin, H., Zhang, X., Huan, Y., Tang, L., . . . Li, L. (2011). Decreased gray matter volume in the left hippocampus and bilateral calcarine cortex in coal mine flood disaster survivors with recent onset PTSD. *Psychiatry Research, 192*, 84–90.

Zhang, L., Plotkin, R. C., Wang, G., Sandel, M. E., & Lee, S. (2004). Cholinergic augmentation with donepezil enhances recovery in short-term memory and sustained attention after traumatic brain injury. *Archives of Physical and Medical Rehabilitation, 85*, 1050–1055.

Zimmerman, M., & Mattia, J. I. (1999). Psychotic subtyping of major depressive disorder and posttraumatic stress disorder. *Journal of Clinical Psychiatry, 60*, 311–314.

Zinzow, H. M., Rheingold, A. A., Hawkins, A. O., Saunders, B. E., & Kilpatrick, D. G. (2009). Losing a loved one to homicide: Prevalence and mental health correlates in a national sample of young adults. *Journal of Traumatic Stress, 22*, 20–27.

Zisook, S., Chentsova-Dutton, Y. E., & Shuchter, S. R. (1998). PTSD following bereavement. *Annals of Clinical Psychiatry, 10*, 157–163.

Zlotnick, C., Donaldson, D., Spirito, A., & Pearlstein, T. (1997). Affect regulation and suicide attempts in adolescent inpatients. *Journal of the American Academy of Child and Adolescent Psychiatry, 36,* 793–798.

Zoellner, L. A., Feeny, N. C., Bittinger, J. N., Bedard-Gilligan, M. A., Slagle, D. M., Post, L. M., & Chen, J. A. (2011). Teaching trauma-focused exposure therapy for PTSD: Critical clinical lessons for novice exposure therapists. *Psychological Trauma: Theory, Research, Practice, and Policy, 3,* 300–308.

Zohar, J., Amital, D., Miodownik, C., Kotler, M., Bleich, A., Lane, R. M., & Austin, C. (2002). Double-blind placebo-controlled pilot study of sertraline in military veterans with posttraumatic stress disorder. *Journal of Clinical Psychopharmacology, 22,* 190–195.

Index

About the Authors _____

John N. Briere, PhD, is Associate Professor of Psychiatry and Psychology at the Keck School of Medicine, University of Southern California, and Director of the Psychological Trauma Program at Los Angeles County + USC Medical Center, where he consults and teaches in the emergency room, burn unit, and inpatient psychiatry. A past president of the International Society for Traumatic Stress Studies (ISTSS), he is recipient of the Robert S. Laufer Memorial Award for Scientific Achievement from ISTSS, the Award for Outstanding Contributions to the Science of Trauma Psychology from the American Psychological Association (Division 56), and designation as Highly Cited Researcher (Behavioral Sciences) by the Institute for Scientific Information. He is author of a number of books, articles, and psychological tests in the areas of trauma and interpersonal violence, and has a long-standing interest in the clinical applications of meditation, mindfulness, and compassion. His website is http://johnbriere.com.

Catherine Scott, MD, is Assistant Clinical Professor of Psychiatry and the Behavioral Sciences at the USC Keck School of Medicine. Her educational background includes Harvard College, Columbia University College of Physicians and Surgeons, and psychiatric residency training at Cornell and USC. She was formerly Medical Director of the Psychological Trauma Program at Los Angeles County + USC Medical Center, and the Associate Medical Director of the Psychiatric Emergency Service at Los Angeles County + USC Medical Center, where she taught and supervised resident physicians and medical students in the assessment and treatment of trauma-related disorders arising from sexual and physical violence, torture, child abuse, and other forms of interpersonal violence. Although continuing to teach, Dr. Scott stepped down from administrative duties in order to pursue writing and research projects. Her clinical and research interests include human rights, women's issues, and the remediation of sexual violence and its effects.

Contributing Authors

Janelle Jones, MD, is a psychiatrist in Denver, Colorado. She completed her residency at the University of Southern California, where she received additional training in trauma. In addition to practicing in several health systems in Colorado, she continues to work in the psychiatric emergency room of Los Angeles County + University of Southern California Medical Center, where she supervises physicians-in-training. Dr. Jones is experienced in treating trauma survivors and has a particular focus on working with women in correctional settings. Specific interests include the psychobiology and psychopharmacology of posttraumatic stress disorder.

Heidi Ardern, Ph.D., is a psychologist in Denver, Colorado. While earning her Ph.D. at Nova Southeastern University, she worked closely with Lenore Walker, Ed.D., in researching the experiences of battered women. Since that time, Dr. Ardern has devoted much of her professional time to working with survivors of trauma in correctional, medical, and inpatient psychiatric settings. She also conducts volunteer psychological evaluations of refugees for a human rights clinic. Dr. Ardern works in private practice in Longmont, Colorado, and is a lecturer at the University of Colorado-Denver

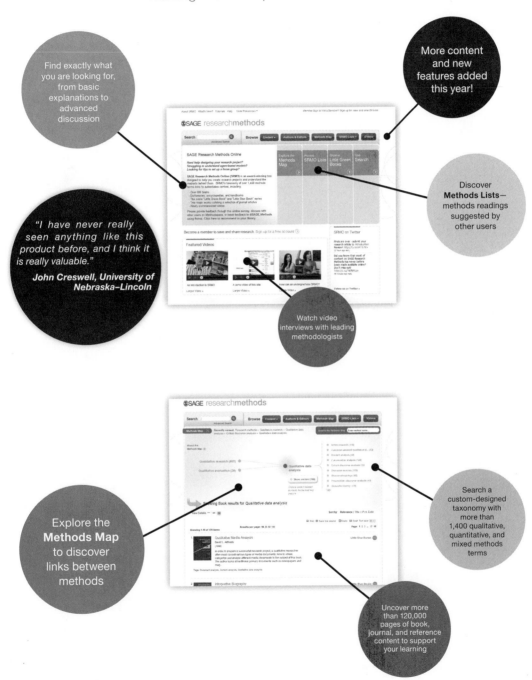

⑤SAGE research**methods**

The essential online tool for researchers from the world's leading methods publisher

Find exactly what you are looking for, from basic explanations to advanced discussion

More content and new features added this year!

"*I have never really seen anything like this product before, and I think it is really valuable.*"

John Creswell, University of Nebraska–Lincoln

Discover **Methods Lists**— methods readings suggested by other users

Watch video interviews with leading methodologists

Explore the **Methods Map** to discover links between methods

Search a custom-designed taxonomy with more than 1,400 qualitative, quantitative, and mixed methods terms

Uncover more than 120,000 pages of book, journal, and reference content to support your learning

Find out more at
www.sageresearchmethods.com